# REFLECTIONS ON NATIVE-NEWCOMER RELATIONS:
## SELECTED ESSAYS

The twelve essays that make up *Reflections on Native-Newcomer Relations* illustrate the development in thought by one of Canada's leading scholars in the field of Native history – J.R. Miller. The collection, comprising pieces that were written over a period spanning nearly two decades, deals with the evolution of historical writing on First Nations and Métis, methodological issues in the writing of Native-newcomer history, policy matters including residential schools, and linkages between the study of Native-newcomer relations and academic governance and curricular matters. Half of the essays appear here in print for the first time, and all use archival, published, and oral history evidence to throw light on Native-newcomer relations.

Miller argues that the nature of the relationship between Native peoples and newcomers in Canada has varied over time, depending on the reasons the two parties have had for interacting. The relationship deteriorates into attempts to control and coerce Natives during periods in which newcomers do not perceive them as directly useful, and it improves when the two parties have positive reasons for cooperation.

*Reflections on Native-Newcomer Relations* opens up for discussion a series of issues in Native-newcomer history. It addresses all the trends in the discipline of the past two decades and never shies away from showing their contradictions, as well as those in the author's own thinking as he matured as a scholar.

J.R. MILLER is a Canada Research Chair and professor in the Department of History at the University of Saskatchewan.

*J.R. Miller*

# Reflections on Native-Newcomer Relations

## Selected Essays

UNIVERSITY OF TORONTO PRESS
Toronto Buffalo London

© University of Toronto Press Incorporated 2004
Toronto  Buffalo  London
Printed in Canada

ISBN: 0-8020-8723-X (cloth)
ISBN: 0-8020-8669-1 (paper)

Printed on acid-free paper

**National Library of Canada Cataloguing in Publication**

Miller, J.R. (James Rodger), 1943–
Reflections on native-newcomer relations : selected essays / J.R.
Miller.

Includes bibliographical references.
ISBN 0-8020-8723-X (bound)      ISBN 0-8020-8669-1 (pbk.)

1. Indians of North America – Canada – History.   2. Indians of
North America – Canada – Government relations.   3. Indians of North
America – Canada – Historiography.   4. Canada – Race relations –
History.   I. Title.

E92.M545 2004      971.004'97      C2004-900889-7

University of Toronto Press acknowledges the financial assistance to its
publishing program of the Canada Council for the Arts and the Ontario Arts
Council.

University of Toronto Press acknowledges the financial support for its
publishing activities of the Government of Canada through the Book
Publishing Industry Development Program (BPIDP).

*To Bill and Marley Waiser,*
*colleagues and friends*

# Contents

# Acknowledgments

Bill Harnum, vice-president (scholarly publishing), and Gerald Hallowell, then history editor at University of Toronto Press, suggested the compilation of the present volume. I hope that they are satisfied with the consequences of their suggestion. Jill McConkey, Gerry Hallowell's able successor in the history post, was energetic and imaginative in shepherding the collection through the various processes associated with academic publishing, and Ken Lewis was a careful copy editor. I am grateful to all of them for their work.

Most of the essays are the result of research funded by the Social Sciences and Humanities Research Council of Canada, whom I thank most warmly. Over the last twenty years, SSHRC's grants provided essential resources for work on residential schools, Indian policy, and Native-newcomer policy issues.

As usual, my wife, Mary, has been a steadfast source of encouragement and helpful criticism during the process of putting this collection together.

I benefit from being associated with colleagues in the Department of History, University of Saskatchewan, whose advice and encouragement have been unfailing. Also essential has been the hard work of my secretary, Lawrene Toews. My faculty colleagues, along with the many graduate students and faculty from other universities who are thanked in the notes, are very much appreciated, to the point of my saying explicitly that they are not responsible for the shortcomings that remain. In particular, a new colleague, Keith Thor Carlson, has offered valuable suggestions and corrections on many topics, especially those dealing with Native-newcomer history in his native British Columbia. Finally and most important, I am, as usual, greatly indebted both intellectually and personally to Marley and Bill Waiser, to whom this volume is dedicated.

# REFLECTIONS ON NATIVE-NEWCOMER RELATIONS:
## SELECTED ESSAYS

# Introduction

An invitation to assemble a book of essays is cause for both reflection and selection. When Bill Harnum and Gerald Hallowell of University of Toronto Press asked me to prepare the present volume, the opening led to a consideration of where the Native-newcomer history field has been and where it is now going. It is obvious, as is pointed out in several of the essays here, that the field has evolved and matured dramatically over the past thirty years. One manifestation of that greater maturity is the attention to a wider range of subjects over which indigenous and immigrant peoples had dealings within Canada during the last four centuries. Whereas in the 1970s what little literature there was on Native-newcomer relations tended to focus on the fur trade, Christian missions, and diplomacy and war, in the twenty-first century specialists in the field are as likely to concentrate on identity, treaties, state policy, Aboriginal agency, and a host of other topics in addition to the original preoccupations. Historians and others interested in the Native-newcomer theme have often created as many questions as they have answered by their research, but the overall result of their labours during the past three decades is a richer and more complex, if not more definitively and thoroughly analysed, domain of history than previously was available. The deepening and enrichment of Native-newcomer history has also contributed to the increasing complexity and revelatory power of general works of Canadian history, although much here, too, remains to be done to integrate the findings of recent decades into the larger historical narrative.

When it came time to select the essays for this collection, I was conscious that what I had to offer was not completely representative of the field of Native-newcomer history as a whole. Although I had been working on the theme steadily since 1983, when I initiated a study of the history of residential schooling for Native children, there was only a limited range of topics on which I could comment with anything like authority. For one thing, my research interests were located primarily in English-speaking Canada, more particularly the West, where I had lived and worked since 1970. Consequently, there is relatively little commentary in my work on early French Canada, which, fortunately, has a small army of specialists to cover it. Moreover, my detailed research concentrated on policy issues such as schools and treaties, although I had been drawn into consideration of methodology, reflection that is an inevitable part of any historical field, but especially pressing for a non-Native investigator dealing with Native peoples.

Fortunately, my intention was not to specialize in the history of Native peoples in Canada, but in the history of relations between them and non-Natives who came to this land. Increasingly in recent years I have chosen to characterize this theme in our history as 'Native-newcomer history' rather than the history of settler-Native relations, as was fashionable in some quarters in earlier years. Given Canada's reliance on the extraction and export of natural resources through most of its history, the term 'settler,' with its connotation of agricultural colonist, lacked the several dimensions I prefer to capture when referring to the immigrant peoples. The newcomers to Canada who interacted with the indigenous populations have as often been fishers, miners, forest workers, and members of the service industries as farmers. Another attraction of Native-newcomer history is that it is a field that belongs to all in Canada because all of us are either indigenous or immigrant peoples. Hence, there is no need for jealousy or boundary-setting when it comes to doing Native-newcomer history. That is how I have chosen to characterize my own expertise, and that is the theme running through the essays in this volume.

This particular collection is far more modest in its range than is the field from which its contents are drawn. It focuses on historiography and methodology relevant to Native-newcomer history, the history of Indian policy issues, the role of the Crown in a couple of aspects of the Native-newcomer relationship, and the relevance of the theme to some academic issues of the present day. My interest in policy questions is the outgrowth of the first major topic in Native-newcomer history that attracted me, residential schools. Since that work, I have gone on to explore other issues such as treaties and the relationship between Native-newcomer history and other public policy issues. As a result, I have been drawn to consider questions of historiography and methodology as I worked on various topics in the field. My methodological and historiographical reflections resulted in a number of conference papers from which I selected the first four chapters of this collection. These choices, obviously, reflect my own interests and concerns over the past twenty years, but they by no means exhaust the possibilities.

The historiographical selections span more than fifteen years of developments in the field. The first essay, 'Bringing Native People In from the Margins,' was a paper I gave at a conference in Italy in 2001. It was an attempt to reflect recent developments in English-Canadian historical writing on Native peoples as well as some possibilities for the future of the field. The examination of Métis historiography was commissioned in the mid-1980s by the co-editors of the *Canadian Historical Review,* who thought that the time was ripe – with the inclusion of Métis and Inuit in the constitutional definition of 'Aboriginal peoples' in 1982 and the centenary of the Northwest Rebellion and the execution of Louis Riel in 1985 creating a surge of interest in the topic – for an examination of the numerous recent scholarly works that had begun the process of expanding understanding of mixed-blood peoples, particularly in the prairie West. The co-editors' instincts were sound, because study of the Métis and other Aboriginal peoples has steadily expanded since the mid-1980s. Although the focus of these two essays differs, with one concentrating on First Nations and the other on the Métis, together they still provide some sense of how English-Canadian historical writing developed from the middle of the 1980s until the end of the century.

The genesis of the two methodological pieces lay in presentations originally made at the University of Saskatchewan. '"I can only tell what I know,"' which was composed for a 1994 interdisciplinary conference on 'Authority and Interpretation,' attempted to explore the impact and implications of recent methodologies, notably postmodernism and feminist epistemology, for Native-newcomer history especially, and more generally for academic freedom. At its heart, the argument was that by undermining academic researchers' claim to be pursuing truth these new approaches unintentionally weakened the case for freedom of inquiry. The latter, freedom of inquiry, was justified principally by the former, the claim of researchers to be pursuing truth. If the truth was unknowable or if a major way of knowing was experiential and beyond verifiability, where did this leave the search for truth and the right to academic freedom? '"I can only tell what I know"' attracted a hostile response by the distinguished specialist in subaltern studies who was the principal commentator at the conference, as well as by two eminent women's historians of Canada.[1] (It also was unloved by one of the anonymous readers of the manuscript of this work, who described it as 'a classic period piece in its naïveté.') The critics rejected the questions raised about the impact of new approaches but, so far as I could see at least, did not address the concern about the foundations of academic freedom. It certainly is a 'period piece' insofar as it reflected concerns about writing on Aboriginal peoples and other peoples of colour in the early 1990s, but its preoccupation with an enduring matter such as the defences for academic freedom seems to me neither dated nor naïve.

The reception of the other methodological piece, 'Reading Photographs, Reading Voices,' was less exciting. Originally conceived as a lecture at the University of Saskatchewan for a series organized by the vice-president (academic) that tried to expose the community to developments in various specialties, it attempted to answer some of the questions that were current about the propriety and methodology of non-Native scholars conducting research on topics that involved mainly Aboriginal people. In its spoken version, it included an audio excerpt and many slides, including slides of works of art. Subsequently it was published in the first edition of a collection that attempted to explore the many challenges of doing research that concerned Native peoples.[2] The methodological preoccupations of this essay are no longer as pressing in the Native-newcomer field as they were in the mid-1990s, when it was written. Since then, the use of non-literary sources, including especially oral history, has become largely taken for granted. 'Reading Photographs, Reading Voices' reflects concerns of a decade ago.

The first of the four essays that constitute the section on policy also 'enjoyed' a rocky reception. I wrote 'Owen Glendower' in the late 1980s during a period of detailed research on the history of residential schooling in Canada. It struck me at the time that much of the writing that was appearing on the history of Native-newcomer relations tended to overemphasize the impact of malevolent intentions of missionaries and bureaucrats, and not to pay much heed to the many and ingenious ways that First Nations communities resisted these attempts to control, coerce, and remake them. In short, it seemed to me that there had been too much about Native victimhood and not enough about Native agency in the historiography of the previous fifteen years. While it was easy to understand how this developed, the stress on newcomer malice and Native victimhood was neither accurate nor helpful. Since the researchers of the 1970s and 1980s tended to rely heavily on governmental and church archives for their evidence, they sometimes fell into the assumption that what bureaucrats and missionaries *wanted* to happen was *what happened*. Very often, as I was finding out through my own research, including interviews, on residential schooling, the non-Natives' intent was effectively resisted by the Native targets. The 'Owen Glendower' piece was intended to redress the balance of interpretation by making a case for Native agency. Alas, it was interpreted by two graduate students who have since gone on to produce fine scholarly works as trivializing Native suffering by exaggerating the degree to which agency translated into effective self-defence.[3] The discussion between the two critics and two of the authors whose work they examined raised issues that still have relevance to researchers working in the field today.

The other three essays grouped under the policy heading have produced fewer ripples. 'Great White Father Knows Best' was composed in the immediate aftermath of the Oka crisis of 1990 in an effort to explain the deep historical roots of the confrontation and to highlight the culpability of the Department of Indian Affairs and Northern Development, whose procedures for resolving land claims had proven completely ineffectual in dealing with the complex issues at Oka/Kanesatake. It is included here partly because of the inherent importance of the topic, and partly as a reminder that the government of Canada is no closer to solving the land ownership problem that underlay the Oka crisis than it was when its troops supplemented Quebec provincial police in the summer of 1990. 'Canada and the Aboriginal Peoples, 1867–1927' was commissioned by the Canadian Historical Association for its Historical Booklets Series. It was to be complemented, I was told, by another study that would carry the examination of policy onward from 1927, but so far no such examination has appeared. 'The State, the Church, and Indian Residential Schools in Canada' was prepared at the invitation of Queen's University historian Marguerite Van Die for a conference on religion and public life in Canada that was held at her university in the spring of 1999 and later published in a collection she edited.[4]

The material on the Crown's relations with First Nations grew out of an interest in the symbolic role of the monarchy in treaty-making and a Canadian regional peculiarity. In western Canada, First Nations give great prominence to their link to the Crown, even carrying Union Jacks in their colour party on public ceremonial occasions. This interest is just one of many examples of the way in which I, like many researchers, have been influenced by my surroundings. Although the monarchy, as is argued in 'Petitioning the Great White Mother,' has been important to First Nations throughout Canada, in the West the emphasis on the personal link seems especially pronounced. Equally, research on the making of the numbered treaties underlined the degree to which both government and First Nations invoked the symbol of the Crown in their negotiations in the 1870s. These influences resulted in conference papers presented at the University of London in 2001 on 'petitioning' and at the University of Edinburgh in 2002 on the Crown and western treaty-making. Somehow it seemed fitting that these papers were disseminated in British institutions.

The final section of this collection contains two of the papers I have written on academic issues that have a connection to my interest in Native-newcomer history. Because of personal interests and local circumstances, I found myself heavily involved with my university's faculty association from 1978 to 1982, and later with its board of governors from 1989 to 1992. These involvements strengthened a long-standing interest in academic governance, an interest that in my case has always manifested itself in playing the role of commentator rather than practitioner. Both papers included in this collection to a great extent concern the issue of academic leadership. 'Devil's Island' was composed for a meeting of western regional faculty associations – ironically, in the middle of my term as a member of my university's board of governors – in Saskatoon, and it was partly inspired by the fact that it was presented not long after the Oka crisis. The paper also reflected a growing concern with an emerging style of academic leadership that was separating the top Canadian university administrators from the faculty from whose ranks they almost invariably had come. Increasingly, central administrators were *from* but not *of* the academic community, with results that were unsettling. Although readers have suggested that this essay is not scholarly, I think it belongs in a collection such as this because it is an example of how the study of the past, in this case contemplation of the distinctive qualities of the Iroquois Confederacy, can serve as a commentary on the present and its preoccupations. To me academic writing should concern itself with applying lessons learned from scholarly investigations to the contemporary realm, as well as with the dissemination of the results of curiosity-driven research. The distinguished American scholar of Native-newcomer relations James Axtell has contributed notably to American understanding of academe, while Australia's premier scholar of Aboriginal-European relations, Henry Reynolds, has given his fellow citizens the benefit of his scholarly insights with commentaries on issues of the day.

'Aboriginal Peoples and the Academy' originated as a public lecture that I was obligated to give at my university as a consequence of receiving the Distinguished Researcher Award. In it I attempted to address some of the questions that were becoming prominent, especially in western Canada, about the place and role of Aboriginal people and Aboriginal topics in the modern Canadian university. Responses to these issues are still evolving. This presentation, too, was controversial at the time, because it challenged other views of the place and role of Aboriginal people and Aboriginal topics in the university. There is an ongoing debate, in western Canadian universities especially, over whether subjects dealing with Aboriginal peoples should be diffused through the curriculum and institution for the contribution and benefit of all, or reserved to the control of Aboriginal scholars. My position in that debate, a discussion that is likely to continue for some time to come in western Canada at least, is that an integrated, inclusive approach is better for all involved.

In a sense, these academic preoccupations provide some chronological consistency to the selection of the essays. At the heart of one of the earliest pieces, '"I can only tell what I know,"' was the issue of how new methodologies and ways of understanding the past were affecting a practice, academic freedom, that for the better part of a century has been central to the university's vitality and credibility in Western society. 'Devil's Island' explored issues of university governance and leadership that became especially pronounced in the 1980s and 1990s, while 'Aboriginal Peoples and the Academy' probed an ongoing and still evolving opportunity for North American universities. In other words, these selections very much reflect the continuing interests and preoccupations of the author.

### Notes

1 The conference commentator was Gayatri Spivak of Columbia University. The Canadian colleagues who reacted negatively to an unfinished draft of the paper that circulated without my knowledge were Joy Parr ('Gender History and Historical Practice,' *Canadian Historical Review* (CHR) 76, no 3.

[Sept. 1995]: 354–76, esp. 357–60) and Veronica Strong-Boag ('Contested Space: The Politics of Canadian Memory,' *Journal of the Canadian Historical Association*, NS 5 [1994]: 3–17, esp. 4).

2 Jennifer S.H. Brown and Elizabeth Vibert, eds, *Reading beyond Words: Contexts for Native History* (Peterborough, ON: Broadview Press, 1995), 460–81. Broadview Press graciously said that it had no objection when I withheld the article from the second edition for publication here.

3 Robin Brownlie and Mary-Ellen Kelm, 'Desperately Seeking Absolution: Native Agency As Colonialist Alibi?' *CHR* 75, no. 4 (Dec. 1994): 543–56. The other targets were Doug Cole and Ira Chaikin's *An Iron Hand upon the People: The Law against the Potlatch on the Northwest Coast* (Vancouver/Toronto: Douglas & McIntyre, 1990); and Tina Loo's 'Dan Cranmer's Potlatch: Law As Coercion, Symbol, and Rhetoric in British Columbia, 1884–1951,' *CHR* 73, no. 2 (June 1993): 125–65. Cole and I responded in *CHR* 76, no. 4 (Dec. 1995): 628–39; and Kelm replied, ibid., 639–40.

4 Marguerite Van Die, ed., *Religion and Public Life in Canada: Historical and Comparative Perspectives* (Toronto: University of Toronto Press, 2001), 109–29.

# HISTORIOGRAPHY

# Bringing Native People In from the Margins: The Recent Evolution and Future Prospects of English-Canadian Historiography on Native-Newcomer Relations

I do not consider it incumbent upon me to enter into an account of the Indian races of North America. The subject demands much attention, and to be understood in the view of race, language and customs, would occupy many pages. It forms a special field of enquiry, and is totally independent of the History of Canada, except so far as it bears upon the relations of the European and Indian races. I have, therefore, in these pages confined myself to the record of events, without entering into ethnological details, considering that they would only lead to an undesirable interruption of the narrative.

– William Kingsford, *History of Canada* (1888), 2: 166

William Kingsford, an engineer and amateur historical investigator who is often described as the 'dean' of late-nineteenth-century historians in English Canada, typifies the ills that long beset the writing of history about the relations of Native peoples and newcomers. First, Kingsford assumed that First Nations had a place in Canadian history only when and where they interacted with European newcomers, such as in the fur trade in New France or the colonial phases of European imperial wars in the eighteenth century. Furthermore, Kingsford took the view that any description of the character, customs, and contributions of First Nations themselves would be 'an undesirable interruption of the narrative.' That is why he never found space in his history of Canada to 1840 for treatment of Native people and their history. Nowhere in the ten volumes of the work!

Such thinking, for the most part, remained typical of English-Canadian scholarship on Native peoples for another eighty years. By and

large, historical writing in English Canada parallelled historical scholarship in Quebec in this era. If Quebec historians remained preoccu-
pied from Garneau till the 1960s with the theme of *la survivance*, the
survival of the French-Canadian people after 1760 in a continent dominated by English-speaking communities, anglophone writing was different in its chosen theme rather than its obsessive character. For a long
time, as historiographers such as Maurice Careless and Carl Berger
have convincingly pointed out, English-Canadian historians wrote of
Canada as a part of the triumphant British imperial story, shifting in
many cases after the Great War to an approach that emphasized our
constitutional struggle for autonomy within the British Empire, or
Commonwealth. Such Anglophile interpretations did, it is true, at least
note Indian warriors who played a helpful role in defending the
Empire and Canada against the upstart republicans to the south. But
the motivations of the First Nations who fought with the British and
Canadians in the American Revolutionary War or the War of 1812 were
not probed, it being assumed, apparently, that the self-evident virtue
and constitutional superiority of the British made such explanations
superfluous. Even when English-Canadian historiography became
more consciously North American after 1945, Native peoples still
remained neglected. And it goes without saying that during the biographical flurry of the 1950s, 1960s, and early 1970s, anglophone academic historians with one exception did not find their subjects among
the Native peoples of Canada's past.[1]

The lamentable state of academic historical writing on Native people
and the history of their interactions in Canada with European newcomers was finally noticed and analysed at the end of the 1960s. When
Jim Walker surveyed a wide range of general Canadian histories, he
concluded, 'The picture of the Indian as a human being that is presented by writers of Canadian history is confusing, contradictory and
incomplete. Clearly he [*sic*] is not often considered to be deserving of
serious attention, or his [*sic*] society of scholarly analysis ... The other
general histories consulted mention the Indian only in passing, and
invariably on occasions of white-Indian contact ...' Implicitly, Walker
concluded that historical writing about Aboriginal peoples in Canada
had not advanced very far beyond the work of the 'dean,' who wrote
four generations earlier. Walker's conclusion was not far off what
Kingsford had written in matter-of-fact style: '... it is evident that the
Indian is considered totally peripheral to the study of Canada.'[2]

The state of English-Canadian scholarship about Aboriginal people in Canada gives rise to a number of obvious questions. Why did historians ignore the activities of Native peoples? If historians were not writing about Aboriginal people, were any other scholars in English Canada? More important, when did this neglect begin to fade, and why? What have been the major trends in scholarship, especially historical scholarship, about Aboriginal people over the past thirty years? And are there any indications of where this scholarship is headed as the twenty-first century begins?

English-Canadian writing on the First Nations and other Native peoples began outside the academy in the nineteenth century and only slowly found a comfortable and nourishing home in universities as the twentieth unfolded. As had been the case earlier in Quebec, in English Canada the earliest writings on Aboriginal peoples were the products of Christian missionaries and self-trained amateurs who developed a curiosity about the indigenous population of the still-young country. Clergy who wrote on Aboriginal peoples ranged from the Methodist minister and Mississauga chief Peter Jones (Sacred Feathers or Kahkewaquonaby) in Ontario to the Oblate father A.G. Morice, who in the late nineteenth century and early decades of the twentieth carried out inquiries into a variety of First Nations in British Columbia and the prairie region. The clerics were joined by enthusiastic amateurs such as Horatio Hale in Ontario and C.M. Tate in British Columbia, to mention only two of the more accomplished of this group. Although a University of Toronto academic, Daniel Wilson, contributed in the late nineteenth century to the study of indigenous peoples – he is credited with creating the now problematic term 'prehistory' – Wilson's appointment was professor of history and English literature. Wilson's anthropological initiatives notwithstanding, no academic was appointed to teach anthropology full-time in an English-Canadian university until T.F. McIlwraith joined the University of Toronto faculty in the 1920s.[3]

There was other research on Native peoples done in these years, but it was conducted by social scientists outside the academy. The contributions of anthropologists associated with museums and government agencies such as the Geological Survey of Canada were noteworthy, but of limited utility. Their inquiries were dominated by an ethnological or ethnographic approach, a descriptive, static mode of investigation that stemmed directly from these scholars' dedication to what is usually termed 'salvage anthropology.' What motivated ethnographers was the desire to record as much as they possibly could about indigenous peoples' languages, social structures, and spiritual beliefs before they disappeared. Some, such as Daniel Wilson or the New Zealand–born anthropologist Diamond Jenness, were driven by their belief that First Nations were literally a 'vanishing race.' (Jenness nowadays is notorious for concluding the historical portion of his 1932 volume, *The Indians of Canada*, with: 'It is not possible now to determine what will be the final influence of the aborigines on the generations of Canadian people still to come. Doubtless all the tribes will disappear. Some will endure only a few years longer, others, like the Eskimo, may last centuries.')[4] Other ethnographers, such as the highly influential German-born scholar Franz Boas, were motivated by a concern to record Natives' cultural attributes before the 'purity' of Aboriginal societies was diluted by intermarriage and prolonged contact and interaction with non-Natives.[5]

The ethnographic approach to the study of indigenous peoples was problematic because it was a descriptive portrayal that rendered Natives static and unchanging. Accordingly, it was of little help to historians, whose principal preoccupation was and is with change over time. Moreover, as Aboriginal critics have pointed out in more recent decades, the ethnographic approach tended to freeze them, take them out of history, and render them irrelevant to the larger population about them. If anthropology made a limited and disquieting contribution directly to the study of Aboriginal peoples, it did have an important by-product. It was in an anthropology department, the University of Toronto's, that T.F. McIlwraith supervised the dissertation of a young New Brunswicker, A.G. Bailey, who would go on to publish the thesis in 1937 as *The Conflict of European and Eastern Algonkian Cultures, 1504–1700: A Study in Civilization*.[6] As Bruce Trigger has pointed out, Bailey's work was the first example of a genre that would become important in the 1970s and 1980s, the ethnohistorical approach.

Other social scientists such as sociologists and academic lawyers did not contribute any more usefully to scholarship on Aboriginal peoples prior to the 1970s than anthropologists. Sociologists remained focused on community and institutional studies for many decades after the discipline's emergence as a Canadian academic specialty in the twentieth century. Even when sociologists' interests turned towards questions of ethnicity or race, for a long time the groups they chose for study were eastern European and Asian nationalities whose entry into Canada had often ushered in lengthy and difficult periods of adjustment. For their part, academic lawyers, who later would become highly influential in studies of Aboriginal peoples, were conspicuous by their absence until 1970. Federal legislation was a factor in the lawyers' absence. In 1927, Parliament amended the Indian Act to make giving or soliciting funds for pursuit of claims a criminal offence. Until it was rescinded in 1951, this amendment had a chilling effect on research and litigation about land claims and issues of what today would be called Aboriginal title. Indeed, taking the steam out of the claims campaign, particularly in British Columbia, was a principal motive for amending the Indian Act in 1927. However, by reducing the prospects of for-profit legal research on First Nations land issues, the amendment discouraged research into Aboriginal matters by lawyers, including academic lawyers. As the Supreme Court of Canada noted in the 1990 *Sparrow* decision, Aboriginal legal rights, especially involving land, 'were virtually ignored' by Canada's lawyers. The highest court noted that 'for fifty years after the publication of Clement's *The Law of the Canadian Constitution* (3rd ed. 1916), there was a virtual absence of discussion of any kind of Indian rights to land even in academic literature.'[7] Not until 1970, when Peter Cumming and Neil Mickenberg published *Native Rights in Canada*, did lawyers' neglect of Aboriginal law begin to wane.[8]

It would be misleading to leave the impression that no work was published in English Canada on Native peoples prior to the 1970s. However, the exceptions can be counted on a few fingers. Bailey's work was pioneering, of course, although it had little impact on historians until it was reissued by a major press in 1969. Harold Innis published *The Fur Trade in Canada*, and although Arthur Ray has recently rehabilitated Innis's coverage of the role of Natives in the trade to some degree, the work focused on economic matters that largely avoided Aboriginal people and their concerns.[9] Innis, incidentally, was responsible for dissuading a major Canadian historian from doing research on New France, a period that might have led him to comment on Native history. According to Donald Creighton, who used to tell this story to his graduate students, in the late 1920s Creighton was considering switching his research field from eighteenth-century France and consulted his senior colleague Innis about the advisability of undertaking research on New France. The more experienced economic historian advised against the move because, as Creighton reported Innis's advice, 'Parkman has done it.'[10] Perhaps this event can be added to the list of malignant influences for which the Boston historian was responsible that Bruce Trigger has catalogued.[11]

Parkman, Innis, and Creighton aside, some other scholars were writing about Aboriginal people in the first half of the twentieth century. Military historian George Stanley published *The Birth of Western Canada: A History of the Riel Rebellions* in 1935; it was to dominate for a half a century academic understanding of the response of Plains First Nations and Métis to Canada's penetration of the western interior. While Stanley was exceptional in devoting considerable attention to the aims and policies of the federal government in relation to Aboriginal peoples in the West, unfortunately he depicted the federal government's approach to treaty-making with western First Nations in the 1870s as far-sighted and provident. This benign interpretation dominated historians' perception of federal Indian policy and western development for half a century.[12] A similar comment could be made about the work of French anthropologist Marcel Giraud in the 1930s, research he published in 1945 as *Le Métis canadien: Son rôle dans l'histoire des provinces de l'Ouest*. This detailed description of western Métis also had a lasting impact upon academics', particularly historians', view of Native peoples. Giraud's influence in some ways was negative because his inquiry was based on assumptions about social evolution that led him to look for Métis 'development' towards a Euro-Canadian norm, an approach that was intensified by his reliance on Roman Catholic missionaries for suggestions about which Métis informants he should interview and study.[13]

If Jim Walker was critical of English-Canadian historical writing about Native peoples in 1970, it was with good reason. With only a couple of exceptions, historians had devoted no attention to the topic in the eighty years since Kingsford had dismissed Aboriginal history as an 'undesirable interruption' of his ten-volume narrative. Bailey's work was significant but still largely undiscovered; Stanley's contribution was noteworthy but daunting for most other historians who looked westward. Anthropologists were largely mired in an ethnographic approach that tended to freeze Aboriginal societies in time and remove them from the flow of history, or, in Giraud's case, interpreted what they saw and heard in the field through evolutionary or developmental assumptions that took it for granted that Native 'progress' consisted of becoming more like non-Natives. Sociologists, still struggling for autonomy and recognition in some institutions down to the middle of the century, were developing research questions and methods that could have been applied profitably to indigenous peoples. However, sociology's gaze remained fixed on social groups undergoing adjustment, whether they were immigrant communities in western Canada or francophones and anglophones in the Eastern Townships of Quebec. Academic lawyers seem to have been deterred, at least in part, by the legislated reality that until the 1950s there was no profit potential in work on First Nations' land issues. In any event, the lawyers proved no more interested in research on Aboriginal peoples than their historical, anthropological, or sociological colleagues down to the 1970s.

The decade in which Walker published his critique, and Cumming and Mickenburg broke the ice for lawyers with *Native Rights in Canada*, introduced decisive change. The 1970s ushered in a new and large-scale scholarly interest in Aboriginal peoples that requires explanation. The new-found academic interest in Aboriginal peoples and their histories of interaction with non-Natives in part reflected a growing consciousness of Native affairs that stemmed from contemporary political and social influences. The emergence of the civil rights movement, and in particular the activities of the American Indian Movement, tended to strengthen a growing awareness of Third World and indigenous peoples' conflicts with more economically advanced nations of the so-called First World. In western Canada the urban migration of First Nations groups in search of employment opportunities that had been going on at least since the post-war years brought Native peoples into the presence and consciousness of non-Natives, including academics. The civil rights movement and social change in western Canada especially began to assume the appearance of two examples of a worldwide decolonization movement, something that Saskatchewan Métis historian and activist Howard Adams and British Columbia First Nations leader George Manuel would point out in the 1970s.[14]

Not unrelated to the increasing social mobility of Native peoples was the initiation of government-sponsored inquiries such as the Hawthorn Report of the mid-1960s, which involved many social scientists, especially anthropologists, in a consideration of the socio-economic conditions in which First Nations and other Aboriginal groups found themselves in modern, prosperous Canada.[15] The election of the first Trudeau government, with its promise to create a 'Just Society,' excited hopes, while the same ministry's White Paper of 1969 on Indian policy provoked united Indian protest and sparked reflection about social scientists' complicity in federal government policies that were now being revealed as duplicitous in their origins and dangerous to First Nations in their effects. The firestorm of First Nations protest against the White

Paper, including the brilliant polemic *The Unjust Society*, by Alberta Indian leader Harold Cardinal, captured a great deal of attention.[16] If such events as the Hawthorn Report and the White Paper fiasco particularly affected anthropologists and sociologists, academic lawyers found inspiration in *Calder*, the 1973 landmark Aboriginal title decision concerning the Nisga'a. The federal government's subsequent creation of an Office of Native Claims in 1974 to deal with First Nations' land claims also attracted the attention and efforts of a steadily widening circle of historians. For example, Dr John Tobias, an American with a Ph.D. in German history from the University of Alberta, switched his research interests to First Nations' interactions with the Canadian government during and after his employment as a researcher with the Federation of Saskatchewan Indians (now Federation of Saskatchewan Indian Nations). Contemporary influences and opportunities, in other words, drew academics in history and social sciences much more compellingly to the study of Aboriginal topics.

Also influential, particularly among academic historians, were methodological fashions and interests that came to North America in these years from France and Britain. Thanks in no small part to the pioneering work of the French *Annales* school of historians and innovative English social historians such as E.P. Thompson, academic history found itself being reoriented from a concern principally with the high-born and influential in society to detailed study of the marginal, the dispossessed, and the alien. This European influence was intensified among some researchers by growing American scholarly interest in the history of slavery and African Americans. Canadian historians, as is sometimes lamented, have moved from the 1970s onward steadily away from a preoccupation with political, constitutional, diplomatic, and military history towards various branches of social history. So one in the 1970s began to find more systematic study of women, the working poor, immigrants, minority ethnic and racial groups, and, increasingly, the indigenous populations of Canada.

To some extent this change in intellectual fashions in academic research mirrored a social change that the universities themselves had experienced in the 1960s. In an era of unprecedented Canadian prosperity and a dramatic expansion of the public sector, including universities, the social groups who previously had been excluded or underrepresented – women, working-class youth, 'New Canadians,' and ethnic and racial minorities – began to flood into the academy in search of the credentials that would, politicians promised in the 1960s, guarantee them secure employment and lifelong affluence.[17] Although few Aboriginal students would follow the trail of academic credentials to doctorates and positions in Canadian universities until the 1980s and 1990s, non-Native historians began to pay more attention in their research to Indians, Métis, and Inuit – just as their colleagues were doing with immigrants, women, children, African Canadians, and a variety of hitherto neglected groups.

For anthropologists, in particular, the 1960s and 1970s were trying, but ultimately stimulating, years. Anthropologists experienced a crisis of conscience in this period, a rapidly spreading realization that their work had done little to help Native peoples and sometimes had been a powerful tool in the hands of governments and corporations that used their findings to oppress or exploit indigenous societies. The results of this trauma were a shift among some anthropologists to 'action anthropology' and research in the service of the research subjects, a new interest in government policies directed at Aboriginal peoples, and the development of a new methodology or approach that is usually referred to as ethnohistory. An example of the 'action anthropology' movement is University of Calgary anthropologist Joan Ryan, whose 1978 *Wall of Words: The Betrayal of the Urban Indian* was the result of her work with the Calgary Urban Treaty Indian Alliance, which, Ryan argued, had been undermined by bureaucrats in the Department of Indian Affairs.[18] Anthropologists' new interest in government policy was exemplified memorably by the late Sally Weaver's 1981 monograph *Making Canadian Indian Policy*, which dissected the White Paper initiative of 1969 and exposed it as the duplicitous and wrong-headed document that it was.[19]

Ethnohistory, another product of anthropology's rethinking of its approach to the study of Native peoples, had a wider impact than 'action anthropology' and policy studies by anthropologists once it emerged, mainly in United States in the 1970s. It was not surprising that historians embraced it, for it was merely a different way of reading the kinds of sources with which historians had long been familiar. Besides, although historians had largely forgotten the fact, a historian, A.G. Bailey, had been the first Canadian scholar to employ the method. Bailey's pioneering work illustrated that the ethnohistorical approach or method is congenial to historians because it involves mainly documentary records. The method, which consists essentially of using anthropology's insights about Aboriginal people to interpret documents written about them by non-Natives, allows historians to extract important information about First Nations from Europeans' documents. It requires the investigator to look through the surface of descriptions and attributions of motive for underlying meaning.[20] As a result, historians, now sometimes referring to themselves as ethnohistorians, have been busily rereading utterly Eurocentric sources such as the *Jesuit Relations*, the annual propaganda exercises of the Society of Jesus in Canada, shoving aside the priests' sometimes racist comments and interpretations to bring out what was going on among the Algonkin, Huron, or Iroquois in Indian country. Fine examples of the contributions that the ethnohistorical method can make are to be found in the works of Bruce Trigger, James Axtell, and Cornelius Jaenen.[21]

These changes in anthropology were significant for historians because their developing interest in the history of Native peoples was bringing them ever more frequently into association with practitioners of other disciplines. Historians pursuing new social history topics began to look to cultural anthropologists for clues that would allow them to practise the new technique known as ethnohistory, to sociologists for a better understanding of mass social processes, to historical geographers for an improved appreciation of the impact of the terrain and environment on collectivities in remote regions, and even to legal scholars for the beginnings of an understanding of how some of the ordinary people that historians were now studying found themselves enmeshed in the coils of the law and with what results. An emphasis on social history, especially involving Native peoples, led to greater cross-fertilization and methodological convergence of historians and social scientists.

Two other disciplinary or methodological influences have become important, especially from the 1980s onward. Academic lawyers, as has been convincingly pointed out by political scientist Alan Cairns,[22] moved into legal research and legal activism on Aboriginal matters. In addition to the stimulus to historically oriented legal research provided by land claims after the *Calder* decision, the struggles over and implementation of the Charter of Rights and Freedoms after 1982, the battles over finding a place for Aboriginal rights in the proposed Meech Lake Accord and the Charlottetown Accord, and the research approach of the Royal Commission on Aboriginal Peoples from 1992 until 1996 brought academic lawyers into the field in large numbers. In many respects, they, along with a few political scientists, have become the chief proponents of Aboriginal causes in English Canada, and their work cannot be ignored by any historian interested in the history of Native-newcomer relations.

In other words, since Walker criticized the historical profession for its neglect of Aboriginal peoples in 1970, an enormous change has occurred in historians' preoccupations, research subjects, and contributions. Influenced by contextual factors such as growing Aboriginal assertiveness and personal factors such as their own class and gender, and taking note of parallel developments in other disciplines, some historians of Canada have turned to the study of Native peoples and of their interactions with non-Natives in Canada. In the process, they have found themselves frequently leagued with investigators from other fields, such as anthropologists, lawyers, and other social scientists. The result methodologically has been a greater awareness among historians of theoretical and methodological developments in other disciplines, and, notably in the case of ethnohistory, a borrowing of tools and techniques from these allied colleagues. There can be little doubt that in approach and quantity, at least, the historiography dealing with Native-newcomer relations has changed dramatically since 1970.

What do these changes mean in practice for the historiography of this field? What difference have these new interests, allies, and approaches made to historians' understanding of the history of Canada? These innovations have enriched our understanding of Canada's history in a variety of ways, from subject matter, to research questions, to methodology. The result of these innovations is a picture of Canada that is richer, more rounded, and more complex than was available to students down to the 1960s in Canada. Something else significant has happened in the course of conducting this research over the last thirty years. Researchers' focus has begun to shift from what might be called the 'headquarters' perspective of the European group involved in Native-newcomer relations to Indian country, where the interactions occurred.

Although the new research at first focused on familiar topics in Canadian history, by the 1980s investigators had begun to open up new areas of inquiry. Carl Berger observed in the revised edition of his overview of English-Canadian historiography in 1986 that the increased volume of work on Native peoples still concentrated on traditional areas of research such as New France and the fur trade.[23] Trigger's and Jaenen's work, of course, dealt with New France, and the contributions of historical geographers Conrad Heidenreich and Arthur J. Ray took up the Huron in New France and the role of First Nations in the Hudson's Bay

Company trade.[24] However, although these interests seemed in some ways traditional, there was in fact significant innovation. As the subtitle to Ray's landmark study *Indians in the Fur Trade* – specifically *Their Role As Hunters, Trappers and Middlemen ...* – revealed, there was now a much greater emphasis on the actions of the First Nations in these activities. From work like Ray's, as well as Daniel Francis and Toby Morantz's counterpart on eastern James Bay, Indians as agents rather than victims began to emerge.[25]

What was happening in the apparently traditional field of fur-trade studies in Canada was exactly what occurred in the equally conventional American research area of imperial warfare in eighteenth-century North America.[26] In due course, the areas of research in which the growing ranks of Native history researchers interested themselves expanded beyond traditional fields such as New France and the fur trade. In spite of the dead hand of George Stanley's interpretation in *The Birth of Western Canada*, the Prairies stimulated a new interest in studying the history of government policies towards First Nations because of two seminal works that appeared in 1983–4. First, John Tobias's article 'Canada's Subjugation of the Plains Cree,' by portraying government aims and methods as malignant, devious, and destructive, awakened interest in what Canada was up to.[27] Tobias's approach would be extended to other policy areas, notably agriculture and reserves, in the work of Sarah Carter.[28] A year after Tobias published his article, Gerald Friesen issued his influential *The Canadian Prairies: A History,* which was remarkable for the way in which it wove the latest in scholarship on Aboriginal people into the history of the region, yielding a richer and more complete picture than anything that had previously been available.[29] Friesen's work was soon followed by Brian Titley's meticulous dissection of Indian Affairs deputy minister Duncan Campbell Scott, and in due course by a historical treatment of British Columbia that also foregrounded First Nations from the pen of Jean Barman.[30]

However, it was not just conventional research areas such as the fur trade or regional studies that benefited from historians' new concern with Aboriginal peoples. Also important to the flourishing of the historiography that became so noticeable by the 1980s was the fact that some researchers asked new questions of familiar material. Again, the fur-trade field provides the most striking examples. As noted, generations of scholars had examined the fur trade as an imperial or metropolitan commercial venture, but Ray advanced understanding by looking at the same evidence with additional questions. He wanted to know, not just how the commerce functioned, but also what the role of First Nations in it had been. In a similar way, two of the new generation of female academics who were now to be found in history departments made a dramatic contribution in the same field. Where Ray had interrogated the Hudson's Bay Company records about the roles played by Indians in the trade, Jennifer Brown and Sylvia Van Kirk approached the trading companies' archives with questions about the place and contributions of Native women to the Hudson's Bay Company and the Nor'westers. Although Brown did her doctorate in anthropology at Chicago and Van Kirk hers in history at the University of London, both ended up in the Hudson's Bay Company archives in the late 1970s. The result of their coincidental investigations was coincidental publication of their monographs in 1980. Brown's *Strangers in Blood: Fur Trade Company Families in Indian Country* and Van Kirk's *'Many Tender Ties': Women in Fur-Trade Society, 1670–1870*, though different in focus as their subtitles show, both contributed enormously to the reinterpretation of Native-newcomer interactions.[31] This work not only deepened our understanding of Canadian history enormously, it also inspired others, including a sociologist who re-examined missions in New France from a novel angle, to take another look at Native-newcomer relations to uncover the place, actions, and contributions of Aboriginal women to history.[32]

In addition to finding new answers about Native people by asking new research questions, the post-1970 historiography also contributed substantially by employing new research methods. The impact of ethnohistory, that blend of anthropology and history, has already been mentioned. Also important was a technique that came to Native-newcomer history from the discipline of anthropology. Oral history, or interviewing, had developed spontaneously in the research of Hugh Dempsey, who since the 1970s has done so much to make the post-contact history of the Blackfoot Confederacy, and the Kainai (Blood), in particular, better known. In a series of biographical studies that in some respects culminated in his fine portrait of Mistahimusqua (Big Bear), Dempsey used the oral history resources of First Nations communities, with some of which he had personal connections, to add new dimensions to our understanding of that consummate Prairie diplomat during the difficult decades of declining bison, inter-tribal war, epidemic disease, and the coming of Canadian rule.[33]

The influence from anthropology on oral history research is even more evident in the work of a northern specialist, Julie Cruikshank. The way in which the findings of oral history research can revise historians' understanding is well demonstrated in one of Cruikshank's articles on Yukon history. The incident that was rewritten in non-Native accounts as a result of Cruikshank's interviews with Tagish informants in southern Yukon was the 'murder' of two non-Native prospectors in the 1890s by Natives. In earlier accounts written from documentary sources, the deaths were seen as acts of senseless, treacherous violence. The non-Natives were murdered without warning by two men, the Nantuck brothers, after the Natives and non-Natives had passed a couple of days in apparently amicable socializing. However, according to the account that Cruikshank took down from Tagish informants, the outsiders had not been murdered, but executed according to the will of the community. In the eyes of the Tagish, the outsiders were accountable for the deaths a couple of years earlier of Natives who mistook arsenic that earlier prospectors had left behind for flour. Local people had consumed the powder, and some of them had died as a result. When the later prospectors, whom the locals regarded as being of the same clan as those who had earlier left the fatal powder behind, failed to make amends during two days of visiting and tea-drinking, the Nantuck brothers on behalf of the Tagish community carried out the capital sentence their clansmen had incurred and they had failed to mitigate by conciliatory actions.[34]

As these few, highly selective examples indicate, Canadian historians' interest after 1970 in the place of Native peoples in Canadian history has dramatically altered the way that history is written and taught. Although researchers' preoccupation with Native peoples at first concentrated on familiar topics of study, it was not long before inquiry began to branch out into other fields. In particular, although Robert Surtees had noted in the introduction to his 1982 bibliography, *Canadian Indian Policy*, that the topic had 'attracted remarkably little attention from historians and other scholars,'[35] one consequence of expanded interest in Native people in the 1980s was much more extensive treatment of subjects such as treaty-making and reserve policy, the Indian Act, and First Nations responses to these government initiatives. A major part of the increasing scope of research in the field since the 1970s has been the willingness of researchers not just to examine neglected topics, but also to use different research questions and even unfamiliar research methods. Asking the fur-trade records, Where were the Native women, and what were they doing? proved enormously productive. So, too, has the employment of ethnohistorical techniques in examinations of Christian missions to Native peoples.

These innovations since 1970 have resulted in an understanding of Canada's history that is, as noted earlier, more complex and rich. If historians and their allies in other disciplines have not yet succeeded in putting Aboriginal people at the centre of Canadian history, they have certainly brought Native groups in from the margins and accorded them a prominent place in the story. A few examples must suffice. As Jim Walker's critique showed, it was unthinkable before 1970 to begin an English-language general history of Canada with a Native creation story, as Doug Francis, Richard Jones, and Donald Smith have done in the first of their two-volume text *Origins*.[36] Similarly, in *History of the Canadian Peoples*, Margaret Conrad, Alvin Finkel, and Cornelius Jaenen constantly keep the experience of Native people front and centre for the undergraduate students for whom their text is intended.[37] Both these works are the antithesis of what Walker found thirty years ago. Finally, in 1970, could one imagine a multi-episode history of Canada on the national television network in prime time that accorded an enormous amount of attention to First Nations, Métis, and Inuit? (In 1970, could one imagine a prime-time history of Canada on television, period?) And yet that is precisely what the creators of *Canada: A People's History* did in 2000.

The episodes of *Canada: A People's History* also illustrated something else significant about change in the writing of Native-newcomer history over the past thirty years: the researcher's gaze or focus has begun to shift from 'headquarters' to 'Indian country.' The point can be appreciated best by contrasting earlier studies with later efforts. In fur-trade studies, for example, there is a world of difference between the metropolitan perspective of an E.E. Rich and the historical point of view of Arthur Ray and Frank Tough in their studies.[38] In the latter cases, the investigator's focus is very much on the resource hinterland where Native-newcomer interactions occurred. While the newer generation of scholars does not neglect the impact of decisions taken in London on Native people and their relations with Europeans, the story is very much concentrated on what occurs in Indian country. Another good example of the shift in the historian's gaze is found in the area of policy studies. No longer are researchers content to investigate the terms of the Indian Act and the thinking of the Department of Indian Affairs in their efforts to understand what happened to relations in the West, say, after treaties were concluded, the buffalo economy collapsed, and First Nations increasingly became administered peoples. Ever since the ground-breaking work of Tobias, Titley, and Carter, researchers have realized that a more accurate interpretation is produced by investigating the impact of policy as it was administered on the ground, rather than as it was conceived in Ottawa. A great deal of the increased richness and complexity of the revised picture of Native-newcomer relations derives from this shift in focus – from headquarters to Indian country.

While there have been many advances in the post-1970 historiography of Native peoples and their relations with non-Natives, there is also much work unfinished. If the foregoing remarks have outlined some aspects of the recent evolution of English-Canadian historiography in this field, what are likely to be some of the future prospects?

In some areas, the process of shifting the gaze and deepening the perception of the relationship will continue along lines similar to those that have opened up in recent years. As historians become anxious to gain a better understanding of the Native-newcomer historical relationship from the Aboriginal as well as the European perspective, more research will be undertaken to pursue this goal. Such an approach is qualitatively different from the ethnohistorical method that has been such a boon to the field during the past few decades. Ethnohistory is at its heart the reinterpretation of Europeans' evidence to uncover the perceptions, actions, and aspirations of the indigenous peoples on whom the European sources were commenting. Examples of this are common and familiar. Historians have reread missionary sources, particularly for New France, to uncover how groups such as the Huron, Montagnais, or Iroquois reacted to the arrival and intrusion of Europeans. Similarly, students of nineteenth- and twentieth-century missionary contact with Aboriginal peoples have reinterpreted documentary evidence produced either by the missionaries themselves or under their auspices. Examples include petitions to the Department of Indian Affairs penned on behalf of First Nations by missionaries, or student compositions in residential school newsletters. Such sources can be revealing when probed with the ethnohistorical approach. However, in the twenty-first century we are likely to see more research and writing that is based on Aboriginal sources, or on both indigenous and newcomer evidence.

Advancing into this expanded realm of research is both exciting and daunting. The potential to achieve a better understanding of the

Native-newcomer relationship by seeing it reflected in both Native and outsider commentaries is cause to pursue what will undoubtedly be a difficult research strategy. The difficulties come from a number of sources, most of them rooted in Native peoples' resentment and suspicion of non-Native researchers because of what they regard as high-handed and disrespectful treatment of their communities by outsiders who lacked both empathy and common cause with the Native informants they wished to study.[39] Native communities complain that they are tired of having anthropologists or historians fly into their communities, carry out research whose purpose is probably murky and almost certainly has nothing to do with the community's goals, and then depart, probably never to be heard from again. Worse, sometimes Native communities have been shocked to discover much later what was written about them as a result of these lightning raids. Another problem as some Aboriginal communities see it is that researchers often wish to extract oral traditions and songs that are usually sacred to the community, and each of which is exclusive to the person or family who has the right to tell or sing it. In many cases, there is a strict Native protocol governing when and how such traditions may be divulged. All too often these considerations have been unknown or, if known, disregarded by researchers who treated the story or song as just another artifact. It will take many years and considerable effort to overcome the understandable reluctance of at least some Native communities to make their knowledge available to researchers.

It is difficult to decide if recent granting council measures assist with that task or make it more difficult. In September 1998, the (then) Medical Research Council, the Natural Sciences and Engineering Research Council of Canada, and the Social Sciences and Humanities Research Council of Canada (SSHRC) issued a *Tri-Council Policy Statement: Ethical Conduct for Research Involving Humans* (*TCPS*) to govern all university-based research that uses people as informants or subjects. The *Tri-Council Policy Statement* facilitates needed advances into research that will incorporate the insights of Aboriginal communities insofar as it counsels researchers to adopt respectful methods and provides them with references to research protocols, such as those developed by the Royal Commission on Aboriginal Peoples and the Association of Canadian Universities for Northern Studies, that do enjoy the confidence of Native organizations and scholars. However, the *Tri-Council Policy Statement* also sets up a regime – gauntlet might be an appropriate metaphor – of research ethics boards in universities to which researchers are obligated to submit their research plans involving humans prior to commencing investigation. In the uncertain environment created by the implementation of a novel research protocol involving all three of the principal granting councils in Canada, institutional research ethics boards have understandably reacted hesitantly. Often these ethics review boards err on the side of caution, raising innumerable questions and objections, and not infrequently attempting to impose requirements on researchers that are not justified by the *Tri-Council Policy Statement* itself. No doubt in time the implementation and interpretation problems of the *Tri-Council Policy Statement* will be worked out, but until that time researchers interested in Native peoples who want to include community observation and interviews in their methods will find themselves challenged by the new research ethics environment that has been created.

While researchers wait for the happy day when the *Tri-Council Policy Statement's* provisions for research in and with Native communities and individuals are well understood by both researchers and research ethics boards, there are other ways of acquiring the desired Aboriginal evidence. One approach that was applied successfully by two Saskatchewan historians, Blair Stonechild of the Saskatchewan Indian Federated College, now First Nations University of Canada, and Bill Waiser of the University of Saskatchewan, is to conduct the research in Native communities with a bicultural team. Their initiative proved highly effective, resulting in a valuable, revisionist study of the Northwest Rebellion, *Loyal till Death*.[40] Another approach that can yield similarly beneficial results is the work of Aboriginal scholars who are trained in Euro-American or Euro-Canadian universities as well as schooled in and sensitive to their own communities' history and values. For example, John Borrows, a legal historian, has produced a number of articles that combine the knowledge of his own community, the Chippewas of Newash, with conventional legal research and even documentary history investigation to produce scholarship that shows clearly the benefits of bicultural research methods.[41] Relying upon both documentary sources and the evidence of a wampum, a First Nations form of record-keeping, Borrows makes a plausible case for reinterpreting the Royal Proclamation of 1763, not as a unilateral British Crown document, but as a treaty between the United Kingdom and a large number of First Nations. Such work illustrates the potential of a bicultural research strategy to provide insights from the Aboriginal point of view as well as the European perspective on some of those portions of our past that involve intense Native-newcomer interaction.

Turning from methods to topics, there is obviously no shortage of possibilities. One area in which more research would be welcome is regional studies. As noted earlier, the Prairies and British Columbia have benefited from histories that accord Native peoples a prominent place, and Yukon and the Northwest Territories have also been the sites of important monographs dealing with Native peoples and their relations with outsiders.[42] Parallel studies that deal with Ontario, Quebec, and the Maritimes are highly desirable. No doubt the central provinces will be best approached by separate studies on their northern and southern Aboriginal populations. Another example of an area where approaches of the past thirty years could be extended is policy studies. We do not know, for example, how many status Indians enfranchised, much less how and why they gave up their Indian civic identity for Canadian citizenship. Similarly, while we have a clear idea of what Ottawa was trying to achieve from 1869 on with its legislation to promote or compel use of Euro-Canadian elective institutions of governance in First Nations, we have no inkling of how often the Department of Indian Affairs exercised the draconian powers the Indian Act gave it to impose elective institutions, or how such measures were received by the communities themselves. Finally, although a good deal has been accomplished in recent decades in studying health and health care, much remains to be done here as well as concerning another perennial favourite, Native education. To give only one instance, we need to know what the effect of the federal government's adoption of the 1973 policy of 'Indian control of Indian education' has meant on the ground, on reserves and in northern communities. Much remains to be done on the history of government policy aimed at Aboriginal peoples.

Finally, this historiographical field is now sufficiently mature that comparative studies can be carried out with profit. The obvious parallels between the American and Canadian experiences, especially in eighteenth-century military affairs as well as treaty and assimilation policy, have already led some scholars to explore the comparisons.[43] However, there remain a large number of possible comparative topics featuring American and Canadian experiences. And the possibilities of comparison in policy and other areas among Canada, Australia, and New Zealand are almost untapped.[44]

Indeed, although significant progress has been made in the study of Native peoples and the history of their relations with non-Natives in Canada, there is still a great deal to do. Thanks to changes in the social composition of university researchers, there has been a dramatic broadening of the research agenda to include non-elites, including Aboriginal peoples. One looks forward hopefully to the further diversifying of the research community, and in particular to the arrival of more scholars of Aboriginal ancestry. Thanks, too, to innovations in methodology and approach, we are acquiring a better understanding of the complex reality of the Native experience after the arrival of Europeans. Again, there is every reason to hope that the research community is following a trajectory that will lead to a better grasp of the Native-newcomer experience from the Native as well as the newcomer perspective. Students of Native history and the history of Native-newcomer relations in Canada cannot say of their field what the Royal Commission on Aboriginal Peoples claimed – prematurely, perhaps – for the place of Aboriginal peoples and their causes. 'Within a span of 25 years,' RCAP asserted, 'Aboriginal peoples and their rights have emerged from the shadows, to the sidelines, to occupy centre stage.'[45] It would be ludicrous to claim that Native history is at centre stage of Canadian history, but clearly it has moved well in from the margins. And certainly it is no longer the case that Canadian historians, and Canadians in general, regard that history as 'an undesirable interruption of the narrative.'

## Notes

An earlier version of this essay was presented to the 'Recasting Canadian History in the Wider World: Towards New Perspectives for the Twenty-First Century' conference, Sestri Levante, Italy, 4–6 May 2001. The research on which it is based was generously supported by a Standard Research Grant from the Social Sciences and Humanities Research Council of Canada.

1  The exception was George F.G. Stanley, whose biography, *Louis Riel* (Toronto: Ryerson), was published in 1963.
2  James W. St G. Walker, 'The Indian in Canadian Historical Writing,' in Canadian Historical Association, *Historical Papers 1971*, 21, 38–9. Although published in 1971, the paper was presented the previous year.
3  Bruce G. Trigger, *Natives and Newcomers: Canada's 'Heroic Age' Reconsidered* (Montreal and Kingston: McGill-Queen's University Press, 1985), 39; Douglas Cole, 'The Origins of Canadian Anthropology, 1850–1910,' *Journal of Canadian Studies* 8, no. 1 (Feb. 1973): 33–45, esp. 35.

4 Diamond Jenness, *The Indians of Canada*, 7th ed. (Toronto: University of Toronto Press, 1977; 1st ed., National Museum of Man, 1932), 264.

5 Cole, 'Origins,' 34, 40, 43–4; Trigger, *Natives and Newcomers*, 18–19.

6 Saint John: New Brunswick Museum, 1937. A second edition was issued by University of Toronto Press in 1969.

7 *R. v. Sparrow [1990] 1 S.C.R. 1075* at 1103.

8 Peter A. Cumming and Neil H. Mickenburg, eds, *Native Rights in Canada*, 2nd ed. (Toronto: Indian-Eskimo Association of Canada, 1972; 1st ed., 1970).

9 H.A. Innis, *The Fur Trade in Canada: An Introduction to Canadian Economic History*, rev. ed. (Toronto: University of Toronto Press, 1956; 1st ed., Yale University Press, 1930). See A.J. Ray's introduction to the most recent edition of *The Fur Trade in Canada* (Toronto: University of Toronto Press, 1999), v–xix.

10 Personal recollection.

11 On Parkman's negative influence, see Trigger, *Natives and Newcomers*, 9ff.

12 Arthur J. Ray, Jim Miller, and Frank Tough, *Bounty and Benevolence: A History of Saskatchewan Treaties* (Montreal and Kingston: McGill-Queen's University Press, 2000), 206–7.

13 Marcel Giraud, *Le Métis canadien: Son rôle dans l'histoire des provinces de l'Ouest* (Paris: Institut d'ethnologie, 1945), translated and introduced by George Woodcock as *The Métis in the Canadian West*, 2 vols (Lincoln and London: University of Nebraska Press, 1986). For Giraud's acknowledgment of his reliance on Oblate missionaries, see his 'Foreword' in *The New Peoples: Being and Becoming Métis in North America*, ed. J. Peterson and J.S.H. Brown (Winnipeg: University of Manitoba Press, 1985), xii. For critiques of Giraud's analysis, see J.R. Miller, 'From Riel to the Métis,' *Canadian Historical Review* 69, no. 1 (March 1988): 3–4; and Frank Tough, 'Race, Personality and History: A Review of Marcel Giraud's "The Metis in the Canadian West,"' *Native Studies Review* 5, no. 2 (1989): 59, 74–5, 88, 89n11.

14 Howard Adams, *Prison of Grass: Canada from a Native Point of View* (Toronto: new press, 1975; Fifth House, 1989); George Manuel and Marcel Posluns, *The Fourth World: An Indian Reality* (Toronto: Collier-Macmillan, 1974).

15 H.B. Hawthorn, ed., *A Survey of the Contemporary Indians of Canada: Economic, Political, Educational Needs and Policies*, 2 vols (Ottawa: Indian Affairs, 1966–7).

16 Harold Cardinal, *The Unjust Society: The Tragedy of Canada's Indians* (Edmonton: Hurtig, 1969).

17 For an example of the impact of the 1960s by a scholar who is himself a product of that era, see Greg Kealey, 'Writing about Labour,' in *Writing about Canada: A Handbook for Modern Canadian History*, ed. John Schultz (Scarborough, ON: Prentice-Hall, 1990), 160–1.

18 Joan Ryan, *Wall of Words: The Betrayal of the Urban Indian* (Toronto: Peter Martin Associates, 1978).

19 Sally M. Weaver, *Making Canadian Indian Policy: The Hidden Agenda, 1968–1970* (Toronto: University of Toronto Press, 1981).

20 The literature on ethnohistorical methodology is extensive, but a useful beginning can be made with Trigger, *Natives and Newcomers*, 164–72. Trigger is himself a brilliant exemplar of the method. See his *Children of Aataentsic: A History of the Huron People to 1660*, 2 vols (Montreal and Kingston: McGill-Queen's University Press, 1976).

21 James Axtell, *The Invasion Within: The Contest of Cultures in Colonial North America* (New York: Oxford University Press, 1985); Cornelius J. Jaenen, *Friend and Foe: Aspects of French-Amerindian Cultural Contact in the Sixteenth and Seventeenth Centuries* (New York: Columbia University Press, 1976). For Trigger, see preceding note.

22 Alan C. Cairns, *Citizens Plus: Aboriginal Peoples and the Canadian State* (Vancouver: UBC Press, 2000), 169–70, 175–88, on which this passage is based.

23 Carl Berger, *The Writing of Canadian History: Aspects of English-Canadian Writing since 1900*, 2nd ed. (Toronto: University of Toronto Press, 1986; 1st ed., 1976), 298–301.

24 Conrad Heidenreich, *Huronia: A History and Geography of the Huron Indians* (Toronto: McClelland and Stewart, 1971); Arthur J. Ray, *Indians in the Fur Trade: Their Role As Hunters, Trappers and Middlemen in the Lands Southwest of Hudson Bay, 1660-1870* (Toronto: University of Toronto Press, 1974).

25 Daniel Francis and Toby Morantz, *Partners in Furs: A History of the Fur Trade in Eastern James Bay, 1600–1870* (Kingston and Montreal: McGill-Queen's University Press, 1985).

26 This parallel, which cannot be explained more fully here, is dealt with in J.R. Miller, 'Owen Glendower, Hotspur, and Canadian Indian Policy,' *Ethnohistory* 37, no. 4 (Fall 1990): 386–8; reprinted in this volume.

27 John L. Tobias, 'Canada's Subjugation of the Plains Cree, 1879–1885,' *Canadian Historical Review* 64 (Dec. 1983): 519-48.

28 Sarah Carter, *Lost Harvests: Prairie Indian Reserve Farmers and Government Policy* (Montreal and Kingston: McGill-Queen's University Press, 1990).

29 Gerald Friesen, *The Canadian Prairies: A History* (Toronto: University of Toronto Press, 1984).

30 E. Brian Titley, *A Narrow Vision: Duncan Campbell Scott and the Administration of Indian Affairs in Canada* (Vancouver: University of British Columbia Press, 1986); Jean Barman, *The West beyond the West: A History of British Columbia* (Toronto: University of Toronto Press, 1991).

31 Jennifer S.H. Brown, *Strangers in Blood: Fur Trade Company Families in Indian*

*Country* (Vancouver: University of British Columbia Press, 1980); Sylvia Van Kirk, *'Many Tender Ties': Women in Fur-Trade Society, 1670–1870* (Winnipeg: Watson & Dwyer, [1980]).

32  Karen L. Anderson, *Chain Her by One Foot: The Subjugation of Women in Seventeenth-Century New France* (New York and London: Routledge, 1991). There is now a substantial literature on Native women in areas such as resource industries and Christian missions throughout the country.

33  Hugh A. Dempsey, *Big Bear: The End of Freedom* (Vancouver: Douglas & McIntyre, 1984). Other works by Dempsey that exemplify the same resources and results are *Charcoal's World* (Saskatoon: Western Producer Prairie Books, 1978), *Red Crow: Warrior Chief* (Saskatoon: Western Producer Prairie Books, 1980), and *The Gentle Persuader: James Gladstone, Indian Senator* (Saskatoon: Western Producer Prairie Books, 1986).

34  Julie Cruikshank, 'Oral Traditions and Written Accounts: An Incident from the Klondike Gold Rush,' *Culture* 9, no. 2 (1980): 25–34. Cruikshank is also renowned for her landmark study *Life Lived like a Story: Life Stories of Three Yukon Native Elders*, with Angela Sidney, Kitty Smith, and Annie Ned (Vancouver: UBC Press, 1990).

35  Robert J. Surtees, *Canadian Indian Policy* (Bloomington: Indiana University Press, 1982), 1.

36  D. Francis, R. Jones, and D.B. Smith, *Origins: Canadian History to Confederation*, 3rd ed. (Toronto: Harcourt Brace, 1996), 1–2.

37  Margaret Conrad, Alvin Finkel, and Cornelius Jaenen, *History of the Canadian Peoples*, Vol. I: *Beginnings to 1867* (Toronto: Copp Clark, 1998); Alvin Finkel and Margaret Conrad, *History of the Canadian Peoples*, Vol. II: *1867 to the Present* (Toronto: Copp Clark, 1998).

38  E.E. Rich, *The Fur Trade and the Northwest to 1857* (Toronto: McClelland and Stewart, 1967); Ray, *Indians in the Fur Trade*; Frank Tough, *As Their Natural Resources Fail: Native Peoples and the History of Northern Manitoba, 1870–1930* (Vancouver: UBC Press, 1996).

39  See, for example, Marie Battiste and James Sa'ke'j Youngblood Henderson, *Protecting Indigenous Knowledge and Heritage: A Global Challenge* (Saskatoon: Purich, 2000); and Linda Tuhiwai Smith, *Decolonizing Methodologies: Research and Indigenous Peoples* (London and New York: Zed Books, 1999).

40  Blair Stonechild and Bill Waiser, *Loyal till Death: Indians and the North-West Rebellion* (Calgary: Fifth House, 1997). One measure of the book's impact was that it was shortlisted for the Governor General's Award for non-fiction.

41  For historians, probably his most interesting contribution is 'Wampum at Niagara: The Royal Proclamation, Canadian Legal History, and Self-Government,' in *Aboriginal and Treaty Rights in Canada: Essays on Law, Equity, and*

*Respect for Difference*, ed. Michael Asch (Vancouver: UBC Press, 1997), 155–72 and 256–67.

42  Ken Coates, *Best Left As Indians: Native-White Relations in the Yukon Territory, 1840–1973* (Montreal and Kingston: McGill-Queen's University Press, 1991); Kerry Abel, *Drum Songs: Glimpses of Dene History* (Montreal and Kingston: McGill-Queen's University Press, 1993).

43  Roger L. Nichols, *Indians in the United States and Canada: A Comparative History* (Lincoln and London: University of Nebraska Press, 1998); Robert Allen, *His Majesty's Indian Allies: British Indian Policy in the Defence of Canada, 1774–1815* (Toronto: Dundurn, 1993); Hana Samek, *The Blackfoot Confederacy, 1880–1920: A Comparative Study of Canadian and U.S. Indian Policy* (Albuquerque: University of New Mexico Press, 1987); Carol L. Higham, *Noble, Wretched, and Redeemable: Protestant Missionaries to the Indians in Canada and the United States, 1820–1900* (Albuquerque: University of New Mexico Press, 2000); and Jill St Germain, *Indian Treaty-Making Policy in the United States and Canada, 1867–1877* (Lincoln and London: University of Nebraska Press, 2001). I am indebted to Jim Carroll of Iona College, who drew the Higham title to my attention.

44  A significant exception is Andrew Armitage, *Comparing the Policy of Aboriginal Assimilation: Australia, Canada, and New Zealand* (Vancouver: UBC Press, 1995).

45  Royal Commission on Aboriginal Peoples, *Final Report*, Vol. 1: *Looking Forward, Looking Back* (Ottawa: RCAP, 1996), 216.

# From Riel to the Métis

Although miscegenation must have been one of the earliest and most common effects of the expansion of Europe, its consequences have been relatively little studied by historians of Canada. Indeed, one of the few general histories of the western mixed-blood population suggests – only half-jokingly, one suspects – that the Métis people of Canada were founded nine months after the landing of the first European.[1] Perhaps because of traditional historiographical emphases, a limited methodological sophistication, or simply as a consequence of racist inhibitions on the part of Euro-Canadian historians, who dominated the field until recently, the history of the Métis has not received much concerted and systematic attention from academic historians.

How have the limitations of our historiography, methodological backwardness, and prejudice accounted for this scanty treatment? The emphases of the first generations of Canadian historians on political themes, such as national consolidation and the achievement of autonomous status, or on economic development, drew those investigators to documents that were confined to the elites of early Canadian society. The questions that Canadian historians first asked and the materials to which they put those interrogatories were not such as to lead investigators to an examination of the lives of mixed-blood peoples. So long as Canadian historical methodology was of the from-the-top-down variety, the Métis remained invisible unless they impinged on a Great Man, such as Sir George Simpson or Sir John A. Macdonald, or unless one of them was, like Louis Riel, a Great Man in his own right. Finally, the ethnocentric and racist prejudice and preferences of many historians made them reluctant, however unconsciously, to acknowledge the presence, much less the importance, of Canadians of mixed racial background. The Abbé Lionel Groulx, with his strenuous denials of miscegenation in New France, was only one example of this widespread, racially inspired blindness.[2]

So it was that early studies of the Métis treated that community within a Eurocentric and historiographically elitist framework. In general, the mixed-blood population only received serious attention when its activities intersected with European commercial companies or Canadian politicians. Perhaps owing to the legacy of Groulx, there was little attention to the Métis in the history of New France and the early colonial period of French Canada. Among economic historians, there was some notice of the role that the offspring of unions between Hudson's Bay or North West Company men and Indian women played, especially in the nineteenth century. But even this perspective, as the later research of social historians would point out, was an extremely limited one. One would almost have thought, from reading Canadian history at least, that the Métis did not exist until they became enmeshed in the rivalries of Montreal and Bay traders, menaced Lord Selkirk's settlement plans, destroyed the Bay monopoly in 1849, or frustrated Macdonald and McDougall in the Red River district in 1869.

Early studies by George Stanley and Marcel Giraud that *did* attempt to examine the role of the Métis displayed many of these historiographical constrictions and methodological shortcomings. For G.F.G. Stanley the Métis, whether of Red River or Saskatchewan, were merely part of a 'frontier' of hunters and nomads that resisted before succumbing to an advancing frontier: 'Both the Manitoba insurrection and the Saskatchewan rebellion were the manifestation in Western Canada of the problem of the frontier, namely the clash between primitive and civilized peoples.'[3] The consequences of viewing the Métis through these Turnerian glasses were enormous. In the first place, Stanley tended to see all the people of mixed blood in the West as essentially the same. They were, after all, just part of the same frontier phenomenon. Consequently, *The Birth of Western Canada* discounted differences of denomination and levels of affluence that existed among the Métis, even within the Red River colony. Second, Stanley's perspective resulted in a blending of the stories of Indians and Métis in the insurrection of 1885. The Indian followers of Poundmaker and Big Bear who 'rose' in the spring of 1885 were portrayed as part of a concerted campaign of insurrection led by Riel. Why the southern Indians, who were even worse off than those in the Saskatchewan country, failed to take up arms; why so few of the more northerly Indians resorted to violence; why leaders such as

Poundmaker and Big Bear appeared to have exerted themselves to minimize bloodshed; and why they ultimately surrendered – all these were discomfiting questions that were not addressed by a treatment of the events of 1885 as the clash of two frontiers. This distorted perception of what occurred at Red River in 1869 and in the Saskatchewan country unfortunately set the pattern for most later accounts of these clashes.[4]

Another pioneer in Métis studies, a contemporary of Stanley's, demonstrated a different type of deficiency in his view of the subject. Marcel Giraud's *Le Métis canadien* (1945) is usually, and rightly, described as monumental, a paragon of painstaking research. Giraud's ethnographic study of the emergence of the mixed-blood communities in the West was based on field observations, vast researches in the Hudson's Bay Company Archives in London, and exhaustive reading of every secondary source available to him. Its appearance at the end of the German occupation of France was testimony to the author's perseverance and energy. But, though the study was monumental and painstaking, it was not without its faults; and these shortcomings were attributable both to Giraud's own assumptions and prejudices and to some of his sources. George Woodcock's 'Translator's Introduction' to the handsome reissue of *Le Métis canadien*, brought out in two volumes under the title *The Métis in the Canadian West*,[5] is at pains to stress that Giraud does not make ethnocentric judgments about the Métis. Says Woodcock: '... where judgments exist in *Le Métis canadien* they can be taken as relative to the changing situation of the West and not as absolute.'[6]

However, Giraud was very much in the grip of interpretations that attributed certain characteristics to particular nationalities or races, and he was unconsciously influenced by some of his sources. So one finds references to 'the inflexibility of the Anglo-Saxon temperament' and to the fact that Highlanders were 'frugal.'[7] The easy-going, convivial francophones got along with both Indians and mixed-blood peoples because of their temperament. Giraud also found that Native societies tended to be 'less evolved' and European communities 'more evolved.' Whether a particular branch of the Métis community was more or less 'evolved' usually turned out to be a matter of the degree to which it accepted or spurned the clergy's urgings to give up nomadism and embrace sedentary agriculture.[8] The explanation of this bias resided in the methodology Giraud employed in his field research. As noted, he relied on Catholic missionaries for information and for suggestions as to which Métis he should interview.[9]

The fact that Giraud's investigations were partially shaped by missionaries and those Métis of whom the clergy thought most highly, as well as by his own subscription to notions of ethnic or racial characteristics, imparted to *The Métis in the Canadian West* a number of disquieting features. Various groups were evaluated according to the degree to which they had 'evolved' towards a European or Euro-American standard of economic and social activity, rather than the extent to which they had adapted to their natural environment and economic opportunities. Furthermore, the Métis were portrayed as the malleable objects on which other, more 'evolved' groups worked. Accordingly, the sense of Métis nationalism that had begun to develop early in the nineteenth century was portrayed largely as the product of the machinations of the Nor'westers, rather than an understandable response to economic encroachment, commercial antipathies, and, later, increasing racism. Finally, in this version the events of 1869 and 1885, as well as the recriminations that followed the resistance and insurrection, led to 'The Disintegration of the Métis As a Group.'[10]

The accounts that George Stanley and Marcel Giraud produced in the 1930s and 1940s set the tone for Métis studies for a long time. In their different ways, and in spite of their quite distinctive approaches, they resembled one another in their refusal to treat the Métis as a people and a subject worthy of study in their own right. Stanley's interests may have been military and political while Giraud's were ethnographic, but in both cases the Métis were seen within a distinctively European framework of interpretation. Stanley's sources reinforced this Eurocentric tendency; Giraud's more innovative methods of investigation were offset by Eurocentric assumptions and 'filters.' For Stanley, the Métis were important as the principal constituent of the 'frontier' that unsuccessfully resisted the expansion of a more mature economy. Giraud purported to take the Métis more on their own terms, but he too saw them to a large extent as the product of European influences. Some 'evolved' and succeeded; most 'disintegrated' after Euro-Canadian society crushed them in 1885.

When scholars began to pay renewed attention to the Métis in the 1970s, it was initially within the framework that earlier scholars had established. This meant that the Métis entered the ken of these scholars when their activities impinged on the doings and aspirations of European and Canadian society. More obviously, still, it was not so much the Métis as the Great Men of their community – especially Riel – who attracted attention. Indeed, Riel has always served as a mythic figure whom a variety of groups have used to interpret, not the Métis, but themselves in the guise of history. Even before Riel was executed, French-Canadian nationalists had begun to transform him into a symbol of Quebec's political impotence and vulnerability within Confederation. The fact that Ontario critics of French Canada began in the summer of 1885 to attack Riel as a French, Catholic rebel made him into a symbol of Quebec militancy, rather than Native resistance, and drove French Canadians to embrace the Métis leader as a surrogate and champion of themselves.[11]

In the twentieth century, Riel proved a useful rallying point for politicians of all sorts, including the leaders of Native organizations that were beginning to find their political voice. This process reached a culmination of sorts in 1978 when the Association of Métis and Non-Status Indians of Saskatchewan (AMNSIS) petitioned the federal cabinet for 'a posthumous pardon for David Louis Riel.'[12] Western regional leaders joined in the process, Saskatchewan Liberal premier Ross Thatcher intoning that 'we of 1968 face a situation which is similar in some respects' to that of the 1880s. 'If Riel could walk the soil of Canada today, I am sure his sense of justice would be outraged as it was in 1885.'[13] Not to be outdone, Liberal prime minister Pierre Trudeau exploited Riel as a symbolic victim of nationalistic intolerance. Observed the champion of participatory democracy and multiculturalism: 'Riel and his followers were protesting against the Government's indifference to their problems and its refusal to consult them on matters of their vital interest ... Questions of minority rights have deep roots in our history ... We must never forget that, in the long run, a democracy is judged by the way the majority treats the minority. Louis Riel's battle is not yet won.'[14] And, of course, Riel and his 'adjutant' Gabriel Dumont became Canadian versions of anti-imperialist guerilla fighters in the febrile orations of student radicals of the later 1960s and the 1970s.[15]

A refreshing gust of realism blew away much of this rhetoric when political scientists and sociologists turned to examine Riel in the 1970s. University of Calgary political scientist Thomas Flanagan foreshadowed his iconoclastic analysis in the 1974 article 'Louis "David" Riel: Prophet, Priest-King, Infallible Pontiff.'[16] Before Flanagan could loose his fully developed ideas on the Canadian academic world, a more traditional study of Gabriel Dumont by George Woodcock appeared.[17] Flanagan and Woodcock together represented the continuation of the traditional preoccupation with the Great Man approach, now with novel twists.

Woodcock, of course, came to Dumont from a background in which philosophical anarchism was at least as important as literary analysis. To Woodcock, Dumont and the Métis represented one of the last examples in North America of the liberated and self-regulating communities that he so much admired. The hunters in pursuit of the bison manifested an 'anarchic egoism, tempered by mutual respect among the strong and by generosity towards the weak. Bakunin, who stressed the virtues to be found in people not entirely absorbed into modern industrial society, would have loved, if he had known them, these free hunters who were his contemporaries.'[18] The 'Republic of St. Laurent' of the 1870s, and to a lesser extent Batoche of the 1880s, are a sort of anarchists' Utopia in the Woodcock account. But Woodcock's approach by way of the inner dynamics of a pre-industrial, semi-tribal community did make a major contribution: it sketched a possible explanation for Dumont's willingness to follow Riel while disagreeing with his strategy in the spring of 1885. As Dumont put it, 'I yielded to Riel's judgment ... although I was convinced that, from a humane standpoint, mine was the better plan; but I had confidence in his faith and his prayers, and that God would listen to him.' According to Woodcock, Dumont followed because of a combination of traditional loyalty to a leader, pious faith in a religious appeal, and the strong personal bonds that had been forged by Riel's earlier political success.[19]

Flanagan's initial interest was with why Riel led rather than why the Métis followed. In his important *Louis 'David' Riel: 'Prophet of the New World,'* Flanagan reinterpreted the Métis leader, not as a madman, but as a messianic prophet who stood in a long line of prophetic advocates in Western history.[20] Reinterpreting the numerous writings Riel left behind, Flanagan stressed Riel's emphasis on the coming apocalypse and his radical ideas on religious reform to place the Métis leader in a lengthy tradition of millenarian leadership. Riel was, he claimed, 'more prophet and miracle worker than political leader,' the Northwest Rebellion was 'a politico-religious movement,' and Riel's actions were consistent with those of 'other millenarian leaders.'[21] The implications that could and would be drawn from Flanagan's reinterpretation were numerous and important.

First, Flanagan himself pursued his interest in the Métis Great Man within the confines of what was becoming known as 'The Riel Project.' A team headed by George F.G. Stanley was assembling an edited and annotated collection of everything Riel wrote that was still extant in time for the centenary of the Rebellion of 1885.[22] Flanagan's own work on the volume dealing with material written between Riel's acceptance of an invitation to return to Canada in 1884 and his execution in 1885 led him to produce another work that was decidedly not part of the centenary celebrations. In *Riel and the Rebellion: 1885 Reconsidered*, Flanagan argued against the position, championed by AMNSIS in 1978, that Louis Riel deserved a full, posthumous pardon. The Métis case was not that Riel deserved to be pardoned because of insanity, but because he had been driven to rebellion by an insensitive government. Flanagan argued that Riel should not be pardoned because he was, individually, responsible for the insurrection. The objective conditions that justified rebellion in liberal democratic theory did not exist in the Saskatchewan country in 1884–5, and Riel was pursuing personal objectives as well as Métis claims. Needless to say, Flanagan's revision, which resembled no scholar's interpretation of 1885 so much as it did Donald Creighton's, caused a storm of controversy. There were calls for Flanagan's dismissal from his academic position and denunciations of him as a racist. The Métis of Saskatchewan now announced that they no longer sought a pardon for the simple reason that Riel had done nothing wrong. It was the government of Canada, not Louis Riel, that needed forgiveness. The work of Woodcock and Flanagan on the politically climactic moment of 1885 served to focus attention on a crucial question that no one seemed able to answer. Why did the Métis follow Riel in the spring of 1885 as he departed from the agenda on which all had agreed in the summer of 1884? Woodcock had provided a provocative answer at the personal level of Dumont. But what of the Métis community as a whole? Two new answers emerged, significantly, from quite distinct areas of social history. That development, it would turn out, was an indicator of where studies on the Métis were headed in the 1980s.

The most ambitious attempt to explain why the Métis followed Riel came from a sociologist of religion. Gilles Martel of the Université de Sherbrooke employed the model developed by Maria Isaura Pereira de Queiroz that explained that messianic leaders emerged at critical times in the development of peoples, especially groups that were being buffeted by social and economic change. His carefully constructed *Le Messianisme de Louis Riel*[23] sought both to establish that the conditions of dislocation and marginalization prevailed among the Métis at Red River and Saskatchewan, and that Riel was the sort of messianic figure whose claims were accepted in such conditions. There were, however, difficulties with the model as Martel applied it in the Canadian West from the 1860s to the 1880s. First, it was by no means clear that the Métis in the Saskatchewan were experiencing the trauma that seemed necessary to prepare for upheaval. Second, there was almost no evidence that those who followed Riel understood any of the messianic ideas to which he subscribed. Finally, the theory conveniently ignored the very large numbers of mixed-blood residents in Red River and Saskatchewan who did not follow Riel. Frits Pannekoek had made a sustained, though controversial, argument about the earlier resistance that stressed that Red River was a divided community in which the English-speaking or 'country born' peoples were opposed to Riel.[24] (A number of scholars, most notably Irene Spry, have vigorously rejected this analysis.)[25] And the theory did not seem to explain how it was that of the mixed-blood community of thirteen hundred in the valley of the South Saskatchewan, only two hundred and fifty were at Batoche when it fell in May 1885.

The second attempt at explanation came from a different sort of social history, a community study of Batoche. Diane Payment's *Batoche (1870–1910)* was not only a significant example of the social history that was becoming increasingly important; it was also an instance of the work of a 'public historian.'[26] Payment's work cast doubt on Martel's sociological interpretation as applied to the 1880s by showing that the Métis of Saskatchewan had been adjusting well to changing economic circumstances prior to the coming of the branch-line railway in 1890–1. It also provided evidence for disunity in the Métis community in 1885, pointing out that probably one-third of those with Riel at Batoche had participated only under duress.[27] But Payment also provided a tantalizing suggestion that might prove to be an important part of the explanation for whatever unity of mind and purpose existed between Riel and his followers. She suggested that the Métis had developed a syncretic religion from traditional Indian animism and Catholic Christianity.[28] Perhaps that religious amalgam had predisposed the Métis to recognize and follow a leader like Riel, who spoke the language of religion in explaining political and military campaigns. If correct, Payment will have provided a link between the newer social history concerns and the older political and military preoccupations with the Great Man of the Métis.

Social history did not immediately have the field of Métis studies all to itself in the 1980s; several political and military histories continued to explore the field. Walter Hildebrandt, another Parks Canada investigator, provided a valuable corrective to many of the generalizations about the climactic days of the 1885 campaign in *The Battle of Batoche.*[29]

Don McLean, a sociologist who taught for several years at the Gabriel Dumont Institute, attempted to mount an answer to Flanagan. McLean constructed an argument that the federal government and local entrepreneurs fomented rebellion in 1885 to justify further appropriations for the foundering Canadian Pacific Railway, in the one case, and to bring badly needed hard money into the Saskatchewan country, on the other.[30] McLean's study must hold the record for the number of times such formulations as 'must have' or 'it is very likely' or 'it is difficult to find direct evidence' appear.[31]

Conspiracy theories aside, solid work was also being done in the traditional political history area of biography. Murray Dobbin's *The One-and-a-Half Men* was an interesting analysis of two Métis political organizers in the twentieth century, written from a Marxist perspective.[32] Dobbin was one of the first to dabble in the murky waters of provincial governments' relations with the Native community, a stagnant pond that badly needs scholarly stirring up. Another fascinating study in Métis political leadership came from the pen of Hugh Dempsey of the Glenbow-Alberta Institute. One of the intriguing aspects of Dempsey's biography of his father-in-law, Senator James Gladstone, was that it was an analysis of a Métis who had chosen (and struggled hard) to become a status Indian, going on to play an important economic and political leadership role from the 1940s to the 1960s.[33] Like all of Dempsey's work, *Gentle Persuader* was a sensitive and sympathetic depiction of the Native peoples in their interaction with the political apparatus dominated by Euro-Canadian society.

However, if some historians and social scientists continued to interest themselves in the military and political history of the Métis community, their more numerous colleagues were beginning to examine the Natives from a variety of social history perspectives. Indeed, the most exciting development in the historiography of the Métis in the past generation has been the attention devoted to it by social historians. In this, perhaps, the study of the mixed-blood communities is historiographically similar to most areas of Canada's story. Like the history of labour, which moved away from a fascination with climactic events and powerful organizations to a concern with the everyday experience of working-class people, Métis history gradually forsook its obsession with Riel or fur-trading companies for an examination of life in the numerous mixed-blood communities. The types of social history that have been brought to bear during this evolution of the field were several. They included women's history, family and childhood history, and local history. Probably the most productive avenues of investigation thus far have been women's and family history, in particular the work of Sylvia Van Kirk of the University of Toronto and Jennifer S.H. Brown of the University of Winnipeg.[34]

Although the principal works by these two scholars were superficially similar, as noted earlier, their approaches were in fact quite distinctive. Van Kirk's *'Many Tender Ties'* and Brown's *Strangers in Blood* were concerned with the social side of the fur trade in western and northern Canada from the beginning of the Hudson's Bay Company's contact, though both emphasized the later part of the eighteenth century and the nineteenth century because of the thinness of the documentary evidence from the earlier period. Both works drastically revised and substantially enriched our understanding of the fur trade and the distinctive western Canadian society that that commerce had helped to create. A greater appreciation of the importance of Indian women and their Native children of both genders to the trade was only one way in which these scholars deepened our understanding. Their insights into the shift of European men's taste in women from Indians to Métis to Caucasians helped to trace the onset and growth of racism in nineteenth-century western Canadian society, while simultaneously adding another dimension to our understanding of the emergence of Métis nationalism and resistance to Canadian imperialism.

But there were also important differences between the approaches employed in *Strangers in Blood* and *'Many Tender Ties'* that were signalled in their subtitles. Brown's study had as its subtitle *Fur Trade Company Families in Indian Country*; Van Kirk was interested in *Women in Fur-Trade Society.* Of necessity, both paid considerable attention to the Native and female side of the relationships, as well as to the offspring of those relations. But Van Kirk was especially interested in the women, and, although she did not ignore the fate of male offspring of country marriages, she understandably concentrated on the matrimonial and other fates of the daughters of these unions. Brown's interests were more extended, and to some degree their wide-ranging nature explained the fact that *Strangers in Blood* had less of a focus than did *'Many Tender Ties.'* Brown was interested in the formation of families and, to a lesser degree, social organizations, such as business partnerships, in which in the eighteenth and nineteenth centuries clan, kin, and friendship links had been very important. Consequently, she devoted more attention to family and business enterprise formation, to the evolving patterns of childhood among both anglophone and francophone fur-trade families, and to the ways in which both these families and these commercial enterprises had related to their local, transcontinental, and transoceanic context.

Some measure of Brown's more extended interests could be found in the historiographical models that she employed. She placed particular reliance on Peter Laslett's *The World We Have Lost*[35] to explain both family formation and small business organization in fur-trade country. From this model, she derived fascinating insights that went far to explain the relationship between economic and marital motives in seventeenth- and eighteenth-century families and the ease with which such a custom as 'placing' or 'turning off' Native spouses had been adopted by European males. Similarly, her adoption of Japanese sociologist Chie Nakane's concept of 'the vertical society' to analyse the Hudson's Bay Company provided her with a useful explanatory tool that allowed her to dissect and display the inner operations and outer appearance of the business partnerships in which the Baymen had participated.[36]

But Brown's employment of these models from other disciplines and other fields of history also demonstrated some of the weaknesses of the social history approach. It was understandable that social historians reached for other models: those available were so sophisticated and the field to be reworked was so intimidating. However, the application of a model derived from an alien environment could cause difficulties. Van Kirk indirectly pointed out one problem about borrowing the interpretive scheme of someone such as Laslett when she insisted that the usual European distinctions between public and private spheres simply did not apply: 'Fur-trade society, as in both Indian and pre-industrial European societies, allowed women an integral socio-economic role because there was little division between the "public" and "private" spheres.'[37] Given that difference, was it wise to apply concepts from British social history to family formation and business history in fur-trade country in the late eighteenth and nineteenth centuries?

In a somewhat parallel fashion, social historians such as Brown might have been more cautious in borrowing from sociologists, even ones as talented as Japan's Nakane. Nakane's 'vertical society' model was a fascinating interpretive searchlight turned on Japanese society. But did it work as well for links between British entrepreneurs? Were partnerships structured like Japanese families, even the extended families of the business and industrial world? Furthermore, Nakane's work was highly controversial and not universally accepted within Japanese academe. There was also a competing model in Takeo Doi's *The Anatomy of Dependence*, which emphasized *amae* – dependence, or the urge to be loved – as an interpretive tool to explain the group orientation of Japanese society and business.[38] There might well have been more clues to linkages within fur-trade enterprises in Doi than in Nakane.

The emphasis on women's and family studies pioneered so ably by Brown and Van Kirk has advanced Métis historiography by providing important new insights. By taking the viewpoint of the female partner in these *mariages à la façon du pays*, these scholars gained a new insight into what had previously been considered sexual exploitation at the hands of European men. Both pointed out the differing attitudes towards marriage, and towards dissolution of the matrimonial bond, that prevailed among many Indian peoples, and both argued convincingly that what Europeans took for amoral casualness had merely been a different attitude to sexual mores. Such insights enabled students of fur-trade social history to appreciate properly such things as 'serial polygamy' and 'turning off,' practices that had hitherto been referred to with barely suppressed sniggers by male scholars. The female-oriented approach has also helped students of the fur trade to understand fully the invaluable economic and diplomatic role of Native women in exploration and commerce in early Canadian history. Since the work of Van Kirk and Brown, it has become almost ritualistic to refer to this important function.[39] A feminine emphasis has greatly expanded and deepened our understanding, not just of the emergence of a Métis community, but of the functioning of the western and northern fur trade as a whole.

Increasingly, family-oriented studies began to blend into another type of social history – the small community study. In some respects there was nothing new in this. John E. Foster had begun the process of scholarly investigation of a small, predominantly Métis community more than fifteen years ago in his doctoral thesis on the country-born of Red River.[40] More recently, a growing band of scholars has undertaken the systematic investigation of far-flung Métis communities, and in the process they have gone far to free Métis scholarship of what is sometimes referred to as 'Red River myopia.'[41]

The best example of this broader vision in Métis studies was *The New Peoples*, the papers of the 1981 Conference on the Métis in North America, which was held at the Newberry Library in Chicago. The conference, which was addressed by Marcel Giraud, brought together many of the younger scholars at work on various aspects of Métis history and culture. Jacqueline Peterson of the University of Washington gave a useful overview of her work on the many mixed-blood communities of the Great Lakes area of the United States, while John S. Long discussed 'halfbreeds, Indians, petitioners and Métis' in northern Ontario, and T. Nicks and K. Morgan dealt with the development of Grande Cache and the emergence of Aboriginal identity among the mixed-blood people of that area.

These representative chapters from *The New Peoples* illustrated nicely the variety and richness of recent community-oriented research. Peterson's careful scholarship should compel many people, including Marcel Giraud, to re-evaluate their generalizations about the Métis, because Peterson found that the communities she examined so thoroughly had evinced a sense of Métis nationalism long before the tensions between rival fur-trading companies in Rupert's Land supposedly engendered that feeling of ethnic pride and aspiration. Long's work was one of the few reminders one could find that the Métis, contrary to most of the historiography dealing with them, were not a purely western Canadian phenomenon. In fact, what was remarkable was the absence of studies of mixed-blood communities in Quebec and the Maritime provinces, to say nothing of British Columbia and the far north. If 'Red River myopia' is being cured, it is not being replaced by excellent peripheral vision.

But in many ways the most fascinating study in *The New Peoples* was the one by Nicks and Morgan on Grande Cache, which combined the talents of an anthropologist and a geneticist. These scholars employed both traditional scholarly investigations of written sources with oral history and with family reconstruction and record linkage. Moreover, Grande Cache was not so much the product of fur-trade company penetration as it was of the migration of Iroquois-descended freemen. Finally, the Grande Cache Métis of northern Alberta behaved in divergent ways at the time of the coming of treaties and Ottawa-directed policies aimed at Indians and mixed-blood peoples. The hunters and trappers of Grande Cache accepted Métis scrip, while others among their relatives – apparently the more sedentary and agriculturally inclined of them – entered Treaty 6. In the twentieth century, the Métis of Grande Cache only slowly and belatedly developed a sense of Aboriginal identity. It was not until 1972 that, 'with the assistance of white cultural brokers,' they put forward an Aboriginal claim to land.[42] 'For the Grande Cache people, adopting a Métis identity does not mean that they have lost sight of themselves as a distinct social group. Identifying themselves as Métis achieves quite the opposite effect – it ensures their continued distinctiveness in a social, political and economic environment now dominated by Euro-Canadian immigrants.'[43] How many other unexplored mixed-blood communities does this pattern fit? It might well be that the model Nicks and Morgan have developed can be applied to other Métis communities with profit.

It seems highly likely that the short-term future of Métis studies lies in the sort of sophisticated analyses that Nicks/Morgan and Peterson have produced. At least one study, that of the Fort Vancouver Native community in Washington, is being undertaken from the perspective of the history of children and of families.[44] Another examination is being made, along the lines of Peterson's work on the Great Lakes Métis and their diffusion, on the migration of Red River Métis to the Oregon territory in the 1840s.[45] What the intensive study of specific communities has shown thus far is that many of our generalizations are flimsy, and that the Métis experience is an extremely diverse one. Payment's excellent study of Batoche, for example, showed clearly that the traditional view that 1885 had been a devastating blow to the South Saskatchewan Métis simply will not hold up. They adjusted economically, socially, and politically, and continued to be a coherent and successful group until they were swamped by European immigrants in the first decade of the twentieth century. The more individual studies are multiplied, the more we are likely to find our restricted focus on one story widened to include the heterogeneity of mixed-blood experience in different topographic and economic zones of the continent.

However, in some ways Métis studies will probably become even more tightly focused and microscopic. For one thing, there should be increasing attention to Métis arts and crafts. 'In Search of Métis Art,' by Ted Brasser, though it only scratched the surface of the artistic and artisanal production of the Métis, suggested strongly that there was a fascinating field to be developed.[46] The 1985 exhibition 'The Métis,' which was mounted at the Glenbow Museum and recorded by Julia D. Harrison in a well-illustrated work called simply *Métis*,[47] similarly suggested that handicrafts and artwork would repay further study. In addition, language and literature require more attention. The distinctive Métis language(s) known as Michif have received some attention.[48] More seems in order. At the same time, what of the bardic tradition, whose existence, if nothing else, is known? What beyond Pierre Falcon constituted it? Does it survive?

Recent efforts have been made to recover the Métis literary and everyday voices. A powerful autobiographical statement by Maria Campbell, *Halfbreed*, touched many Métis deeply, while bringing home to the majority population in a direct way many of the problems of contemporary Métis society.[49] A more recent collection, gathered apparently in commemoration of the 1885 rising, was less successful. *No Feather, No Ink* contained many poems about Great Men such as Riel and Dumont, but little by Métis people themselves.[50] In marked contrast was Irene Poelzer's successful effort to record the views of a group of Métis women from northern Saskatchewan communities. *In Our Own Words* was noteworthy for the deliberately unstructured way in which the interviews were conducted and for the manner in which the results of the interviews were subjected to content analysis by trained social scientists.[51] The result was a poignant account of living the life of a Métis woman that had both the immediacy of first-hand testimony and analysis by scholars who did not obtrude on the subjects themselves. More such investigations would be most welcome.[52]

Métis studies would also benefit from zeroing in on the Métis in another sense. Though we know an increasing amount about specific Métis communities thanks to people such as Peterson, Payment, and the Nicks/Morgan team, we do not know as much as we should about relations within those communities. There has been a fierce debate over internal relations in Red River in the 1850s and 1860s, with Pannekoek insisting that the community had been divided between francophone and anglophone, and Spry dismissing that argument and contending that the divisions that existed were along class lines. Payment's study of *Batoche* emphasized the differences between the Métis bourgeoisie, who had tended to cosy up to authority both in 1885 and afterwards, and the rest of the population, which had been much more volatile politically. We need to know more about these divisions, if such they were.

We must, in short, study class as a factor among the Métis. There has been some fruitful analysis of the Hudson's Bay Company labour practices after the amalgamation of 1821.[53] And fur-trade historians have frequently commented in passing on relations between bourgeois and voyageurs, factors and servants. We need to know more about some of the Métis business success stories such as Letendre *dit* Batoche or Pascal Breland. If Spry was correct in her contention that the lines of cleavage in heterogeneous communities such as Red River had been along class or occupational group lines, such analysis will deepen our understanding of those communities. If not, we will still know more about the economic history of the Métis than we do now.

However, while Métis scholarship needs in some ways to become more tightly focused, it also must simultaneously become more diffused. This is so in at least two senses: the artificial barrier between Métis and Indians should be obliterated; and Canadian Métis should be examined within a comparative, international framework. At the present time, students of Indian history and the history of mixed-blood communities barely communicate with each other. Those who are interested in the history of Indian-White relations systematically avoid, as though in some blind obedience to the dictates of the Indian Act of 1876, any consideration of the Métis. The most recent example of this approach was Brian Titley's study of Indian Affairs bureaucrat Duncan Campbell Scott.[54] In a note, Titley explained that once the Métis took scrip, they 'no longer came under the jurisdiction of the federal government and therefore are not of immediate concern in this study.' But in discussing the making of Treaty 9, he was driven to mention them in passing.[55] And discussion of Indian education is misleading without some attention to the fact that mixed-blood, and even Euro-Canadian, children frequently attended the schools that Ottawa thought it was supporting solely for Indian children.

Other recent publications besides Titley's *A Narrow Vision* make clear the perils involved in sticking rigorously to the Indian group. Hugh Dempsey's biography of James Gladstone was in fact the story of a Métis who not only had become 'Indian,' but emerged as an important leader of the 'Indian' community. Jennifer Brown reminded us in *Strangers in Blood* that Mandelbaum some time ago explained that the 'Parkland People,' who are regarded officially as Plains Cree, were in fact descendants of mixed marriages.[56] Books by Yerbury, Thistle, and Francis and Morantz that supposedly dealt with 'Indians' in the fur trade in various parts of the country invariably had to mention the importance of mixed-blood people in the trade.[57] The most painful example of the folly of trying to ignore one community while studying the other was David Mulhall's biography of Father A.G. Morice. As Jacqueline Gresko has pointed out, Mulhall did not seem to recognize that the 'French of the Mountains' that Morice had used to communicate with the Babines of northern British Columbia was in fact Michif, the Métis tongue.[58] And, in the camp of the other solitude in Native studies, Nicks and Morgan have shown in the case of the groups they studied how artificial was the distinction between Métis and Indian. Investigators of both Indian and Métis history topics really must ask themselves how much longer they are willing to allow obsolete statutory distinctions that were developed in Ottawa in pursuit of bureaucratic convenience and economy to shape their research strategies. All the evidence seems to be that the dead hand of the Department of Indian Affairs is exerting a pernicious influence.

It is also important that Canadian scholars in Métis and other Native studies extend their horizon to include other countries where the interaction of Aboriginal peoples and European newcomers produced miscegenation. Certainly comparisons with countries such as the United States, New Zealand, and Australia, in which British and other colonial expansion encountered indigenous peoples, seem potentially fruitful. To take but one of many possible examples, a recent study of Presbyterian missionaries in the United States in the nineteenth century suggested that *Métissage* had had an impact on the internal relations of at least one Indian people. In this case, partially assimilated 'Choctaw halfbreeds' constituted a large part of the 'progressive' camp within the Choctaw nation that advocated acculturation and adaptation to the White people's ways.[59] Such comparative endeavours may be difficult among indigenous peoples who reject the notion of mixed-blood identity, but they seem worth pursuing for the light they might shed on developments in Canada.[60]

There are other obstacles, besides the inherent difficulties in studying similar experiences in a number of countries, to the successful pursuit of further studies of the Métis. One major hurdle that seems to be causing problems is politicization, which takes at least two forms: self-censorship and partisanship. Scholars who work with Native communities frequently find themselves confronted with the question of whether or not to publish a scholarly opinion that might run counter to the current political objectives of the community they are studying. Examples abound. The introduction to *The New Peoples* agonized over whether or not to capitalize the word 'Métis' because of the political implications that either the upper or the lower case might carry.[61] Hugh Dempsey's Preface to his biography of James Gladstone concluded, 'As this book, in part, deals with the history of the Blood Reserve, I also submitted the manuscript to Roy Fox, the head chief, and his council, for their approval.'[62] Both academic and public historians need to think through carefully what their stance should be towards subject groups who have both moral claims and political agendas to pursue.

Partisanship is an equally serious potential danger. Among some Native organizations there is a strongly held view that scholars are like politicians: those who are not with them are against them. The treatment to which Thomas Flanagan was subjected after the publication of *Riel and the Rebellion* was a particularly ugly example of that attitude. Some academics are predisposed to take a favourable, partisan position; others might be intimidated into doing so or remaining quiet. This, too, is a point of professional ethics that anyone working on subjects that might have a political interest to Native groups ought to consider carefully.

Not completely unrelated to the corrupting influence of censorship and partisanship is the menace of venality. As Inuit, Indian, and Métis land claims proceed to the courts with increasing frequency, there are multiplying opportunities for historians, anthropologists, sociologists, and others to earn large fees as consultants and witnesses. Still more dangerous is the fact that it is usually the government that has the longer purse and therefore offers the greater pecuniary attraction. This is a problem with which the Canadian historical community is only beginning to grapple. Historians are going to have to think about if, and on what terms, they are going to participate in remunerative judicial jousting so as to maintain not only their own integrity, but also that of their discipline.

While problems are numerous in Métis history, there is every reason for optimism about its prospects. During the past fifteen years, the study of mixed-blood communities has made rapid progress. It has broken free of its old fixation with the Great Man, and it has been partially cured of 'Red River myopia.' This field has become much more than the study of Louis Riel and his activities. To a considerable extent, the field has moved 'From Riel to the Métis.' Thanks largely to the influences of other disciplines such as anthropology and sociology, as well as the powerful stimulus that has come from the expansion of social history, investigators have begun to examine carefully Native women, childhood, and far-flung communities that had hitherto been ignored. Much remains to be done, both in attempting broader, comparative analyses and in examining individual communities more minutely. It promises to be a formidable task. However, if the students of the Métis show as much energy and imagination in the next generation as they have in the recent past, there is every reason to look forward eagerly to the results of their labours.

### Notes

This essay is reprinted from the *Canadian Historical Review* 69, no. 1 (March 1988): 1–20. I should like to thank my colleague W.A. Waiser for numerous helpful suggestions concerning it.

1 D.B. Sealey and A.S. Lussier, *The Métis: Canada's Forgotten People* (Winnipeg, 1975), 1.
2 B.G. Trigger, *Natives and Newcomers: Canada's 'Heroic Age' Reconsidered* (Kingston and Montreal, 1985), 34–5.
3 G.F.G. Stanley, *The Birth of Western Canada: A History of the Riel Rebellions*, 2nd ed. (Toronto, 1960; 1st ed. 1936), vii.
4 A welcome exception is G. Friesen, *The Canadian Prairies: A History* (Toronto and London, 1984), esp. chapters 6–7 and 10.
5 Lincoln and London, 1986.
6 Ibid., 1: xiv.
7 Ibid., 287, 444.
8 For example, ibid., 2: 160–1
9 'Foreword,' in *The New Peoples: Being and Becoming Métis in North America*, ed. J. Peterson and J.S.H. Brown (Winnipeg, 1985), xii.
10 Giraud, *Métis in the Canadian West*, vol. 2, title of Part Six.
11 A.I. Silver, *The French-Canadian Idea of Confederation, 1864–1900* (Toronto, 1982), chapter 8.
12 James Sinclair to P.E. Trudeau, 22 Sept. 1978 (mimeograph); reproduced as the frontispiece in *Louis Riel: Justice Must Be Done* (Winnipeg: Pemmican Publications, n.d.).
13 Quoted in ibid., vi.
14 Ibid., iii.
15 D. Owram, 'The Myth of Louis Riel,' *Canadian Historical Review* (CHR) 63, no. 3 (Sept. 1982): 328, 335. See also ibid., 329–33.
16 *Journal of Canadian Studies* 9, no. 3 (Aug. 1974): 15–25.
17 G. Woodcock, *Gabriel Dumont: The Métis Chief and His Lost World* (Edmonton, 1975). See also Woodock's poem 'On Completing a Life of Gabriel Dumont,' *Canadian Forum* 55 (Nov. 1975): 24.
18 Woodcock, *Dumont*, 36.
19 Ibid., 191-2.
20 T. Flanagan, *Louis 'David' Riel: 'Prophet of the New World'* (Toronto, 1979).
21 Ibid., 141, 149, 186.
22 G.F.G. Stanley et al., eds, *The Collected Writings of Louis Riel / Les Ecrits complets de Louis Riel*, 4 vols (Edmonton, 1985).
23 G. Martel, *Le Messianisme de Louis Riel* (Waterloo, 1984), esp. 1–8.
24 F. Pannekoek, 'The Anglican Church and the Disintegration of Red River Society, 1818–1870,' in *The West and the Nation: Essays in Honor of W.L. Morton*, ed. C. Berger and R. Cook (Toronto, 1976), 72–90; and 'The Rev. Griffiths Owen Corbett and the Red River Civil War of 1869–70,' *CHR* 57, no. 2 (June 1976): 133–49.

25  I.M. Spry, 'The Métis and Mixed-Bloods of Rupert's Land before 1870,' in Peterson and Brown, eds, *The New Peoples*, 95–118.

26  D. Payment, *Batoche (1870-1910)* (Saint-Boniface, 1983). Payment has reiterated her basic arguments while extending the period analysed in 'Batoche after 1885: A Society in Transition,' in *1885 and After: Native Society in Transition*, ed. F.L. Barron and J.B. Waldram (Regina, 1986), 173–87. Payment is a historian with Parks Canada.

27  Payment, *Batoche*, 67n77.

28  'The Métis Homeland: Batoche in 1885,' *NeWest Review*, May 1985, p. 12.

29  W. Hildebrandt, *The Battle of Batoche: British Small Warfare and the Entrenched Métis* (Ottawa, 1985).

30  D. McLean, *1885: Métis Rebellion or Government Conspiracy?* (Winnipeg, 1985).

31  Ibid., 120–1. Undoubtedly more is to be expected from D.N. Sprague's *Canada and the Métis, 1869–1885*, which is forthcoming from Wilfrid Laurier University Press.

32  M. Dobbin, *The One-and-a-Half Men: The Story of Jim Brady and Malcolm Norris – Métis Patriots of the Twentieth Century* (Vancouver, 1981).

33  H.A. Dempsey, *The Gentle Persuader: James Gladstone, Indian Senator* (Saskatoon, 1986).

34  S. Van Kirk, *'Many Tender Ties': Women in Fur-Trade Society, 1670–1870* (Winnipeg, [1980]); J.S.H. Brown, *Strangers in Blood: Fur Trade Company Families in Indian Country* (Vancouver, 1980).

35  New York, 1965.

36  Chie Nakane, *Japanese Society* (Berkeley and Los Angeles, 1970).

37  Van Kirk, *'Many Tender Ties,'* 4.

38  T. Doi, *The Anatomy of Dependence* (Tokyo, 1973).

39  See, for example, D. Francis and T. Morantz, *Partners in Furs: A History of the Fur Trade in Eastern James Bay, 1600–1870* (Kingston and Montreal, 1983), 84, 90–1; J.C. Yerbury, *The Subarctic Indians and the Fur Trade, 1680–1860* (Vancouver, 1986), 91; Paul C. Thistle, *Indian-European Relations in the Lower Saskatchewan River Region to 1840* (Winnipeg, 1986), 16.

40  J.E. Foster, 'The Country-Born in the Red River Settlement: 1820–1850' (Ph.D. diss., University of Alberta, 1972).

41  Quoted by T. Nicks and K. Morgan, 'Grande Cache: The Historical Development of an Indigenous Alberta Métis Population,' in Peterson and Brown, eds, *The New Peoples*, 173.

42  Nicks and Morgan, 'Grande Cache,' 172.

43  Ibid., 178.

44  J. Pollard, 'Growing Up without the Means of Grace: Cultures and Children

in the Pacific Northwest' (Ph.D. diss., University of British Columbia, in progress).

45  M. Patola, 'Red River Migration to Oregon, 1840–1856,' (M.A. thesis, University of Saskatchewan, in progress).

46  In Peterson and Brown, eds, *The New Peoples*, 221-9.

47  J.D. Harrison, *Métis: People between Two Worlds* (Vancouver/Toronto, 1985).

48  For example, J.C. Crawford, 'What Is Michif?' in Peterson and Brown, eds, *The New Peoples*, 231–41; 'Speaking Michif in Four Métis Communities,' *Canadian Journal of Native Studies* 3, no. 1 (1983): 47–55.

49  M. Campbell, *Halfbreed* (Toronto, 1973). Concerning the authenticity and immediacy of this work for Native peoples, see Emma LaRoque, 'The Métis in English Language Literature,' *Canadian Journal of Native Studies* 3, no. 1 (1983): 91.

50  *No Feather, No Ink* (Saskatoon, 1985).

51  D.T. Poelzer and I.A. Poelzer, eds, In *Our Own Words: Northern Saskatchewan Métis Women Speak Out* (Saskatoon, 1986), esp. xviii.

52  Although enough published accounts to provide a complete picture would be beyond the means of Canadian scholarship, recording of oral testimony on tape seems a feasible alternative. An excellent start has been made in many parts of Canada, most notably the Métis Oral History Project of the Provincial Archives of Manitoba.

53  P. Goldring, 'Papers on the Labour System of The Hudson's Bay Company, 1821-1900' (Parks Canada paper, 1979).

54  E.B. Titley, *A Narrow Vision: Duncan Campbell Scott and the Administration of Indian Affairs in Canada* (Vancouver, 1986).

55  Ibid., 206n32, 212–13n35.

56  Brown, *Strangers*, 217.

57  For example, Thistle, *Indian-European Relations*, 81-2.

58  D. Mulhall, *Will to Power: The Missionary Career of Father Morice* (Vancouver, 1986), 53. Mulhall has numerous references (39, 78, 81, 125) to Métis that appear potentially important, but he does not follow up. Gresko's critique is contained in a review of Mulhall that is soon to appear in the *NeWest Review*.

59  M.C. Coleman, *Presbyterian Missionary Attitudes toward American Indians, 1837–1893* (Jackson, Mississippi, and London, 1985), 58–9, 61.

60  Ron Bourgeault, assistant professor of Native studies, University of Saskatchewan, learned that Maori leaders with whom he spoke while in New Zealand in 1986 rejected the notion of *métissage*. They told him that a person was either Maori or White.

61  Peterson and Brown, eds, *The New Peoples*, 6–7.

62  Dempsey, *Gentle Persuader*, viii.

# METHODOLOGY

# 'I can only tell what I know':
# Shifting Notions of Historical Understanding
# in the 1990s

During the litigation surrounding the first James Bay hydroelectric project in Quebec in the 1970s, a number of Native witnesses appeared in Euro-Canadian courts in support of an attempt by the Cree to stall development in lands that they considered theirs. Naturally, these witnesses were administered the usual oath that bound them to tell the truth, the whole truth, and nothing but the truth – on at least one occasion with unexpected results. One Cree hunter hesitated when the clerk read out the usual form of words. Then he responded: 'I'm not sure I can tell the truth ... I can only tell what I know.'[1] Historians in the 1990s are increasingly finding themselves in the position of that Cree who found court ritual puzzling some twenty years ago. Although most of us – at least those of us who are now in mid-career – were trained in a tradition that assumed that the pursuit of truth was the underlying purpose of the discipline, we increasingly are finding our confidence shaken by a number of forces and influences. The comfortable nineteenth-century intellectual world on which until the past quarter-century academic tradition in the humanities unquestioningly reposed seems to be undermined by contemporary forces that are both political and intellectual. In particular, the movement that is usually termed Political Correctness, the growing strength of new methodological systems such as feminist scholarship, and a burgeoning interest in cross-cultural and interracial studies are combining to make us less and less confident that we can tell any truth, let alone the whole truth and nothing but the truth. Like the Cree witness, we find ourselves having to acknowledge, 'I can only tell what I know.'

It was all so simple and appealing back in graduate school days, wasn't it? Although students in the humanities rarely felt the need to articulate such justifications prior to the 1980s, everything that historians and other students of the human condition did was based on a nineteenth-century set of assumptions that was widely shared in the Western world at least. In fact, the foundation of this hegemonic intellectual approach had been articulated much earlier, most notably in John Milton's boast that no one ever saw Truth bested in a free and unconfined clash of ideas. In the nineteenth century this tradition was codified and popularized by the likes of John Stuart Mill, and in our own century its academic adherents found themselves buttressed by the triumph of academic freedom in Western universities. The other element that used to make up the comfortable intellectual world of historians was a tradition of critical methodology that came principally from Germany. Historians borrowed the criterion of verifiability of conclusions, imposing on their discipline the humanities variant of the bench scientist's requirement that any claim could be supported or refuted by replicating the experiment. For historians this meant an obligation to produce their evidence accurately, cite the sources of their evidence fully, and acknowledge the existence of contrary material if such there were. In such a methodological regime, other scholars who doubted one's conclusions could – not precisely run the experiment again – but check the sources to ensure that the conclusions being drawn from them were appropriate and sound. With liberalism's rationale for free inquiry, Rankean methodology, and, not incidentally, modern academic safeguards such as academic freedom and tenure, historians would be able to search the past for historical Truth.

To historians still trying to practise their craft in the 1990s, it seems the arrival of that liberal utopia is delayed. Indeed, some days it even sounds as though the world in which we try to practise our craft is marching determinedly backward towards a dystopia in which no one knows, much less proclaims, the truth any more. As noted above, the reasons for this are found principally in contemporary political and intellectual trends. The forces that are usually termed Political Correctness sometimes confine or even close off completely the scope of investigation, ensuring that whatever 'truth' emerges will be partial at best. More significant, though, are changing fashions in scholarship, especially feminist methodology but also including some aspects of postmodernist thought, that strike at the heart of the assumptions underpinning the intellectual edifice historians 'of a certain age,' at least, once took for granted. Finally, for historians who try to work across the boundaries of culture and race, there are additional challenges to the epistemological foundations of their intellectual abode. All of these – Political Correctness, new methodologies such as feminist interpretations, and cross-cultural inquiry – account for present-day angst among some historians, bewilderment among others, and apoplexy in a few.

Among the challenges facing history's claim to authority in the 1990s, the least of these is Political Correctness. In spite of all the hue and cry that one hears and reads about 'tenured radicals' and 'leftist' students combining to stifle free inquiry and open debate, there probably is no reason to worry about long-term damage from PC to the systems of inquiry with which we are familiar. This is not to say that there have not been attempts to gag those who espoused views that were politically unpopular, whether the critics understood them or not. In Canada most of these episodes have arisen, significantly, in the social sciences rather than in the humanities discipline of history. And, while the most notorious of them were certainly troubling for their targets, they all passed in time.[2] Before academics in the humanities become too self-congratulatory about the fact that it was their socially scientific colleagues who attracted most of the PC ire, they should bear in mind two things. One reason that humanities researchers have not on the whole been the targets of those who would limit or distort academic inquiry is that their subjects are considered much less relevant than those in the social sciences. Their invulnerability is the result of irrelevance, not invincibility. Secondly, within the humanities there are variants of Political Correctness that, while not attracting as much attention as censorship or political retribution, are much more insidious and potentially damaging.

These two enemies within are self-censorship and cultural appropriation. A clear-cut case of self-censorship comes from New Zealand and was reported to the annual meeting of the Canadian Historical Association at the University of Victoria in 1990. Professor Kerry Howe of Massey University told a session of historians that their colleagues in his country had for close to two decades eschewed serious study of the 1841 Treaty of Waitangi, a fundamentally important event and document in the history of relations between indigenous Maori and *pakeha* intruders. Howe explained that in recent years no one in academe had worked on this subject because any conclusions that historians could legitimately draw from the treaty would run counter to the political agenda and arguments that Maori organizations had been making. Of course, *pakeha* historians were already anxious and uncomfortable because their work embraced members of a different racial group.[3] A milder variant of this problem might be developing in Canada over a fundamental interpretation of part of the written constitution, the British North America Act of 1867 (Constitution Act 1867). Thanks to a combination of Québécois nationalist propaganda and social scientists' uncritical support, the concept of Confederation as a 'compact' or entente between two ethnic founding peoples has become well entrenched. Following a vigorous scholarly debate in the 1960s and 1970s, most historians and political scientists dropped disputation over whether or not the unification of Canada in the 1860s represented an unwritten pact to share and develop the new state on the basis of cultural and linguistic equality. Although most academics abandoned the question, politicians remained attached to the notion of Confederation as a cultural or ethnic compact. Naturally, the journalists have played no little part in keeping the compact view of Confederation front and centre, to the point that *Maclean's* magazine in commenting on the aftermath of the 1992 referendum on the Charlottetown constitutional accord reported in suitably shocked tones that most Canadians apparently did not view Canada as a compact of French and English.[4]

More recently the compact theory of Confederation has received highly publicized support from no less a personage than the Royal Commission on Aboriginal Peoples. One of the commission's published research papers declares Confederation to be a cultural compact and seeks to graft Aboriginal peoples onto that entente, the better to support their case for constitutional recognition of Aboriginal self-government.[5] In January 1994 the minister of Indian affairs announced that the new Liberal government accepted the royal commission's position on Aboriginal self-government and was prepared to implement it in short order. This series of events raises a conundrum for Canadian historians with an interest in Aboriginal subjects. It remains to be seen whether historians whose view of the nature of the Canadian federation differs will attack the royal commission's publication for historical inaccuracy or whether they will censor themselves in a good cause – support for Aboriginal self-government. Both the New Zealand and Canadian instances suggest that within the halls of academe one of the greatest dangers of Political Correctness is the temptation to censor oneself lest telling the truth as one knows it undermine support for a political cause with which one is sympathetic.

The same insidious danger arises over the issue of cultural appropriation, in spite of the fact that there are many effective arguments that scholars in the humanities might deploy to justify investigation of gender, racial, and ethnic groups other than their own. Those working on topics involving social groups different than their own might stand on the nineteenth-century canon, declaring that open and unfettered inquiry is the essence of academic inquiry – part of our mission statement, to use the cant of our own day – and those who argue to exclude cross-cultural investigation are advancing illegitimate propositions. A related argument might be the classical one. *Nil alienum*: I am human; I count nothing human foreign to me.[6] Or one might use a more refined, materialistic argument to retain access to at least some part of another culture's experience. So, for example, while one might concede that there are in Native society some practices, such as certain songs and dances, whose ownership and right of performance inhere exclusively in an individual or a particular family, other aspects of those societies are common to all and accessible. So, to continue the example, while one might not presume to reproduce a ritual song owned by an individual without permission, much as one might not reproduce a poem for fear of breaching copyright, one could investigate and write about the more public aspects. Finally, one could mount a utilitarian argument against the foes of academic cultural appropriation. For example, if non-Native people are excluded from researching and speaking about Aboriginal societies, who will write the history of the Beothuk, the original 'red Indians' of Newfoundland? They died out totally by 1829.

Although numerous robust arguments exist with which to defend scholarly work across racial and ethnic lines, there remains a problem. The real danger, of course, is that none of these arguments will be mounted, and that some historians will abandon a particular field in deference to those who shout 'cultural appropriation.' In other words, self-censorship and cultural appropriation can become linked, as in the case of a Canadian historian who during an academic visit to the University of Saskatchewan in 1992 said that she might move out of the field of Native history in part because of the criticism she had received from Native people during her presentation. We already know that New Zealand historians no longer probe the Treaty of Waitangi, and we fear that in Canada the hegemony, at least among journalists, of the compact view of Confederation will lead historians simply to censor themselves rather than confront the relatively few champions of Political Correctness within the groves of academe. The long-term implications of such craven behaviour, as will be noted later, are ominous in the extreme.

A much more powerful influence on the historian's presumption to authority is the emergence during the last few decades of new methodologies, particularly within the humanities area. It would be as tiresome as it is beyond the scope of this paper to attempt to list all the innovations in academic inquiry that have combined to cast into doubt the confident assumption that historians used to share with Leopold von Ranke that they were recovering the past *wie es eigentlich gewesen*, or essentially as it was. However, two aspects of recent scholarly investigation, new cultural history and feminist methodology, are particularly relevant, both because of their widespread influence and because of the way that they are redefining historians' understanding of what their subject is about and what it can accomplish.

The complex of interpretive styles that are usually grouped under the heading 'the new cultural history' share a healthy scepticism about the validity of anything being truly what it appears to be. Whether it is historians of text dismantling the structure and prose of a work to lay bare some inner meaning that either amplifies or contradicts the surface, or followers of Foucault holding any manner of concept whose reality we thought we 'knew' up to demystifying examination, cultural historians make it clear that inquirers cannot expect to reconstruct the past *wie es eigentlich gewesen*, if only because they do not accept that there is a fundamental source whose meaning and significance, unchanging and absolute, can be uncovered and used to test the meaning and significance of historical events and phenomena. So, for example, a legal historian in Canada used Foucault as part of her examination of the law against the potlatch among North West Coast Indians between 1885 and 1951. Using Foucault's notion of power as decentred and diffuse, she was able to explain the intermittent, incomplete, and often counterproductive effect of state attempts to use this law to extirpate the sharing ritual among these Native groups.[7] And, of course, innumerable studies have found that 'race' or 'gender' are not solid, immutable characteristics, but, rather, guises and identities that are always socially constructed and often can be altered. So, for example, Joy Parr's comparative study of work forces in two Ontario industries, a female-dominated textile factory and a male-dominated furniture firm, reveals unmistakably how the communities contended over and ultimately constructed dramatically different notions of 'proper femininity' or 'manly virtue' in the context of work routine and labour relations confrontations.[8] A parallel case involving race is found in coastal Labrador, where the community definition of a 'settler,' a term that, ironically, connoted Aboriginal ancestry, varied from time to time, depending upon the benefits or liabilities attached to that status.[9] Race, like gender and the power of the state, turns out to be an indeterminate quality rather than a solid substance, an elusive disguise rather than a fixed identity.

For traditional historians, the growing influence of the agnostic styles of historical inquiry that march under the banner of cultural history or cultural studies is seriously disquieting. While it is often easy for the conventional follower of Clio to see the advantages to be found in using methodological tools from a variety of disciplines – literary analysis, anthropology, law, psychology – it is less reassuring to contemplate the other cardinal feature of cultural history. As well as blurring the boundaries between methodologies and disciplines, the practitioners of cultural studies also destroy the notion of a bedrock or benchmark reality against which other phenomena can be examined and classified.[10] If nearly everything about people and their products turns out to be socially constructed, then there is no norm, no firm foundation. For historians this realization is the equivalent of a Platonic philosopher discovering that there are no ideal forms, only material reflections and human interpretations. In other words, the figures flickering on the wall of the cave are the only reality humankind will ever have to contemplate and interpret. Among historians, as among Platonic philosophers, if some find this revelation exhilarating and liberating, others find it disquieting and immobilizing. If there is no objective reality – if, to misquote Gertrude Stein, there is no there there – the conventional historian is at a loss as to what is being sought.

Feminist theory and feminist interpretations in history have had a profoundly unsettling, if also dramatically energizing, impact on the practice of history over the past two or three decades. There should be no mistaking the fact that those who began by looking for the women who had been left out of conventional history and ended up constructing new methods of inquiry and new schools of interpretation have profoundly changed our understanding of the history of most Western societies, including Canada. To take only one example for purposes of illustration, Canadian historians of women revolutionized our understanding of what was probably the most important economic activity of early European groups in the northern part of North America. While historians of Canada had long recognized the importance of the fur trade, and while Harold Innis had recorded its outlines in an important, if turgid, tome in 1930, we really knew little of the trade's social aspects until two historians approached the subject anew with the question 'Where were the women?' front and centre. The result of their novel inquiries was *'Many Tender Ties'* and *Strangers in Blood*, which uncovered not just the contribution of Native women to the fur trade but also a role for Native men that turned out to be much more complicated and influential than had previously been thought.[11] As these contributions from Jennifer Brown and Sylvia Van Kirk, as well as many other recent works, show, the revelations made by the researches of historians of Canadian women, both in supposedly tried and true topics and dramatically new ones, enriched and deepened Canadian historiography.

Simultaneously, the methodology employed by Canadian historians of women subtly challenged traditional modes of inquiry, interestingly in a manner that paralleled the unsettling influence of cultural history techniques and assumptions. The methodological novelty of feminist inquiry can perhaps best be summed up by saying that it places much more emphasis on *experiential* evidence than did traditional history, which tended to discount anything personal and emotional as suspect because it was partial or non-objective. As Professor Ruth Pierson has explained extremely well, the reason that female and feminist historians began to search for the internal and the personal was that they usually could not find women and women's experience when they looked at the public events and external forms of evidence that historians had traditionally used and, accordingly, traditional archivists had collected. Following Joan Kelly, Pierson pointed to 'oppositional consciousness,' the reaction a female inquirer experienced when she looked at a historical event or personage and either did not find female representation or found it misrepresented and denigrated by male interpreters of sources that failed to embody women's experience. The dawning of this oppositional consciousness – a variation of what an earlier generation of scholars might have referred to as cognitive dissonance – caused historians of women to search out the personal experiences and explanations of historical figures, or to posit the superiority of such personal evidence over other forms. In Pierson's words: 'In a hierarchy of knowledges we women's historians, particularly we feminist women's historians, have assigned a privileged place to knowledge claims based on "lived experience."'[12]

Among other things, this new approach drove women's historians to make considerable use of oral history in order to recapture the experience of women who historically were not deemed significant enough to have their records collected and analysed by male archivists and historians. 'In response to the invisibility and/or misrepresentation of women, it became a major goal of reclaiming women's history to enable women of the past to "speak with their own voices." In order to get at "women's experience," the methodology of oral history, in the absence of women's otherwise recorded voices, was valorised as validating women's lives. The "valorization" of women's "lived experience" was enhanced by the notion that it figured in the birth of feminist consciousness.'[13]

If this privileging of the interior and the personal, this valorization of 'lived experience' rather than formally recorded deeds, has made it possible to open up uncharted and important fields of inquiry, it has also raised new and unsettling questions. Driven by a desire to uncover the experience and contribution of women who had been ignored, historians of women have painted a large number of missing figures back into the national portrait, with the result that the depiction of the community's history is fuller and more rounded than it has ever been before. At the same time, however, the emphasis of feminist approaches on the personal and experiential points to some of the same sources of disquiet as did the cultural history approach. If the most 'privileged' evidence is lived experience, can there be any evidentiary bedrock, any foundation against which to measure other phenomena for their validity and representativeness? Is it worrisome that something as fundamental as 'gender' is described as 'a process, changing over time' rather than an entity?[14] If oral history records of lived experience contradict formal, official records in archives, how do we adjudicate between them? This is by no means a hypothetical question for researchers seeking to use both official records and oral history. For example, I have been told by a Mi'kmaq informant that her experience at a residential school was that she was frequently kept out of class for long stretches to help with kitchen work, but the Indian Affairs records for the school indicated that she was routinely in her classroom the one-half of each day that she was supposed to be. In this case, the contradiction was easily resolved in favour of the oral history version, because it was well known that school reports to Indian Affairs were regularly doctored to make school administrators look better and that keeping students out of class to help run the institution was common practice.[15]

The feminist emphasis on the personal and experiential leads to two other complications. First, *experience* is not a synonym for *knowledge*, at least as we have traditionally construed that word. To have been part of an event does not necessarily entail understanding the why and the wherefore of that event. Indeed, the more deeply involved one is in a complicated occurrence – such as a massive military manoeuvre during wartime, for example – the less likely an individual participant is to emerge with a sound grasp of what occurred, why it occurred in the way it did, and what the consequences and implications of the occurrence were.[16] If it be answered that this is a non-issue because there is no TRUTH, only socially constructed versions of reality that vary with time, place, and people, then academic inquirers are setting themselves up to have the foundation of all their activity, academic freedom, destroyed for reasons I will explain in due course.

The final unsettling implication of the feminist approach to the historical record that flows from its emphasis on the private, the internal, and the experiential is that it courts the danger of fencing off areas of inquiry. If the legitimacy of inquiry is rooted in oppositional consciousness, and if the experiential is privileged over the recorded, then it will be ever easier for successive groups to insist that they alone have the knowledge (i.e., the experience) to permit a proper investigation of past events. In other words, an emphasis on the primacy of personal experience creates an incentive to insist upon exclusiveness, or, to put it plainly, privileged access. Men cannot do the history of women because they lack the oppositional consciousness that is a prerequisite to doing it properly. White women cannot do Native women's history or the history of other women of colour because they lack the proper experience. Heterosexual women of colour cannot investigate lesbians' history for the same reason. And so it could go, in ever-diminishing, concentric circles until historical inquiry disappears entirely. It would be horribly ironic if that should be the fate of feminist innovations in historical awareness and methodology. It would be ironic that the methodological innovation that has made the greatest contribution to our historical understanding in this century should end up driving inquiry into such narrow and exclusive channels that the relevance of one researcher's work to another disappears and most meaningful communication ceases. It would also be ironic if this dark scenario became reality because women's history began by expanding historical understanding and making it more inclusive. How horrid if it should indirectly and unintentionally end up making the discipline parochial to the point of picayune and exclusive to the point of atomism.

The ambiguity and agnosticism of cultural studies or the dangerous potential for diminution and irrelevance to the larger community in the experiential emphasis of feminist approaches are only part of the explanation of historians' uneasiness in the 1990s. Investigation across

ethnic and racial boundaries, especially in the area of the history of
Native peoples and of relations between indigenous and immigrant
peoples in North America, has created similar challenges over the past
few decades.

In many respects, the difficulties and opportunities in the Native history area are only a subset of those that social historians in general have
found when they have turned to trying to recover and explain the historical experiences of previously inarticulate and unremarked groups.
Women, of course, were a major component of the previously ignored,
but so were working-class communities, immigrants and ethnic groups
in general, and racial minorities. As social historians attempted to
locate and illuminate these slighted social elements, they found that
they had to turn to new techniques and new sources. Did the archives
contain little information on post-1945 Italian immigrants? One answer,
then, was to interview members of that community and by employing
oral history to compensate for archival deficiencies. Similarly, if official
repositories of records could help us but little in knowing how the vast
majority of working people who were not organized in trade unions
responded to the advent of the factory system and the discipline of life
in an occupationally segregated urban area, then other materials could
be pressed into service. In particular, what are referred to in the trade as
'routinely generated data' – manuscript census records, pollbooks kept
by returning officers in the era prior to the secret ballot, police arrest
blotters, church baptismal and marriage rolls, and even mind-numbing
school records – could be used to turn up the volume on the hitherto
mute. And so with ethnic minorities, economically disadvantaged
classes, and racial groups, this is what has been and is being done to
make their voices heard. These sources have been used to amplify the
historical experience of groups.

As noted, in some respects inquiries in the history of Native peoples
and of their relations with European newcomers can be understood as a
particular example of that social history contribution. However, that is
not all of the story of investigating Native history, or of the ways in
which such cross-cultural or interracial inquiries have cast doubt on the
comfortable verities of conventional history. To simplify the many-fac-
eted problem of cross-cultural inquiry, one could begin by quoting Seneca – not the Iroquois nation but the Roman savant. 'They change their
skies but not their minds who cross the seas in ships,' noted Seneca.[17]
The observation is useful for understanding, for example, that French
explorers and missionaries often attempted to interpret the behaviour

of North American Indians within a European framework of assumptions, values, and aspirations. Seneca's insight applies as well to historians from one culture, the Caucasian, who attempt to 'cross the seas' in their inquiry by voyaging to the land of another racial group, in this case Aboriginal peoples. If they do not learn to change their minds as well as their skies, such researchers will come to grief.

An example or two of the complexities of interpreting behaviour and data across racial bounds might help to make Seneca's abstraction more concrete and pertinent to the subject under examination here. Rupert Ross, a Euro-Canadian lawyer who has written illuminatingly about doing justice in a cross-cultural setting, recounts the example of groups from two different First Nations who met and held a ritual feast prior to a sports tournament. Among the visiting Cree, the polite thing to do was to consume everything placed before you; among the Mohawk hosts etiquette required providing guests with more food than the visitors could consume. As might be anticipated, an unintended and unwitting contest developed between the satiated visitors and exasperated hosts. The two groups became more irritated with each other instead of, as the ritual repast was intended to make them, more congenial towards each other.[18]

A somewhat more intractable interpretive problem arose from an incident during the 1890s gold rush in the Klondike. In 1898 Joe Nantuck and Dawson Nantuck, two Tagish men, killed one and wounded the other of a pair of Euro-Canadian prospectors for reasons that were unclear to the non-Natives. What seemed to make the event more heinous and less comprehensible was the fact that the assailants had made several apparently friendly visits to the prospectors' camp prior to the attack. For many years the bloody incident was depicted in history books as an act of wanton cruelty, an event of mindless bloodthirstiness. However, when an anthropologist trained both in oral research and in the cultural values of the Native people of the area probed the matter further, she discovered that the death of the outsiders had been a form of group retribution, or justice, to use the European term. The Tagish community regarded all White men as members of the same nation or clan. They sought compensation or retribution for an earlier death of two of their number that had been caused by prospectors who had left a can of arsenic behind with fatal consequences. The men who were attacked had first been given a chance to atone and make redress. That was why the Native men had visited their camp and eaten with them before the violence. It was only when it had become clear that the two new prospectors were not going to offer compensation for the earlier wrongdoing of their clansmen that they were put to death by the Nantuck brothers on behalf of the Tagish. It took over eighty years for this second, Aboriginal perspective on the deaths to become known in non-Native accounts.[19]

More complex still than cross-cultural interpretive puzzles in the area of social ethics and justice are those that touch on the even more internal matters of sacred belief. A particularly good example of this difficulty has been pointed out by American historian David Edmunds, a major writer on Native warfare and diplomacy in the late eighteenth and early nineteenth centuries. Edmunds recently has straightened out historians about the relative importance of two Shawnee leaders who are prominent in both American and Canadian history. Indeed, Tecumseh and his brother, The Prophet, figure conspicuously in the background and early stages of the War of 1812. Tecumseh was a skilled and influential chief who worked for many years to forge an alliance of interior nations against the expansionist American republic, a strategy that led him to work with the British and British North Americans in spite of Britain's record of treachery in its treatment of Indian allies. Most historians have focused on the role of Tecumseh, leaving in the background the work of his brother, who is usually depicted as having prepared the ground for Tecumseh's diplomacy by disseminating a nativist religious movement among many interior peoples. However, Edmunds tells us, the foregrounding of Tecumseh and the downplaying of The Prophet distort – reverse, in fact – the reality in the Aboriginal societies from which the two came. In Shawnee and other societies, it was The Prophet who was much the more influential of the two.[20] Once again, the complexity of working across a racial boundary confounded Euro-American scholars and undermined their confidence in their ability to interpret events in Native history accurately.

A closely related area that has caused problems for historians trying to untangle the complexities of Native communities has been politics and public decision-making mechanisms. This, like diplomacy and alliance, has been viewed as an important area of history because events there often impinged on the development of European societies in North America. Political and diplomatic rhetoric, for example, is grounded in the social structures and values of the communities from which the politicians and diplomats hail. When those societies differ fundamentally, the result can be misunderstanding by contemporaries and misinterpretation by later generations of historians. No single

event in Canadian history illustrates this truism better than the negotiations surrounding land treaties in the 1870s in western Canada. When
Cree spokesmen referred to themselves as the Queen's children and
asked that the Queen's government 'pity us,' Euro-Canadian negotiators and their governments usually interpreted these pleas as implicit
confessions of subordination and dependence. In reality, as a historian
who had been doing research for a Native political organization for several years pointed out in the 1980s, the implied message was exactly the
opposite. In Cree society, childhood was a time of great autonomy and
self-indulgence, a period when adults had an obligation to gratify and
provide for the needs of youth.[21] Using the language of childhood
implied a desire for continued autonomy, not dependence.

A similar misunderstanding occurred with the Cree chief Mistahamusqua, or Big Bear as he was known to Euro-Canadians, a failure to
communicate meaningfully that might have contributed to a later massacre. When Big Bear said during negotiations at Fort Pitt in 1876 that
he 'feared the rope around my neck,' the Canadian government
thought that he was afraid of being hanged, and perhaps it and its min-
ions harboured negative attitudes to the Cree chief as a consequence. In
reality, Mistahamusqua, chief in a Plains culture in which the horse was
extremely important, was saying he feared the horse's bridle: he
rejected Canadian law, or sovereignty, and consequently would not
take treaty.[22] The misunderstanding and the government's misinterpretation of what he meant contributed to the harsh measures that Ottawa
employed in an attempt to force Big Bear into treaty. Indirectly, they
helped to fuel the unrest among his followers that erupted in the so-
called Frog Lake Massacre in the spring of 1885. For a long time, historians who did not fully appreciate what Big Bear meant or understand
that he favoured peaceful, diplomatic means over force, depicted him
and his followers inaccurately as willing, united participants in the
rebellion of 1885. Only recently, thanks both to more sensitive readings
of Cree diplomacy by non-Native scholars and detailed oral history
work by an Indian historian, has the non-participation of First Nations
in the violence in 1885 been uncovered.[23] The slowly dawning awareness among historians that they have for decades perpetrated these
misconceptions about Native peoples because of their own incomplete
understanding of Aboriginal values and political behaviour has been
sobering.

In this regard, Aboriginal political procedures have a direct bearing
on what is construed as 'truth' in their own societies. Unlike Euro-

Canadian processes, Native political decision-making is consensual, requiring an opportunity for at least the prominent people to have their say and sufficient time to bring general acceptance, if not universal agreement, on a particular viewpoint or decision. Whereas the adversarial political process among non-Natives is based on the assumption that the product of a clash of ideas will be the position that is best for the group, or the policy equivalent of truth, in most Aboriginal societies the 'truth' is the consensus that the group reaches after lengthy consultation and reflection. It was because consensus and truth were assumed to be synonymous that the Cree hunter in the Quebec courtroom in the 1970s had to respond to the oath, 'I'm not sure I can tell the truth ... I can only tell what I know.' The truth, in his universe, would be the consensus reached after all participants told what they knew.

As difficult as untangling etiquette or diplomatic and political processes across a racial border can be, it is child's play alongside efforts to understand fully the components of personal and group identity among various Aboriginal communities. For the better part of a decade, historians and anthropologists wasted a great deal of effort trying to answer the question of whether the Europeans' impact on northeastern woodlands peoples had altered their attitudes towards the physical world and fur-bearing animals in particular.[24] Even more challenging than the issue of Native people's relationship to the natural world is that of sexual identity, at least in the case of one Athapaskan group that has been documented.[25] In this case, 'Paul' informed a visiting anthropologist that he was really 'Rose,' the dead sister of his cousin 'Mary.' That Paul was the reincarnation of the dead 'Rose' was known and accepted in the community, as was shown by the people's behaviour in a number of areas. Young women in the community would not date Paul, males did not invite him to drinking parties in the nearby bush, and even lascivious graffitti in a building used by members of both sexes for drinking and sex acknowledged Paul's sexual duality.[26] Paul, himself, was troubled by the fact that he would never marry if he stayed in the community; the local missionary priest was not aware of the cross-gender reincarnation; and historians who examine the issue are reminded of the difficulties of making evaluations and offering interpretations across cultural frontiers.

The growing interest among historians in Canada in exploring both the history of Native peoples and the story of their historic interactions with

European newcomers, then, is another source of uncertainty in the historical profession in the 1990s. Like the challenges of Political Correctness, especially in its seductive temptation to self-censorship in response to charges of cultural appropriation or for fear of damaging an important Native political initiative, the complexities of interpreting the actions of a society whose social structures, ethical systems, and political processes are dramatically different from your own are anxiety-inducing. In some ways, as well, the methodological challenges that arise when historians attempt to work across racial and cultural lines are like those created by postmodernism in general and feminist methodologies in particular. With their emphasis on the internal, the personal, and the experiential, all these areas of historical inquiry sow doubt about the possibility that the search for historical truth can ever succeed. Instead of the solid foundation historians once had in nineteenth-century liberal thought, Germanic methodology, and tenure conferred by the work of generations of academic politicians, historians in the 1990s often feel that they stand on shifting sands of understanding about what is real, what is absolute, what is enduring, or what is universal.

The problem is not that uncertainty prevents historians from doing their work. As is already happening, historical investigators can learn the assumptions and techniques of cultural studies and feminist theory, they can develop insights into the ways of other societies by studying what ethnographers have discovered and recorded, and they can – as is increasingly the case – rely on fellow investigators from the other racial or cultural groups to probe the recesses more effectively. Being able to do the work of historians amidst the swirl of methodologies and interpretive styles is not the problem. The real danger lies much deeper.

The reason that shifting notions of historical interpretation threaten the discipline of history, indeed all the disciplines in the humanities, is that they undermine the one precondition for research that inquirers cannot do without. That prerequisite is what we call academic freedom, the freedom from constraint and retribution that responsible researchers enjoy no matter where their inquiries lead them. The challenge that new methodologies bring to this essential condition is found in the implication that there is no single truth that can be uncovered by inquiry. If everything is socially or otherwise humanly constructed, if texts have no inherent meaning, if one cannot discern what is real, then inquiry can never lead to truth. Of course, it might be possible to define 'truth' as the process of seeking whatever answer the researcher turns up, or as the consensus of views on a particular issue. The former would parallel what some gender historians posit; the latter would be to embrace a North American Aboriginal understanding of truth. However, if neither of these semantic defences succeeds, researchers in history and other humanities disciplines will be in difficulty. The sole justification for academic freedom is that it is necessary to permit the pursuit of truth to occur through free and unfettered investigation. If there is no truth, there is no point in pursuing it. If there is no social utility in the pursuit of truth, there will be no academic freedom for pursuers.

Researchers in the humanities should be concerned about shifting notions of method and interpretation in the 1990s because that condition threatens to move them from being researchers protected by academic freedom to clones of university administrators or faculty in religious institutions. Neither university administrators nor theology school faculty enjoy genuine academic freedom because they do not need it. They do not need it because they already have the Truth. (Faculty in denominational institutions get it from God, and administrators get it from government. Indeed, it might be asked if university administrators distinguish between the two sources.) The implications of this for other academics are obvious. If the pursuit of truth can, by definition, never be anything but a series of aimless probes into intellectual outer space, the social utility of academic freedom ceases to exist.

Those who respond that this concern is unwarranted because people in authority will understand and accept the utility of what scholars are doing, should bear in mind a cautionary tale that shows how well-intentioned theories can have unforeseen, negative consequences. Many in Canada cheered in 1992 when the Supreme Court of Canada shifted its criterion in cases of alleged pornography from the traditional 'community standards' test to a question of whether the disputed work could promote 'harm.' In the case of *Regina v. Butler* the highest court found that films in an 'adult' video store in Winnipeg were 'degrading' and 'dehumanizing' to women and, therefore, were obscene. The decision adopted the legal reasoning popularized by American feminist legal scholars Andrea Dworkin and Catharine MacKinnon. Indeed, MacKinnon, who had assisted the Women's Legal Education and Action Fund in preparing their brief on the case, described the Butler decision as '"good for women."'[27] The Butler decision was followed by a rash of border seizures of allegedly obscene materials, most of it homoerotica, by Canada Customs officials. According to the newsletter *Censorwatch*, one-quarter of Canada's feminist bookstores had material seized or held up by Canada Customs by the end of 1993. As a lesbian spokesperson complained later at a conference in Toronto, '"You handed them post-modern language, the language they had been looking for, the 'degrad-ing and dehumanizing' language and now they are busting our bookstores."'[28] The ultimate irony occurred when Andrea Dworkin's *Pornography* was rejected at the border by Canada Customs clerks because some of the material Dworkin quoted was held to be obscene.[29] The aftermath of the Butler case demonstrates that well-intentioned scholarly approaches can have devastatingly negative consequences.

The sad story of the Butler decision is something champions of post-modernist styles of research, including historical investigation, should contemplate. In a democratic society there is no way of controlling what the political and bureaucratic classes, left to their own devices and public opinion polls, will do with academic arguments. Those who believe strongly in the necessity to retain academic freedom should be alert to the pitfalls inherent in some of the scholarly fashions that are so influential in the 1990s. Tread softly when you walk the shifting sands of method and interpretation in the 1990s, because you could end up among the bureaucrats and the divines.

### Notes

1  James Clifford, 'Introduction: Partial Truths,' in *Writing Culture: The Poetics and Politics of Ethnography,* ed. James Clifford and George E. Marcus (Berke-ley: University of California Press, 1986), 8
2  This refers to incidents such as the demand by some Métis students for the dismissal of political scientist Tom Flanagan at the University of Calgary for publishing work presumed critical of Louis Riel; demands for the dis-missal of psychologist Phillip Rushton of the University of Western Ontario for disseminating studies that argued Caucasians and Africans were intel-lectually and morally inferior to Asians; and similar demands concerning anthropologist Jeanne Cannizzo of Scarborough College (University of Tor-onto) for curating the Royal Ontario Museum exhibit 'Into the Heart of Africa.' Flanagan was never seriously threatened; Rushton, though greatly inconvenienced, survived academically thanks in no small part to a univer-sity president who defended academic freedom vigorously; and Cannizzo, unfortunately, had to take sick leave to get away from an atmosphere poi-soned by students who disrupted her classes and university administrators

who failed to defend her right to teach and research freely. Eventually, Professor Cannizzo left Scarborough.

3 Kerry Howe, 'The Treaty of Waitangi: History As Prescriptive Ideology' (unpublished paper delivered to the annual meeting of the Canadian Historical Association, University of Victoria, June 1990), *Journal of the Canadian Historical Association*, NS 1 (1990): 322.

4 *Maclean's*, 4 Jan. 1993, pp. 28–9. 'Significantly, almost seven out of ten often reject the primary principle upon which the nation was founded – namely, that Canada was a contract between English and French, where each other's rights would be recognized explicitly in our laws and institutions' (29).

5 Royal Commission on Aboriginal Peoples, *Partners in Confederation: Aboriginal Peoples, Self-Government, and the Constitution* (Ottawa: Ministry of Supply and Services, 1993), esp. 22–6.

6 Terence, *Eunuchus*, Prog. 41: 'Homo sum; humani nil a me alienum puto' (*Oxford Dictionary of Quotations*, 3rd ed., 544).

7 Tina Loo, 'Dan Cranmer's Potlatch: Law As Coercion, Symbol, and Rhetoric in British Columbia, 1884–1951,' *Canadian Historical Review* 73, no. 2 (June 1992): 125–65. Professor Loo's explicit references to Foucault are in her conclusions (165).

8 Joy Parr, *The Gender of Breadwinners: Women, Men, and Change in Two Industrial Towns* (Toronto: University of Toronto Press 1990).

9 Evelyn Plaice, *The Native Game: Settler Perceptions of Indian/Settler Relations in Central Labrador* (St John's: Institute for Social and Economic Research, Memorial University of Newfoundland, 1990). Other examples of racial identity being socially constructed are the Grande Cache Métis and the 'country born' of Red River, as depicted respectively in Trudy Nicks and Kenneth Morgan, 'Grande Cache: The Historical Development of an Indigenous Alberta Métis Population,' in *The New Peoples: Being and Becoming Métis in North America*, ed. Jacqueline Peterson and Jennifer S.H. Brown (Winnipeg: University of Manitoba Press, 1985); and Frits Pannekoek, *A Snug Little Flock: The Social Origins of the Riel Resistance 1869–70* (Winnipeg: Watson & Dwyer, 1991).

10 Such a longing for a norm or benchmark is, of course, 'foundationalism: The doctrine that inquiry or thought can actually be grounded on pregiven principles that are true beyond mere belief or assumption. Postmodern analysis shows us that no such principles or truths exist, and that any attempt to establish or prove that they do is merely an exercise in "self-constituted logic"' (Henry Beard and Christopher Cerf, *The Official Politically Correct Dictionary and Handbook*, rev. ed. [New York: Villard Books 1993; 1st ed., 1992], 27).

11  Sylvia Van Kirk, *'Many Tender Ties': Women in Fur-Trade Society, 1670–1870* (Winnipeg: Watson & Dwyer, [1980]); Jennifer S.H. Brown, *Strangers in Blood: Fur Trade Company Families in Indian Country* (Vancouver: University of British Columbia Press, 1980).

12  Ruth Roach Pierson, 'Experience, Difference, Dominance and Voice in the Writing of Canadian Women's History,' in *Writing Women's History: International Perspectives*, ed. Karen Offen, Ruth Roach Pierson, and Jan Rendall (Bloomington and Indianapolis: Indiana University Press, 1991), 83, 93. I am indebted to Professor Sarah Carter of the University of Calgary, who kindly supplied me with a copy of the Pierson article.

13  Ibid., 93.

14  'History offers unique contributions to the study of such a multifaceted and creative, but also an inherently unstable and contradictory concept. For gender operates at every level: the psychic, interpersonal, institutional, cultural and social, Above all, the creation and reproduction of gender is a process, changing over time' ('Why Gender and History?' [editorial], *Gender & History* 1, no. 1 [Spring 1989]: 2).

15  Interview with Muriel Waldvogel, Mississauga, Ontario, 25 June 1987. Ms Waldvogel had checked Indian Affairs records in the regional office in Amherst, Nova Scotia, herself.

16  The point was also made by Sandra Martin in a 'Cross Current' column in the *Globe and Mail*, 31 October 1990, concerning the Allied bombing of Dresden in 1945, a copy of which was also provided to me by Professor Carter.

17  Quoted in A. Brian McKillop, *A Disciplined Intelligence: Critical Inquiry and Canadian Thought in the Victorian Age* (Montreal: McGill-Queen's University Press 1979), frontispiece.

18  'The Cree, anxious to show respect, ate and ate until they were more than a little uncomfortable. They considered the Mohawk something akin to gastro-intestinal sadists intent on poisoning them. The Mohawk, for their part, thought the Cree ill-mannered people intent on insulting Mohawk generosity' (Rupert Ross, *Dancing with a Ghost: Exploring Indian Reality* [Markham, ON: Octopus, 1992], 2).

19  Julie Cruikshank, 'Oral Traditions and Written Accounts: An Incident from the Klondike Gold Rush,' *Culture* 9, no. 2 (1989): 25–31.

20  R. David Edmunds, 'Tecumseh's Native Allies: Warriors Who Fought for the Crown,' in *War on the Great Lakes: Essays Commemorating the 175th Anniversary of the Battle of Lake Erie*, ed. William J. Welsh and David C. Skaggs (Kent, OH, and London, England: Kent State University Press, 1991), 56–7, esp. 61–2.

21  John L. Tobias, 'The Origins of the Treaty Rights Movement in

Saskatchewan,' in *1885 and After: Native Society in Transition*, ed. F. Laurie Barron and James B. Waldram (Regina: Canadian Plains Research Center, 1986), 248.

22  John L. Tobias, 'Canada's Subjugation of the Plains Cree, 1879-1885,' in *Sweet Promises: A Reader on Indian-White Relations in Canada*, ed. J.R. Miller (Toronto: University of Toronto Press, 1991), 215.

23  Tobias, 'Subjugation of the Plains Cree'; A. Blair Stonechild, 'The Indian View of the 1885 Uprising,' in *Sweet Promises*, ed. Miller, 259–76. Professor Stonechild is working with my colleague Professor W.A. Waiser on a new history of the rebellion that incorporates considerable oral history research among Native groups.

24  The debate was initiated by Calvin Martin, *Keepers of the Game: Indian-Animal Relationships in The Fur Trade* (Los Angeles: University of California Press, 1978). Among the many responses, one that indicated the complexity of Aboriginal attitudes was Adrian Tanner, *Bringing Home the Animals: Religious ideology and the Mode of Production of the Mistassini Hunters* (London: C. Hurst, 1979). By the late 1980s most scholars had rejected Martin's interpretation as oversimplified and ahistorical.

25  Jean-Guy Goulet, 'Religious Dualism among Athapaskan Catholics,' *Canadian Journal of Anthropology* 3, no. 1 (Fall 1982): 9–10. I am indebted to Professor Donald B. Smith of the University of Calgary for bringing this article to my attention.

26  'The walls of this house are covered with drawings of male and female figures having sexual intercourse, and drawings of hearts and of genitals. Among these drawings I noticed two hearts, one with a cherry within, the other with a penis within. These two hearts, one next to the other, are surrounded by the following inscription: "Paul never broke his cherry. I don't know how to break Paul's cherry, but someday I break [*sic*] his cherry for her"' (ibid., 10).

27  National Coalition against Censorship, 'MacKinnon/Dworkin "Theories" Flunk Reality Test,' *Censorship News* 4, no. 50 (1993); 'Northern Closure,' *The Nation*, 27 Dec. 1993, p. 788.

28  'MacKinnon/Dworkin "Theories" Flunk Reality Test.' See also 'Canada's Morals Police: Serious Books at Risk?' *New York Times International*, 13 Dec. 1993.

29  John Preston, 'Whose Free Speech?' *Censorship News* 4, no. 50 (1993).

# Reading Photographs, Reading Voices: Documenting the History of Native Residential Schools

The tasks of uncovering and recounting the history of the residential schools for Inuit and status 'Indian' children that existed in Canada until the late 1960s present many challenges. Three groups were involved in the creation and operation of these institutions, but the available records on these groups are not uniform in either quantity or quality. Aboriginal peoples, government, and Christian churches were all participants in the residential school story, but only the latter two entities created written records that, along with personal recollections, were systematically collected and preserved for the benefit of later generations. The constructive use of what materials exist often is further handicapped by an unacknowledged aversion to denominational records on the part of many twentieth-century investigators. Possibly unknowingly, scholars have often neglected or simplified the missionaries' role. In the increasingly secular atmosphere that has prevailed in Canada since the middle of the last century, a tendency has developed to ignore religious figures, their actions, and their records.[1]

In the case of the Aboriginal peoples' involvement in schooling, the principal difficulty has been that most archival repositories have not collected much material generated in their societies. Ironically, a substantial portion of the written records that Native groups did create concerning their interaction with missions and schools is to be found in the denominational archives that researchers have largely ignored. Because much of the existing literature on residential schooling has failed to bring out Native roles in and contributions to residential schooling, the picture that is available is at best a two-dimensional depiction, often presented in stark black and white without many of the colour tones that are usually present in any rendering of human affairs.

One peculiarity of the history of residential schooling is that Canadians, although they have never had a fully rounded treatment of the phenomenon made available to them, are inclined to think that they know the tale well because these institutions have been in the news a great deal during the past five years. A major event that created a false sense of knowing the residential school story occurred in 1990, when Phil Fontaine, head of the Assembly of Manitoba Chiefs, made public the fact that he, like many others, had been a victim of abuse at the Fort Alexander residential school that a Roman Catholic missionary order operated. Fontaine's revelations surfaced just as spectacular details of widespread mistreatment of orphans at Mount Cashel in Newfoundland and the Alfred institution for boys in Ontario were becoming known. They instantly sparked interest in Native residential schools as yet another setting in which abuse of defenceless children had taken place over many decades. Fontaine's initiative encouraged other victims to come forward and tell their stories, just as it stimulated major newspapers, magazines, and television news shows to prepare stories on the issue. Subsequently, the public hearings that the Royal Commission on Aboriginal Peoples conducted in various parts of Canada kept the subject of abuse in these schools alive in the popular media. Finally, in August 1994 the First Nations Health Commission of the Assembly of First Nations, the umbrella political organization for status Indians in Canada, issued a report that alleged that physical, sexual, and emotional abuse had been so widespread in residential schools that it was almost universal.[2] As a consequence of this barrage of publicity, many Canadians in the 1990s came to believe that they understood all too well what these custodial institutions had been about. The heavy documenting of one aspect of residential school life left the impression that it was the entire story.

However, among the many things that Canadians did not know about the subject was that residential schooling has a lengthy, if mixed, history in their country. In fact, the earliest boarding schools – or seminaries as they were known – were developed in seventeenth-century New France by Récollet and Jesuit priests, and Ursuline sisters. Because these early French initiatives all failed, forays into residential schooling were abandoned in the late seventeenth century. An attempt by a British missionary body a century later to establish what it called an 'Indian College' for young Native children in colonial New Brunswick similarly did not succeed in educating and training Mi'kmaq and Maliseet children.[3] Nonetheless, two other colonial efforts soon followed, one in Red River (Manitoba) under a Church of England missionary named John West in 1820, the other later in the same decade when the forerunner of what would become known as the Mohawk Institute was established near Brantford, Upper Canada (later Ontario).[4] Initially with Native cooperation, more institutions – then called 'manual labour schools' – were set up in southern Ontario in the 1850s; finally, the Shingwauk Home was established near Sault Ste Marie in the 1870s. This Anglican school, which still survives as part of Algoma University College, was the product of both missionary interest and Aboriginal initiative. The local Ojibwa chief, Shingaukonce, had asked in the early 1830s for the creation of a mission, and later his son, Chief Augustin Shingwauk, called for the establishment of a 'teaching wigwam' to prepare the youth of their people for a future with the European newcomers.[5]

The modern phase of residential schooling, the era whose results have been in the news so much, began in 1883 when three schools of a novel type were created in what were then the North-West Territories (now Saskatchewan and Alberta). The 'industrial schools' that were established were usually located well away from reserves and were intended by the federal government and Christian missionary bodies that ran them to do three things: to provide a basic academic training; to teach the children usable economic skills, including trades such as carpentry and blacksmithing; and to assimilate them culturally. The system that began with three industrial schools and a number of pre-existing boarding schools in 1883 expanded for the next half century, reaching at its height a total of eighty institutions. Although all of them were financed in part by the federal government, they were run by the churches. Roman Catholic missionary orders, both male and female, were in charge of about 60 per cent of the schools; Anglicans, about one-third; and Methodists and Presbyterians, the remainder. For most of the residential school system's existence, only one-third to one-half of status Indian children were enrolled, and a much smaller fraction of all Native children came under their influence. Part of the reason for the incomplete coverage was Native resistance to the schools' harsh discipline and overwork of children, and their inadequate academic and vocational teaching. Increasingly in disfavour and subject to criticism after the Second World War, these schools were phased out in the 1960s as the Department of Indian Affairs moved towards a policy of integrated schooling.

For the historian, the research challenge that Native residential schools present is to tell their long and complex story as systematically and comprehensively as possible. Although we have fragmentary accounts, there exists as yet no historical overview of the educational experiment as a whole. One reason for this lack is the sheer size of the task. It requires recovering the experiences and views of three distinct sets of actors – Native peoples, government, and missionaries. Compounding the problem of scale is the shortage of conventional records for Native peoples. The records of politicians and bureaucrats like Indian Affairs deputy minister Hayter Reed are conveniently arranged for researchers in archival repositories such as the National Archives of Canada in Ottawa.[6] Similarly, the various church denominations have seen to it that the records of many missionaries and teachers are collected and available in archives from Victoria (Sisters of St Ann) to Toronto (General Synod Archives and United Church of Canada Archives), to Ottawa (Archives Deschâtelets of the Oblates), and to Montreal (Sisters of St Ann and Daughters of the Heart of Mary). Records of some Aboriginal clergymen, such as the well-known Mississauga, Peter Jones, exist in government and church repositories.[7]

What are lacking, though, are records that tell the stories of the children who attended and of their families. What was it like for Inuit children to be taken far up the Mackenzie River to an Anglican school such as Hay River, which was located in alien, forested territory where limited gardening was carried out using dogs to pull the plough? What was the reaction of Dene children from small settlements in northern Alberta when they got their first glimpse of the Methodists' enormous Edmonton Indian Residential School? More generally, what was it like to live and learn, work and play, be cared for or mistreated on a day-to-day basis in one of the eighty residential institutions run by missionaries on behalf of Ottawa between the 1880s and 1960s? The records of Native peoples, like those of many other groups that the dominant Euro-Canadian society has until recently regarded as marginal, for the most part remain uncollected. For the researcher who wants to sketch the history of Native residential schools, the challenge is to find the means to recover and recount the experiences – good, bad, and indifferent – of the Inuit and Indian children and of the families and communities they left behind, sometimes never to be seen again.

The appropriate way to respond to that challenge is to multiply the lines and techniques of inquiry. The papers of politicians, bureaucrats, and missionaries must be utilized, of course. In particular, a research approach known as ethnohistory can help us to extract the submerged experiences of Native peoples from the records of the dominant Euro-Canadians. Ethnohistory, which combines insights about Aboriginal societies derived from anthropology with the traditional sources and methods of history, may help to amplify the muffled voices of Native children and their families that are sometimes found in archival records.[8] For example, one can find letters, petitions, remonstrances, and protests from Aboriginal people, often mediated through missionary interpreters. Similarly, one can uncover in denominational archives fragments of children's writing, often in the form of school newsletters. All of these kinds of sources can and must be pressed into service.

Ultimately, however, written sources and collections cannot do the job as fully and effectively as one would like. Other forms of evidence and other techniques of inquiry are needed to recapture Native experiences of residential schooling as fully as possible. In particular, the contributions of visual and oral history are vital components in the multidisciplinary research strategy that is necessary to tell the story of residential schools.

Visual images are of great value in helping a researcher to grasp fully residential school experiences and to convey them vividly and forcefully to the reader. Many of the sensations that Native children experienced in the residential school environment were alien or frightening, and particular exercises of imaginative reconstruction are required to appreciate them properly. How intimidating it was coming to school for the first time, perhaps at night to the Methodists' school in Edmonton, can be understood better when the strangeness is perceived in pictorial form (see fig. 1). Another example is the powerful visual religious message that Roman Catholic residential school children were given. The famous (or infamous) teaching aid that Oblates and female religious used in many institutions, often known as Lacombe's Ladder, makes clear, in a way that mere words cannot, how frightening missionaries' depiction of the road to Hell might have been to impressionable children (see fig. 2). When one notes, too, that the lost souls on the path to perdition were mainly Aboriginal while those on the upward road to Paradise were Caucasian, one begins to appreciate how the evangelical message often served to reinforce the denigration and undermining of Native culture and belief that were central to the mandate of these schools.

Residential school experiences can be vividly reconstructed if visual images are juxtaposed to documents. Consider, for example, the 'half-day system,' which in theory trained students in practical skills during the 'half-day' that they spent working in barn or yard or about the school. (The other half-day, of course, was supposed to be spent learning academic subjects in the classroom.) The discrepancy between the theoretical justification of the half-day labour system and the onerous reality is perceived upon careful scrutiny of illustrations of children at

1 Edmonton school at night, 1936 (Provincial Archives of Alberta, A 13457)

work. If, for example, one sees a picture of a couple of boys cutting wood into stove lengths, it may mean little at first glance (see fig. 3). However, if we contemplate the reality of how much wood was required for the furnaces at Chooutla residential school near Carcross in the southern Yukon, it becomes clear that the volume of routine labour extracted from the Tutchone and Tlingit schoolboys at this Anglican school went far beyond anything justified by the theory that underlay the half-day system (see fig. 4). Naturally, the official records of government and the churches do not dwell on how hard-worked the children at Chooutla and other schools were. And complaints of former students about excessive labour may not register strongly or concretely in written form. The pictures make the scope and weight of the labour burden on students starkly clear.

Similar examples of how visual images can make students' experiences speak more forcefully to later generations may be drawn from the propaganda pictures that the Department of Indian Affairs used to illustrate what it was trying to accomplish in the residential schools (see fig. 5). In 1900 the department's annual report emphasized pictorial contrasts of dress and grooming between Quewich and his children in order to celebrate the success of the Lebret school in Saskatchewan. The photographs vividly evoked the cultural assimilation program that such schools were designed to carry out. The lengths to which bureaucratic propagandists were willing to go similarly come out in the before-and-after pictures of Thomas Moore, a student at the Regina Industrial School prior to the First World War. The obviously staged quality of figures 6 and 7 testifies as eloquently to the federal government's reliance on propagandistic techniques as it does to Ottawa's hope of working a cultural transformation in residential school students.

Literary artifacts of the residential school experience also help to convey aspects of how students remember their experience – for both good and ill. Mi'kmaq poet Rita Joe makes clear the pain that she felt, and feels, as a result of attending the Shubenacadie School in Nova Scotia, in a poetic remembrance entitled 'Hated Structure':

> I for one looked into the window
> And there on the floor
> Was a deluge of a misery
> Of a building I held in awe
> Since the day
> I walked into the ornamented door.[9]

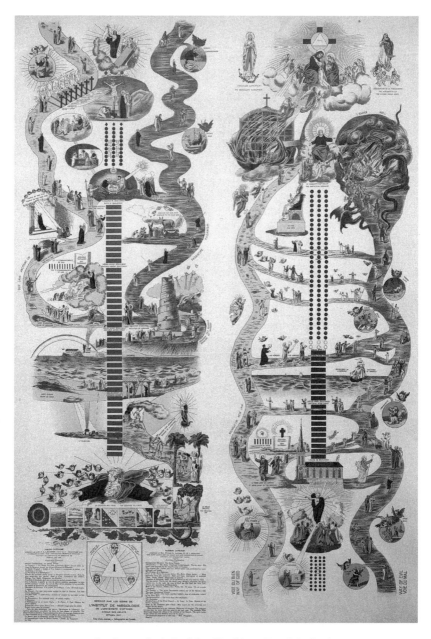

2   Lacombe's Ladder (Archives Deschâtelets)

3  Splitting wood at Tsuu T'ina (Sarcee) School, ca. 1890s (Glenbow Archives, NC-21-9)

4   Woodpile at Chooutla School, Carcross, Yukon (Yukon Archives, Anglican Diocese of Yukon Records, box G-142, Album 7, #1044)

Equally revealing are students' recollections, written and oral, of a more positive nature. The youthful pleasure with which two middle-aged Regina women remembered and sang for an interviewer the school song for St Paul's, the high school division of the Oblates' school at Lebret, Saskatchewan, in the 1950s, is suggestive of some fond memories held by these former students:

St Paul's forever.
Junior, Senior High.
Teach us to live and love,
laugh and never deny.

Pride of the Valley,
We'll keep your honour true.
Always the dearest and
the best of the love for you.[10]

One of these singers also wrote a letter to the editor of the *Regina Leader-Post* defending Lebret School from many of the charges of abuse that have been made in recent years. At least this residential school evokes some positive recollections.[11]

The singing of a school song remembered many years later by a pair of former students leads directly to consideration of the major contribution that can be made by oral history. Oral history evidence is invaluable for understanding and depicting all those nooks and crannies of everyday life in the residential school that are not found in the official record because they were not considered important enough to be reported by missionary or bureaucrat. These details are significant and revealing. Consider, for example, a tale of how the girls at St Joseph's residential school in Spanish, Ontario, managed to defy the rules and communicate with boys in the Jesuit-run institution across the road, something that was usually hard to do given the rigid segregation of the sexes in these institutions until the 1950s. The priest who came each morning to the sisters' establishment to say Mass did not know that for each visit a forbidden message written lovingly on a scrap of paper was craftily tucked into his hatband. Nor did he realize that the deferential girl who took his hat and coat would retrieve the message before placing his apparel in the cloakroom. After saying Mass, the good father was handed his hat by another apparently submissive girl, who had secreted a return message in the hatband. And so the Jesuit would

5   Quewich and children (National Archives of Canada, C37113)

6   Thomas Moore before attending Regina Industrial School (Saskatchewan
Archives Board R-A8223-1)

7   Thomas Moore after attending Regina Industrial School (Saskatchewan Archives Board R-A8223-2)

make his way back to the boys' school, where another pair of hands would extract the hidden note and pass it on to its intended recipient. No official document in any archives could inform us about such subterfuges. Only an interview with someone who was there allowed the retrieval of that detail of subversive school life.

Interviews with former students and staff have brought out very clearly more serious areas of the residential school experience. For example, both former staff and students raised, explicitly or implicitly, the topic of gender distinctions in the schools. Time and again former students answered questions about activities and recreation in ways that show clearly how residential schools constructed and reinforced notions of gender. Boys did outdoor work, while girls spent their half-day of supposedly instructive labour in the kitchens and sewing room, or in cleaning the hallways and other spaces of the buildings. That is not to say that vocational instruction in the schools adhered absolutely to separate gender spheres. Recollections and pictures tell us that sometimes girls, such as those at the female-run school at Spanish, Ontario, worked in the barns as boys did, though never at the same time as boys. Likewise, boys sometimes learned to bake bread, or a favoured male student was sometimes chosen to wait on table in the staff dining room.

The shortcomings of both instruction and supervision also emerge clearly from oral histories. Classroom instruction was often rudimentary and culturally inappropriate, as Euro-Canadian teachers with no training in cross-cultural education attempted in sterile settings to convey in a foreign tongue the contents of a curriculum that was little altered from that of non-Native schools. The differentiation between females and males continued to manifest itself in these settings, too. In the area of recreation, for example, boys recalled their active and intense involvement with sports as one of the too-infrequent bright spots in their stay at boarding school. From the earliest days, when efforts were made to inculcate cricket at Lebret, until the middle of the twentieth century when federal budgets began to supply equipment to hockey teams such as the 'Blackhawks' at Brandon residential school in Manitoba or Latuque, Quebec's, 'Indiens du Québec,' who participated in a tournament held in conjunction with the Quebec Winter Carnival in 1967, sports were vitally important.[12] (The contrast between the rudimentary equipment of the 'Blackhawks' and the first-class gear of the 'Indiens' also confirms that funding for residential schools was much better in the 1960s than it had been during the Depression.) However, it is also revealing that, while one learns of hockey teams known as the

'Indiens du Québec' or the Brandon 'Blackhawks,' one rarely hears of a lacrosse team being started or encouraged at a residential school. That is an interesting omission, given the Aboriginal origins of that game in eastern and central North America.

Women who attended residential school recounted dramatically different memories about recreation. If the sports for boys were sometimes culturally inappropriate, as in the case of cricket, the males were at least provided with athletic activities. For females, there was essentially no physical recreation available. Although girls such as those at the United Church school at Portage la Prairie were often able to join organizations such as the Canadian Girls in Training (CGIT), and girls at Catholic schools were encouraged to join sodalities oriented towards devotional practices, there was little else for them to do. For most girls, recreation consisted of conversation and playing with dolls, although boys were able at some institutions to play table hockey or even pool when outdoor activities were not possible. In a few exceptional cases, girls could avail themselves of some activities that were at least interesting, such as the dance troupe at the Kamloops School, which also boasted an outdoor swimming pool.[13] Such diversions, however, were the exception rather than the rule.

In general, oral histories reveal a routine of school life that at best was monotonous and at worst destructive. For most it was an unaccustomedly structured life of rules, bells, and punishments for infringements. Sewing class was usually recalled as only slightly less tedious than the obligatory attendance at chapel. The routine sometimes was relieved by parental visits, easily in the case of the Anglicans' Alert Bay School in British Columbia or Shubenacadie in Nova Scotia, where the residential school was close to the village. But parents in the North whose children attended such schools as Chooutla or even Aklavik at the mouth of the Mackenzie River found it difficult to visit their offspring. Over time, visiting became more difficult at some schools. At Lebret in the Qu'Appelle Valley of Saskatchewan, for example, the hospitality that was shown to parents in the first decade after 1883 was replaced by discouragement. Indian Affairs officials had intervened vigorously to prevent frequent parental visits, arguing that they disrupted the work of the schools. This episode illustrated another generalization about residential school administration: missionary principals and staff, who worked closely with Native children and their families, were often more sympathetic than Indian Affairs bureaucrats, who were remote geographically or emotionally – or both – from the schools.

The memories collected through oral history inquiry also show that the absence of parental contact permitted neglect and mistreatment to develop and even to flourish.[14] Negative aspects of residential school life included poor clothing, about which both men and women have remarked ever since. Numerous former students also complained about inadequate medical care and negligence when it came to preventing illness. Teachers at residential schools oversaw not just inappropriate curriculum, but also a student body that often included some children who ought not to have been in class in their infectious state. Both governmental and church records contain evidence that this happened because hard-pressed principals often accepted unhealthy students to ensure maximum revenue from federal per capita grants. Photographs and interviews with former students and staff confirm that these dangerous conditions were allowed to exist. The existence of disease in classrooms, and its spread in overcrowded dormitories, inevitably resulted in serious illness and death. Oral history inquiries also corroborate other evidence of overwork, mistreatment, and both physical and sexual abuse.

The use of oral history evidence to study the history of residential schooling inevitably carried with it a number of challenges and questions. Perhaps the first and most substantial was to try to ensure that informants were treated with sensitivity, consideration, and respect – especially respect for privacy. The key to meeting this challenge was the notion of 'informed consent,' on which all bodies that oversee research with human subjects insist and which all reputable investigators practise. Potential interview subjects, whether they were being questioned by the principal investigator or by an interviewer hired for the purpose, first heard a description of the research project on the history of residential schooling, the nature and purpose of the oral history portion of the investigation, and the rules and guidelines surrounding the collection and use of their memories. The interviewer told them that they should feel free to answer or decline to answer as they saw fit, as well as the fact they had the right to terminate the interview at any point. It was also explained that they could restrict the use of answers to particular questions. To protect their privacy if they wished to do so, they had the right to be identified either by name or by the institution and years they attended. Finally, potential informants were told that the tapes and notes of the interviews would be disposed of as they wished. These materials could be deposited in an archives that the researcher chose so as to be available to future investigators, placed in a repository that the interview subject chose, returned to the subject, or destroyed.

A variation on the interview was the questionnaire, which was administered by mail. In these cases, potential respondents received a written version of the explanations and options that an interview subject was provided orally, and they were asked to indicate on the completed questionnaire if they wished any of the information restricted and where they wanted the questionnaire deposited once the research project was completed. In a few cases, respondents to a questionnaire provided their answers on audio tape, a format that often led them to answer specific questions more expansively than they might have otherwise. Both face-to-face interviews and questionnaires provided valuable information on everyday life in residential schools, and both types of inquiry yielded these data while protecting the privacy of individual respondents and their control over the knowledge they furnished.

Consideration of the safeguards that are called for in a program of oral history research leads fairly logically to another controversial aspect of this style of investigation. The debate over 'voice' and 'appropriation' that has been so strident, if not usually enlightening, during the past few years has not exempted the use of recollections of Aboriginal informants and other people of colour from its censorious consideration. According to some critics, it is not appropriate for a non-Native investigator to attempt to tell the stories or speak in the voice of people of another cultural or racial group. It should be noted that there are, indeed, aspects of Aboriginal culture in which it is not appropriate for non-Natives to participate. Certain songs or dances in some Aboriginal cultures belong to particular individuals or families. It is as wrong for someone else to tell or perform these rites without permission as it would be in non-Native society for someone to break copyright by performing another's play. A somewhat analogous example is the oral tradition that the Gitksan and Wet'suwet'en peoples put before the courts of British Columbia in the late 1980s in order to demonstrate their relationship to and ownership of the lands they claimed. Their texts formed a complete and integral account, rather than isolated bits of evidence, and they needed to be told in their own right and in their own context. Extracting them from their cultural matrix as the court system demanded, and using them for purposes of another people, distorted their meaning and character.[15]

However, not all oral history material partakes of ritual or sacred tradition. Informed respondents often may willingly recount histories in which they have been involved. Those histories are not an 'oral tradition' lifted whole from the Native environment, but rather recollections given freely by informed participants. Their answers, rather than resembling a potlatch song that has meaning and validity only when sung by the person who possesses the right to sing it and in its own culturally defined context, are oral equivalents of the bureaucrat's recording of the events in a residential school from the governmental point of view. Their spoken words are the only way of recovering and preserving records of some activities and experiences that were considered too minor to be caught in the official paper net or too scandalous to be preserved by those whose negligence or wrongdoing they exposed.[16]

The historical investigation of residential schools involves – some might say implicates – both Aboriginal peoples and non-Native peoples, and both can contribute in vital ways to understanding the history of these institutions. The schools were the device by which an unsympathetic majority sought to assimilate and culturally eliminate a racial minority, but that very fact ensures that their story belongs to both racial communities. This biracial reality is necessarily reflected in any reputable research into residential schooling. Properly conducted oral history research will elicit information not only from former students, but also from former members of the schools' staffs. The importance of relying on both former staff and former students for oral history evidence about residential schools is exemplified by the story recounted earlier about the priest whose trips across the road to the girls' school at Spanish, Ontario, to say Mass each day made him an unconscious conveyor of secret messages between romantically inclined boys and girls. The existence of that practice was uncovered solely because of an interview conducted with a female religious who had worked for many years at the Spanish girls' school.[17] It would appear that the Daughters of the Heart of Mary community at Spanish knew what was going on all the time. We would not have known about it without the use of interviews.

What documents should one use, then, to recover and recount the history of Native residential schools? The answer reflects the nature of the historical phenomenon. Because residential schools are a historical artifact of a process by which a numerically and politically dominant society tried to assimilate a racial minority, and because their creation and operation involved Native peoples, missionaries, and officials, we need an expanded definition of 'documentation,' one that allows the recovery of the recollections of all the participants. Researching the history of residential schools requires an integrative style of scholarship that combines the insights and revelations of many forms of memory.

While these recollections include not only the written records of both church and state, and the smaller amount of Native testimony preserved in the repositories of denominations and governments, they should encompass a wide range of other evidence as well. It is essential to consider why Alberta artist George Littlechild chose in his painting *Red Horse Boarding School* to depict the school without any windows.[18] In comparison, the works of art that students of Alert Bay School produced for the Pacific National Exhibition in 1936 illustrate that not all principals and instructors denigrated or discouraged all expressions of Native culture.[19] It is necessary to examine cultural artifacts such as the Christian passion play that the Oblate missionaries staged at their school at Mission, BC, before audiences of thousands, and to contemplate the rich ironies of these enactments, which an uncharitable newspaper editorialist referred to as 'Christian Potlatches.'[20] And, finally, it is essential to collect and listen empathetically to the oral histories of both former staff and former students to obtain a well-rounded picture of what residential school life was like, synthesizing all the available evidence responsibly and respectfully.

How should the researcher handle the documents so assembled? It is essential to view the sources in context in order to appreciate the ways in which their creators have mediated and presented their observations and recollections. Is a student's story of a hard-hearted adult who weeps at a cinematic portrayal of children's hardship, and then spurns children who ask for help outside the theatre, merely a formulaic story? Or might the apparently familiar tale be a residential school inmate's allegory of the cruelties and insensitivities of supervisors and teachers? If it is important to peruse any document to understand it properly in its context, it is also vital to peer into its gaps and listen for its silences. Just as it is worth noting that the pictures of boys playing games rarely reveal a lacrosse team, so it is necessary to look carefully at the children's clothing for evidence about the quality of the care they were receiving. Similarly it is important in conducting and using interviews to listen for the things informants do not say, or express in opaque and oblique fashion. The researcher must try to interrogate the silences and scan the omissions.

The history of the residential school experience embraces the hopes, hurts, successes, and sufferings of many people. To document it, we must listen carefully and actively to as many voices as we can, and integrate the diversity of evidence that results into interpretive accounts that will speak directly of and to all groups.

## Notes

This essay appeared in the first edition of Jennifer S.H. Brown and Elizabeth Vibert, eds, *Reading beyond Words: Contexts for Native History* (Peterborough, ON: Broadview Press, 1996).

1 L.H. Thomas noted the failure to take into account the Christian socialism of North America's first socialist government in 'The CCF Victory in Saskatchewan, 1944,' *Saskatchewan History* 34, no. 1 (1981): 1–3; Ruth Compton Brouwer, in 'Transcending the "Unacknowledged Quarantine": Putting Religion into English-Canadian Women's History,' *Journal of Canadian Studies* 27, no. 3 (1992): 47–61, pointed out how historians of women have neglected the sphere in which nineteenth-century Canadian women were probably most active outside the home.

2 Assembly of First Nations, First Nations Health Commission, 'Breaking the Silence' (mimeo, August 1994).

3 Judith Fingard, 'The New England Company and the New Brunswick Indians, 1786–1826: A Comment on the Colonial Perversion of British Benevolence,' *Acadiensis* 1, no. 2 (1972): 29–42; Grace Aiton, 'The History of the Indian College and Early School Days in Sussex Vale,' *Collections* [New Brunswick Historical Society] 18 (1963): 159–62.

4 Winona Stevenson, 'The Red River Indian Mission School and John West's "Little Charges," 1820-1833,' *Native Studies Review* 4, nos. 1-2 (1988): 129–65; Canada, *Sessional Papers 1929-30, vol. 2, Annual Report of the Department of Indian Affairs for the Year Ended March 31, 1930,* 15–16; Jennifer Pettit, 'From Longhouse to Schoolhouse: The Mohawk Institute, 1834–1970' (unpublished paper, Canadian Historical Association Annual Meeting, 1994).

5 *Augustin Shingwauk, Little Pine's Journal: The Appeal of a Christian Chippeway Chief on Behalf of His People* (Toronto: Copp, Clark, 1872; facsimile edition, Sault Ste Marie: Shingwauk Reunion Committee, 1991); Jean L. Manore, 'A Vision of Trust: The Legal, Moral and Spiritual Foundations of Shingwauk Hall,' *Native Studies Review* 9, no. 2 (1993–4): 1–21.

6 National Archives of Canada (NA), MG 29, E 106, Hayter Reed Papers.

7 For example, the Archives of Victoria University in the University of Toronto have rich Jones materials.

8 See James Axtell, 'Ethnohistory: An Historian's Viewpoint,' *Ethnohistory* 26,

no. 1 (1979): 1–13; and 'Some Thoughts on the Ethnohistory of Missions,' *Ethnohistory* 29, no. 1 (1982): 35–41. Also useful are Bruce G. Trigger, *Natives and Newcomers: Canada's 'Heroic Age' Reconsidered* (Montreal and Kingston: McGill-Queen's University Press, 1985), chapter 4; and 'Ethnohistory: Problems and Prospects,' *Ethnohistory* 29, no. 1 (1982): 1–19.

9  Rita Joe, 'Hated Structure: Indian Residential School, Shubenacadie, N.S.,' in *Song of Eskasoni: More Poems of Rita Joe* (Charlottetown: Ragweed Press, 1988), 75. I am indebted to editor and friend Gerald Hallowell, who brought this poem to my attention.

10  Interview with Elizabeth Yuzicappi and Pat Lacerte, 6 February 1992, Regina. The interview was conducted by Maynard Quewezance. 'The Valley' was the Qu'Appelle Valley of southern Saskatchewan.

11  Pat Lacerte to editor, *Regina Leader-Post*, 31 January 1992. I am indebted to Maynard Quewezance, who kindly provided me with a copy of the clipping containing this letter.

12  Western Canada Pictorial Index, University of Winnipeg, EWA026408432 (Brandon 'Blackhawks,' 1936); NA, PA 185843 (Latuque 'Indiens').

13  Celia Haig-Brown, *Resistance and Renewal: Surviving the Indian Residential School* (Vancouver: Tillacum Library, 1988), 71–2; Royal British Columbia Museum, PN 6660 (dancers); PN 6665 (swimming pool).

14  The importance of Sunday visits and how they shielded some children from physical abuse are recurrent themes in Isabelle Knockwood, *Out of the Depths: The Experiences of Mi'kmaq Children at the Indian Residential School at Shubenacadie, Nova Scotia* (Lockeport, NS: Rosewood Publishing, 1992), 27, 32–3, 44, 78–9, and 123–4.

15  See the helpful comments of Julie Cruikshank, 'Oral Tradition and Oral History: Reviewing Some Issues,' *Canadian Historical Review* 75, no. 3 (1994): 403–18.

16  Note, for example, the heavy reliance on oral history evidence in 'Breaking the Silence.'

17  Interview with a Daughter of the Heart of Mary, 16 October 1990, Montreal.

18  I am indebted to Donald B. Smith of the University of Calgary, who brought this oil painting to my attention.

19  Vancouver Public Library, 9359, Pacific National Exhibition (1936), Display of Indian Art and Artifacts by Students of Alert Bay School.

20  Royal British Columbia Museum, PN 8788. The reference to 'Christian Potlatches' is quoted in an article on Father Paul Durieu by Jacqueline Gresko, in the *Dictionary of Canadian Biography* 12 (1990), 283.

# POLICY

# Owen Glendower, Hotspur, and Canadian Indian Policy

> *Owen Glendower*: I can call spirits from the vasty deep.
> *Hotspur*: Why, so can I, or so can any man;
> But will they come when you do call for them?
> – Shakespeare, *Henry IV, Part I*

Scholarly writing on Canada's Indian policy of the late Victorian period has lagged behind analysis of other aspects of Native-newcomer relations. Like American academics, Canadians have made an impressive start on revising the understanding of economic, military, and social relations in the seventeenth and eighteenth centuries. However, discussions of nineteenth-century assimilative policies have persisted in an older tendency to treat the Indians as objects rather than agents, victims rather than creators, of their history. The existing literature usually examines missionaries' requests for the suppression of cultural practices such as the potlatch and notes how their desires coincided with the government's anxiety to prevent Indians from squandering their capital or wasting their time. The standard interpretation then makes a logical leap from such policies as forbidding the Sun Dance or establishing residential schools to an implicit conclusion that such measures assimilated Indians.

In short, this traditional version of government policy towards Canada's Native peoples tends to treat as synonymous the aims and results of legislation banning traditional cultural practices or inhibiting Native movement. Such treatments remind one of nothing so much as Shakespeare's dialogue between Hotspur and Owen Glendower. When the boastful Glendower claims, 'I can call spirits from the vasty deep,'

Hotspur responds, 'Why, so can I, or so can any man.' Calling them is not the point. What matters is the response. 'But will they come when you do call for them?'[1] Canada legislated to control and assimilate Indians late in the nineteenth century. But did the measures work? Were the Indians simply victims of these policies?[2]

This view of late-nineteenth-century policy as efficacious resembles older, outmoded views of economic, military, and social relations between Canada's indigenous peoples and European newcomers. For a long time the literature on the fur trade, for instance, treated the Indians and Inuit as victims of rapacious European traders.[3] Following Francis Parkman, military historians talked about the 'use' of Indians by various European powers in the wars of the eighteenth century in North America.[4] Similarly, accounts of Christian missions in early New France emphasized the heroism of the Jesuits while paying little attention to the activities of those whom they proselytized.

Unlike the conventional treatment of late Victorian Indian policy, however, the traditional picture of the Indian as victim of European merchants, generals, and missionaries has of late been revised. Scholars like A.J. Ray and Robin Fisher have demonstrated that Indians both in the Hudson's Bay Company lands and on the Pacific were in control of the commerce in furs: Natives successfully insisted that the fur trade be carried on according to their formulas, and for purposes largely determined by them.[5] This work has been amplified and enriched by social historians who, while probing the role of Native women in fur-trade country, discovered that the social side of the commerce in peltries was controlled by Native societies, too.[6] And scholars such as Axtell, Eccles, Jaenen, and Trigger have reassessed the social and intellectual relations between Indians and Europeans in New France. They have demonstrated that missions were planted in the interior of North America primarily because the Native peoples regarded them as a manifestation of the exchange of personnel with which they had for centuries cemented commercial liaisons. Jesuits were allowed into Huronia to maintain the commercial and military alliance between the Huron and the French.[7] 'Heroic' missionaries were hostages to the exchange of furs; Jesuits were 'martyrs' to commercial ambitions.

The military relationship of the colonial period has also been reinterpreted to portray the Indian peoples as agents rather than objects. This development in Canadian historiography has paralleled American writing on military relations.[8] To Canadian audiences, Upton explained that the Mi'kmaq did not fight as the tools of the French, but rather that they embraced Catholicism and the French alliance as their best defence against the Anglo-Americans, whom they feared. And students of the American War of Independence have demonstrated conclusively that Indians operated, not as 'pawns' or 'tools,' but according to carefully worked-out calculations of where their self-interest lay.[9] Woodlands Indians perceived that their interests lay with the more northerly, commercially inclined European power rather than with the agriculturalists to the south.[10] Pontiac sought to repel the Anglo-American farmers who were poised to sweep across the Alleghenies after the Peace of Paris in 1763. The Brant family led the Mohawk to support the British in the Revolutionary War for personal and familial reasons and because of calculations that the British posed a lesser threat to their lands than the Americans. Tecumseh and the Shawnee Prophet were operating during the War of 1812 on the same strategy that was designed to deter the advance of the agricultural frontier.[11]

What these specialists in economic, social, and military history have done is to restore indigenous peoples to their active role in Canadian history. They have demonstrated that the Native peoples, at least in the early phases of contact, controlled the fur trade, that they pursued their own interests in military matters, and that they shaped the social and intellectual relationship. Similarly, some works on education and civil policy-making in the early decades after the War of 1812 have recognized an active Indian role. Mississauga and other Indians north of the lower Great Lakes encouraged and supported efforts to educate their young until they recognized that the missionaries and government sought to assimilate Native youths as well as make them literate. And legislative initiatives in the 1850s to assert political control over Indians in the central colony of British North America encountered stiff resistance.[12] Unfortunately, studies of Indian-White relations after Confederation in 1867 have thus far proved largely resistant to reinterpretation.[13] It is now time for another look at Canada's version of the policy of the Bible and the plough.

This policy, though foreshadowed in pre-Confederation programs in central Canada, became fully developed only after 1867. Legislation of 1869 and 1876, which was re-enacted in the Indian Act of 1880, presumed to define who was an Indian and to interfere with Indian self-government. At the same time, inducements were held out to Indians to encourage their 'advancement' towards full citizenship by offering those in eastern Canada the federal franchise in 1885 and by making 'allotments' of reserve land available to Indians who wished to take possession of individual plots. However, as had been the case with similar experiments earlier, Indians proved uninterested in acquiring electoral rights or freehold tenure and remarkably resistant to so-called enfranchisement, or adoption of standard citizenship status.[14] Bureaucrats responded to parallel failures in the 1870s and 1880s by resorting to what Indian commissioner Edgar Dewdney described as '"sheer compulsion."'[15]

Officialdom's inclination towards coercion culminated in a series of measures that were designed to control Indians politically and alter them culturally. Amendments to the Indian Act in 1884 prohibited the potlatch, or 'the Indian dance known as the "Tamanawas"' of the Pacific Indians, while in 1885 department regulations instituted a 'pass system' designed to control movement. In western Canada, Indians who wished to travel off their reserve were expected to obtain a pass signed by the agent. The pass system was designed to inhibit the movements of Indian diplomats, to discourage parental visits to residential schools, and to provide the North West Mounted Police (NWMP) and Indian agents with the authority to stop Plains Indians from participating in ceremonies such as the Sun Dance or the Thirst Dance on distant reserves. These coercive measures were aimed at assimilating Indians by attacking their religious rituals, removing their children from home influences, and preventing their travelling when there was work to be done in the fields. They were viewed as a necessary part of a broad campaign to inculcate agriculture in the prairie West that embraced subdivision of reserves into individual lots and enforced avoidance of mechanized horticulture.[16] These policies were stiffened in 1894–5 by legislation that permitted regulation of Indian children's attendance at school and by further legislation that attacked the cultural practices of both Pacific and Plains Indians by banning 'giveaway' dances or ceremonies that involved self-mutilation. Finally, in 1898 a new government withdrew the 1885 offer of the right to vote from eastern Canadian Indians.[17]

These Canadian policies were based on both British and American practices. In the British North American colonies in the middle decades of the nineteenth century, Christian missionaries and civil government had combined to promote both sedentary agriculture and education.[18] After the formation of the Dominion of Canada and the acquisition of the western plains by the new state in the 1860s, there was an increasing tendency among Canadian policy-makers to look to the United States as well as to British colonial policy for suggestions as to what should be done. The destructive American Indian wars of this period were quickly rejected as a model for Canada's integration of its new lands. Recognizing that they had 'to make up their mind to one of three policies – viz: to help the Indians to farm and raise stock, to feed them or to fight them,' Canadian officials chose the first option for reasons of both economy and humanitarianism.[19] However, if the American military was not an appropriate model for Canadian policymakers, other aspects of American Indian policy were. Programs such as allotting lands in individual plots in an effort to break up the reserves and atomize members of bands were largely copied from the Dawes scheme.[20] And planning in the late 1870s for a new educational policy led the federal government to send a commissioner south to investigate what its neighbours were doing by way of residential schooling.[21] Finally, the thorough cooperation of state and Christian church for the prosecution of these policies was both reminiscent of contemporary American approaches and consistent with British and British North American practice.

More important than the sources of these policies of assimilation was their effect. On the whole, scholars have treated policy intent and effect as similar, if not identical, largely because they concentrated on government fiat and documents. That assimilation and coercion were the objectives of the group of policies there is no doubt. But what were the effects? Did the measures work?

Consider, for example, the notorious pass system that was set up in 1885. First, it is important to note that little about the operation, as opposed to the purpose, of the system is known. We do not know for certain how long even a pretense of enforcing it was maintained.[22] And even while it was official policy in the prairie provinces, its effects appear to have been very mixed. For one thing, it does not seem to have been implemented uniformly in the 1880s. Hayter Reed, commissioner after Dewdney's elevation to the cabinet, referred in correspondence with his deputy minister in 1891 to 'regulations already issued, but so far disregarded' when talking about Natives' mobility.[23] Agents and farm instructors, who lacked the power and the time to make Indians obey the pass regulations, attempted to hand the duty off to the NWMP.[24] But the leaders of the NWMP had serious doubts about the system and their role in enforcing it. They believed that the requirement that Indians get a pass before leaving their reserve would not stand up in court. They also feared that if Indians tested it through litigation, their victory would discredit the whole system of law enforcement. In the aftermath of the Northwest Rebellion of 1885, the horsemen were most concerned not to undermine the law and themselves by attempting to enforce invalid regulations. They dragged their feet in response to agents' requests for help and, at times, refused outright to enforce the restrictions of the pass system.[25]

Indian Affairs bureaucrats themselves recognized the weakness of their position and were reluctant to provoke a confrontation over passes. The department's instruction to its agents was 'to issue Passes to Indians who they know will leave in any case, and so preserve an appearance at least of control, and a knowledge of their movements.'[26] It is also clear that many agents were less than thorough in their administration of the pass system. One disgruntled Mountie complained to Commissioner Reed that one of the latter's agents had given a pass to 'the biggest whore master in the band,' a man who 'had six squaws with him.'[27] In sum, what little is known about the actual operation of the pass system suggests not so much that it was effective in controlling the Indians as that it was very often a nullity.

There is similar reason to doubt the efficacy of the 1884 and 1895 measures against the potlatch and 'giveaway dances.' An 1884 amendment to the Indian Act threatened anyone 'who engages or assists in celebrating the Indian festival known as the "Potlach" or in the Indian dance known as the "Tamanawas"' with a jail term.[28] The federal government soon found that enforcement was a problem. The provincial government of British Columbia, which quarrelled constantly with Ottawa over Indian Affairs matters, was uncooperative about enforcement of the bans on 'Potlach' and 'Tamanawas.' And the federal government had few officials on the Northwest Coast through whom to compel compliance with the law.[29] Agents were helpless in most parts of the Coast. At the first announcement by a group of Indians that they intended to defy the ban, the local agent avoided a confrontation by acquiescing, giving as his justification the explanation that the scheduled potlatch was not really a potlatch at all.[30] The young anthropologist Franz Boas noted several years after the prohibition was legislated that '"there is nobody to prevent the Indians doing whatsoever they like."' He observed that an Indian who had been appointed a constable and supplied with a uniform and flag by the agent for the purpose of preventing unlawful feasts and dances responded strangely. Since his appointment, '"he dances in his uniform with the flag."'[31] Little wonder that the Kitwanga Indians in 1890 dismissed the anti-potlatch law, saying it '"was as weak as a baby."'[32]

When the occasional agent did try to enforce the ban, matters only got worse from the government's point of view. The agent at Alert Bay made the first arrest under the 1885 prohibition in 1889. Acting in his capacity as justice of the peace, he tried the accused and extracted a plea of guilty. Apparently in error, the agent or his superiors then committed the prisoner to trial in Victoria, the provincial capital. When friends of the accused Indian applied for a writ of habeas corpus, the justice immediately granted it on the grounds that the prisoner had already been tried and convicted. However, the jurist went on in a remarkable series of *obiter dicta* to lay waste the 1884 ban. He explained that the statute lacked a proper definition of 'Potlach' and that the other prohibited celebration, the 'Tamanawas,' was '"unknown."' Finally, he speculated that the accused, who knew no English, probably had not understood the earlier proceedings. The judge thought, on reflection, that '"there would be some difficulty in convicting at all under the Statute."'[33] As the distraught agent who had begun the series of events lamented, the incident rendered the 1885 ban '"a dead letter."'[34]

Although a more precisely framed amendment in 1895 got around the legal difficulty, it did not lead to immediate or effective enforcement of the prohibition on potlatching. There is abundant evidence that the supposedly forbidden celebrations went on long after 1895, though no potlatcher served a prison sentence till 1920.[35] (In 1909 a Methodist missionary on Vancouver Island plaintively asked his superiors, 'Can nothing be done with the Dominion Government to compel the enforcement of the Act which prohibits Potlatching?' When the principal of a residential school wanted to find out when a particular 'great potlach' was to take place, he wrote the agent to inquire – hardly evidence that potlatching was something kept hidden from the agent.)[36] A crackdown stopped the festivities for a few years, but by 1927 those Indians who still wanted to potlatch were back at it. It took the Great Depression and culture change to suppress it temporarily in the 1940s.[37] It would revive during a general rediscovery of traditional rites, crafts, and arts in the 1960s and later.

What is too often neglected in discussions of the anti-potlatch campaign is the role of Indian converts. The initial ban in the 1880s was a direct response to pressure from such Indians, as well as from missionaries and Indian Affairs officers.[38] Observers on the Northwest Coast noted that the minority who supported prohibition of the potlatch were Christian converts and young people who faced many decades of paying out before they could look forward to reaping their reward from the

redistributive ritual.[39] Certainly there is evidence of pressure to enforce
the ban from Christian converts in British Columbia. In 1888 government commissioners appointed to establish reserve limits in the Nass
River area heard complaints from Indian opponents of the potlatch.
They explained that they had protested to Indian Affairs officials about
the practice. The officials had counselled them to 'go to the heathen,
and advise them to stop Potlaches, but the heathen laughed at us.' They
were pleased when they heard reports that the government was going
to do something about the practice.[40] In 1893 the council at Kitimaat,
British Columbia, ruled that 'any person in the village of Kitimaat who
gives a feast or Potlach will be punished by a fine of One hundred and
forty Dollars,' while the 'Chiefs of Kispiox' in 1914 asked for government and church help in stopping the potlatch and 'old fashioned feasts
or feasts in memory of the dead.'[41] Converts apparently absorbed some
of the outlook of the non-Indian majority. When a spokesperson for a
Kwakiutl band in 1919 wanted to 'give you a few reasons' why the potlatch ban 'should not only stand but ... also be strongly enforced,' she
began with a patriotic argument. Here, 'people as a whole will never
own Allegiance to the Government or King as long as they are allowed
to practice their Allegiance to the Potlatch system, for to them this
excludes every other Government.' 'No Potlatchers,' she claimed, 'volunteered to serve overseas.'[42] As late as 1936, a public meeting at Alert
Bay was the scene of a vigorous debate between Christians and traditionalists over the potlatch and marriage customs.[43]

If not all coastal Indians opposed banning the old ways, neither did
all the purveyors of new beliefs favour coercion and suppression.
Some missionaries thought coercion unnecessary and undesirable.
'Leave the thing alone as far as the old people are concerned; educate
along definite lines with the young people and ten years at the outside
should see the end of the problem,' one argued.[44] Even the Department
of Indian Affairs on occasion promoted supposedly forbidden traditions. Ironically and unintentionally, it encouraged the officially illegal
dances by conveying to the World Exposition of 1893 in Chicago a
troupe of Kwakiutl who staged the illicit dances.[45]

Because a pattern similar to the anti-potlatch campaign is found in
the forbidden dances of Plains Indians, we should be skeptical about
the effectiveness of nineteenth-century prohibitions of these celebrations. Pressure for action against festivals such as the Sun Dance of the
Blackfoot Confederacy or the Thirst Dance of the Cree and Saulteaux
sometimes came from Christian converts among the Indians them-

selves. Church of England canon H.W. Gibbon Stocken claimed to be 'writing ... at the earnest & repeated request of several of our leading Blackfoot Christians' when he asked the deputy minister for energetic action against the 'native dances, now so largely indulged in.'[46] An Indian agent among the Dakota reported that 'there were two cliques or factions on this reserve, a pagan faction and a Christian faction ... The Christians wanted to legislate the pagans into the church, first by stopping their recreations and forcing along certain lines and the pagans worked in opposition to the Christians.'[47] Indian missionaries on the plains, like converts on the Northwest Coast, often advocated suppression. The Dakota John Thunder, a Presbyterian missionary in Manitoba, argued for action against giveaway dances, which he thought retarded his people's moral growth as well as their economic advance.[48] On the other hand, there were rare non-Native missionaries who defended Indians' right to carry out these dances. The Methodist John McDougall explained to a western audience that the Sun Dance, like the Thirst Dance, was 'a religious festival.' 'And,' he added, 'I altogether fail to see why in these days of our much boasted religious liberty anyone should interfere with a few Indians in the exercise of their faith.'[49] But Plains Indians did not have much need of the efforts of someone like McDougall. They proved quite adept at resisting, evading, and defying efforts to stamp out the Sun and Thirst Dances.

Local Indian leaders, some of them the products of residential schools, resorted to formal protests to the government, sometimes with the aid of Euro-Canadian lawyers whom they retained, against the agents' efforts to interfere with their dancing.[50] Residential school graduates like Dan Kennedy were also known to employ their influence against the missionary on the reserve, using the argument that removal of the cleric would put an end to interference with traditional dancing.[51] Indians also became adept at exploiting differing attitudes among White authority figures to defeat those who wanted to interfere with them. Numerous Plains bands cited the missionary McDougall in justification of their attempts to carry on with their dances.[52] In the 1890s the Blood Indians decided to ignore their agent, who threatened prosecution as they arranged a medicine pipe dance, at least partly because they knew that other agents on the Piegan and Blackfoot reserves were permitting dancing there.[53] As the years went by, it became increasingly common for Indians to use lawyers to combat Indian Affairs and for local officials to lament their charges' greater familiarity with the law and with legal weapons.[54]

Evasion was often employed by Plains Indians intent on maintaining their religious traditions in the dance. One of the easiest ways was simply to wait until the Indian agent was not expecting a dance and then hold it, as Samson's band did in the Hobbema Agency in Alberta.[55] Another method was to seek informal approval for a modified version of the forbidden dance and then to carry out the traditional ceremony. Under the 1895 amendment to the unenforceable 1884 provision on dancing, only celebrations that involved giving away property or self-mutilation were outlawed. It was a fairly simple matter for Indians to persuade the agent that they were going to hold a 'modified' dance and then to indulge in the forbidden practices.[56] In theory, agents were supposed to use the pass system to prevent Indians from travelling to other reserves to participate in dances. Near the west-central Saskatchewan town of Battleford, the Cree of the Poundmaker and Little Pine bands hit on an ingenious stratagem. Since their reserves were contiguous, they built their dance hall on the boundary line so that no official could interfere.[57] And when the Poundmaker band had to replace their community hall, they made sure they built the new one well away from the prying eyes of agent and missionary. The dancing continued largely undetected.[58] Farther south, on the File Hills Farm Colony, which was designed as a Christian home for ex-pupils of the residential schools, Indian dancing also went on clandestinely.[59]

Finally, there were cases in which the Indians simply defied both law and agent. An agent in northwestern Ontario who tried to dissuade a shaman from carrying on traditional feasts and dances found that the conjurer 'only laughed' at him.[60] On Red Crow's Blood reserve, after several years in which the Indians had carried on modified versions of their dances, the agent in 1900 decided to prevent dancing altogether. He withheld the beef tongues that were essential to the ritual, but Indians who were employed by the Mounted Police as scouts quietly obtained tongues from police larders. Next, the agent threatened to withhold rations from any Indian who participated in the Sun Dance. When Red Crow threatened to slaughter every head in his considerable herd to feed his people, the agent capitulated, 'and never again was the ceremony denied to them.'[61]

Plains Indians proved so adept at resisting, evading, or defying the bans on ceremonial dancing that agents and missionaries were compelled to proceed cautiously and often to try to redirect, rather than stamp out, these activities.[62] Agents who knew that they could not suppress dancing tried to create interest in alternatives such as sports days and other summertime festivals.[63] And the Anglican missionary on the Blackfoot reserve, following in a long Christian tradition, tried to defeat 'pagan' ritual by adopting and modifying it. He 'made a bid for the transformation of' the tobacco dance by creating 'a ceremony very much like the old one of "Beating the bounds" which has almost gone out of the Church.' He formed his converts into a procession headed by a 'cross of green wood' and marched them 'round the camp stopping at the East, South, west [sic] and North. Then we formed up in the centre of the camp and planted the cross.'[64] Moreover, agents and missionaries found that efforts to discourage dancing ran up against Euro-Canadian populations that wanted the dances included in their summer fairs in order to sell tickets.[65] Efforts to stamp out dancing, like those aimed at the potlatch, proved largely ineffective because of both Euro-Canadian and Indian obstacles.

Even residential schools, which are often described as the most coercive of church-state instruments of assimilation, were no more representative of effective policy than prohibitions on Indians' traditional cultural and religious practices. These schools – a joint enterprise of the federal government and major Christian denominations, a blend of British and American practice[66] – sought to remove the children from 'the demoralizing and degrading influences of the tepees' and surround them with an environment of bourgeois Christian values.[67] Here the children would be made over into acquisitive, individualistic Christians who would, ultimately, make the pass system and prohibitions on dancing or potlatching unnecessary. Residential schools were intended to lead to 'not only the emancipation of the subjects thereof from the condition of ignorance and superstitious blindness in which they are, and their parents before them were sunk, but converting them into useful members of society and contributors to, instead of merely consumers of, the wealth of the country.'[68]

Residential schools are usually treated as though they were effective in capturing Indian children and in crushing their will and identity. It is sometimes said that 'it was the rule at that time that all treaty Indian children had to attend an Indian boarding school.'[69] The authority of the Department of Indian Affairs was supposedly used to ensure that children were not only sent to these schools but also kept there. At the schools, Native children were strictly forbidden to practise any Native traditional observances or to speak their own languages. Residential schooling, in short, typified the totalitarian and assimilative spirit of Canada's Indian policy in the later Victorian era and the first half of the twentieth century.[70] It amounted, as a candid missionary put it, to an effort to 'educate & colonize a people against their will.'[71] But is this view accurate for anything more than the intentions of those who ran the residential schools? There is no doubt that the institutions were intended to convert children to Christianity and to equip them with the skills to become self-supporting in or alongside Euro-Canadian society. But what was the result?

First, the conventional view of residential schools fails to note that the system never reached more than a minority of young Indians and Inuit. There were never more than eighty residential schools supported by the government in the entire country. Atlantic Canada did not have any until Shubenacadie was established in Nova Scotia late in the 1920s, and even thereafter most Indians in the region went to day schools or to no school at all. Much the same holds true for Quebec, where vast areas were without residential schools. In southern Ontario there were only four, and in northern Ontario many large districts lacked boarding or industrial schools. The prairie provinces, British Columbia, and the far north were the most thoroughly covered regions, not because a far-sighted federal government systematically provided full coverage, but because denominational competition among Oblates, Anglicans, Methodists, and Presbyterians fostered the rapid multiplication of missions and schools in these areas. In some cases, Indian bands petitioned unsuccessfully for the erection of a residential school for their children.[72] Many children, even in the West and the North, completely escaped the residential schools. As one Stoney put it, 'I didn't even go to one hour of school because I am an Indian.'[73] Thousands of young Indians similarly escaped the clutches of residential schools.[74]

Even where residential schools existed, they proved singularly difficult to keep filled with students. Missionaries in the early years were forever complaining that agents either failed to help them recruit students or even worked actively against their efforts to procure them.[75] Even after the department acquiesced in 1894 to the missionaries' cries for compulsory attendance legislation, the problem persisted. In 1908 a Methodist principal complained that 'there is no law to compel an Indian to educate his child,' and in 1906 the Anglican Mission Board in the Diocese of Calgary contended that Indians 'send their children to school when it suits them to do so, and they keep them at home for the same reason. The only exception to this rule is, the children are allowed to please themselves whether they go or not.'[76] Even allowing for clerical hyperbole, it is clear that attendance remained a problem. If this were not so, why did principals make numerous, expensive 'recruiting' trips in search of students, and why did men of the cloth resort to bribing parents to get their children?[77] Once students were obtained for the schools, how could they be kept? To take only one example, Joseph Shaw was admitted to Coqualeetza Institute on 19 August 1901; he disappeared on 1 November 1903 and remained a truant till formally discharged on 3 September 1905. (He did, however, pay a visit to the school in 1906.)[78] In understaffed schools it was a lot of trouble to chase students. Agents were often uncooperative or distracted, and the police hated the chore of retrieving unhappy runaways. When the constabulary presented the bill for their services as truant officers, the evangelists became unhappy too.[79]

It is not clear that the schools, assuming they procured and held on to the students, were very successful in eradicating traditional Indian religion and cultural practices. Certainly most schools tried to force the children to conform to Euro-Canadian standards, especially in the highly visible areas of dress and grooming. It was standard procedure to scrub the students and shear the boys' hair on arrival, a practice that caused consternation in children for whom cropped hair was a sign of mourning.[80] Even after the student got over the shock of thinking that one of his loved ones had died after he left home for the school, he did not necessarily get over the rough subjection to Euro-Canadian grooming. One fellow who became a Christian worker among the Indians 'never forgave the woman who cut his hair while he slept and if he followed the inclination of his own heart he would throw off all the education & go back where he would never see a white man.'[81]

One area of school life that requires reconsideration is the matter of suppressing Indian languages, usually held to have universally occurred. This seems to be an exaggeration. It would have been strange for evangelists who had laboured hard to master Indian tongues – and there were many of them among the Oblates and Church Missionary Society workers in the nineteenth century, in particular – not to use their linguistic skills with the children, if only outside classrooms. In many schools, at least one church service on Sunday was conducted in the Indian language, especially in those mission districts where the school chapel was also the mission's church.[82] A Methodist missionary one Sunday 'held service in the schoolhouse, and had the privilege of preaching the glorious Gospel to an earnest people in the "language wherein they were born," which, after all, is the only way to reach the hearts and thoughts of any congregation.'[83] At Lejac School, 'they used to pray one week in

Indian and one week in ... English.'[84] In British Columbia schools the rule was, 'we must not talk Indian (except when allowed),' while at some other institutions, such as the Blood Anglican school, students were able to use their own language after seven o'clock in the evening.[85] Some schoolmasters were criticized for their indifference about language.[86] But was it realistic to think all use of Indian languages could be stopped? Many schools were like Morley, Alberta, where the teachers knew that 'the children were not supposed to speak Stoney, but they really couldn't stop them.'[87]

There were even rare examples in which the schools turned out to be the place where students actually became acquainted with their culture. The daughter of parents who lived on the File Hills ex-pupils' colony in Saskatchewan recalled that 'we didn't speak Cree in our house as our parents spoke two different languages.' However, when she 'went to school we learned some Cree from our schoolmates but we often found that what we learned wasn't in good taste when we repeated it to our parents.' She picked up a little Cree at school, though she never mastered the language.[88] But this daughter of supposedly converted parents also recalled that she 'learned a lot about our Indian culture and some of the language, even though we weren't allowed to speak it at school.' On occasion 'we went down to the lake to dance a pow-wow. We used a pail for a drum and Gracie Squatepew was always our main singer.'[89]

The language question could even provoke the parents to intervene in the operation of the schools, on at least one occasion in a surprising fashion. The Anglican missionary on the Blood reserve in southern Alberta was visited by a delegation of parents whose leader told him, 'I came to see you about teaching my children. They tell me that you are teaching them syllabics in the Blackfoot language.' This man said that the parents thought that this 'is wrong. We want you to teach the children the English tongue, and not syllabics. They have their own language and we have ours. Teach them English and we will be satisfied.' The missionary acceded to the delegation's desire: 'I dropped teaching them syllabics right away. There the matter ended so far as the Bloods were concerned.'[90] There were other pressures generated from among Indians in favour of the use of English. When a school population contained children from two or more language groups, English was promoted as a medium of communication that all could use.[91] Residential schools were not always the oppressive institutions they were thought to be in the area of the suppression of language, and

Indian parents sometimes had a significant role in the operation of these schools.

The traditional view that residential schools rigidly separated children from their parents, their homes, and their bands also should be qualified. Again, there can be no doubt that this was hoped for by government officials, who wanted the schools to socialize children away from the ways of their parents. But it frequently was not the result. Many of the boarding institutions were located close to, or even on, the reserves from which their inmates came. The Mohawk Institute in Ontario was close to the Six Nations Reserve. Crowstand in east-central Saskatchewan was on the reserve of the Cote band. In southern Alberta, in particular, the boarding schools run by the Catholics and Anglicans were located on the reserves of the Sarcee, Piegan, Blackfoot, and Blood Indians. Proximity enhanced parental control of the children's movement. When 'Running Rabbit made bother about his girl remaining in the Home' on the Blackfoot reserve, it was easier for the principal to 'let her go' than to resist.[92] Similarly, at Alberni on Vancouver Island, the Presbyterian school was only a hop, skip, and jump from the 'rancherie,' or Indian encampment.[93] While the more elaborate 'industrial schools' that the Department of Indian Affairs began to establish in 1883 were deliberately located far from reserves, there were always many fewer of these than of boarding schools. Most children in residential schools were not kept away from home influences for long periods. Many of them visited home at least every weekend, whatever the theory of residential schooling might have held.

For other reasons also there was a great deal more interaction between the home and the child than Indian Affairs would have liked. The children at these schools were notorious for running away whenever they became homesick or angry at the discipline or fed up with the poor food and hard work. The diary of an Anglican missionary in southern Alberta in 1917 contains at least seventeen instances, many of them multiple escapes, of children running away during the year.[94] The high incidence of runaways was part of the reason that schools such as the Anglican Blood institution provided a weekend 'monthly holiday,' as well as generous Christmas, Easter, and summer breaks.[95] On Kuper Island in British Columbia, the principal pleaded with the Department of Indian Affairs for longer summer holidays, arguing that the parents would take the children salmon fishing regardless of what he or Ottawa said.[96] The flow of personnel went the other way, too. The pass system notwithstanding, Indian parents often made their way from their reserves to the school to visit their children. The principal at Lebret School in southern Saskatchewan constructed an 'Indian porch' to house the unauthorized visitors, defending his action to annoyed Indian Affairs officials by saying that it was necessary to prevent the parents from removing their children from the school.[97] All such instances suggest that residential schools did not always keep parents and children apart, and that parents sometimes had some influence over the schools' operation.

Indeed, there were cases for which it would be more accurate to say that the Indians were the guiding force behind the foundation of the residential school. Northwest Coast Indians demanded that the Presbyterians provide residence facilities at Alberni in which their children could stay while they were absent to work in the sealery or in the canneries.[98] Those at Kitimaat petitioned the Methodists in 1896 for a home and offered to help with the construction and maintenance of such a facility.[99] In the north, a missionary reported that 'at Whitefish Lake some forty miles from Lesser Slave Lake ... [a] Boarding School has just been erected because the Indians would not send their children to the School at the latter place.'[100]

As revealing as these examples are, they pale beside the exceptional case of the Cecilia Jeffrey School in the Lake of the Woods district, near the Ontario-Manitoba boundary. In 1898 the Indians at Shoal Lake petitioned the Presbyterians in Winnipeg for a school, and two years later they were reported to be 'not only willing but anxious for a boarding school.' The local missionary warned that they 'will lose confidence in us and have no further use for us' if the church did not move to meet their wishes.[101] In January 1902 an extraordinary meeting of missionaries and Ojibwa chiefs negotiated an agreement that should be quoted at length for the benefit of people who believe that residential schools were imposed on Indians and run totally by the clergy:

1st. That while children are young and at school they shall not be baptized without the consent of their parents but if when they reach years of understanding they wish to be baptized, relations and friends shall be invited to the baptism ...

4th. That a number of children shall be sent now and if they are well treated more shall be sent ...

6th. Little children (under 8 years) shall not be given heavy work and larger children shall attend school, at least half of each school day ...

8th. That parents shall be allowed to take their children to their religious festivals, but only one child at a time and the child shall not remain away over night ...

9th. That in case of a child running away, police aid shall not be used, but the parents shall bring back the child.[102]

As this contract made clear, the Ojibwa not only were responsible for the establishment of the school but largely dictated the terms on which it was to operate. Proselytization was forbidden, children could leave to observe traditional religious rites, and the police were not to be used to force runaways back.

Over the following few years, the Cecilia Jeffrey School continued as it had begun – under Indian control. When the Indians became annoyed because the staff made the children kneel for prayers and the matron meted out harsh discipline, they warned the local missionary that they wanted the original agreement obeyed. If 'we keep our promises they will send more children but if they think we are trying to use the school as a trap to get them in and make Christians of them against their parents [sic] wishes, they will perhaps withdraw even the scholars we have now.' The church's capitulation on the kneeling issue quieted the parents somewhat, but the protests against the matron continued.[103] The Cecilia Jeffrey case illustrated that Indians sometimes had considerable control over their children's schooling.

Parental efforts to control if and when their children entered a residential school, and how they were treated when they did, took many forms. It was quite common to keep the children out of school at the end of the summer where seasonal employment made doing so economically attractive. As the principal of the Coqualeetza Industrial Institute in the Fraser Valley noted, 'It is difficult to persuade the Indians to allow their children to come to school till after the fishing season closes.'[104] Once the children were in school, parents could sometimes influence the curriculum, as when they preferred instruction in English to syllabics. And they persisted in visiting the schools to check up on their children over the objections of Indian Affairs officers.

Parents also had ways of responding to school officials whom they found obnoxious. The mildest form of resistance to an unpopular staff member was to petition the Department of Indian Affairs to remove the person.[105] The fact that 'the Indians from the Prince Albert District have sent in a remonstrance against the conduct of the school' was a contributing factor in the dismissal of the principal at the Battleford Industrial School.[106] Indian resistance to objectionable schooling could also be violent. At the Jesuit school on Manitoulin Island in Ontario, a boy who took exception to the unfamiliar corporal punishment grabbed his teacher by the throat and roughed him up.[107] On the Blackfoot reserve, an Indian Affairs employee was killed and the missionary-principal and his family forced to flee for their lives in 1895.[108] Another spectacular altercation between a parent and a staff member took place at the File Hills School in 1949.[109] At the Kamloops School, a music instructor who had mistreated students was forced to leave, and when he returned as a teaching brother the next year, an Indian leader went to the school and successfully demanded his removal.[110] Incidents of violent resistance are not numerous in the documentary evidence (usually interviews and private correspondence between missionaries and their church's headquarters staff), but it is important to remember that missionaries were not likely to advertise their unpopularity.

More often, passive resistance was just as effective as petitions and violence were. Because of the way that the schools were financed, a certain amount of parental cooperation was essential to their survival. Since funding was based on the number of students physically present, a decline in attendance hurt the missionary organization's finances. The churches involved always found revenues from per capita grants less than their needs; therefore, a drop in enrolment-related grant revenue made a tight budgetary situation critical.[111] Denominational competition compounded the financial problem and increased the need to conciliate Indian parents. When schools of different churches occupied the same district, competition for students arose. For example, parents who were unhappy with the Methodist Coqualeetza Institute in British Columbia simply transferred their children to the Roman Catholic school on Kuper Island.[112] One consequence of competition among the schools was bribery of parents to send their children to a particular school. Another was that parents, who almost always preferred to send their children to the school closest to their home, acquired bargaining power with school officials. Institutions with reputations for mistreating or overworking children or for housing them in unhealthy conditions found recruiting more difficult. In the opinion of a bishop, the death of seven students in the Anglican school at Hay River was likely 'to make recruiting impossible' in their home community the following season.[113] Parental complaints about the inadequate number of teachers and staff in their schools led the Anglicans to appeal to their members for helpers: 'We are literally fighting for our continued existence as a Missionary Church in this area due to the highly organized campaign of the roman [sic] Church against us.'[114]

The price of failing to meet such challenges by placating the parents was the demise of the schools. The Calgary Industrial School closed because it was too distant from the reserves and because the presence of other schools on the reserves gave parents alternatives.[115] As a Presbyterian missionary said of the situation in Saskatchewan, it was 'almost impossible to get some of the Indians to send their children to a school on the reserve, and, of course, it is even more difficult to secure recruits for schools at a distance.' Distance and a poor reputation for health conditions worked against the Presbyterians' Regina Industrial School. In western Manitoba, the 'Regina School is looked upon with disfavor. It is a long way off and of the seven who were sent there only one is alive today, all the rest dying of tuberculosis. The parents are really afraid to let their children go.'[116] In spite of Herculean efforts by the Presbyterians, enrolments at Regina could not be increased sufficiently, and it closed. A similar pattern developed at an Oblate school in Alberta after the First World War. Because 'Indians seem to be more and more opposed to the idea of sending their children to Dunbow,' the local bishop came 'to the conclusion that it is better to end the struggle and send back to their respective reserves, or to the Lebret School, the few pupils actually in the Dunbow school.'[117]

Some parents fought long-term campaigns to force a school to operate as they wished. Between 1922 and 1934 the Roman Catholic Indians at Fort Frances in northwestern Ontario demanded a meeting with the provincial of the Oblates, asked for an investigation of the school's administration, withheld their children, and began to urge the Department of Indian Affairs to establish a day school. Finally, they got the principal replaced.[118] Such manifestations of organized parental resistance occurred frequently in the schools of all denominations.[119]

By means ranging from evasion to resistance, passive or violent, parents made their children's educational experiences tolerable. In unusual cases, such as the Cecilia Jeffrey School, they could set the terms on which the school was run and enforce them by withholding their children.[120] More common were the tactics of protesting, petitioning, sending the children to a competing institution, or boycotting the schools altogether. This is not to argue that the events at Cecilia Jeffrey, Lestock, Fort Frances, or Regina were typical of all residential schools. Rather, it is to suggest that the conventional picture of residential schools as totalitarian institutions run arbitrarily by all-powerful missionaries and bureaucrats is also not universally accurate.

Nor should this analysis be read as arguing that interference and coercion did not occur. Dances were interrupted and dancers prosecuted.[121] Moreover, even an ineffective pass system or an unenforceable prohibition on cultural practices could have a deterrent effect, dissuading Natives from exercising their right to move or to celebrate religious traditions.[122] This examination of Indian policy is merely an attempt to test the conventional picture of aggressive government and missionaries controlling and reshaping Indian peoples.

Students of Canadian Indian policy need to adjust the conventional picture of residential schools as well as the generally accepted view of policies aimed at political control and cultural assimilation. The pass system and the prohibitions on dancing and the potlatch were seldom or ineffectively applied. Indian peoples after the middle of the nineteenth century may have subsided into numerical inferiority to Euro-Canadian society, they may have passed into a period of economic and military irrelevance to Canadians at large, and they may have been subjected to policies intended to transform them into Christian, bourgeois citizens. However, just as their ancestors often shaped the conduct of the fur trade and served as equal partners in military alliances in the seventeenth and eighteenth centuries, Indian peoples of the late nineteenth and early twentieth centuries were actors who pursued their interests and struggled to preserve their identity. They resisted, evaded, and defied efforts to control their decision-making, limit their traditional rites, and deprive them of their children. If we distinguish between the intentions of churches and government, on the one hand, and the effects of the policies, on the other, we might find that Canada's Native peoples persist throughout time as active, if lamentably ignored, actors in the country's history.

### Notes

This essay first appeared in *Ethnohistory* 37, no. 4 (Fall 1990). I should like to express my appreciation to the Social Sciences and Humanities Research Council of Canada, whose grants financed its research; to thank W.A. Waiser, a colleague who provided helpful suggestions for revisions of earlier drafts; and to acknowledge the assistance of Janice Acoose, a student who suggested several ideas and sources to me, as well as that of the anonymous referees of *Ethnohistory*.

1  William Shakespeare, *Henry IV, Part I* (Folger ed.), III, i, 57–9.
2  For examples of the conventional view of the Indian as passive victim see

Bruce Sealey and Verna J. Kirkness, eds, *Indians without Tipis: A Resource Book by Indians and Metis* (Agincourt, ON, 1973), 33; James S. Frideres, *Native People in Canada: Contemporary Conflicts*, 2nd ed. (Scarborough, ON, 1983), 33; Donald Purich, *Our Land: Native Rights in Canada* (Toronto, 1986), 121–2.

3  Stanley B. Ryerson, *The Founding of Canada: Beginnings to 1815*, new ed. (Toronto, 1960), 86–8, 262.

4  Jack M. Sosin, 'The Use of Indians in the War of the American Revolution: A Re-Assessment of Responsibility,' *Canadian Historical Review* 46 (June 1965). See also George F.G. Stanley, 'The Indians in the War of 1812,' *Canadian Historical Review* 31 (June 1950).

5  Arthur J. Ray, *Indians in the Fur Trade: Their Role As Hunters, Trappers, and Middlemen in the Lands Southwest of Hudson Bay, 1660–1870* (Toronto, 1974); Robin A. Fisher, *Contact and Conflict: Indian-European Relations in British Columbia, 1774-1890* (Vancouver, 1976), chapters 1–3. See also Kenneth Coates, 'Furs along the Yukon: Hudson's Bay Company–Native Trade in the Yukon River Basin, 1830–1893,' *BC Studies*, no. 55 (Autumn 1982): 56–68.

6  Sylvia Van Kirk, *'Many Tender Ties': Women in Fur-Trade Society, 1670–1870* (Winnipeg, [1980]); Jennifer S.H. Brown, *Strangers in Blood: Fur Trade Company Families in Indian Country* (Vancouver, 1980). For examples of other fur-trade scholars who agree with Van Kirk and Brown, see Daniel Francis and Toby Morantz, *Partners in Furs: A History of the Fur Trade in Eastern James Bay, 1600–1870* (Kingston, ON, and Montreal, 1983), 53, 90; Paul C. Thistle, *Indian-European Trade Relations in the Lower Saskatchewan River Region to 1840* (Winnipeg, 1986), 9, 16; J. Colin Yerbury, *The Subarctic Indians and the Fur Trade, 1680–1860* (Vancouver, 1986), 71–2, 91.

7  Bruce G. Trigger, *Natives and Newcomers: Canada's 'Heroic Age' Reconsidered* (Kingston, ON, and Montreal, 1985), chapter 5, esp. 260–71. See also James Axtell, *The Invasion Within: The Contest of Cultures in Colonial North America* (New York, 1985), esp. chapter 5; William J. Eccles, *The Canadian Frontier, 1534–1760* (New York, 1969), 44–5; Cornelius J. Jaenen, *Friend and Foe: Aspects of French-Amerindian Cultural Contact in the Sixteenth and Seventeenth Centuries* (New York, 1976), 67–8.

8  Among the most important American influences have been Barbara Graymont, *The Iroquois in the American Revolution* (Syracuse, NY, 1972), and the following works by Francis Jennings: *The Invasion of America: Indians, Colonialism, and the Cant of Conquest* (Chapel Hill, NC, 1975); 'The Indians' Revolution,' in *The American Revolution: Explorations in the History of American Radicalism*, ed. Alfred F. Young (De Kalb, IL, 1976), 319–48, esp. 322; *The Ambiguous Iroquois Empire: The Covenant Chain Confederation of Indian Tribes*

*with English Colonies from Its Beginnings to the Lancaster Treaty of 1744* (New York, 1984); 'Iroquois Alliances in American History,' in *The History and Culture of Iroquois Diplomacy: An Interdisciplinary Guide to the Treaties of the Six Nations and Their League*, ed. Francis Jennings (Syracuse, NY, 1985), 37–65; *Empire of Fortune: Crowns, Colonies, and Tribes in the Seven Years' War* (New York, 1988).

9  Leslie F.S. Upton, *Micmacs and Colonists: Indian-White Relations in the Maritimes, 1713–1867* (Vancouver, 1979), 26; Sydney F. Wise, 'The American Revolution and Indian History,' in *Character and Circumstance: Essays in Honour of Donald Grant Creighton*, ed. J.S. Moir (Toronto, 1970), 200.

10  Jaenen, *Friend and Foe*, 192; Jennings, 'The Indians' Revolution,' 336–41.

11  E. Palmer Patterson, *The Canadian Indian: A History since 1500* (Don Mills, ON, 1970), 84. Again there are strong historiographical parallels in the United States: R. David Edwards, *Tecumseh and the Quest for Indian Leadership* (Boston, 1984), esp. chapters 7–8, and *The Shawnee Prophet* (Lincoln, NE, 1983), chapter 6 and epilogue; Colin G. Calloway, *Crown and Calumet: British-Indian Relations, 1783–1815* (Norman, OK, 1987), esp. 22 and chapter 8.

12  Hope Maclean, 'The Hidden Agenda: Methodist Attitudes to the Ojibwa and the Development of Indian Schooling in Upper Canada, 1821–1860' (M.A. thesis, University of Toronto, 1978); John S. Milloy, 'The Early Indian Acts: Developmental Strategy and Constitutional Change,' in *As Long As the Sun Shines and Water Flows: A Reader in Canadian Native Studies*, ed. Ian A.L. Getty and Anthony S. Lussier (Vancouver, 1983), 56–64; Donald B. Smith, *Sacred Feathers: The Reverend Peter Jones (Kahkewaquonaby) and the Mississauga Indians* (Lincoln, NE, 1987), esp. chapters 8–12.

13  Important exceptions to this generalization include E. Brian Titley, *A Narrow Vision: Duncan Campbell Scott and the Administration of Indian Affairs in Canada* (Vancouver, 1986); Jacqueline J. Gresko, 'Qu'Appelle Industrial School: White "Rites" for the Indians of the Old North-West' (M.A. thesis, Carleton University, 1970); Hana Samek, *The Blackfoot Confederacy, 1880–1920: A Comparative Study of Canadian and U.S. Indian Policy* (Albuquerque, 1987), esp. chapter 6.

14  Milloy, 'Early Indian Acts,' 59–61.

15  John L. Tobias, 'Canada's Subjugation of the Plains Cree, 1879–1885,' *Canadian Historical Review* 64 (Dec. 1983): 534.

16  Sarah A. Carter, 'The Genesis and Anatomy of Government Policy and Indian Reserve Agriculture on Four Agencies in Treaty Four, 1874–1897' (Ph.D. diss., University of Manitoba, 1987), esp. chapter 5. I am grateful to Dr Carter for allowing me to use her dissertation.

17  Useful summaries of these policies are Titley, *A Narrow Vision*, esp. chapters

3, 5, 6, and 8; James R. Miller, *Skyscrapers Hide the Heavens: A History of Indian-White Relations in Canada* (Toronto, 1989), chapters 11–12.

18 See note 12.

19 David Laird (lieutenant-governor and Indian commissioner of the Northwest Territories) to minister of the interior, 17 April 1878, National Archives of Canada (hereafter cited as NA), Ottawa, Records of the Department of Indian Affairs (hereafter cited as RG 10), Western Canada Files (hereafter cited as Black Series), vol. 3664, file 9825; Miller, *Skyscrapers*, 161–2.

20 Sarah A. Carter, 'Two Acres and a Cow: "Peasant" Farming for the Indians of the Northwest, 1889–97,' *Canadian Historical Review* 70 (March 1989): 38–9.

21 Nicholas F. Davin, 'Report on Industrial Schools for Indians and Half-Breeds,' 14 March 1879, NA, Sir John Macdonald Papers, vol. 91, 35428.

22 Sarah A. Carter, 'Controlling Indian Movement: The Pass System,' *NeWest Review,* May 1985, pp. 8–9; Carter, 'Genesis and Anatomy,' 302–12. See also Purich, *Our Land,* 129–32; F. Laurie Barron, 'The Indian Pass System in the Canadian West, 1882–1935,' *Prairie Forum* 13 (Spring 1988): 25–42; and B. Bennett, 'Study of Passes for Indians to Leave Their Reserves' (mimeo, Treaties and Historical Research Centre, Department of Indian Affairs and Northern Development, Ottawa, 1974), esp. 7–8. I am grateful to John Leslie of the Treaties and Historical Research office for providing me with a copy of the Bennett paper.

23 RG 10, Black Series, vol. 3675, file 11, 411-4, H. Reed to L. Vankoughnet, 20 May 1891.

24 See, for example, Glenbow-Alberta Institute Archives (hereafter cited as Glenbow Archives), S.B. Lucas Papers (M 699), file 9, diary, July 1896.

25 Roderick C. Macleod, *The North-West Mounted Police and Law Enforcement, 1873–1905* (Toronto, 1976), 146; Barron, 'Pass System,' 35–7; Carter, 'Genesis and Anatomy,' 307–8. For evidence that the department knew it had no legal basis for attempting to restrict Indians to their reserves, see J.D. McLean (assistant deputy and secretary) to H.E. Calkin, J.P., 22 August 1913, RG 10, Black Series, vol. 4076, quoted in Bennett, 'Study of Passes,' 6.

26 NA, MG 29 E106, Hayter Reed Papers, vol. 14, H. Reed to Hon. T. Mayne Daly, 25 March 1893. It is significant, too, that the printed 'General Instructions to Indian Agents in Canada,' issued in 1913 and reissued in 1933, nowhere mentions passes (Glenbow Archives, Blackfoot Indian Agency Papers [M 1785], box 3, file 15).

27 Reed Papers, vol. 17, Lawrence W. Herchmer to Hayter Reed, 7 February 1891.

28 Statutes of Canada 1884 (47 Victoria), c. 27, Sec. 3. My discussion has been

greatly influenced by an unpublished manuscript on the potlatch by Douglas Cole and Ira Chaikin, which Professor Cole kindly allowed me to read.

29  Cole and Chaikin, potlatch manuscript, 51–2, 55.
30  Ibid., 46–8.
31  Franz Boas, 'The Indians of British Columbia,' *Popular Science Monthly* 32 (1888): 636; and 'The Houses of the Kwakiutl Indians, British Columbia,' *Proceedings of the United States National Museum II* (1888), 206; quoted in Cole and Chaikin, potlatch manuscript, 50–1.
32  Quoted in ibid., 59.
33  Ibid., 52–4.
34  Quoted in ibid., 54.
35  Royal British Columbia Museum (hereafter cited as RBCM), Anthropological Collections Section, nos. 250, 834, 2777 (examples only); Provincial Archives of British Columbia (hereafter cited as PABC), Sound and Moving Images Division (hereafter cited as SMID), tape 965-1, Mrs Edward Joyce interview; Cole and Chaikin, potlatch manuscript, 122, 168.
36  United Church of Canada Archives (hereafter cited as UCA), Toronto, Alexander Sutherland Papers, box 5, file 97, C.M. Tate to A. Sutherland, 5 November 1909; PABC, Add. MS. 1267, Kuper Island Industrial School Papers (hereafter cited as Add. MS. 1267), vol. 3, 266, G. Donckele to W.R. Robertson, 23 May 1903.
37  Cole and Chaikin, potlatch manuscript, chapters 6–9.
38  NA, Correspondence of the Secretary of State, vol. 54, no. 4355, order in council, 7 July 1883 (gazetted 4 August 1883).
39  Cole and Chaikin, potlatch manuscript, 43.
40  Glenbow Archives, Edgar Dewdney Papers (M 320), report of meeting of reserve commissioners, Agent Todd, and Indians on board the steamer *Douglass*, 8 September 1888, p. 1394.
41  PABC, H/D/RI3/RI3.II, G.H. Raley Collection, notice of Kitimaat Council, 10 November 1893; ibid., H/D/RI3.9 (III), Kispiox chiefs' statement of 13 February 1914.
42  Mrs. S. Cook to deputy superintendent general of Indian Affairs (D.C. Scott), 1 February 1919, quoted in Daisy (My-yah-nelth) Sewid Smith, *Prosecution or Persecution* (N.p., 1979), 20. Supporters of non-Christian tradition could use Christians' arguments effectively, too. One wrote to the Indian Affairs office in Ottawa to inform them that he intended to hold a potlatch. '"I don't think there are [*sic*] no wrong in it, if you only look up the 10 chapter of St. Mark, ver. 17–21, in the Bible, you will see that I am just going to do the right"' (Dan Quatell to J.D. McLean, 14 July 1922; quoted in ibid., 72).

43 Archives of the Anglican Diocese of British Columbia, Victoria, Text 198, file 50, report of 'Special Meeting Held at Alert Bay, June 1, 1936.'

44 Church of England General Synod Archives (hereafter cited as GSA), Toronto, Papers of the Missionary Society in Canada (hereafter cited as Series 75–103), Records of the Indian and Eskimo Residential School Commission (hereafter cited as IERSC 2–15), box 23, 2433, minutes of commission, 14 May 1940, quoting Rev. F. Earl Anfield.

45 Douglas Cole, *Captured Heritage: The Scramble for Northwest Coast Artifacts* (Vancouver, 1985), 129–30.

46 RG 10, Black Series, vol. 3825, file 60, 511-1, H.W. Gibbon Stocken to deputy superintendent general of Indian Affairs, 6 January 1900.

47 Ibid., vol. 3826, file 60, 511-3, J. Hollies to David Laird, 15 February 1912.

48 John Thunder to David Laird, 16 July 1907, RG 10, Black Series, vol. 3569, file 95-2, cited in Peter Douglas Elias, *The Dakota of the Canadian Northwest: Lessons for Survival* (Winnipeg, 1988), 117.

49 Clipping from *Winnipeg Free Press News Bulletin*, 27 November 1907, RG 10, Black Series, vol. 3825, file 60, 511-2. See also ibid., J. McDougall to F. Pedley, 24 May 1906. On another occasion, McDougall went so far as to charge that campaigns against dancing were a violation of treaty undertakings that he, like other missionaries, had helped to convince Plains Indians to accept in the 1870s (letter to the editor, *Christian Guardian* [Methodist], 8 July 1914, pp. 19–20).

50 RG 10, Black Series, vol. 3825, file 60, 511-2, Levi Thomson to F. Oliver, 19 March 1906, enclosing petition dated 9 March 1906; ibid., file 60, 511-1, 208133, extract from report of the Muskowpetung's agency (copy), December 1900; ibid., file 60, 511-2, E.H. Yeomans to secretary, Indian Affairs, 11 July 1907. Indians had to rely upon non-Native lawyers because no status Indian in Canada, so far as is known, was admitted to the bar until the 1950s (information supplied by Don Purich, Director, Native Law Centre, University of Saskatchewan). Concerning Indian petitions *re* dancing, see ibid., Chief Thunderchild and C. Fineday to commissioner of Indian Affairs (copy), 28 June 1907; ibid., 339198, T. Cory to secretary, Indian Affairs, 13 March 1909; ibid., file 60, 511-3, notes of representations made by delegation of Indians from the west, A. Gaddie, interpreter, Ottawa, 24 January 1911.

51 UCA, Presbyterian Church of Canada, Foreign Mission Committee, Western Section, Indian Work in Manitoba and the Northwest (hereafter cited as PC, FMC, UC, IWMNW), box 4, file 59, E. MacKenzie to R.P. McKay, 7 March 1904.

52 RG 10, Black Series, vol. 3825, file 60, 511-2, G. Mann to Indian commis-

sioner David Laird, 3 July 1906, and marginal note by Laird; ibid., J.P.G. Day to commissioner, 4 July 1908.

53  Hugh Dempsey, *Red Crow, Warrior Chief* (Saskatoon, 1980), 208, 212. Similarly, *re* a Saulteaux band, see RG 10, Black Series, vol. 3825, file 60, 511-2, J.P.G. Day to Indian commissioner, 4 July 1908.

54  RG 10, Black Series, vol. 3825, File 60, 511-2, E.H. Yeomans to secretary, Indian Affairs (copy), 11 July 1907; ibid., file 60, 511-3, R. Logan to secretary, Indian Affairs, 8 February 1912; ibid., G.H. Gooderham to secretary, Indian Affairs, 19 July 1912.

55  Ibid., File 60, 511-2, G. Mann to Commissioner, 22 July 1907.

56  Ibid., File 60, 511-2, W.S. Grant to Secretary, Indian Affairs, 2 July 1906; ibid., H. Nichol to secretary, Indian Affairs, 16 February 1911; ibid., file 60, 511-3, Father J. Hugonard to H. Nichol, 16 January 1913. In another instance, the Indians intended to keep their promise to conduct only a 'modified' dance, but a latecomer to the festivities carried out self-mutilation rites, to the consternation of the attending Euro-Canadian officials. See 'The Last Rain Dance,' told by Standing through the Earth, in *Earth Elder Stories*, by Alexander Wolfe (Saskatoon, 1988), 61–4.

57  Interview with Gordon Tootoosis, Poundmaker Reserve, 7 May 1987. It is extraordinary to note in the official records how infrequent are the references to the actual or even contemplated use of the pass system to prevent movement between reserves to attend festivals. See RG 10, vols. 3825–6, file 60, 511, passim.

58  Stan Cuthand, 'The Native Peoples of the Prairie Provinces in the 1920's and 1930's,' in *One Century Later: Western Canadian Reserve Indians since Treaty 7*, ed. Ian A.L. Getty and Donald B. Smith (Vancouver, 1978), 40.

59  Eleanor Brass, 'The File Hills Colony,' *Saskatchewan History* 6 (Spring 1953): 67. See also her *I Walk in Two Worlds* (Calgary, 1987), 13, 25.

60  RG 10, Black Series, vol. 3825, file 60, 511-2, R.S. McKenzie to secretary, Indian Affairs, 24 October 1903.

61  Dempsey, *Red Crow*, 213–24. In the Blood chronicles, 1900 was recorded as the year when '"Yellow Buffalo Stone Woman put up the Sun Dance by force."'

62  For an example of the Department of Indian Affairs's pusillanimity concerning taking action against dancing, see Glenbow Archives, Blood Agency Papers (M 1788), box 4, file 23, series of letters by A. de B. Owen, Joseph Howe, J.A. McGibbon, and D. Laird, 26 June to 16 July 1902.

63  RG 10, Black Series, vols 3285–6, passim. See also Titley, *Narrow Vision*, 170; Dempsey, *Red Crow*, 210.

64  Glenbow Archives, Tims Papers (M 1234), box 1, file 7, J.W. House to J.W.

Tims, 19 June 1939. The missionary was under no illusions about how successful this syncretic ploy was likely to be. 'At the end of the ceremony I am quite sure they went back to their old customs,' he noted. Blending Christian and Indian practices could backfire on the missionaries. One who tried to dissuade some Blackfoot from holding the dance they made 'in preparation for tobacco sowing' on a Sunday received the reply that it was all right to hold the dance on a day of prayer because 'they were going to pray' (ibid. [M 1233], box 2, file 22, J.W. Tims diary, 15 May 1887).

65 See, for example, University of Calgary Archives, Anglican Diocese of Calgary Papers, box 8, general files 64, F.W. Godsal to Canon Hogbin, 13 July 1910, and unidentified newspaper clipping entitled 'The Indians and the Exhibition.' In 1895 the *Calgary Herald* (10 July) had claimed that the Cree chief Piapot held his dance every year under the nose of the Indian Affairs Department in Regina, charging twenty-five cents' admission to the White folk who drove out from the territorial capital to see the ceremonies. In *Proceedings of the Church Missionary Society, 1895–1896* (London, 1896), 395, there is a report from the Battleford area of Christian Indians backsliding into being 'present at the heathen Sun Dance, the interest in which revived in a painful degree in the summer of 1895, encouraged, Mr. Inkster says, by the morbid curiosity of white men and women.' Again, there are numerous more examples in RG 10, Black Series, vols 3825–6, file 60, 511, passim.

66 The parallels between U.S. and Canadian practice are many. See, for example, Margaret Connell Szasz and Carmelita Ryan, 'American Indian Education,' in *Handbook of North American Indians*, Vol. 4, *History of Indian-White Relations*, ed. Wilcomb E. Washburn (Washington, DC, 1988), 288–95; Frederick E. Hoxie, *A Final Promise: The Campaign to Assimilate the Indians, 1880–1920* (Lincoln, NE, 1984), esp. chapters 2, 8.

67 *Calgary Herald*, 10 February 1892.

68 Report of the Department of Indian Affairs for 1891, Canada, *Sessional Papers, No. 14* (1892), x.

69 Brass, *Two Worlds*, 4.

70 See, for example, Purich, *Our Land*, 132–4.

71 UCA, Presbyterian Church of Canada, Foreign Mission Board, Missions to the Indians of Manitoba and the North West (hereafter cited as PC, FMB, MIMNW), box 3, file 55, H. McKay to R.P. McKay, 25 October 1903.

72 RG 10, School Files, vol. 6038, file 157-1-1, petition of Massett, BC, Council to agent, 20 January 1914; A. Sutherland Papers, box 5, file 95, C.M. Tate to A. Sutherland, 28 November 1905.

73 Nakoda Institute Archives, Oral History Program, box 1, Norman Abra-

ham interview. Compare the comment of a chief who said that he was glad that they had 'a Reserve that the white man cannot encroach upon; but there are three things that I do not wish to see within the boundaries of our Reserve. I don't want Christianity, I don't want a school, and I don't want the law. I don't want Christianity, because we wish to follow the ways of our fathers. We are Indians, and we intend to remain Indians. I don't want schools, because I want the children to be happy and free from restraint. I don't want the law because we are good people. We never do anything wrong, and we have no use for the law' (*Proceedings of the Church Missionary Society, 1898–1899* [London, 1899], 424).

74  Indeed, most Indian children for a long time escaped any kind of schooling. In 1888, when the official Indian population of Canada was 124,589, there were only 6,127 enrolled in all types of schools for Indians in Canada (Report of the Department of Indian Affairs for 1888, Canada, *Sessional Papers, No. 16* [1889], 308, 317). On the File Hills Agency in Saskatchewan in 1889, only one-third or one-quarter (depending on whether one believes the school inspector or the Indian commissioner) were in school (RG 10, Black Series, vol. 3824, file 60, 470, J.A. Macrae to commissioner, 24 July 1889). For a close study of the inadequate coverage of British Columbia by residential schooling, see James Redford, 'Attendance at Indian Residential Schools in British Columbia, 1890–1920,' *BC Studies*, no. 44 (Winter 1979–80): 41–56.

75  Tims Papers (M 1234), box 1, file 12, J.W. Tims to bishop of Calgary, 2 July 1895. That Tims might have had some ground for complaint is borne out by the register of Old Sun's School for 1894–1908, in which 22 of the 128 young people did not appear (Glenbow Archives, Calgary Indian Missions Papers [M 1356], box 1, file 7, Old Sun's Boarding School, history of pupils for September 1894). For a time in the early 1890s, the department itself did not try 'to enforce too rigidly attendance at schools. Everything that is likely to irritate the Indians is to be avoided as much as possible' (Hayter Reed Papers, vol. 17, H. Reed to Mr Wright, 31 January 1891). Reed was concerned about Indian unrest in the United States at the time.

76  A. Sutherland Papers, box 7, file 33, Arthur Barner to A. Sutherland, 19 September 1908; GSA, GS 75-103, IERSC 2-15, box 18, file Nov./05–Oct./06, John Hines to 'Hon. and Dear Sir,' 29 November 1906.

77  Brass, *Two Worlds*, 6. See also UCA, PC, FMB, MIMNW, box 1, file 21, H. McKay to R.P. McKay, 9 January 1901; ibid., file 32, quarterly report for Round Lake ... 31 December 1901. We have 'to pay $15 to $20 for any child that we get into the school,' admitted the Presbyterian missionary, although in his official quarterly report he mentioned only that his Roman Catholic

opponents on the reserve 'pay $15 or $20 for a pupil & many of the Indians will give their children to those who pay most for them' (A. Sutherland Papers, box 7, file 127, John McDougall to A. Sutherland, 2 March 1906; ibid., box 6, file 118, A. Sutherland to A.R. Aldridge, 3 March 1908).

78 United Church of Canada, Conference of British Columbia Archives, Vancouver, Coqualeetza Institute, Register of Admissions and Discharges, no. 157. See also ibid., no. 141, Simon Green: admitted September 1900, did not return from holiday July 1908, discharged officially 30 June 1909, 'visited the school at Christmas 1911.'

79 GSA, GS 75-103, IERSC 2-15, box 20, IERSC Minutes, 382, minutes of 23 October 1924. At Kuper Island, when five ran off, two priests were out in a boat looking for them till four in the morning. The man who, 'with a warrant,' returned the children and the canoes they had stolen got a '$25 fee for returning the 5 pupils' (Add. MS. 1267, vol. 31, daily journal for 1924, entries for 2, 4, and 5 January 1924). See also Macleod, *NWMP and Law Enforcement*, 147–8.

80 Mike Mountain Horse, *My People the Bloods*, ed. H. Dempsey (Calgary, 1979), 15–16; Dan Kennedy (Ochankugahe), *Recollections of an Assiniboine Chief*, ed. James R. Stevens (Toronto, 1972), 54.

81 UCA, PC, FMB, MIMNW, box 3, file 54, H. McKay to R.P. McKay, 25 October 1903.

82 Tims Papers (M 1234), box 2, file 21, seven pages of prayers in syllabics on the letterhead of Calgary Industrial School. Concerning preaching in the Blackfoot language, see ibid., file 15, annual report to Church Missionary Society (draft), 31 January 1901. See also the banner in an Indian language in Christ Church Anglican Church, Alert Bay, BC, RBCM, Anthropology Collections Section, no. 2305. Concerning Wikwemikong, see Regis College Archives, 'Synopsis of the History of Wikwemikong' (typescript), entries for 1854 and 1860; ibid., J. Paquin, 'Modern Jesuit Indian Missions'; and ibid., Ontario Indian Missions Papers, file 'Correspondence, Spanish, 1926–1936,' C. Belanger to Father Walsh, 19 February 1936.

83 John McDougall, *Christian Guardian*, 27 January 1891, p. 51.

84 PABC, SMID, tape 3533-3, Sister Patricia, S.C.J., interview. At the church on the Stoney reserve, the church service was translated into Stoney. 'Prayers are offered in Stoney by some of the men and in English by the Ministers' (Telfer Collection [J. Telfer], 'The Stoney Indians' [typescript, n.d.]).

85 PABC, H/D/RI3/RI3.7, Raley Collection, file of papers on Coqualeetza Industrial Institute and other schools, 'Rules,' A.E. Green, inspector of Indian schools, 28 October 1906. At the Cariboo School, 'we talk Shuswap when we're alone' (PABC, SMID, tape 3532-2, Celestine and David Johnson

interview). A student who attended Sechelt during 1915–16 said that, while they were encouraged to speak English, 'I wouldn't say [we were] punished' for speaking their own language (PABC, SMID, tape 960-2, Clarence Joe interview). See also, *re* Williams Lake, ibid., tape 3533-1 (transcript), Sister Patricia, S.C.J., interview, Glenbow Archives, Nurse Jane Megarry Memoirs (M 4096), third (beige) book, 191.

86  Archives Deschâtelets, L 531 .M27C, Codex historicus 1907–20 for Lestock School, 15, instructions of provincial (J.P. Magnan, O.M.I.), 27 March 1909; ibid., L 535 .M27L 149, Brother Leach to [provincial?], [1923], reporting that the principal at Lestock 'prefered [*sic*] the children to speak in their own language.' Concerning the willingness of school authorities to allow an Indian language to be used when outsiders were not around, see PABC, SMID, tape 361-1, Joe C. Clemine interview.

87  Telfer Collection, notes of a conversation with Miss Jean Telfer, 16 May 1979.

88  Brass, *Two Worlds*, 13, 64.

89  Ibid., 25. This lady's interest in Cree traditions was stimulated sufficiently that she collected and published a volume of legends and stories: Eleanor Brass, *Medicine Boy and Other Cree Tales* (Calgary, 1978). The Kuper Island Conduct Book lists many instances of infractions that involved 'Indian dances,' 'talking Indian,' and 'Forbidden Games' (Add. MS. 1267, vol. 38, conduct book, 1891–5).

90  Glenbow Archives, S.H. Middleton Papers (M 839), box 2, file 7, S.H. Middleton to R. Forsberg (copy), 7 November 1960. It is also worth noting that at a day school that a Dakota band established themselves, instruction was 'in both Dakota and English' (Elias, *Dakota of the Canadian Northwest*, 73). And an Indian woman told a reporter that her father, himself highly educated, favoured her learning English early in life (undated clipping from *Weekend Magazine*, UCA, E.E. Joblin Papers, box 2, file 7).

91  PABC, SMID, tape 3858-1, Mary Englund interview. The same informant (ibid.) said that parents took great pride in children who mastered English. John Jeffrey, a former student at the Chapleau, Ontario, school and an Anglican clergyman, also noted that the widely differing backgrounds of the students at Chapleau made the use of English appropriate (audio tape, December 1989, in possession of author).

92  Tims Papers (M 1234), box 1, file 2, diary, 8 September 1891. For a similar case in British Columbia, see Add. MS. 1267, vol. 3, 733–4, G. Donckele to W.R. Robertson, 23 July 1905.

93  UCA, PC, FMB, Missions to the Indians in British Columbia (MIBC), box 1, file 10, B. I., Johnston to R.P. McKay, 20 February 1896.

94  Tims Papers (M 1233), box 2, file 22, journal for 1917. In an interview, a

former teacher (name withheld by request) who had served briefly at the Mohawk Institute in 1934 told me that he could not recall a day when no children ran away from the school. A request from Jesuit missionaries that the department withhold annuities from parents who failed to return schoolchildren after holidays was firmly turned down. See Regis College Archives, Wikwemikong Papers, 'Various Correspondence 1909–1912,' J.D. McLean to Rev. C. Belanger, S.J., 25 July 1910.

95 Middleton Papers, box 2, file 4, school diary for 1945, entries for 2 March, 1 April, 4 May, 23 June, 1 September, and 25 December. Significantly, before adopting the policy, the principal held a 'Meeting of Parents at the Reserve re Holidays' on 9 December. At Sechelt 'the children got home sometimes for weekends' to the nearby reserve (PABC, SMID, tape 3533-3, Sister Patricia, S.C.J., interview). There were also Saturday afternoon visits home at Kitimaat (PABC, microfilm 1360, Margaret Butcher Journal, 17 April 1917), and, at Kuper Island, once a month 'four deserving students of the senior class' received a weekend leave (Archives of the Sisters of St Ann, RG 2, Series 39, Kuper Island school papers, file 'Chronicles 1944–1954,' entry for 29 October 1948).

96 Add. MS. 1267, vol. 1, 433, G. Donckele to W.H. Lomas, 3 July 1894. The same principal confessed that he was at a loss to know how to stop parents from withdrawing their children (ibid., 583, G. Donckele to A.W. Vowell, 30 April 1895).

97 Reed Papers, vol. 18, J. Hugonard to E. Dewdney, 5 May 1891. There was a cabin to house parents overnight at the Cariboo School. See PABC, SMID, tape 3530-1, Lily Squinahan interview. See also Add. MS. 1267, vol. 31, daily journal for 1924, entry of 27 May. For comments concerning the 'Indian parlor' at Williams Lake, see ibid. tape 3533-1 (transcript), Sister Patricia, S.C.J., interview. And 'the parents of the pupils come from all parts of the Blood reserve to attend the Church service and to visit with their children after the service' (Megarry Memoirs, third [beige] book, 238). See also Telfer Collection, 'The Stoney Indians.'

98 UCA, PC, FMB, MIBC, box 1, file 1, J.A. McDonald to H. Cassells, 12 January 1892; A. Sutherland Papers, box 6, file 108, J. Edward Rendle to A. Sutherland, 8 October 1909.

99 PABC, H/D/RI3/RI3.II, Raley Collection, file on Kitimaat, Chief Jessea and 41 Indians to 'Dear Brothern [sic],' 23 March 1896. The 'Sechelt nation' built and at least partially maintained their school (PABC, SMID, tape 960-1, Clarence Joe interview).

100 GSA, GS 75-103, IERSC 2-15, box 18, file Nov./05–Oct./06, W.D. Reeves to S.H. Blake, 15 October 1906.

101  UCA, PC, FMB, MIMNW, box 1, file 14, T. Hart to W. Moore, 12 September
1898; ibid., file 20, A.G. McKitrick to R.P. McKay, 14 December 1900.

102  Ibid., box 2, file 33, J.C. Gandier to R.P. McKay, 14 January 1902, and
'agreement' of same date.

103  Ibid., box 2, file 35, A.G. McKitrick to R.P. McKay, 7 March 1902; ibid., file
38, same to same, 2 June 1902; ibid., file 41, Indian petition dated 22 September 1902; ibid., box 3, file 47, A.G. McKitrick to R.P. McKay, 11 March
1903; ibid., file 55, J.O. McGregor to R.P. McKay, 27 November 1903.

104  A. Sutherland Papers, box 5, file 89, R. Cairns to A. Sutherland, 18 August
1906.

105  Ibid., box 3, file 74, A.W. Vowell to Rev. Dr Campbell, 13 May 1905, enclosing petition from Indians against a principal. See also Archives Deschâtelets, L 281 .M274 31, list of complaints against the administration of Lebret
School; GSA, GS 75-103, IERSC 2-15, box 22, 1847, minutes of 17 July 1934,
*re* Lac la Ronge School.

106  Reed Papers, vol. 14, H. Reed to Archdeacon J.A. Mackay (copy),
9 November 1894.

107  Regis College Archives, J. Paquin, S.J., 'Modern Jesuit Indian Missions in
Ontario.'

108  *Alberta Tribune*, 12 October 1895; *Toronto Globe*, 4 July 1895; *Canadian
Churchman*, 11 July 1895; Tims Papers (M 1234), box 1, file 12, J.W. Tims to
bishop of Calgary (draft), 2 July 1895; Reed Papers, vol. 14, H. Reed to T.
Mayne Daly (copy), 25 June 1895. Ian A.L. Getty, in 'The Failure of the
Native Church Policy of the CMS in the North-West,' in *Religion and Society in the Prairie West*, ed. Richard Allen (Regina, 1974), 30, points out that
the Blackfoot had petitioned the government in 1892 to remove the missionary, whom they regarded as 'too bossy.' The crisis in 1895 led to his
transfer to another reserve.

109  UCA, United Church of Canada, Woman's Missionary Society, Home Missions, Indian Work, file 9, L. McLean to J.P.B. Ostrander, 17 February 1949.
Concerning a girl's attack on a nun at Lebret, see Archives Deschâtelets, L
286 .M27L 226, J.P. Magnan (O.M.I.) to G. Leonard, 18 June 1930.

110  Celia Haig-Brown, *Resistance and Renewal: Surviving the Indian Residential
School* (Vancouver, 1988), 102. At the same school, a father who was
angered when his daughter's head was shaved seized the priest responsible '"and shook him up"' (ibid., 103).

111  At the Anglican Sarcee School, for example, the government grant in 1915
was $100 per pupil, when operating costs per child were just over $160.
During the remainder of the First World War, the discrepancy grew larger
(Glenbow Archives, Calgary Indian Missions Papers (M 1356), box 1, file 5,
J.W. Tims's annual reports to the Church Missionary Society for the years

ended March 1915 and 31 December 1919). In 1949 the Anglicans claimed that the financial shortfall in the school's operation that was attributable to under-enrolment was $51,200 (GSA, GS 75-103, IERSC 2-15, Box 29, Indian School Administration circulars, Circular 14/49, 29 April 1949).

112 Add. MS. 1167, vol. 2, 561, G. Donckele to A.W. Vowell, 7 July 1900.

113 GSA, Bishop Lucas Papers (M 75-1), box 3, file 'Correspondence A-M 1925,' Bishop Lucas to T.B.R. Westgate, 20 June 1925. See also Add. MS. 1267, vol. 1, 602, G. Donckele to A.W. Vowell, 1 June 1895; microfilm 1360, Margaret Butcher Journal, 17 April 1917.

114 GSA, GS 75-103, IERSC 2-15, ISA, box 25, reports of superintendents with minutes of Executive Committee, 1927–52, file 1947, circular of Alderwood to clergy, 14 January 1947.

115 Tims Papers (M 1233), box 1, file 6, 'Impressions Regarding Missionary Effort ... Jan. 6, 1909.' For examples of opposition to sending students to far distant schools in British Columbia and Alberta, see A. Sutherland Papers, box 6, file 108, J. Edward Rendle to A. Sutherland, 8 October 1909; ibid., box 7, file 132, 'Report of the Red Deer Industrial Institute for ... 1907,' by Thompson Ferrier.

116 UCA, PC, FMB, MIMNW, box 4, file 66, F.F. Dodds to R.P. McKay, October 1904; ibid., file 72, F.O. Gilbart to R.P. McKay, 28 April 1905. On the difficulties at the Regina School, see also Titley, *Narrow Vision*, 80–2.

117 Archives Deschâtelets, HR 6676.C73R 8, Mgr Grandin to Mgr J.T. McNally, bishop of Calgary, 22 February 1922. For background, see RG 10, School Files, vol. 6039, file 160-1, part 1, D.C. Scott to W.J. Dilworth, 9 March 1915; ibid., Dilworth to Scott, 20 March 1915.

118 Archives Deschâtelets, L 912 .M27C 195 and 199; ibid., L 913 .M2.7L 63, 102, 104, and 108. Unfortunately, the next generation of parents had to take up the struggle against another unpopular priest thirty years later. See ibid., 291, group letter of Indians to father provincial, May 1962.

119 See, for example, ibid., L 531. M27C 2, Codex historicus for school at Lestock, SK, 16 December 1934.

120 There are indications that some parents imposed limits on the duration of their children's stays at Kuper Island School when it was starting up. See Add. MS. 1267, vol. 40, 43, quarterly return for quarter ended 30 September 1896, remarks. See also ibid., 47, quarterly return for quarter ended 31 December 1896.

121 RG 10, Black Series, vol. 3825, file 60, 511-1, extract from Sgt Saul Martin's report from Fort Qu'Appelle, SK, 28 June 1902; *Toronto Globe*, 27 May 1903.

122 'The Last Rain Dance,' 64.

# Great White Father Knows Best:
# Oka and the Land Claims Process

In their 1961 presentation to the Joint Committee of the Senate and House of Commons on Indian Affairs, the Oka Indians made a simple request:

> The Oka Indians wish that the Oka lands be given the status of a reserve. It has all the characteristics of it, with a resident agent of the Department, but it has not the legal status that would enable the band to have a perpetual use vested in it for their enjoyment and that of their children and descendants. What future is there for the Oka Indian?[1]

Nothing was done about the Indians' request through the 1960s, with Indian and Northern Affairs Canada taking the view that there was no serious problem because Ottawa was administering the Mohawk lands at Kanesatake as though they were a properly established reserve.[2] As the 1970s opened, there was 'still a widespread feeling among Indian people that the problems of Oka are far from settled.'[3]

As Canadians know all too well, in 1991 the 'widespread feeling among Indian people' was justified, while Ottawa's complacent self-confidence was not. Through the 1970s and 1980s, the dispute over title to lands occupied by Mohawk Indians adjacent to the Quebec town of Oka went from bad to worse. The Indians took advantage of a new land claims process that the federal government had devised after the pivotal Calder decision of 1973; they registered a demand, not for the recognition of the lands at Kanesatake as a 'reserve,' as had been requested in 1961, but as unsurrendered land held by Aboriginal title. When that comprehensive claim was rejected in 1975 by the Office of Native Claims (ONC), the Kanesatake Mohawk then initiated another claim, a specific claim to the lands. This, too, was rejected by the federal authorities in 1986. However, the federal minister of Indian Affairs offered to look for alternative methods of redressing the band's grievance. The federal government 'recognized that there is an historical basis for Mohawk claims related to land grants in the 18th century.' In 1989 Ottawa proposed a framework agreement for bringing about land reunification.[4] That was rejected by the Kanesatake Indians because it did not seem likely to produce enough land to meet their needs, and it appeared not to address either 'the long standing problems or unique character of Kanesatake.'[5]

Through the later 1980s, the unresolved issue of title to the lands occupied by Mohawk on Lake of Two Mountains rapidly degenerated. On the Indian side, rising frustration was exacerbated by the growing influence of a new form of Native militancy, the Warrior Society. On the non-Native side, impatience and acquisitiveness combined to produce an attack on a disputed piece of land. In the Euro-Canadian community there was growing exasperation that the continuing dispute over lands adjacent to Oka was thwarting development. Specifically, a plan to expand a privately owned nine-hole golf course to eighteen holes by acquiring and incorporating a forested tract that the municipality owned, but that the Indians claimed as their own, became a source of contention. In preparation for a confrontation over the disputed land, some Kanesatake Mohawk erected barricades in the contested area on 11 March 1990. In due course, the town and golf club decided to proceed, securing an injunction from Quebec's Superior Court on 26 April. The Mohawk ignored the court order. A second injunction procured on 26 June was also rejected by the Indians. And on 10 July, Mayor Ouellette requested Quebec's provincial police force to enforce the injunction by tearing down the roadblock. An assault by one hundred police officers the next day resulted in an exchange of gunfire, the death of a police corporal, and an eleven-week stand-off that involved Mohawk, police, and 2,500 Canadian soldiers at Kanesatake and Kahnawake. The last of the hold-out Warriors, their Mohawk supporters, and a few journalists walked out to waiting army and police on 26 September 1990. Canada, Quebec, and the Mohawk of Kanesatake are still evaluating the consequences.

How did a dispute over a relatively small parcel of land culminate in violence, death, and a demoralizing confrontation in a country that prides itself on acceptance of diversity, pursuit of accommodation, and a long tradition of peaceful compromise? Much of the commentary

since the end of the Oka crisis has concentrated on specific, local, immediate factors. The Mohawk Warrior Society is portrayed either as a collection of righteous militants pursuing a sacred constitutional principle
or as a band of goons. The local residents of Oka and Châteauguay are
long-suffering neighbours or red-necked hooligans. The Sûreté du
Québec are uniformed thugs or inexperienced law-enforcement officers
trying to mediate in a hopelessly polarized situation. Quebec is either
the most tolerant and generous of provinces in its treatment of Aboriginal peoples or the home of a nationality becoming increasingly unwill-
ing to permit dissent by distinctive ethnic and racial minorities. Ottawa
is to blame either for mollycoddling the Mohawk with promises of
accommodation after their claims were rejected, or for failing to act
decisively after the rejection of the second, specific claim in 1986 to
acquire and transfer to the Indians enough lands to accommodate their
wishes. Where in this welter of charges and countercharges do the roots
of the exceptional and lamentable eleven-week stand-off at Kanesatake
lie?

The origins of the events of the summer of 1990 at Oka lie in none of
the immediate and local factors on which attention has focused since
late September 1990. Rather, the violence over the land dispute at Oka
is the product of an attitude or disposition on the part of the government of Canada that stretches back at least a century and a half – an
outlook that it knows best what serves the interests of indigenous peoples and that it alone can solve their problems. The implication of this,
of course, is that the same sort of confrontation and possibly violence
that disfigured life in Kahnawake and Kanesatake in 1990 can – and
are likely to – happen elsewhere. If the real reason for the trouble is a
long-standing approach by the federal government to relations with
Native peoples, and if the origins of the violence lie not in specific and
local factors but in national policy, then obviously there is great potential for a repetition of the Oka tragedy in other parts of the country
where there is competition for land and resources between the First
Peoples and the newcomers. To understand better both the general
nature of the Oka problem and its potential to recur elsewhere, it is
necessary to consider the aged, extensive, and alarming roots of the
conflict.

Prior to the invasion of the valley of the St Lawrence by Europeans
in the sixteenth century, the territory near what the intruders would
call Lac des Deux Montagnes, or Lake of Two Mountains, was used by
some of the indigenous people who are known to scholars as the St

Lawrence Iroquoians. In the opinion of the Assembly of First Nations there had been Aboriginal presence at Kanesatake since at least one thousand years before the birth of Christ, and in the seventeenth century the Five Nations 'took the land from the french [*sic*] in retaliation for Champlain's raid on their territory.'[6] Non-Native scholars hold that sometime in the latter part of the sixteenth century, between the explorations of Jacques Cartier and Samuel de Champlain, the so-called 'St. Lawrence Iroquoians' withdrew from the St Lawrence region, abandoning the area to a variety of Algonkian peoples. These dwellers of the Ottawa River valley, being migratory hunter-gatherers, extensively used the territory in which Oka was later established. They travelled over it, fished in its waters, and hunted in its nearby woods. In general, there was little or no permanent occupation of the lands on the north side of Lake of Two Mountains by Indian groups.

By a grant in 1717, confirmed in 1718, a tract of land three and one-half leagues in front and three leagues deep was set aside by the French Crown for the Gentlemen of St Sulpice of Paris as a refuge for a mixed group of Indians to whom they had been ministering since the 1670s. (The parcel of land was augmented by an additional grant by the Crown that was made in 1733 and confirmed in 1735.)[7] This mixed group of Nipissing, Algonkin, and Mohawk had in 1696 reluctantly transferred from the Mission de la Montagne near Ville Marie (later Montreal) to the Sault au Récollet on the north side of Montreal Island as European settlement of the future Montreal began to present obstacles to successful evangelization of these mission Indians. But even the more northerly Sault au Récollet eventually came within the pernicious ambit of European influence, and the Sulpicians once more became anxious to move their charges to a more remote and less morally menacing location. Again with reluctance, the Indians relocated, being persuaded by the missionaries that the move was for their own good. The French, whose concept of divine-right kingship entailed a belief in the Crown's ownership of all lands in New France, purported to grant the land on Lake of Two Mountains 'in order to transfer there the mission of the said Indians of Sault au Recollet' on 'condition that they shall bear the whole expense necessary for removing the said mission, and also cause a church and a fort to be built there of stone at their own cost, for the security of the Indians ...'[8] In 1743 there were approximately seven hundred Indians – mostly Six Nations Iroquois and Huron, but also including Algonkin and Nipissing – at the Lake of Two Mountains mission.[9]

Title to the lands to which the mixture of Mohawk and Algonkians repaired on Lake of Two Mountains was never free from challenge. Neither the terms of the Capitulation of Montreal nor the Royal Proclamation provided much protection to the Indian occupants. The Capitulation promisingly stated that the 'Indian allies of his most Christian Majesty [France], shall be maintained in the Lands they inhabit; if they chuse to remain there; they shall not be molested on any pretence whatsoever, for having carried arms, and served his most Christian Majesty; they shall have, as well as the French, liberty of religion, and shall keep their missionaries.'[10] The Royal Proclamation of 1763, whose definition of 'Hunting Grounds' reserved for Indians did not include the area around the Lake of Two Mountains because it lay within Quebec, also contained provisions regulating purchase of Indian lands within existing colonies. However, this protection did not apply to the Oka lands either, because they were held by Europeans to have been allocated by seigneurial grant.[11] A brief and ineffective claim by Lord Jeffrey Amherst was laid after the transfer of Quebec to British rule in the period 1760–3. The so-called 'conqueror of Montreal' argued that these lands should be given to him, inasmuch as the provisions of the Capitulation of Montreal, while they guaranteed free exercise of the Roman Catholic religion, explicitly excluded the Sulpicians from their protections of conscience, custom, and lands. However, the British authorities saw no more reason to humour Amherst's pretensions to Sulpician or Indian lands than they did his preposterous desire for the Jesuits' estates.[12]

Amherst's claim came to nothing, but tension soon developed between the Sulpicians and their Indian charges over use of and title to the lands on which Natives and clerics resided. By 1781 a disagreement between the priests and Indians over division of revenue from non-Indians who kept their cattle on the lands at Oka led the Sulpicians to state bluntly that the Indians had no right to the lands. The resulting confrontation led the Natives to present their claims to the British authorities in 1781, 1787, and 1795.[13] The Indians' case rested on several bases. They had once possessed, they said, a document granting them the lands on Lake of Two Mountains, but they had surrendered it for safekeeping to the priests, who now denied all knowledge of it. Moreover, during the Seven Years' War their representatives had met with British Indian superintendent Sir William Johnson at Oswegatchie to promise not to fight the British, and to receive confirmation of 'our lands as granted by the King of France.' They had a wampum belt that recorded their possession of the lands. When General Guy Carleton, on a visit, had asked who owned uncultivated lands on the north shore of the lake, the Indians had told him 'that they belonged to the Indians of the lake.' No one contradicted them. Finally, they had been told during the American Revolutionary War that if they fought with the British they would 'fight for your land and when the War is over you shall have it.' All these – missing deed, their own record of taking the land, Johnson's assurance, the lack of contradiction when they said the lands were theirs, and British promises during the American Revolution – constituted good and sufficient 'title' for the Indians on the Lake of Two Mountains.

The Indians' position and other factors began seriously to cloud the Sulpicians' title to the properties at Oka. In particular, in the early decades of the nineteenth century the view increasingly took hold that the Sulpicians' legal position was weak for a technical legal reason. The original seigneurial grant of 1717–18 (expanded by an additional grant in 1733–5) had been made to the Sulpicians of Paris, who transferred their rights to the Sulpicians of Montreal in 1784.[14] But since the Canadian missionary body had no legal existence – that is, it was not legally incorporated by positive law – the Order was legally barred from possessing estates in mortmain, or inalienable tenure. A challenge was raised in 1763 to the Sulpicians' title by an Indian's sale of property to a newcomer, but on that occasion the governor upheld the Order's claim and dispossessed the would-be purchaser.[15] In 1788 the Indians of Oka themselves raised the issue directly with the Crown, claiming title to the lands on which they were located. However, Lord Dorchester's council concluded, on the advice of the colonial law officers, 'That no satisfactory Evidence is given to the Committee of any Title to the Indians of the Village in Question, either by the French Crown or any Grantee of that Crown.'[16] However, no evidence was adduced that either law officers or councillors had made any effort to ascertain what were the bases of the Indians' claim. The abrupt rejection of their case did not deter the Indians, and the dubious quality of the Sulpicians' title was regularly highlighted by a number of petitions from the Aboriginal inhabitants of Oka for the granting of title to them.[17]

Further complications developed in the nineteenth century, especially during a period of heavy settlement following the War of 1812. Often lands were granted to non-Native settlers in the lower Ottawa Valley without consideration of or compensation for the long-standing use of the territory for hunting by Algonkin and Nipissing with ties to

Oka.[18] These encroachments led the Algonkin and Nipissing of Lake of Two Mountains in 1822 to register a claim to land on both sides of the Ottawa River from a point above the seigniory on Lake of Two Mountains as far north as Lake Nipissing.[19] The claim was rejected by British officials in 1827 even though the superintendent general of Indian affairs, Sir John Johnson, strongly supported their position, and was again dismissed by the Executive Council of Lower Canada in 1837.[20]

Still the Sulpicians were obviously worried. In June 1839 the superior of the seminary made a proposal to the Indians that was designed to regularize the Order's claim. The Indians' rights to use, expand, dispose of, or build on the particular plots would be guaranteed, and the Sulpicians would continue to provide the Indians with wood, though it might be cut only where the priests said. The Indians of Oka accepted this proposition.[21] Nonetheless, in order to resolve any technical difficulty and remove any cloud on the title, the legislature in 1840 (reconfirmed in 1841) passed 'An Ordinance to incorporate the Ecclesiastics of the Seminary of Saint Sulpice of Montreal, to confirm their title to the Fief and Seigniory of the Island of Montreal, the Fief and Seigniory of the Lake of the Two Mountains, and the Fief and Seigniory of Saint Sulpice, in this Province; to provide for the gradual extinction of Seigniorial Rights and Dues within the Segniorial limits of the said Fiefs and Seigniories, and for other purposes.'[22] The fact that the representative assembly had been suspended following the Rebellion of 1837–8 in Lower Canada meant that the critical measure could be passed by a small, appointed council. No doubt the authorities wished to reward the Sulpicians for their ostentatious and vocal loyalty during the troubled times in the Lake of Two Mountains region. No one bothered to note that the Indians at Oka had refused to join or aid the *Patriotes*, though pressed to do so.[23]

Legislative disposition of the question of title did nothing to still the rivalry and tension between Indians and priests at Oka. One basis for the quarrel was the Indians' view that the land was truly theirs, and that the Sulpicians were merely trustees for their lands. This fundamental difference of opinion was exacerbated by friction over access to resources in and on the territory, and the conflict worsened steadily through the nineteenth century because of the increasing pressure of settlement in the area. A further complication arose from the fact that different Indian groups at Kanesatake used the territory differently. While the Iroquois at Oka were inclined towards agriculture on lands made available to them by the Sulpicians without charge, the Algonkin and Nipissing tended more to rely upon a hunting economy for which they extensively used a large area of the Ottawa Valley, returning to the Oka area only for two months in the summer. Not surprisingly, then, it was these Algonkian groups that felt more severely the negative impact of inrushing settlers and lumber firms. Their petition to Lord Dalhousie in 1822 began by noting 'That in Consequence of the Increase of Population and the Number of New Settlements on the Lands in which they were accustomed to hunt and the Game getting Scarcer in Consequence thereof' they were being hard-pressed.[24]

The depletion of furs in the region severely affected the economic position of the Algonkians.[25] Major General Darling, military secretary to Governor General Dalhousie, had observed in the late 1820s that Algonkin and Nipissing presented 'an appearance of comparative wealth and advancement in civilization,' while the conditions in which the Iroquois lived 'bespeak wretchedness and inactivity in the extreme.'[26] By the 1840s the condition of the Iroquois was still 'far from prosperous' because of their reliance on an uncertain horticulture. But that of the Algonkin and Nipissing had become 'still more deplorable':

> ... their hunting grounds on the Ottawa, which were formerly most extensive, abounding with deer, and other animals, yielding the richest furs, and which their ancestors had enjoyed from time immemorial, have been destroyed for the purposes of the chase. A considerable part has been laid out into townships, and either settled or taken possession of by squatters. The operations of the lumber-men have either destroyed or scared away the game throughout a still more extensive region, and thus, as settlement advances, they are driven further and further from their homes, in search of a scanty and precarious livelihood. Their case has been often brought before the Government, and demands early attention.[27]

The Algonkin responded to these adverse changes in some cases by migrating to the Golden Lake area west of Bytown, and in others by shifting into a trade in wood for local markets.[28] Their increasing use of the forest resources brought them into conflict with the Sulpician seigneurs, who eventually prohibited free access to wood for commercial purposes.[29]

Denominational conflict soon worsened the situation. The Mississauga minister Peter Jones visited the Lake of Two Mountains settlement in 1851 at the request of his church to try to convert the Indians there to Protestantism.[30] Jones's mission did not enjoy immediate success, but the Methodists continued to proselytize in the area by means of itinerant missionaries. After the Methodists established a mission at Oka in 1868, a large number of the Iroquois in particular converted to Methodism in a symbolic act of rejection and defiance.[31] (Such behaviour has parallels elsewhere: the Catholicism of the Mi'kmaq in the eighteenth century was a badge of their alliance with the French, as well as a creed.) Not surprisingly, given the Sulpicians' view of themselves as owners of the lands and the strong religious feelings of the time, the Order attempted to stomp out Protestantism among the Indians. As early as 1852, Bishop Bourget of Montreal had excommunicated four of the leaders of the Mohawk Indians.[32] In the 1870s the Sulpicians applied pressure by demanding that the Methodist chapel that the Indians and their supporters had erected be torn down and the ringleaders among the Indians be arrested. By court order, the Methodist chapel was dismantled in 1875. Bad feelings degenerated to the point that in June 1877 a fire of mysterious origins destroyed the Catholic church at Oka. The ensuing criminal prosecution of Methodist Indians embroiled the mission inhabitants and large numbers of non-Natives in Quebec and Ontario in bitter controversy for years. The quarrel even attracted the disapproving attention of the Aborigines Protection Society in London and led to inquiries from the Colonial Office.[33] The destruction, threat of violence, and growing political complications finally pushed the government of Canada towards action on the troubled Oka situation.

By the 1870s there was a well-established governmental tradition of trying to solve the Oka problem by either or both of two means: relocating the Indians or resolving the dispute by litigation. In 1853, '16,000 acres of land, in Dorchester, North River, in rear of the Township of Wexford, have been set apart for the Iroquois of Caughnawaga and Two Mountains,' and similar provision of new lands was made at Maniwaki for the Algonkians from Oka in 1853.[34] Many of the Algonkin, seeking new lands for hunting and trapping, removed to the Maniwaki area, but the Iroquois stayed at Oka.[35] As the Oka problem heated up in the late 1860s and 1870s, Ottawa was tempted to repeat such a 'solution' elsewhere. Neither the federal government of Alexander Mackenzie (1873–8) nor that of Sir John Macdonald (1867–73, 1878–91) wanted to grapple seriously with the issue. There were many reasons for their attitude. First, Canadian governments of the nineteenth century could not conceive of Indians having title to lands once Europeans had intruded into an area and begun to use the resources. Furthermore, by the mid-1870s

Ottawa was experiencing considerable difficulties in dealing with the settler society of British Columbia. The government there was recalcitrant and obdurate in its refusal to honour its pledges, made in the agreement by which it united with Canada in 1871, to appropriate land for Indians in that province.[36] No federal government wanted quarrels with other provinces, especially the large and powerful province of Quebec, with its French and Catholic majority and its prickly sensitivity on questions of religion and provincial rights. Consequently federal governments avoided dealing with the Oka issue head-on.

Remonstrances by both the Algonkin and Iroquois at Oka in 1868 quickly turned Ottawa's thought to the possibilities of removal.[37] The Indians' demand in a petition that they 'should have the same privileges as enjoyed by white people' evoked an interesting response, one that captured perfectly the government's thinking about Indians:

> ... the Indians cannot have the same privileges as the white man, as long as the law remains as it is, but it is the intention of the Department to submit a scheme by which Indians could, under certain conditions and with certain qualifications, obtain their emancipation, and become, to all intents and purposes, citizens, as the white men are. But in order that such a measure may obtain the sanction of Parliament, and become law, Indians must not violate the law of the land, nor throw, otherwise, obstacles in the way. They must respect property, be content with their present condition, and be sure that the disposition of the Government is to improve their condition, elevate them in their social position, and prepare them for a complete emancipation.[38]

The petitioners were told that their complaints against the Sulpicians were not well founded, and an order-in-council reconfirming federal government support for the seminary's title was passed.[39] The undersecretary of state also informed the Indian complainants that 'the government has your welfare at heart.'[40] The removal in 1869 of some of the Oka Indians to the upper Ottawa eased the problem temporarily. However, the increasing religious animosity of the 1870s, which threatened to bring on an extended Catholic-Protestant clash as White Methodists rallied to their Red brothers' cause,[41] made it tempting to get the Methodist Indians away from Oka.

By 1877, with the Indians at Oka claiming that they owned the land and resorts to violence becoming increasingly common, matters had come to a head.[42] The government launched an investigation by the

Reverend William Scott, a Methodist clergyman and father of a future deputy superintendent general of Indian Affairs, which upheld the position of the seminary.[43] The department also initiated steps in 1879 to remove many of the aggrieved Indians from Oka to the Muskoka district of Ontario. The establishment of the Gibson Reserve, and removal of Oka Indians to it, turned out not to be the total solution that the government sought. Agreement was reached in 1881 for the province of Ontario to supply, and for the Sulpicians to pay for, sufficient land in the township of Gibson to settle 120 families numbering about 500 persons, and in 1882 some of the Oka Indians settled at Gibson.[44] However, nothing like the expected number relocated. Only about one-third of the Oka Indians moved, and not all of those stayed for long at Gibson.[45] The stay-at-homes remained obdurate even though the ever-helpful Reverend Scott remonstrated with them: 'By moral suasion alone the Department endeavours to accomplish what is deemed best for you.'[46] Since most of the Indians remained on the lands near the Sulpician mission, the Oka land dispute continued to fester during the 1880s and 1890s. The Methodists' continuing interest in the issue, during a time when there was a sufficiently large number of other irritants concerning creed and language, ensured that successive governments in this period remained sensitive to the matter, even if they did nothing effective about it.[47]

Sporadically throughout the 1870s and 1880s, Ottawa explored the possibility of resolving the Oka dispute by its other preferred method, litigation. As early as January 1873, Joseph Howe, minister responsible for Indian matters, extended an offer to a Methodist clerical champion of the Oka Indians to have the government 'pay the cost of the Defense' of 'the Indian to whom you refer as having been imprisoned for cutting wood at Oka.' The government, according to Howe, was 'prepared to carry the case if necessary before the highest tribunals in order that the questions in controversy, between the Two Mountains Indians and the Gentlemen of the Seminary may be judicially investigated and set finally at rest.'[48] Apparently nothing came of this proposal, nor of another effort of the department in 1882 to settle the dispute with a test case before the courts. Although Ottawa offered to pay the costs, in 1882 the parties could not agree on facts to submit to the courts.[49] And so, amid bickering and sectarian strife, the Oka question lumbered on, unresolved, through the 1880s and 1890s.

By 1903 the Laurier government had tired of the dispute and its attendant political liabilities. Religious passions remained strong in the new century, and during the first decade the dispute at Oka over wood-cutting continued to cause friction and political embarrassment for the government. In 1902, for example, Prime Minister Laurier arranged to have an Indian Affairs officer dispatched to Oka, where the 'Indians are becoming threatening,' because 'I am under great obligation to the Superior of the Sulpicians, Father Colin.'[50] Petitions and confrontations continued steadily. Finally, in 1903 a representative of the government suggested to prominent Toronto lawyer N.W. Rowell, who represented the Methodist legal interest in the Oka affair, that 'they were anxious that the matter should be settled, and were prepared that a stated case should be agreed upon between the Seminary and the Indians, and the matter referred to a Court for adjudication, the Department paying the expenses of the litigation.' Official thinking was that 'the Indians have a certain right of possession or use in the property,' but the precise nature and extent of those rights or interests were not clear. It was best, therefore, to refer the contentious and complex matter to the courts at public expense.[51] Not for the last time, Indian Affairs opened its files to counsel for each side, and not for the last time Indian land claims litigation proved a boon to the historical research industry. The Rowell firm, no doubt making good use of taxpayers' dollars, dispatched a legal researcher to Paris to uncover documents that might strengthen the Indians' argument that they were the true owners of the lands at Oka.[52]

Thus began the celebrated case of *Angus Corinthe et al v. The Ecclesiastics of the Seminary of St Sulpice of Montreal*, which eventually emerged from the bowels of the Judicial Committee of the Privy Council in 1912.[53] The Indians' argument combined a number of propositions. The Sulpicians' interest in the lands was only that of a 'trustee for the Plaintiffs'; and the Indians 'have from time immemorial' enjoyed the right to use the commons, cut firewood, and pasture stock. As their formal argument to the Privy Council put it, they claimed 'to be the absolute owners by virtue of the unextinguished Aboriginal title, the Proclamation of 1763, and possession sufficient to create title by prescription [tradition]. Alternatively, the Indians have claimed qualified title under the French grants.' The respondents, the Sulpicians, 'rely mainly on these statutory titles and claim that under these titles, they are the absolute owners of the Seigniory of the Lake of Two Mountains and not merely the owners in trust for the Indians.' In the unlikely event that the high court found that eighteenth-century Indians had possessed some form of title or interest, the present Oka claimants 'could not be their representative as the Appellants are the chiefs of the Iroquois tribe only, and the Iroquois tribe's territory was far from the Island of Montreal and the Lake of Two Mountains.' The Algonkin, who were closest to the land in the eighteenth century, were not, the seminary's factum pointedly argued, suing.

The Corinthe appeal to the Privy Council epitomized the principal features of land claims, which at the beginning of this century were in a most rudimentary state. The Indians relied both on an embryonic notion of Aboriginal title ('from time immemorial' they had used the resources of the tract) and British common law (the Sulpicians exercised title 'merely as trustee' for the Indians). The latter argument was buttressed with their oral tradition, which in many instances was supported by documents recently unearthed in Paris. Counsel for the Sulpicians similarly argued a two-part case. The Order was the proper owner by virtue of the original grant, and, in the event that there could be any dispute about that point, their title had been clarified, recognized, and confirmed by legislative action in 1841.

The judgment – in favour of the Sulpicians – similarly represented the limited nature of indigenous peoples' legal title eighty years ago. Speaking for the Privy Council, Lord Chancellor Viscount Haldane ruled that 'their Lordships thought that the effect of this [1841] Act was to place beyond question the title of the respondents [Sulpicians] to the Seigniory, and to make it impossible for the appellants to establish an independent title to possession or control in the administration ... neither by aboriginal title, nor by prescription, nor on the footing that they were *cestuis que trustent* of the corporation, could the appellants assert any title in an action such as that out of which this appeal had arisen.' However, the court did note that a condition of the 1841 legislative confirmation of Sulpician title had created what in common law parlance would be a charitable trust, an obligation to care for the souls and instruct the young of the Indians at Oka, and that there might be means by which the Indians through governments could force the priests to honour those requirements. In the opinion of the Methodists' legal advisor, given the unlikelihood of the province of Quebec's interesting itself in the matter on behalf of the Indians, serious consideration should be given to pressing Ottawa, 'the guardian of the indians [sic] of Canada,' to compel the Sulpicians to honour their obligations.[54]

The Judicial Committee's ruling, though perhaps appearing odd after the Supreme Court of Canada's finding in the 1990 Sparrow case, is understandable in the context of its times. Legally, the negative finding rested on the propositions enunciated in the important *St Catharines Milling* case of 1889. In that instance, the Privy Council had ruled that there was such a thing as Aboriginal title, but that it constituted merely a usufructuary right and that it was 'dependent on the goodwill of the Sovereign.'[55] This was a view of indigenous peoples' rights that, like the federal government's decision to remove some of the Oka Indians to Gibson township, might reasonably be summed up as the view that the Great White Father knew best what was in the interests of his Red-Skinned Children. It assumed that Aboriginal title was limited to use because title inhered in the Crown, and it posited that the head of state could remove what it had graciously granted ('dependent on the goodwill of the Sovereign'). The implication of this latter point, obviously, was that Parliament and the legislatures, of which the Crown was a part, of course, could also unilaterally extinguish even this limited Aboriginal title. And, with very few and limited exceptions, Indians could not vote for representatives to sit in those chambers.[56] That is what the Judicial Committee held had occurred in the case of the Oka lands by the 1841 statute.

The entire doctrine of a limited Aboriginal title that was dependent on the will of the majority population's political representatives was consistent with the approach that Ottawa took in Indian affairs. The government's assumption was that Indians were in a state of tutelage, were legally 'wards' of Ottawa, and were to be encouraged and coerced by a variety of policies to grow into full Euro-Canadian adulthood. In the meantime, they were legally infantile; Great White Father knew best. The Privy Council decision in the Oka land case in 1912 was completely consistent with these legal and policy positions.

Needless to say, the Indians of Oka accepted neither the ruling nor the doctrine of Aboriginal infantilism that underlay it. In the immediate aftermath of the court ruling, their chief was reported as stating 'that it will not be possible to restrain the people longer, as he has been holding them in check pending the judgment of the court in the matter.'[57] Methodist petitioning of the federal government resulted in no observable consequences,[58] and at Oka conditions reverted to the state that had prevailed before the decision to take the *Corinthe* case through the courts. The principal reason for Ottawa's inaction was the fact that the legal advice it had received was that the Privy Council decision placed no particular obligations on either the Sulpicians or the federal government.[59] The Indians kept complaining to Ottawa after 1912, especially when the Sulpicians from time to time sold off part of the disputed lands.[60] For example, when the Sulpicians were unable to repay $1,025,000 they had borrowed in 1933 from the province of Quebec, the Order handed over one hundred lots to the province, which much later transferred some of the lots to the municipality of Oka for one dollar.[61] In the 1930s the Sulpicians sold their rights to a considerable area, including lands the Indians considered theirs, to a Belgian company that began to enforce its proprietary rights on the Indians with consequent friction.[62] As a result of these occasional sales, settlement at Oka came to resemble a racial checkerboard: Whites and Mohawk lived side by side. Moreover, since the lands at Oka that the Mohawk occupied were not a formal or legal 'reserve' within the meaning of the Indian Act, Indian control was even more tenuous than it otherwise would have been.[63]

The next phase came to a head in 1945. Sulpician land sales having occasioned considerable Mohawk disquiet during the 1930s, Ottawa intervened in a bumbled effort to resolve the dispute and lower the tension between Indians and clergy. Again without consulting the Indians involved, the federal government negotiated an agreement with the Sulpicians, who were nearly bankrupt, to purchase land for the remaining Mohawk at the mission.[64] Although this had the immediate effect of lowering the temperature of the quarrel, it by no means cleared up the underlying dispute over ownership of the whole tract. Non-Indians assumed that the sale meant that Indians in future would confine themselves to their small, scattered plots, which totalled 1,556 acres.[65] The descendants of Indians who believed they once had possessed more than sixty-four square miles now found their holdings reduced to two and one-half square miles. As a western member of Parliament observed in 1961, 'They certainly did get gypped, did they not?'[66] Moreover, since the government failed to follow the terms of the Indian Act by setting the purchased lands aside by order-in-council as a reserve for the benefit of the Indians, this newly acquired parcel still was not legally a reserve. In law it remained merely a settlement, an anomalous status that did nothing to reassure the Indians.

By the end of the 1950s, as noted at the outset, the dispute was becoming troublesome once again. In 1959 the municipality of Oka used a private member's bill in Quebec's legislature to establish a nine-hole golf course on some land that the Mohawk claimed as their own.[67] The town knew that such action was a legal possibility because Indians Affairs had thoughtfully announced in 1958 that the Indians' land at Oka was not a legal Indian reserve. 'These lands do not comprise an

Indian Reserve. The right to occupy the individual parcels became involved over the years, and the Indian affairs branch has been attempting to straighten these matters out. The work is nearing completion.'[68] Oka's ability to secure the special legislation was perhaps explained by the fact that the municipality and the tract in question lay in the premier's constituency.[69] Perhaps the same factor also explains why the Indians who resided at Oka were given no notice of the private measure and no opportunity to argue against it.[70] In any event, the private member's bill transferred some 'common lands' that the Indians had long used for wood-cutting and cattle-grazing into land destined for recreation. 'What was once reserved for Indian use and profit is now reserved for golf,' noted their lawyer.[71] As the Indians said themselves, 'We also consider the building of the clubhouse directly adjacent to our graveyard a desecration and an insult to our sensibilities.'[72]

Once the private member's bill was passed, the Kanesatake Mohawk tried to resist. The Indians asked Ottawa to disallow the private Quebec statute, but John Diefenbaker's government refused.[73] The Mohawk remonstrated about the unsatisfactory status of their limited holdings before the Joint Parliamentary Committee in 1961, telling the parliamentarians, 'We want tribal ownership of land, not the individual ownership which the white man favours.'[74] Once more their protests had no apparent effect.[75] The Joint Committee considered their protests in 1961 and recommended establishing an Indian claims commission, such as the United States had, to deal with the British Columbia and Oka land questions. However, not even this could move either the bureaucratic or political levels of government to action.[76] Whatever Ottawa was doing in an attempt 'to straighten these matters out' in any event was overtaken and rendered irrelevant in the 1970s.

As a result of the *Nisga'a* or *Calder* case in 1973, a new chapter on Inuit and Indian land claims opened. Prior to the court's finding that there was such a thing as Aboriginal title and that it extended well beyond the limited version that the Privy Council had defined in the *St Catharines Milling* case, the prime minister had rejected the notion. In Pierre Trudeau's view, 'We can't recognize aboriginal rights because no society can be built on historical "might-have-beens"'.[77] However, in the Nisga'a case six of seven Supreme Court justices gave powerful support to the concept of Aboriginal title, while rejecting the Nisga'a suit itself. Three of the judges found that legislative action in British Columbia had extinguished Aboriginal title, while the other three did not agree. (The seventh judge found against the plaintiff on a technical point.) In the wake of the *Calder* decision, Trudeau had to recognize that he faced a much more powerful adversary than some mere historical might-have-been in this Aboriginal title. He reportedly responded, 'Perhaps you had more legal rights than we thought you had when we did the white paper.'[78] Given the fact that the ramifications of Aboriginal title were enormous in an era when the Cree of Quebec were battling the James Bay hydroelectric project and a variety of Native groups in the Mackenzie Valley were voicing opposition to northern energy development, some concessions were essential. Trudeau and his government, already battered by the First Peoples' united and vehement rejection of the White Paper of 1969, backed away from the prime minister's rarefied individualist notions and prepared to deal with Aboriginal land claims on a collective, systematic basis.[79] In August 1973, Indian affairs minister Jean Chrétien announced that a new policy would soon be forthcoming.

Beginning in July 1974, Ottawa set up a claims resolution process. Government now recognized two categories of Indian claims, comprehensive and specific. Comprehensive claims were based on the contention that the claimant had an unextinguished Aboriginal right through possession of a territory since time immemorial. The Nisga'a case would have been such a comprehensive claim. Specific claims, which might be about a variety of topics including land, were demands for redress based on an argument that commitments or legal obligations on the part of the government to Indian groups had not been carried out fully and properly. The government would assist in the development of claims cases by funding research by Indian organizations. And an Office of Native Claims (ONC) would become the focal point in Indian Affairs for the claims resolution process for both comprehensive and specific claims. The ONC would investigate claims lodged by Indian organizations and advise the Indian Affairs minister on their strength. If it so advised and Indian Affairs accepted the advice, the claim could then be negotiated. In these negotiations, the ONC would represent the federal government, and, following conclusion of an agreement, the ONC would help to implement and monitor compliance with the claim settlement. Finally, the ONC was also responsible for formulating policies covering the Native claims area.

The claims resolution policy of 1973–4 had a chequered history, largely because it was – and remains – seriously flawed. First and foremost, it was, as usual, the product of the Ottawa bureaucracy. Since it had not resulted from consultation and negotiation, it contained elements that were unacceptable to the Native organizations and was the object of suspicion. Some of these problems concerned the criteria by which Ottawa decided if claims were valid. For example, for comprehensive claims it was necessary to demonstrate that the claim emanated from an organized group, that the group had occupied the territory in question exclusively and continuously from pre-contact times (from time immemorial) to the present, and that the claimant could demonstrate it was the legitimate descendant and representative of the original occupiers. Such criteria ignored both pre- and post-contact migrations of Native groups in response to environmental, economic, and military factors. It appeared to rule out, for example, the claim of the Inland Tlingit to the territory in northern British Columbia and southern Yukon that they occupied in the late twentieth century because that group had migrated there in the nineteenth century.[80] And, of course, it worked against the arguments of a group such as the Oka Indians, who had been contending since at least 1781 that the land they occupied was theirs, because those Indians had taken up residence on the land they now claimed well after the Europeans arrived.

Other difficulties stemmed largely from the legalistic approach that the Ottawa bureaucracy took to the claims resolution process. The governing principle in the ONC's evaluation of specific claims was the doctrine of 'lawful obligation,' a narrow gate through which not all worthy cases could squeeze. And government representatives proved themselves prone to argue technical objections, such as invalidity of oral history evidence and the doctrine of laches (barrier to litigation by passage of time). Such approaches were to be expected from a bureaucracy, but they caused enormous problems. As early as 1980 it was noted that bands and organizations were choosing litigation over negotiation with the Office of Native Claims.[81] The inordinately slow pace of Ottawa's work and the backlog that inevitably developed also contributed greatly to disenchantment with the claims resolution process. Since Ottawa limited the number of comprehensive claims negotiations in which it would engage at any one time, a logjam quickly developed. In 1981 a review of the comprehensive claims resolution process noted that the James Bay and Northern Quebec Agreement was the only such dispute that had been resolved. Thirteen others were in various stages of negotiation.[82] By 1985 a task force set up to review the comprehensive claims process noted that there were six comprehensive claims under negotiation, another fifteen (thirteen of them in British Columbia) that had been accepted by the department and awaited negotiation, seven that were under review, and several more that were expected. As the assessors noted, 'in spite of more than a decade of negotiating, little progress has been made in the settlement of claims.' The task force Chair, Murray Coolican, pointed out that 'at the current rate of settlement it could be another 100 years before all the claims have been addressed.'[83] Things were no better in the area of specific claims: at the end of December 1981, 12 specific claims had been resolved, and 250 more awaited resolution.[84]

The problems with the claims resolution process stemmed from more than just the slow pace and consequent frustration. Many Indian groups objected to the two-fisted role played by Indian and Northern Affairs after the process was formalized in 1973–4. The bureaucracy that granted funds for claims research was the same body that decided how much money would be available to bands and other organizations for a variety of social, political, and economic activities. Many suspected that the arrangement was designed to discourage claimants from pressing their cases too aggressively. Moreover, since the Office of Native Claims both decided which claims were to be accepted for negotiation and then bargained on behalf of the federal government, the process was clearly in contravention of a major tenet of natural justice. If it was true that no one should be judge in his or her own cause, what did one say about the Canadian claims process? More generally, all the high cards were dealt to the government in this unequal game:

> Without exception, an aboriginal party has few resources other than the intelligence, commitment, and skill of its leaders, who must sit across the table from the representatives of the Government of Canada, with their apparently overwhelming resources and power. The government decides which claim is accepted, how much money will be made available to the claimant group for research and negotiation, when negotiations will begin, and the process for negotiations. Except where court action threatens a major development project, the government's patience for negotiation appears unlimited. It is hardly surprising that aboriginal groups have little confidence in the fairness of the process, or in the government's desire for early settlements.[85]

Delay, the double role of Indian Affairs, and lack of progress all added up to a claims process that engendered suspicion and opposition in equal parts.

Because of these discontents, the claims resolution process has been under scrutiny through most of its existence. As early as April 1975, claims issues were part of the agenda of a joint National Indian Brotherhood (NIB) / Indian Affairs committee, a consultation that ended abruptly in 1978 when the NIB pulled out in protest.[86] A review of the comprehensive claims procedures led to a restatement of policy under the title of *In All Fairness* in 1981. This document showed little evidence of influence from the Native community, and it embodied no new thinking in any event.[87] In December of the same year, *Outstanding Business*, a revised statement of specific claims policy, modified arrangements in this area slightly. Although this document observed that 'Indian representatives all stated, in the strongest of terms, that Indian views must be considered in the development of any new or modified claims policy,' there were few signs that Ottawa paid much attention.[88] The adoption of the 1982 constitutional package, with its clause recognizing and affirming 'existing aboriginal and treaty rights,' caused more uncertainty in the Native community about the land claims process.

Above all, Ottawa's constant search for and insistence upon extinguishment of all Aboriginal rights as part of claims resolution became particularly ominous. As the *Report of the Task Force on Comprehensive Claims Policy* (Coolican Report) noted, there were other Aboriginal rights – such as self-government, for example – that were not necessarily integral to a land claim. Why should Inuit and Indians give up whatever other Aboriginal rights they had to get their comprehensive claim settled?[89] When a parliamentary committee, known usually as the Penner Committee, supported First Nations' views on self-government in 1983 by advocating *recognition* of that right, the arguments against accepting extinguishment of Aboriginal rights in order to get a comprehensive claims settlement were strengthened still further.

An abortive attempt to come to grips with these objections was made in 1985 in the Task Force on Comprehensive Claims Policy. Although Chief Gary Potts of the Teme-Augarna Anishnabai noted that this inquiry 'marks the first time since 1763 that government has made an effort to hear from the First Nations of Canada' concerning treaty-making and claims, there was little evidence that hearing led to acceptance.[90] The task force condemned the slow pace of comprehensive claims negotiations, blamed government insistence on extinguishment for much of the problem, and called for a new comprehensive claims policy that would speed up the process and largely shunt aside the troublesome extinguishment issue. However, the *Comprehensive Land Claims Policy* that emerged in 1986, though it claimed later to have dropped its aim of 'blanket extinguishment,' offered nothing concrete to avoid the problem. When all the verbiage was stripped away, Indian and Northern Affairs still had not committed itself to drop extinguishment, persisted in talking about 'granting' rather than 'recognizing' self-government, and was still reserving for itself the role of judge of whether or not a comprehensive claim was worthy of proceeding to negotiations. By the later 1980s the major difference in Ottawa's claims resolution process was one of structure: the Office of Native Claims had been replaced in the middle of the decade by a Comprehensive Claims Branch and a Specific Claims Branch.

In light of the unsatisfactory nature and evolution of the federal government's land claims procedures after 1973, the bitter disappointment of the Oka Indians is easier to understand. They, after all, had always been treated like credulous and dependent children for whom others – Sulpicians, legislature, Methodist clerics, judicial committee, and certainly Indian and Northern Affairs Canada – knew best what was in their interest. After 1974 they found themselves enmeshed in a claims resolution process that was unilaterally created and largely operated by the Great White Father in Ottawa. Given the history of Oka-Kanesatake, it was not surprising that the comprehensive land claim that they launched early in 1975 was rejected a few months later.

On the advice of the Department of Justice, the Office of Native Claims found that the comprehensive claim of the Mohawk of Akwesasne (St Regis), Kahnawake (Caughnawaga), and Kanesatake to a large portion of southwestern Quebec did not rest on unextinguished Aboriginal title. If the Mohawk had possessed the land being claimed when Europeans arrived (and the expert in the Justice Department was inclined to doubt that they had), they had since lost it or given it up. '[I]f the claimants ever did have aboriginal title to the land in question, this title has long been extinguished by the dispositions made of the land under the French regime, by the decision of the Sovereign, after the cession [Conquest], to open the territory to settlement and by the grants made over the years pursuant to this policy.' The Justice Department also believed that the lands the Mohawk were claiming had not been protected by the Royal Proclamation of 1763. In short, 'the native title alleged by the claimants, if it ever existed, was extinguished, first by the French Kings at least with respect to the grants made by them, and, after the cession, by the Sovereign by the exercise of complete dominion over the land adverse to the right of occupancy of the Indians.' However, the same opinion that dismissed the extensive Mohawk comprehensive claim explicitly stated that it did not apply to any 'specific claims which the Mohawks of Oka, St. Regis, and Caughnawaga may have with respect to lands contiguous or near their existing reserves.'[92]

Such reasoning – which showed that in some respects the federal government had not advanced beyond the 1912 judicial committee rationale that was based on the 1889 ruling on *St Catharine's Milling* – ignored several facts. Iroquoians had undoubtedly ranged through and extracted resources from the region at the time of European contact. Particularly the Algonkin and Nipissing at Oka had until at least the 1820s regularly hunted, trapped, and fished in the lower Ottawa Valley from their base at the settlement. Finally, Ottawa has accepted or seems prepared to accept claims from other groups whose records of occupation are no lengthier than that of the Indians at Oka. For example, the Golden Lake band of Algonkin in Ontario are proceeding with a comprehensive claim despite the fact that many of them are the descendants of migrants from Oka.[93] Nevertheless, Ottawa rejected the Mohawk comprehensive claim that included lands at Kanesatake-Oka.

The Kanesatake Indians' specific claim fared no better. Lodged in June 1977, it languished until October 1986, when its contention that the Kanesatake Mohawk had an interest in the territory that should be addressed was rejected. Since 'the Oka Band has not demonstrated any outstanding lawful obligation on the part of the Federal Crown,' Indian and Northern Affairs would not accept the claim for negotiation. However, Ottawa 'recognized that there is an historical basis for Mohawk claims related to land grants in the 18th century,' and 'I [minister Bill McKnight] am willing to consider a proposal for alternative means of redress of the Kanesatake Band's grievance ...'[94] As noted earlier, efforts to carry out a land consolidation scheme at Kanesatake failed in 1989–90. This last attempt at resolution fell afoul of fears that Ottawa was not willing to go far enough to meet Mohawk needs, of divisions within the Kanesatake community, and of the impatience of a municipality and a golf club that wanted to expand the existing course by annexing lands that the Mohawk considered theirs. The result, of course, was the violence of the summer of 1990.

Subsequent to the eleven-week confrontation at Kanesatake, Ottawa behaved in its usual consistently inconsistent fashion. While speaking to the Federation of Saskatchewan Indian Nations in August on the error of using confrontation and violence, the minister of Indian and Northern Affairs Canada, Tom Siddon, observed helpfully that 'while our specific claims process is working, it is *not* working to the satisfaction of Indian people or myself.'[95] In September 1990, Siddon lectured Indian leaders assembled in Ottawa on how they would have behaved during the crisis had they been responsible, good little Indian leaders.[96] Having twice rejected Mohawk land claims, the minister announced during the stand-off at Kanesatake that Ottawa would purchase and hand over to the aggrieved Indians the terrain in question. Once Ottawa had acquired some, but not all, of the disputed land in the autumn of 1990, the minister's representatives proceeded to become embroiled in a frustrating round of talks that led nowhere. By February 1991 the minister, appearing before the Commons committee on Aboriginal affairs, argued that the villain in the Oka story was the traditional system of government by chiefs selected by the clan mothers, a system that one of his predecessors had agreed to have restored in 1969. 'Since 1986, clan mothers have appointed six different councils at Kanesatake,' with resulting instability. The indecisiveness that resulted from traditional Mohawk governance, said Siddon, had made it impossible for the federal negotiator, in spite of eighteen meetings with the band council and municipality after 1989, to reach an agreement. That was why there had been violence, destruction, and death at Oka in the summer of 1990.[97]

The real explanation of the Oka tragedy is not clan mothers. Rather it is the Great White Father, or more precisely the attitude that has long prevailed in Ottawa that government is a paternalistic and benevolent agent that knows better than anyone else what is best for its Red Children. This attitude is indistinguishable from that of the Sulpicians and French government officials who in the seventeenth and eighteenth centuries shifted Algonkin, Nipissing, and Mohawk groups from La Montagne to Sault au Récollet to Oka. It underlay the rejection of repeated Oka Indian demands from the 1780s to the 1830s to regularize their title. It accounted for the legislative fiat of 1841 that registered the Sulpicians' title to the disputed lands, a unilateral declaration that was upheld in the *Corinthe* case in 1912 and, in part, in Ottawa's rejection of the comprehensive land claim of the 1970s. The assumption that Ottawa knew best accounted, too, for the repeated efforts to resolve the controversy at Oka by removing some or all of the Indians – to Maniwaki, to Gibson, anywhere away from the political flashpoint of the moment. And, finally, these attitudes explained the repeated failure of bureaucrats and politicians to respond to Indian petitions to the governor in the nineteenth century, to the joint parliamentary inquiry of the 1940s, and to the inquiry of 1961 that something be done to clear up the mess of the land dispute at Oka-Kanesatake.

The Great White Father in Ottawa is responsible for the Oka crisis, and for the larger mess of the land claims resolution process across the country. Procedures decided on in Ottawa and imposed on Aboriginal organizations have responded to bureaucratic imperatives and ignored Native needs. The continuing, futile attempt to impose a doctrine of extinguishment on Aboriginal rights in the comprehensive claims process is the clearest, most egregious example of that attitude. In spite of repeated demands of Indian and Inuit organizations, in spite of the collapse in 1990 of the tentative Dene-Métis comprehensive claim agreement, in spite of the *Sparrow* and *Sioui* decisions of 1990, and in spite of the 1982 constitutional changes, Ottawa refuses to drop a requirement that stands in the way of clearing up an enormous backlog. Why? Presumably because Ottawa – the Great White Father – knows best.

Just ask the people at Oka.

## Notes

This essay originally appeared in *Native Studies Review* 7, no. 1 (1991). The author is indebted to the Social Sciences and Humanities Research Council of Canada and to the Messer Fund of the University of Saskatchewan, each of which funded parts of the research for this essay. I am also appreciative of the advice and information provided by Robert S. Allen, Deputy Chief, Treaties and Historical Research Centre, Indian and Northern Affairs Canada. He is responsible for saving me from many errors, but not for the ones that remain in spite of his counsel. I have also benefited greatly by a paper by John Thompson, 'A Brief History of the Land Dispute at Kanesatake [Oka] from Contact to 1961,' and from a compilation of copies of documents by Mary Jane Jones, 'Research Report on the History of Disputes at Oka/Kanesatake.' Both these helpful reports have been mimeographed by the Treaties and Historical Research Centre under the title *Materials Relating to the History of Land Dispute at Kanesatake (Oka)* (Ottawa, February 1991). Note that an asterisk (*) at the beginning of a citation indicates that the document has been examined in the corpus of material assembled by Ms Jones rather than in the original location or on microfilm.

1  Emile Colas, legal counsel for the Oka Indians to the Joint Committee of Senate and House of Commons on Indian Affairs, *Minutes of Proceedings and Evidence, No. 1* (Ottawa:-Queen's Printer, 1961), 15 (14 March 1961).

2  Throughout this essay, the contemporary designation, Indian and Northern

Affairs Canada, is used for a department or branch that has been known by various titles since 1880.

3  Treaties and Historical Research Centre (hereinafter THRQ), Indian and Northern Affairs Canada, document 0-44, 'Land Title at Oka' [1973].

4  Indian and Northern Affairs Canada (INAC), press release 1-9029, 27 July 1990; and 'An Overview of the Oka Issue,' press release, July 1990.

5  Canada, House of Commons, Minutes and Proceedings and Evidence of the Standing Committee on Aboriginal Affairs, The Fifth Report to the House, *The Summer of 1990* (Ottawa: May 1991).

6  Assembly of First Nations, 'Kanesatake Background and Chronology,' *Kanesatake (Oka) Update* (20 Nov. 1990).

7  THRC, document K-59, 'Oka 1881-1950.' According to M. Trudel, *Introduction to New France* (Toronto/Montreal: Holt Rinehart and Winston, 1968), 221, a common league equalled 2.76 English miles, while an official league was 2.42 English miles. This essay assumes that the measure of the eighteenth-century grant was in official leagues.

8  Title of concession, 27 April 1717 (translation), document K-59, 'Oka 1881–1950.'

9  R. Cole Harris, ed., *Historical Atlas of Canada, Vol 1: From the Beginnings to 1800* (Toronto: University of Toronto Press, 1987), plate 47 (B.G. Trigger).

10  A. Shortt and A.G. Doughty, eds, Article XL of Capitulation of Montreal, 1760, in *Documents Relating to the Constitutional History of Canada, 1759–1791* (Ottawa: King's Printer, 1918), 33.

11  Peter A. Cumming and Neil H. Mickenberg, *Native Rights in Canada*, 2nd ed. (Toronto: Indian-Eskimo Association, 1972), 85–6.

12  R.C. Dalton, *The Jesuits' Estates Question 1760-1888: A Study of the Background for the Agitation of 1889* (Toronto: University of Toronto Press, 1968), chapters 2–4.

13  Speech of several Indian chiefs to Col. Campbell, 7 Feb. 1781; speech by principal chiefs to Sir John Johnson, 8 Feb. 1787; and letter of Indians to Joseph Chew, 7 Aug. 1795; in Great Library, Osgoode Hall, 'Privy Council vol. 32,' containing 'Factums and Supporting Documents for Angus Corinthe et al v. The Ecclesiastics of the Seminary of St. Sulpice of Montreal' (hereinafter cited as Factums). The cited documents are in the first part (labelled Volume 1) at pp. 93–6, 99–102, and 13–14 respectively.

14  Richard H. Bartlett, *Indian Reserves in Quebec*, Studies in Aboriginal Rights no. 8 (Saskatoon: University of Saskatchewan Native Law Centre, 1984), 6.

15  *Decision of General Gage, military governor, 4 Nov. 1763, G.M. Mathieson's 'Blue Book,' RG 10, vol. 10, 024.

16  *Report of a committee of the Whole Council, 21 April 1789, ibid.

17  INAC, 'Comprehensive Land Claim of Kanesatake Indians,' press release, July 1990.

18  Daniel Francis, *A History of the Native Peoples of Quebec 1760–1867* (Ottawa: INAC, 1985), 14.

19  National Archives of Canada (NA), RG 10, Series A3 (Administrative Records of the Military 1677–1857), vol. 492, pp. 30248–51, claim of Algonkin and Nipissing chiefs, Lake of Two Mountains, 22 July 1822, in form of petition to Lord Dalhousie.

20  *John Johnson to Colonel Darling, April 1823; Darling to Oka Indians in council at Caughnawaga, 5 Oct. 1827; and report of a committee of the Executive Council, 13 June 1837 – all in Mathieson's 'Blue Book.'

21  *'Propositions Made by Messire Quiblier, Superior of the Seminary of Montreal, to the Iroquois Tribe stationed at the Lake of the Two Mountains, and Accepted by Them ... 11 June 1839,' by Father Quiblier, enclosed in D.C. Napier to governor general, 18 July 1839, ibid.

22  2 Vict., c. 50, 8 April 1839; 3 Vict., c. 30, 8 June 1840; 4 Vict., c. 42 [1841] of Consolidated Statutes of Lower Canada 1861. See the memorandum *re* 'Oka Indians' by A.E. St. Louis, Indian Affairs Branch, 26 May 1948, in THRC, document K-59, 'Oka 1881–1950.'

23  Thompson, 'Brief History,' pp. 20-3.

24  RG 10, Series A3, vol. 492, 30251, petition of 22 July 1822.

25  J. McCann-McGill, 'The Golden Lake Land Claim: A Case Study for the Comparison of the Litigation and Negotiation Processes,' honours thesis, Carleton University (reprinted by THRC, summer 1990), p. 11.

26  Quoted in 'Report on the Affairs of the Indians in Canada 1845,' *Journals of the Legislature of the Province of Canada 1844–45*, Appendix EEE, Section II, Part 3.

27  Ibid. Similarly see the testimony of James Hughes, superintendent, Indian Department 16 Jan. 1843, in 'Report on the Affairs of the Indians of Canada,' *Journals of the Legislative Assembly of the Province of Canada 1847*, Appendix T.

28  THRC, document K-19, A.E. St Louis, memorandum on 'Early History of the Algonquin Indians of Golden Lake' [1947].

29  Concerning Indian complaints over wood, see 'Chief Joseph Onasakenrat and Fifteen Others to Hon. Joseph Howe, Superintendent of Indian Affairs, Transmitting Petition of 26 July 1868,' in Canada, *Sessional Papers (No. 55), 1870*, 32–3.

30  Donald B. Smith, *The Reverend Peter Jones (Kahkewaquonaby) and the Mississauga Indians* (Toronto: University of Toronto Press, 1987), 217.

31  NA, RG 10, Red Series, vol. 2029, file 8946, petition of 19 August 1871.

32 Thompson, 'Brief History,' 25.
33 NA, CO 42, vol. 753 (reel B-590), Despatch 30, 'Relations Existing between Seminary of St. Sulpice & Protestant Indians Resident at Oka,' 9 Feb. 1878.
34 'Report on the Petition of the Iroquois Chiefs of the Iroquois Tribes of the Lake of Two Mountains, 9 Oct. 1868,' in Canada, *Sessional Papers (No. 55) 1870*, 42.
35 R.C. Daniel, *A History of Native Claims Processes in Canada, 1867–1979* (Ottawa: Indian Affairs and Northern Development, 1980), p. 78; McCann-Magill, 'Golden Lake Land Claim,' 12.
36 Robin Fisher, *Contact and Conflict: Indian-European Relations in British Columbia, 1774–1890* (Vancouver: University of British Columbia Press, 1977), chapter 8.
37 Joseph Onasakenral [sic] and twelve others to Sir John Macdonald, 10 Dec. 1868, in *Sessional Papers (No. 55) 1870*, 4-5.
38 Report on the petition of the Algonquin Indians of the Lake of Two Mountains, 26 Oct. 1868, ibid., 41.
39 Report on the petition of the Iroquois chiefs of the Iroquois tribes of the Lake of Two Mountains, 9 Oct. 1979, ibid., 42; Daniel, *Claims*, 78.
40 Etienne Parent to Joseph Onasakenrat and other chiefs, 15 March 1869, quoted in Thompson, 'Brief History,' 29.
41 See, for example, Rev. John Borland, *The Assumptions of the Seminary of St Sulpice* (Montreal: Gazette Printing House, 1872).
42 *NA, RG 10, Red Series, vol. 2035, file 8946-4, #200285, memorandum of solicitor-general, 25 Dec. 1897, annex 'a' to P.C. 1727, 1 July 1898.
43 NA, RG 10, Red Series, vol. 725, Rev. William Scott, *Report Relating to the Affairs of the Oka Indians, Made to the Superintendent General of Indian Affairs* (Ottawa: MacLean, Roger & Co., 1883) is the published version. It is curious that the published report's preface (p. 3) claims that the pamphlet was printed at the author's expense, because in August 1883 the deputy superintendent general of Indian affairs indicated that Scott's financial situation was not good. See NA, MG 26 A, Sir John A. Macdonald Papers, vol. 289, 132681-3, L. Vankoughnet to Macdonald, 4 Aug. 1883. Similarly see ibid., vol. 290, 133064-6, same to same, 28 April 1885; ibid., 133068-70, same to same, 4 May 1885; RG 10, Red Series, vol. 2203, file 40,584, Rev. William Scott to Sir John A. Macdonald, 28 Nov. 1882 and 18 April 1884; ibid., L. Vankoughnet to Sir John A. Macdonald, 27 Dec. 1882 and 23 April 1883.
44 Donald J. Bourgeois, 'Research Report on the Mohawks of the Gibson Indian Land Claim,' 21 April 1982, p. 6. I am grateful to Professor Donald B. Smith, who provided me with a copy of this report.
45 NA, Secretary of State Correspondence, RG 6, Al, vol. 54, #7539, Rev. L.

Colin, Superior, Seminary of St Sulpice to J.-A. Chapleau, 6 Nov. 1883; Daniel, *Claims*, 79.

46  Scott, *Report*, 63, Appendix 2, W. Scott to chiefs of Oka Indians, 18 Dec. 1882.

47  For example, *Christian Guardian*, 17 Sept. 1884, 31 Aug. 1887, 7 Sept. 1904; NA, MG 27, II B 1, Lord Minto Papers, vol. 10, page 11, 'Subjects Brought before Lord Minto by the Indian Delegation from St. Regis and Oka, 1901'; Rev. John Borland, *An Appeal to the Montreal Conference and Methodists Generally* (Montreal: Witness Printing House, 1883); Norman Murray, *The Oka Question* (n.p., n.d. [1886]); RG 10, Red Series, vol. 2034, file 8946-3, newspaper clippings 1890.

48  NA, RG 10, Red Series, vol. 2029, file 8946, (draft) Joseph Howe to Rev. John Borland, 24 Jan. 1873.

49  *Ibid., vol. 2035, file 8946-4, unidentified, unsigned memorandum, 13 Oct. 1890; Daniel, *Claims*, 79 and 172n5.

50  NA, MG 26 G, Sir Wilfrid Laurier Papers, vol. 791G, 225747, W. Laurier to Clifford Sifton, 17 Nov. 1902 (copy).

51  United Church of Canada Archives (UCA), A. Carman Papers, box 11, file 59, N.W. Rowell to Rev. Dr Henderson, 1 Aug. 1903; enclosed with Rowell to Rev. Dr Carman, 1 Aug. 1903.

52  I.S. Fairty, 'Reminiscences' [1947], in Law Society of Upper Canada, *Gazette* 12, no. 3 (Sept. 1978): 257–8; Daniel, *Claims*, 82.

53  Unless otherwise noted, this treatment of the case relies upon: *Dominion Law Reports*, 5; 'Corinthe et al. v. Seminary of St. Sulpice of Montreal,' 263-8; and Factums (see note 13).

54  UCA, T.E.E. Shore Papers (accession 78.093C), box 3, file 57, N.W. Rowell to Rev. T.E.E. Shore, 2 Oct. 1912.

55  B. Morse, ed., *Aboriginal Peoples and the Law: Indian, Metis and Inuit Rights in Canada* (Ottawa: Carleton University Press, 1985), 58 (Lord Watson).

56  The 1885 Franchise Act extended the franchise in federal elections to Indians east of Manitoba. The provision was repealed in 1898.

57  Shore Papers, box 3, file 57, N.W. Rowell to T.E.E. Shore, 2 Oct. 1912.

58  Ibid., T.E.E. Shore to Col. S. Hughes, 26 Nov. 1912 (copy).

59  *RG 10, Red Series, vol 2032, file 8946X., part 3, E. Lafleur, 'Opinion As to the Rights of the Iroquois and Algonquin Indians of Oka,' 21 June 1916.

60  *Records of Indian Affairs, file 373/1-1, Bernard Bourdon to W.M. Cory, Jan. 1951.

61  *Ibid., file 373/3-8, memorandum by G. Boudreault, 18 April 1969.

62  *Ibid., file 373/1-1, Royal Werry to W.J.F. Pratt, 16 March 1938. The federal minister did criticize the seminary's disposal of property that the Indians

used at one point, but the context suggested that the protest was a bargaining ploy aimed at reducing the amount that the Sulpicians wanted for their lands at Oka. See T.A. Crerar to Sulpicians, 10 Dec. 1941, in *Minutes of Proceedings and Evidence*, 31–2.

63 Although Bartlett, *Indian Reserves in Quebec*, 6, refers to the 'reserve at Oka,' it was not and is not now a reserve because the lands have never been 'set aside by Order-in-Council as a reserve for the benefit' of the Indians (Daniel, *Claims*, 83).

64 Their lawyer later claimed that the Indians were not informed of the 1945 transaction until 1957. See *Records of Indian Affairs, file 373/30-2-16, Emile Colas to Ellen L. Fairclough, 9 Feb. 1960.

65 Emile Colas, counsel for Oka Indians, *Minutes of Proceedings and Evidence*, 14, 34.

66 Mr F.G. Fane, ibid., 34.

67 *Statutes of the Province of Quebec, 8-9 Elizabeth II, c. 181, *An Act Respecting the Corporation of Oka*, 18 Dec. 1959.

68 Minister of citizenship and immigration to attorney for the Oka Indians, 27 May 1958, quoted in *Minutes of Proceedings and Evidence*, 15.

69 Assembly of First Nations, 'Kanesatake Background and Chronology'; Joint Committee, *Minutes of Proceeding and Evidence*, 14.

70 Oka chiefs to Joint Committee of Senate and House of Commons on Indian Affairs, 20 April 1961, *Minutes of Proceedings and Evidence*, 319.

71 Ibid., 14.

72 Oka chiefs to Joint Committee of Senate and House of Commons on Indian Affairs, ibid., 319.

73 Ibid., 18; *Records of Indian Affairs, file 373/30-2-16, Guy Favreau, assistant deputy minister of citizenship and immigration, to Emile Colas, 9 Aug. 1960.

74 Joint Committee, *Minutes of Proceedings and Evidence*, 14. Their lawyer also took pains to explain that the Indians did not regard themselves as Canadian citizens, did not recognize Canadian law, and especially did not accept the validity of the Indian Act (ibid., 23–5).

75 Ibid., 14; document 0-44, 'Land Title at Oka' [1973].

76 Joint Committee, *Minutes of Proceedings and Evidence*, 614, 615.

77 Don Purich, *Our Land: Native Rights in Canada* (Toronto: Lorimer, 1986), 52.

78 P.E. Trudeau as quoted by Flora MacDonald, MP, 11 April 1973, House of Commons, *Debates*, 3207.

79 On Trudeau, Aboriginal rights, and claims, see J.R. Miller, *Skyscrapers Hide the Heavens: A History of Indian-White Relations in Canada*, 3rd ed. (Toronto: University of Toronto Press, 2000), 328–9, 343.

80 Catharine McClellan, *My Old People Say: An Ethnographic Survey of Southern Yukon Territory*, 2 vols, Publications in Ethnology, no. 6 (Ottawa: National Museums of Canada, 1975), 1: 45–50.

81 Daniel, *Claims*, 227.

82 *In All Fairness: A Native Claims Policy – Comprehensive Claims* (Ottawa: Supply and Services Canada, 1981), 29–30.

83 *Living Treaties Lasting Agreements*, Report of the Task Force to Review Comprehensive Claims Policy [Coolican Report] (Ottawa: Indian Affairs and Northern Development, 1985), 13: 'Three claims have been rejected on the basis of their having been superseded by law.' As of 15 March 1991, according to the deputy chief of the Treaties and Historical Research Centre, nineteen comprehensive claims awaited settlement. During the winter of 1990–1 the federal government 'announced the lifting of the six-claim limit on the number of comprehensive claims the government will negotiate at any time' and moved to set up a task force on 'how tripartite negotiations' with Native groups and provinces might proceed (INAC, *Transition*, special edition, February 1991).

84 *Outstanding Business: A Native Claims Policy – Specific Claims* (Ottawa: Indian Affairs and Northern Development, 1982), 13: 'Twelve claims had been settled involving cash payments of some $2.3 million. Seventeen claims had been rejected and five had been suspended by the claimants. Negotiations were in progress on 73 claims and another 80 were under government review. Twelve claims had been filed in court and 55 others referred for administrative remedy (e.g., return of surrendered but unsold land).'

85 Coolican Report, 78.

86 Daniel, *Claims*, 230–1.

87 *In All Fairness*, esp. 17.

88 *Outstanding Business*, 16. The document claimed, however, that Indians' 'views have been taken into consideration by the government in developing new policy initiatives.'

89 Coolican Report, iii, 30, 40, 43. See also p. 14 *re* impact of constitution of 1982.

90 Ibid., ii.

91 *Comprehensive Land Claims Policy* (Ottawa: Supply and Services, 1986 [the title page nonetheless bears the date '1987']), 12, 18, 23. For the minister's claim that 'blanket extinguishment' was dropped as a requirement in 1986, see his statement to the House of Commons in September 1990 in *Transition* 3, no. 12 (Dec. 1990): 3.

92 Paul Ollivier, associate deputy minister, Department of Justice, to P.F.

Girard, Office of Claims Negotiation, INAC, 26 Feb. 1975. A photocopy of this document, which was obtained by means of an application under the Access to Information Act, is in the possession of the author.

93 McCann-Magill, 'Golden Lake Land Claim,' esp. 11–12.

94 INAC, press release, 'An Overview of the Oka Issue,' 3; Bill McKnight to Grand Chief Hugh Nicholas, 14 Oct. 1986; R.M. Connelly, Specific Claims Branch, to Chief Nicholas, 10 May 1984. Photocopies of the McKnight and Connelly letters were obtained via the Access to information Act and are in the author's possession.

95 *Transition* 3, no. 9 (Sept. 1990): 1.

96 *Globe and Mail*, 11 September 1990.

97 Ibid., 20 February 1991.

# Canada and the Aboriginal Peoples, 1867–1927

Confederation established a federal government with jurisdiction over 100,000 to 120,000 'Indians and lands reserved for the Indians.' The responsibility brought with it a challenge vast and complicated. At the time and across the continent, diverse Aboriginal communities found themselves in various states of interaction with Euro-Canadians. The Canadian government faced the monumental task of developing policies for this heterogeneous population. The dimensions of the job and the pressures of time were but two of the factors that help to explain why Canada made such a poor job of its relations with the Aboriginal peoples in the decades after Confederation.

The Atlantic region alone presented a complex set of conditions. In Newfoundland (not a province until 1949), the last Beothuk died in 1829, her people victims of European disease, especially tuberculosis, and economic competition. By the 1860s, perhaps 150 Mi'kmaq in the interior of the island subsisted, in part through traditional hunting-fishing-gathering practices, and in part through casual employment and sales to settlers. On the Labrador coast, the Inuit exhibited another typical form of cultural interaction through their involvement in trade with Europeans and Christian ministrations by Moravian missionaries. The other Atlantic island province, Prince Edward Island (joining Canada in 1873), was primarily agricultural. Land was set aside for the Mi'kmaq relatively late. 'Reserves' were created at Morell River in 1859 and on Lennox Island in 1870. When it joined the Dominion in 1873, PEI's population included some 300 Mi'kmaq.

Nova Scotia and New Brunswick contained roughly 10 per cent of the 30,000 Indians residing in the four original provinces of the Dominion. Prior to Confederation, settlement and agricultural development in Nova Scotia had marginalized the mainly Mi'kmaq population, resulting in their concentration on Cape Breton and near Shubenacadie in the centre of the province. A system of reserves had not developed, and the colonial administration had allowed squatters to purchase Native lands. Although the proceeds from such sales were supposed to be collected in a fund to support the Indians, little had accumulated by Confederation. Nova Scotia's Mi'kmaq were a demoralized and marginalized people who survived through casual employment, the sale of handicrafts and produce, and alms.

In New Brunswick, where reserves had been created, the situation was little better for the Mi'kmaq, Maliseet, and Abenaki population of about 2,100. Sales of reserved land from the 1840s to the mid-1860s had not produced a very large Indian fund, but had reduced Native lands by about one-sixth. Save in northern New Brunswick, where unharvested timber in some districts permitted the continuation of a subsistence-level economy, most Aboriginal peoples were as dislocated and dependent as those in Nova Scotia. Little wonder, then, that Canada's first deputy superintendent of Indian affairs, William Spragge, said 'philanthropic effort' was required in the Maritimes 'to bring them [indigenous people] up, to at least, the standard of the more advanced Indian communities of the Provinces of Ontario and Quebec.'

Spragge's reference to 'the more advanced Indians' reflected the fact that Quebec's Native population, though highly diverse overall, could be divided into two categories. In the Shield country north of the agricultural lands, the largely Cree, Montagnais, and Naskapi (now Innu) groups continued the hunting-gathering patterns that had existed before the coming of the Europeans. There were pinpoints of Catholic missions in the North, especially near James Bay, but until colonization and hydroelectric development began to push northward in the latter decades of the century, Natives in Quebec's North remained relatively undisturbed. In the South, in the agriculturally oriented river valleys, approximately 5,000 of the province's 8,600 Natives had congregated on reserves.

Most of these reserves, such as Sillery or the forerunner of Oka (Kanesatake), had been mission refuges for groups of Mohawk, Abenaki, Algonkin, and Nipissing who were either alienated from religious traditionalists in their home communities or victims of punishing wars by rival nations. At centres such as Lorette, Becancour, south shore Montreal (Kahnawake), or St Regis (Akwesasne), groups of Natives pursued a mixed economy of traditional harvesting, casual employment in nearby urban areas, and sale of handicrafts and natural goods to Euro-Canadians. If the residents of these Quebec reserves were 'more advanced' in the eyes of the deputy minister, it was principally because the education provided by missionaries in day schools fostered acculturation. Certainly, the perceived 'advancement' of these communities had little to do with state action, for the only important civil enactment in the colonial period had been an 1850 statute that defined for the first time who was an 'Indian.'

Neighbouring Ontario had a more extensive array of civil policies that affected the roughly 12,000 Native peoples who dwelt within its boundaries. In the more southerly regions, which had been populated mainly by groups of Mississauga when officialdom began to plan for their settlement in the 1780s, treaty-making became an especially notable policy development. East of the Ottawa River there were no treaties by which Native occupiers had agreed to surrender or share their lands with the newcomers, although there were important pacts of peace and friendship in Nova Scotia and Quebec. In Ontario, by contrast, a pattern of establishing treaties, or treating with, indigenous occupiers for access to their lands had developed on the foundation of the Royal Proclamation of 1763. Among other things, this imperial edict designated territories west of the Ottawa River and south of the lower Great Lakes as lands 'reserved to them [indigenous people] ... as their Hunting Grounds,' and specified how such tracts might be acquired legally from the Natives. Proclamation policy restricted the right to obtain Aboriginal lands to the Crown's representatives, and required that officials negotiate for land only at a 'public meeting' of Natives 'called for the purpose.' The Proclamation was designed to avoid clashes between intrusive settlers and indigenous landholders by regulating the acquisition of Native lands. In the 1770s and 1780s, the British obtained lands north of the lower Great Lakes by treating with the Mississauga, and this practice was repeated following the American Revolutionary War and the War of 1812 to obtain peaceful access to lands for both Natives, especially the Mohawk, and European settlers in a series of treaties. This method of negotiating surrender of tracts of land in return for compensation continued in the 1820s and 1830s until virtually all of southern Ontario was covered.

The Robinson-Huron and Robinson-Superior agreements of 1850 demonstrated that treaty-making in Ontario was not invariably driven by the requirements of the Royal Proclamation alone. In the mid-1840s, the colonial legislature authorized mining exploration in Ojibwa lands near Lake Huron. Many Ojibwa protested the intrusion, and a group under Chief Shinguakonce of Garden River (near Sault Ste Marie) threatened the miners. Only after the intruders appealed to colonial officials for assistance did the colonial government commission W.B. Robinson to negotiate with the Ojibwa. The resulting Robinson treaties contained several notable features. First, they covered large areas, in contrast to the more limited southern treaties. Second, they promised that Natives could continue to hunt and fish throughout the territory surrendered until the land was occupied. And, finally, the treaties promised to create reserves.

Prior to 1850, the establishment of reserves in the future Ontario had been an *ad hoc* affair. Many early 'reserves' were in fact Christian missions, such as the Methodists' Credit Mission west of Toronto, where the churches evangelized and assisted Natives whose economy was being disrupted by agriculture. In the 1830s, a state-sponsored effort at setting up reserves was initiated in the Coldwater-Narrows region, but this attempt to tie Natives to an agricultural setting proved a failure and was abandoned. After 1846 the colonial government again tried to encourage Natives to relocate and settle, but encountered resistance from Native leaders who feared the loss of the small tracts they still controlled. By Confederation a reserve policy existed in Ontario, although its implementation was intermittent at best.

Enfranchisement represented the other significant policy initiative in Ontario. The government's intention in offering enfranchisement to Aboriginal people was to eliminate their separate status by conferring the rights and duties of Canadian citizenship. In convincing Aboriginal people to accept enfranchisement, the government hoped to bring about voluntary assimilation. The preferred approach was embodied in the Gradual Civilization Act of 1857, which repeated the definition of Indian first enunciated in an 1850 Quebec statute. The Act then, paradoxically, laid out the process by which an 'Indian' might cease to be one. Any adult male who was literate, debt-free, and of good moral character, with approval by a colonial government board, could be enfranchised and given a share of reserve land in freehold tenure. Moreover, his wife and his children and their descendants would be enfranchised along with him. The 1857 Act was noteworthy in its minimal short-term but relatively significant long-term impact. The enfranchisement provision retained importance because it carried over into post-Confederation policy and remained part of the Indian Act until 1985. In its immediate application, however, the provision was ineffective, resulting in the enfranchisement of precisely one man in the period down to the codification of the Indian Act in 1876.

In part because Ontario politicians dominated the federal cabinets in the first few decades after Confederation, the civil policies of treaty-making, reserves, and enfranchisement typified the Canadian government's dealing with Aboriginal people in the West. The acquisition of Rupert's Land from the Hudson's Bay Company was an essential part of the Confederation agreement, and Ottawa turned to integrating the region quickly after 1867. Several diverse nations made up the 45,000 or more Aboriginal communities in the prairie West. In some ways, the most distinctive were the people who called themselves 'the New Nation,' the roughly 12,000 mixed-blood peoples known to scholars as Métis or country-born. They were the offspring of a fur trade that brought both British and *canadien* merchants into contact with the western First Nations, and most were settled near the forks of the Red and Assiniboine Rivers in the future Manitoba. The largely French-speaking and Roman Catholic Métis were more numerous than their anglophone and largely non-Catholic country-born cousins, and the latter may have become equivocal about their racial identity. Collectively they had emerged by the mid-nineteenth century as distinct in the West: a 'New Nation.'

West and north of Red River were smaller settlements of Métis in the Saskatchewan District, as well as many tens of thousands of Plains Cree, Saulteaux (Western Ojibwa), Assiniboine, Dakota, and components of the Blackfoot Confederacy in the future Alberta. The Canadian government viewed the Plains peoples with respect and fear, for their numbers and martial skills made them a formidable potential enemy. However, the vitality of the economy that supported the Plains societies diminished with the steady decline of the buffalo herds. Before Confederation, the competition for this resource widened a gulf between Plains Cree and Blackfoot and culminated in a destructive war. The loss of life to warfare and epidemics brought Plains leaders to search for peace, achieved finally in 1871.

To the west, beyond the mountains, lay dozens of other First Nations that the Canadian government would only slowly come to know. Both in the British Columbia interior and on its lush coast, Aboriginal communities still dominated, though their numbers were diminishing. Relations between British Columbia Indians and Europeans had begun in a maritime fur trade in the 1770s and evolved into a land-based commerce in pelts in the second decade of the nineteenth century, involving the interior and northern peoples as well. By the middle of the nineteenth century, disease had profoundly affected the indigenous population just as the opening of settlement and mining frontiers began to disrupt Aboriginal homelands. Between 1835 and 1885, British Columbia's Aboriginal population declined, principally as a result of disease, from 70,000 to approximately 28,000. A shrinking population was one reason why treaty-making generally did not occur in British Columbia. In addition, mining and other forms of economic development led newcomers to covet Aboriginal lands, giving rise to a growing antipathy by both mother country and colony to recognizing indigenous rights and establishing treaties for access to Native lands. Save for some fourteen treaties covering limited tracts near Victoria, Nanaimo, and at the north end of Vancouver Island, British Columbia entered Confederation in 1871 with its territory uncovered by treaty.

As Ottawa prepared to deal with 'Indians and lands reserved for the Indians' in 1867, then, it faced a large and heterogeneous Native population scattered across many thousands of kilometres. Moreover, no single pattern of interaction between Aboriginal peoples and newcomers had emerged, much less a uniform policy. Only in Ontario had a systematic method of dealing with the indigenous peoples been elaborated.

It was a combination of Ontario tradition, blunders, and threatened resistance that led the Dominion to make treaty hurriedly with the western Native peoples. Canada's efforts to extend its jurisdiction over Rupert's Land in 1869 provoked the resistance of the Métis and some country-born led by Louis Riel, thus stalling the process. In the end, the region entered the Dominion as the Province of Manitoba. Moreover, the Manitoba Act, which spelled out the terms of union, contained a provision for granting 1.4 million acres (567,000 ha) to children of mixed-blood families in recognition that they shared in the 'Indian title' to the region. The Red River Resistance reminded Canada that attempts to assert control before treating with the local population resulted in complications. The Manitoba Act recognized, as well, the need to address 'Indian title.'

The First Nations themselves indicated that the government would be wise to negotiate with them for peaceful access to these lands before settlers arrived in large numbers. A minority voice came from chiefs such as Sweet Grass, who in 1871 sent a message from Fort Edmonton asking the Dominion to make treaty. More numerous were the Indians who delivered warnings that unauthorized intrusion and exploitation would result in difficulties. The Ojibwa in the northwest angle of the Lake of the Woods objected to the passage through their lands of road builders and a military expedition, while Saulteaux near Portage la Prairie warned settlers not to cut wood on their lands. As well, Plains Cree in the Saskatchewan country in 1875 ordered both a telegraph construction crew and a field party of the Geological Survey of Canada to cease and desist. In the same year, the Blackfoot of southern Alberta complained formally that strangers were invading their lands and hunting the buffalo. From intimations such as these, the Canadian government understood that only through negotiation could it promote immigration and settlement without bloodshed in the lands it had purchased from the Hudson's Bay Company. A military 'solution' such as the neighbouring American republic was pursuing with the western Indian nations was simply out of the question on financial grounds alone.

For those Aboriginal leaders who wanted to make treaty – and it is essential to note that not all did – the motivation was fairly clear. The Cree and Blackfoot were every bit as aware of the destruction and expense of Indian wars south of the 'medicine line,' the international boundary, as was the government. They similarly recognized, in part because traders and missionaries in their midst had been telling them so, that settlers were going to come from Canada whether the First Nations were agreeable to the influx or not. In the southern portions of the North-West Territories, some groups such as the Blackfoot also realized that the authority of the Queen's Canadian government had had a beneficial effect since the arrival of the red-coated Mounted Police in 1874. Blackfoot chief Crowfoot would later note gratefully that the horsemen had driven whiskey peddlers out of the Cypress Hills and southern Alberta posts, before the poison could debauch and destroy his people. Finally, and most important, the Plains nations were acutely conscious that the once-vast buffalo herds were dwindling. A number of Plains Cree and Blackfoot leaders were prepared to make treaty because they saw in a new relationship with the Queen's government in Ottawa a source of sustenance, protection, and a means to make a living in a new way at a time of impending crisis. While the Ojibwa and Woods Cree, obviously, were less affected by crisis than the Plains peoples, some leaders among all the Aboriginal communities of the West perceived advantage in regulating the influx of strangers by means of a negotiated relationship with the newcomers' government.

For the Christian missionaries, who, like the Hudson's Bay officers

and policemen, played a minor role in the process, there were two reasons to advocate treaties. As outriders for a Euro-Canadian population,
they shared the expansionist aims of the Dominion and interpreted the
interest of their Native flocks within the framework of Canada's objectives. The Oblates, Anglicans, Presbyterians, and Methodists also were
anxious about the future of the peoples whom they evangelized in the
likely event of the disappearance of the buffalo. Most missionaries
believed that exchanging a migratory hunting economy for sedentary
agriculture was in Natives' long-term economic interest, as much as it
would facilitate Native conversions.

These varying motives underlay attempts in the 1870s to conclude
treaties from the Lake of the Woods to the Rocky Mountains, and from
the 'medicine line' to the northern edge of anticipated settlement. These
motives, assumptions, and objectives combined to produce seven 'numbered treaties' between Canada and the western First Nations between
1871 and 1877. Treaty 1, the Stone Fort Treaty, was negotiated in 1871
with Saulteaux and Swampy Cree in southern Manitoba. This was the
one region of the West where a pre-existing treaty was to be found,
because in 1817 the Selkirk Treaty had secured belated access to Native
lands along the Red and Assiniboine for the Selkirk settlers. Treaty 2,
also signed in 1871, covered southwestern Manitoba. Negotiations for
Treaty 3, the North West Angle Treaty, were initiated with the Ojibwa
and Cree of northwestern Ontario in 1870, but not concluded until three
years later because of Native determination to secure their aims. Treaty
4, the Qu'Appelle, was signed with the Assiniboine, Cree, and Saulteaux of southern Saskatchewan in 1874. Treaty 5 brought the Natives of
central Manitoba into treaty in 1875. Treaty 6, with the Plains Cree, was
signed in two locations, Fort Carlton and Fort Pitt, in August and September of 1876. And, finally, the Blackfoot Treaty, Treaty 7, which covered the portion of Alberta south of Treaty 6, was concluded at Blackfoot
Crossing in 1877.

Treaty-making in the 1870s combined both governmental and
Aboriginal preoccupations. From Ottawa's standpoint, the objective
was to get commitments to surrender land and give obedience to the
Canadian government as expeditiously and inexpensively as possible.
In pursuit of that object, treaty commissioners at first were authorized
to make treaty for land and political control in return for modest initial
payments, annuities (annual payments), and limited reserves to be set
aside for the Native peoples. However, government negotiators usually found fulfilling their mandate difficult in the face of Native

demands and determination. Aboriginal negotiators were influenced by the concepts of relationship and reciprocity. The first meant that they sought assurances of peace and protection from the Crown; some, such as the Plains chief Big Bear, explicitly rejected any notion of Canada's sovereignty, at least until starvation forced him into treaty in 1882. Treaty 6 represents the most fully realized concept of a relationship between Canada and Natives that would protect the latter. This treaty provided assurances of government aid in the event of 'pestilence' or 'famine,' as well as a 'medicine chest.'

For Aboriginal negotiators, achieving a reciprocal pact meant that they got something roughly equal in significance to what they were surrendering. They were giving up the exclusive control and utilization of a large territory, a land base that sustained them. Surely reciprocity meant that in return they would acquire new ways to guarantee their livelihood? The desire to have the treaties reciprocally embody means of subsistence led Native leaders to insist upon promises of farming implements, seed, and livestock; ammunition and twine for hunting and fishing; and even schools on reserves that would prepare their offspring to earn a living in ways approximating Euro-Canadian practice. Indeed, many of the most provident features of the numbered treaties resulted from Aboriginal initiative, not government far-sightedness. The same motives on the Native side led to a steady expansion of terms, most notably in the size of reserves promised, or the magnitude of the initial cash and annual payments. Early treaties promised reserves of 160 acres (65 ha) per family of five, for example, but most later ones quadrupled the figure.

At the end of the bargaining day in 1877, Canada attained its territorial objective, but at a far higher price than it had intended to pay. Most Native leaders believed they had secured their chief goal, a formal relationship with the Canadian government, although they had fallen short of other bargaining objectives. Almost as important as what was achieved was the fact that a significant minority of leaders declined to take treaty between 1871 and 1877. Most prominent among the Plains holdouts were Little Pine and Big Bear, important Cree leaders who would be forced into treaty by hardship after the buffalo dwindled away. Part of Big Bear's reason for holding out was his doubt that Ottawa would do what its treaty commissioners promised. By the early 1880s, western Native leaders concluded that Big Bear had been right. Canada's implementation of the treaties was dilatory, niggardly, and legalistic. Native leaders, who had emphasized creating a relationship when they took treaty, were shocked and disheartened by the government's perfidy. When they and their descendants in the twentieth century talked of government violations of 'the spirit' of the treaty, they were alluding to Ottawa's narrow interpretations, pettifogging enforcement, and grudging modifications of the letter of the numbered treaties.

Although negotiating the numbered treaties in the 1870s was an important chapter in the long history of Aboriginal-White relations, it would not be the last. After 1877 the government took the position that it did not want to treat for more land unless and until Euro-Canadian settlers and entrepreneurs demanded access to Native-controlled regions for economic purposes. That was part of the reason why British Columbia remained almost totally out of treaty until 1899, when Treaty 8 embraced its northeast corner. The onset of northern economic development, particularly the discovery of gold in Yukon, led to the negotiation of Treaty 8. Similarly, Treaty 9 in northern Ontario, Treaty 10 in northern Saskatchewan, and Treaty 5(b) in northern Manitoba were concluded in 1905, 1906, and 1908 in response to growing economic interest in the resources of these northlands. The final treaty of this period, Treaty 11, exemplified the point: it was negotiated with the Dene of part of the Northwest Territories in 1921, a year after oil was discovered at Norman Wells. The rest of the country – most of British Columbia, Yukon, part of the Territories, and northern Quebec – would lie outside formal land treaty.

It was appropriate that the treaties of the 1870s promised both 'reserves for farming lands' and implements and livestock with which to farm, because the phase that followed treaty-making was dominated by a complex of measures known as 'the policy of the Bible and the plough.' As the phrase implies, the policy led to a mix of programs that relied heavily on missionary bodies and aimed at converting Aboriginal people into self-sufficient individuals who would earn their living in ways similar to, and compatible with, those of Euro-Canadians. While the immediate source of this policy was the need to develop programs for Natives on the Prairies and in British Columbia, many of its provisions were extended to First Nations throughout the country. And the most pervasive feature of post-Confederation policy was its assimilationist purpose. As the Indian Affairs Branch put it in 1871, it aimed 'to lead the Indian people by degrees to mingle with the white race in the ordinary avocations of life.'

Continuity between pre- and post-Confederation practice surfaced in the 1869 Gradual Enfranchisement Act. This statute, which applied to Indians in the central provinces only, retained the Gradual Civilization Act's provisions for voluntary enfranchisement. However, it also restricted the definition of 'Indian' status by introducing the notion of a 'blood quantum' or minimum percentage – in this case 25 per cent – Aboriginal heritage, and it introduced an ominous novelty: an attack on Native self-government. The 'blood quantum' remained a criterion of status for only a short time, but the assault on Native governance proved enduring. The 1869 Act allowed government to 'order that the Chiefs of any tribe, band or body of Indians shall be elected,' and potentially to remove 'life Chiefs ... for dishonesty, intemperance or immorality.' These vague criteria were to be interpreted, of course, by federal bureaucrats and politicians.

The governance provisions of the 1869 Enfranchisement Act would remain a core element in federal Indian policy for over a century, but the provisions concerning elective political institutions over time would become more coercive. In the first Indian Act (1876), the federal government broadened its self-bestowed power to depose hereditary chiefs, 'for dishonesty, intemperance, immorality, or incompetency.' An 1880 amendment empowered officials to impose an elected band council on a community whether it wanted European-style electoral procedures or not. More serious still was the Indian Advancement Act of 1884, which expanded somewhat the list of municipal-style powers a band council could have, but authorized Ottawa to depose chiefs whom federal officials considered unfit or unable to discharge their duties. The potentially oppressive provisions of the Advancement Act became a permanent part of federal policy when they were integrated into the Indian Act of 1906. More short-lived was the clause of the general Franchise Act of 1885 that extended the right to vote in federal elections to adult male Indians east of Lake Superior. Enacted by Macdonald over vociferous Liberal objections, this provision was not widely used, and was eliminated in 1898 by the Laurier government.

As significant as the governance provisions were, they were only one part of a broad phalanx of initiatives. Central to the overall policy of the Bible and the plough was the concept of enfranchisement, which would remain part of the Indian Act beyond 1927. Here, as in the governance and other provisions, what novelty crept in during revisions lay in the direction of greater restriction and coercion. The 1869 Enfranchisement Act, for example, strengthened the gender discrimination inherent in the definition of 'Indian' by providing that a female with

Indian status who married a male without status, whether non-Native or simply non-status Indian, would lose her status forever. So, too, would her children and descendants. This discriminatory provision would remain a part of Canadian law until 1985. Another coercive attempt to foist enfranchisement on selected males did not last long. The original Indian Act conferred automatic enfranchisement on any man who graduated from university or entered one of the liberal professions such as law or religion. This measure was removed in the amending Act of 1880, but educated males and members of the professions remained eligible for voluntary automatic enfranchisement. All these provisions had a consistent thread: they sought to whittle down the number of 'Indians,' whether by marriage outside the community, voluntary enfranchisement, or loss of status through advanced education. Indian policy, in other words, aimed at converting 'Indians' into citizens by the dubious legal mechanism of enfranchisement.

Other aspects of the policy of the Bible and the plough, such as schools and measures to attack Aboriginal cultural and spiritual traditions, had the same goal of reducing the number of 'Indians' by assimilation. Missionaries in Upper Canada had emphasized schooling as an assimilation mechanism since the 1820s; in 1846 they and the Indian Department added a type of residential school known as a manual labour school. These institutions, like predecessors in seventeenth-century New France and late eighteenth-century New Brunswick, had invariably proven futile. The problem was that Native peoples, though often wanting their young to learn skills in Euro-Canadian schools, rejected efforts to assimilate their children and took exception to the schools' failure to look after their offspring adequately in residential institutions. In spite of this record, Canada proceeded to re-enact most of the earlier failures from 1883 on. Most of the numbered treaties promised a 'school on reserve,' but government and Christian missionaries believed the on-reserve institutions inadequate both because they were plagued by poor attendance and because they were not effective as instruments of cultural assimilation.

As a consequence of this thinking, Ottawa enunciated a policy in 1883 that stressed what it called 'industrial schools.' These facilities would be operated by the missionary bodies and funded for the most part by the Department of Indian Affairs, which had been set up in 1880. The industrial schools were to train children in trades such as carpentry, blacksmithing, and shoemaking, as well as more modest pursuits such as farming for boys and domestic skills for girls. Both in classroom and workshop these schools, like contemporary educational institutions of all kinds, were gendered landscapes in which males were prepared for gainful employment outside the home and females were trained to manage the domestic sphere. The gendered approach to schooling was as prominent in the day schools, which continued to receive inadequate funding from Indian Affairs, as it was in the residential schools.

Between 1883 and 1923 an extensive school system developed. Industrial schools increased in number after the creation of the first three in the Territories in 1883, but the smaller boarding schools continued as well, and both types coexisted with numerous on-reserve day schools. Although the industrial school system was aimed initially at the Prairie region, it quickly spread to British Columbia and Ontario. In the latter case, it was largely a matter of declaring existing schools, such as the Shingwauk Home in Sault Ste Marie, to be industrial establishments. However, in the early twentieth century new industrial schools were created, particularly in northern and northwestern Ontario. With the exception of the southern shore of James Bay, no residential schools were created in Quebec until the middle of the twentieth century. Similarly, Maritime Canada did not have a modern Native residential school until the opening of Shubenacadie, Nova Scotia, in 1929. Residential schools were not provided in the east because missionaries and bureaucrats assumed that those Natives who lived near Euro-Canadians were sufficiently acculturated not to need custodial institutions, while groups such as the Cree and Inuit in northern Quebec were still making a living by traditional means until well into the twentieth century.

Throughout the country, the number of industrial and boarding schools grew until, at the height of the system's development in the 1920s, there were eighty such operations. Approximately three-fifths were run by the Oblates, Jesuits (one institution), and several organizations of female religious such as the Sisters of Charity, Grey Nuns, and Sisters of Saint Ann. Anglicans operated about one-quarter, while Methodists and Presbyterians were in charge of the remainder. Geographically the residential schools were concentrated in northwestern Ontario, the Prairie region, British Columbia, and the Territories. For administrative purposes, the separate categories of 'industrial' and 'boarding' schools were amalgamated under the heading of 'residential schools' by Ottawa in 1923. As significant as residential schools were, they never housed more than a minority – probably one-third – of status Indian children down to the 1950s.

Even though their coverage was only partial, residential schools had a devastatingly negative impact. The institutions wreaked havoc principally for two reasons: aggressively assimilative practices and inadequate care. For both missionaries and bureaucrats, their primary aim was to convert Indian children to Euro-Canadian ways of life and methods of earning a living. In pursuit of that goal, school operators denigrated Aboriginal culture, usually combatting any use of a Native language aggressively, and tried to force Christian views and values on their charges. Often the assimilative program took precedence over both the academic and vocational training provided, with the result that residential school products were inadequately equipped to compete with Euro-Canadians. In recognition of these deficiencies, the Department scaled back the educational objectives of the schools in 1910, thus reducing their utility. In fact, the failure of residential schools to provide useful instruction to their children caused many parents to reject the institutions.

Parental opposition to residential schools grew as well because they were extremely dangerous places for young children. Diet and other aspects of care were inadequate, the staff were often either too few or ill-trained, the workload on children too heavy, and disease and death were ever-present dangers. The fact that the schools operated on a half-day system in which students spent half their time in the classroom and the other half in work opened the way to excessive demands for child labour, while impairing academic learning. In addition to these shortcomings, many schools harboured brutal workers who victimized children in numerous ways. The most common problem was pervasive use of excessive corporal punishment. As well, children of tender years found no emotional support in institutions governed by rules. Finally, there were instances of sexual abuse, both of student against fellow student and of staff against the children under their care.

The damage caused by Ottawa's schooling initiative, especially residential schools, was also evident in other elements of the policy of the Bible and the plough. Again, the principal targets of measures designed to discourage and suppress Aboriginal cultural and spiritual traditions were Natives in British Columbia and the Prairie provinces. In 1884, in response to demands from missionaries and some Native converts, the Indian Act was amended to outlaw the potlatch, the sharing ceremony that was central to North West Coast First Nations. In 1895, when the initial measure to suppress the potlatch proved unenforceable, the federal government amended the law to be more specific. At the same time, the law broadened the definition of rituals that were prohibited to include some Prairie summer ceremonials such as the Sun Dance of the Blackfoot and the Thirst Dance of the Cree and Saulteaux. The 1895 measure ostensibly meant to limit potentially dangerous practices such as piercing the body during Prairie ceremonials. The fact that the amendment also outlawed any sharing or giving away of property made it clear that Aboriginal values and communal bonds were under attack. The measures against the potlatch and Prairie dance ceremonials were also difficult to enforce; on the Pacific coast, enforcement was sporadic, though sometimes spectacular. The arrest in 1922 of fifty-eight Kwagiulth potlatchers, and the seizure of a vast quantity of ceremonial regalia, provides the clearest example of how disruptive the measure could be. In the Prairie region, enforcement of the 1895 ban on summer dancing was more extensive and persistent, but the prohibition never succeeded in extirpating the practice, though it sometimes created a climate of fear and resentment. The ban on the potlatch and Prairie dancing would be repealed in the 1951 revision of the Indian Act.

It was no coincidence that the industrial schools policy and the potlatch ban both took shape in the mid-1880s. This period, in fact, saw a hardening of attitudes towards Native peoples and increasing resort to coercion. To some degree, this harsher atmosphere resulted from the Northwest Rebellion of 1885; certainly bureaucrats became more willing to use coercion in their dealings with Native peoples after the Métis rising. However, the Rebellion was more excuse than reason, for only a tiny minority of First Nations communities took up arms, and these few usually were cases of hard-pressed young men resorting to violence in the heat of the moment. Nonetheless, the Rebellion gave rise to one of the most notorious elements of Indian Affairs policy. As an emergency measure, the Department in May 1885 prohibited Prairie Indians from being off their reserve without the permission of the Indian agent. The restriction persisted after the cessation of hostilities, becoming known as the pass system. Since the pass system had no legal basis, and since the Mounted Police refused to enforce it after 1892, it is not clear how effective it was or even how long Indian Affairs tried to use it.

The pass system was part of an arsenal of weapons used by Ottawa in its efforts to control and reshape Native behaviour, especially on the Prairies. A particularly pernicious example could be found in ill-advised policies supposedly intended to 'encourage' the development of agriculture among Plains peoples who became destitute after the collapse of the buffalo economy. Officially, Indian Affairs attempted to assist these groups to make the transition to agriculture by supplying them with livestock and equipment, by providing agricultural instructors, and, briefly in the 1880s, by operating demonstration farms near reserves where Indians could observe the successful operation of a Euro-Canadian farm. Unfortunately, the reality was disheartening. Often equipment and other necessities were supplied dilatorily, if at all. Many of the farming instructors had little knowledge of local conditions and the climatic challenges of dryland farming. Nor were the demonstration farms especially helpful, for instructors often preferred to operate these tracts on their own, without making an effort to explain agricultural practices to would-be farmers.

Between 1889 and 1897, while Hayter Reed was influential in Indian Affairs, western reserve agricultural policy was particularly pernicious and damaging. Ottawa had already adopted a so-called severalty policy, mimicking the American Dawes or Allotment Scheme, that encouraged the subdivision of communal reserves into individual plots. Theoretically, individual ownership would encourage entrepreneurship and effort; in reality, reserve farmers frustrated the scheme by ignoring the policy. Since the severalty plan required at least minimal cooperation from bands, Native non-compliance effectively defeated it. However, Reed, first as commissioner (1888–93) and then deputy minister (1893–7), imposed another of his schemes, 'peasant farming,' on some western reserves. The peasant farming policy, which was based on current theories of social evolution, held that Plains peoples must move from migratory hunting through peasant or subsistence farming before they could emerge into large-scale commercial farming that employed modern machinery. Accordingly, they were required to sow seed by hand, cut their grain with sickles rather than mechanized reapers, and extract the valuable grain from chaff with flails rather than mechanical harvesters.

The influence of Indian Affairs in local communities usually prevented implement dealers from selling such equipment, and the fact that the Indian Act made it impossible to mortgage reserve land ensured that bands would not be able to borrow to purchase modern equipment. (A permit system that required reserve farmers to get written authorization from the Indian agent before taking their crop to market also made it difficult to obtain cash.) Indeed, there is reason to believe that opposition from non-Native farmers to what they called 'subsidized competition' for limited local markets was a powerful motive for Ottawa's attempts down to 1897 to pursue the peasant farming folly. While no systematic analysis of this ill-starred policy throughout the Prairies exists, a detailed study of Treaty 4 suggests persuasively that the frustrations of peasant farming visited on reserve farmers pushed many communities back into apathy and dependence on government rations just as immigration and settlement were beginning to make reserve lands valuable. The conjunction of the apparent failure of reserve agriculture and an influx of settlers meant that parcels of reserve land were obtained by a variety of means, many of them unconscionable if not illegal, by Indian Affairs to respond to the demand for land. The effect of misguided developmental policies such as peasant farming was to render most western reserves pockets of hardship rather than sites of development.

As severalty and peasant farming illustrate, Native peoples responded in many ways to the attempts to control them politically, reshape them culturally, and mould them economically. While the detailed research that would allow confident generalizations has not yet been carried out, it would appear that while some groups acquiesced to Ottawa's intrusion, many others resisted vigorously. The Mohawk population at Akwesasne (St Regis), for example, opposed with armed resistance the attempts of Indian Affairs to replace their hereditary political structures with elective institutions. Similarly, many Plains people flouted the prohibitions on dancing, just as numerous North West Coast nations adjusted their potlatch or took their observances underground to avoid the prying eyes of missionaries and agents. In schooling, especially residential schools, the patterns were similar. Some groups, such as the White Bear band in Saskatchewan, simply boycotted missionaries and residential schools as part of a strategy of pursuing a traditional way of life that included a mixed economy rather than farming. Other communities gave the appearance of cooperating with missionaries and bureaucrats, although in many cases traditional practices persisted clandestinely.

Whatever successes Native communities had in combatting the policy of the Bible and the plough, it nonetheless had destructive consequences. Even groups that resisted attempts to change them politically, spiritually, and economically were still subject to the demoralizing impact of official censure and Christian denigration. For children who attended residential schools, these psychological blows were probably even stronger than those experienced by their parents. Moreover, the residential schools inflicted a heavy loss of life on the student populations. During the Great War, the deputy minister of Indian affairs acknowledged in writing that up to half of residential school inmates did not live to use the knowledge they acquired in these institutions. As the horrific rates of disease and death in these schools indicate, the policy of the Bible and the plough had serious consequences for Native peoples, even if the individual measures were often ineffective in their original intentions.

As the twentieth century rolled on, Indian Affairs responded to the failure of its policy of cultural transformation with its usual approach of continuity and change. The continuation of obsolete practices was attributable to bureaucratic dimness and missionary opposition to change. For example, as noted earlier, when entrepreneurs became interested in northern resource development, Ottawa responded with treaties that differed little from the measures that had failed in the Prairies. On the other hand, when the Liberal government of Sir Wilfrid Laurier tried by 1910 to phase out some of the worst residential schools and replace them with what it called 'new improved day schools,' the opposition of the Catholics and some non-Catholic missionaries in western Canada made eliminating schools politically impossible. The best that Ottawa could do was insist on better standards for health and care. With minor tinkering, schooling policy would stumble on until new ideological suppositions and improved finances made real change possible after the Second World War.

A novel aspect of government policy in the twentieth century was greater use of coercion, most notably with the land issue in British Columbia. For example, since schools of all kinds did not seem to work the transformations bureaucrats desired, the Indian Act was changed by a series of amendments from 1894 on to create and enforce compulsory attendance. A similar pattern prevailed with the prohibitions on the potlatch and Prairie dancing. Enforcement difficulties constituted one of the reasons why Parliament in 1918 amended the Indian Act to allow agents, who were also magistrates, to deal with breaches of this measure as summary rather than indictable offences. This alteration allowed agents to act as police and judge, avoiding regular courts that could not always be counted on to convict.

However, a more outrageous example of the greater reliance on coercion was found in enfranchisement. Provisions allowing adult males to give up Indian status and become citizens, a core provision of the Indian Act, had consistently failed to produce sufficient enfranchisements. Finally, at the behest of long-serving official Duncan Campbell Scott, the Union government introduced involuntary enfranchisement for selected males in 1920. Status women who married men without

Indian status had lost their status since the 1869 Enfranchisement Act. A few males who achieved higher education and professional status had been at risk of losing their status from 1876 to 1880. Now Ottawa proposed to strip status from any Indian men whom the Department deemed ready for the change. This involuntary enfranchisement clause was repealed two years later after a change of government, but the fact that it was ever on the books reflected the government's exasperation at the failure of its policy. Involuntary enfranchisement would return to the Act in modified form in 1933 and remain until the 1951 revision.

Unthinking continuity and coercive innovation could also be found in Canada's handling of the British Columbia land question. As already noted, very little territory there was covered by treaty during the colonial period, and the terms of union in 1871 required the province to transfer Crown lands to Ottawa 'in trust for the use and benefit of the Indians.' The national government found that even its modest proposals for reserves in British Columbia provoked strenuous opposition from Victoria. Inability to reach agreement on how much land was to be allocated to reserves produced a breakdown by the 1880s, just as First Nations in British Columbia began to protest against incursions on their lands. Ottawa established a commission to draw up boundaries, but numerous meetings with Native groups in the 1880s and 1890s produced little progress, thanks to stubborn provincial opposition.

On the eve of the Great War, the two levels of government, recognizing that further delay would only worsen matters, established a joint royal commission to review the allocations for reserve lands that had already been made. Although many bands hoped that the McKenna-McBride Commission, as it became known, would produce larger allocations, the results of the commission's work represented a setback. When McKenna-McBride reported in 1916, it recommended making about 47,000 acres (19,035 ha) of existing reserve land available to settlers, compensating the bands with approximately 87,000 acres (35,235 ha) that were usually poorly located and less valuable. These menacing recommendations galvanized many of British Columbia's First Nations into combining forces for political action. Indeed, the land question had earlier stimulated political protest by the Squamish, whose chief, Joe Capilano, in 1906 had travelled to London to petition the Crown, and by the Nisga'a, who in 1913 addressed a petition to the Judicial Committee of the Privy Council. In 1916, British Columbia Natives organized the Allied Tribes of British Columbia, a broadly based movement to combat the McKenna-McBride proposals.

The Allied Tribes agitated energetically against McKenna-McBride without much noticeable result, their campaign culminating in an appearance before a parliamentary committee investigating the question in 1926. Despite their best efforts, the parliamentarians in 1927 rejected their case and confirmed the McKenna-McBride recommendations. The aftermath of this phase of the land question in the province was a 1927 amendment of the Indian Act that serves as a fitting conclusion to the long period of attempted tutelage and control. The 1927 revision of the Act outlawed any organizing or raising/giving of funds for pursuing a Native claim. This violation of freedom of association and of natural justice would remain part of the Indian Act until 1951, when, like modified involuntary enfranchisement and the prohibitions of potlatching and Prairie dancing, it was repealed.

As the extraordinary legislation of 1927 illustrates, in the half-century after Confederation policy moved steadily in the direction of increasing interference, attempted political control, and coercive efforts to transform Native peoples culturally and economically. The few initiatives attempted in the period, such as western treaty-making, were inadequately implemented, and government often persisted with them, as in the North, in spite of their obvious shortcomings. Policy in the Prairie region, especially during the 'peasant farming' phase, produced little economic benefit and soon became linked with oppressive controls such as the permit and pass systems. Educational policy was as much about cultural change as pedagogy, and its implementation in residential institutions caused a great deal of harm. Particularly after 1885, government officials increased their coercion and interference. Policies directed at Métis represented an exception, an aberration really, to this generalization. For a time in the 1890s and early 1900s, missionaries tried to promote Métis colonies, particularly in what became the province of Alberta. Soon these initiatives, too, were diverted to the benefit of incoming non-Native settlers. In the 1930s, following recommendations of the Ewing Commission, Alberta would establish ten 'colonies' for Métis, most of which have survived to this day. In the North between Confederation and the Great War, Canada's principal objective was to avoid incurring obligations to the Aboriginal peoples until southerners began to covet their lands. Perhaps the clearest expression of this wilful neglect of northern peoples was Ottawa's attempt to shirk constitutional responsibility for the Inuit.

Both the consistent purpose and the changing mood of post-Confederation relations with the Aboriginal peoples were captured in descriptions provided by leading politicians over the years. The Indian Affairs Branch in 1871 explained that Ottawa wanted 'to lead the Indian people by degrees to mingle with the white race in the ordinary avocations of life.' By 1887, an impatient Prime Minister John A. Macdonald put it more bluntly: 'The great aim of our legislation has been to do away with the tribal system and assimilate the Indian people in all respects with the inhabitants of the Dominion, as speedily as they are fit for the change.' By 1920, the deputy minister was even more brutally frank. 'I want to get rid of the Indian problem,' D.C. Scott told a parliamentary committee. 'Our object is to continue until there is not a single Indian in Canada that has not been absorbed into the body politic, and there is no Indian question, and no Indian Department.'

In the half-century after Scott's statement, the Aboriginal communities of Canada would begin to rise, organize, and resist the oppressive and assimilative treatment most of them had experienced since Confederation.

## Note

*Canada and the Aboriginal Peoples, 1867–1927 / Le Canada et les peuples autochtones, 1867–1927,* Canadian Historical Association Booklet 57 (Ottawa: Canadian Historical Association, 1997). Reprinted by permission.

## Sources

The simplest approach to the period is via the appropriate sections of general accounts: Olive P. Dickason, *Canada's First Nations: A History of Founding Peoples from Earliest Times,* 3rd ed. (Toronto: Oxford University Press, 2002; 1st ed., McClelland and Stewart, 1992); J.R. Miller *Skyscrapers Hide the Heavens: A History of Indian-White Relations in Canada,* 3rd. ed. (Toronto: University of Toronto Press [UTP], 2000; 1st ed., 1989); and Arthur J. Ray, *I Have Lived Here since the World Began: An Illustrated History of Canada's Native Peoples* (Toronto: Key Porter, 1996). For policies developed by the federal government and/or Christian missionary bodies, a useful starting point is Noel F. Dyck, *What Is the 'Indian Problem'? Tutelage and Resistance in Canadian Indian Administration* (St John's: Institute of Social and Economic Research, 1991). Also invaluable for its systematic coverage is J. Leslie and R. Maguire, *The Historical Development of the Indian Act,* 2nd ed. (Ottawa: Treaties and Historical Research Centre, Indian and Northern Affairs Canada, 1978; 1st ed., 1975). More tightly focused studies can also be helpful. For example, E. Brian Titley's *A Narrow Vision: Duncan Campbell Scott and the Administration of Indian Affairs in Canada* (Vancouver: University of British Columbia Press [UBCP], 1986) provides a good overview of the assumptions behind and components of policy from the 1880s to the 1930s. Next to general accounts the most useful sources are regional overviews.

Regional surveys that provide excellent coverage of Aboriginal issues are Jean Barman, *The West beyond the West: A History of British Columbia* (Toronto: UTP, 1991) and Gerald Friesen, *The Canadian Prairies: A History* (Toronto: UTP, 1984). Within the theme of Native and non-Native relations, the best regional treatments are Ken S. Coates, *'Best Left As Indians': Native-White Relations in the Yukon Territory, 1840–1973* (Kingston and Montreal: McGill-Queen's University Press [MQUP], 1991) and Kerry Abel, *Drum Songs: Glimpses of Dene History* (Kingston and Montreal: MQUP, 1993). For British Columbia, the latter chapters of Robin Fisher's *Contact and Conflict: Indian-European Relations in British Columbia, 1774–1890*, 2nd ed. (Vancouver: UBCP, 1992; 1st ed., 1977) cover the post-1867 period. Some of the same themes are continued by Paul Tennant in *Aboriginal Peoples and Politics: The Indian Land Question in British Columbia 1849–1989* (Vancouver: UBCP, 1990). Unfortunately, Central and Atlantic regions are not as well covered as the West and the North. However, an interesting starting point is Ruth Holmes Whitehead's *The Old Man Told Us: Excerpts from Micmac History, 1500–1950* (Halifax: Nimbus, 1991), and there are insights amidst the polemic in Daniel N. Paul, *We Were Not the Savages: A Micmac Perspective on the Collision of European and Aboriginal Civilization* (Halifax: Nimbus, 1993).

With specialized works, again, the coverage is better for the West than elsewhere. Economic development is considered in Sarah Carter, *Lost Harvests: Prairie Indian Reserve Farmers and Government Policy* (Kingston and Montreal: MQUP, 1990) and Helen Buckley's broader *From Wooden Ploughs to Welfare: Why Indian Policy Failed in the Prairie Provinces* (Kingston and Montreal: MQUP, 1992). For the campaign against the potlatch, see Douglas Cole and Ira Chaikin, *An Iron Hand upon the People: The Law against the Potlatch on the Northwest Coast* (Vancouver: Douglas and McIntyre, 1990), while the assault on Prairie dancing is best examined in Katherine Pettipas, *Severing the Ties That Bind: Government Repression of Indigenous Religious Ceremonies on the Prairies* (Winnipeg: University of Manitoba Press, 1994). A detailed history of residential schooling is J.R. Miller, *Shingwauk's Vision: A History of Native Residential Schools* (Toronto: UTP, 1996). Further guidance can be found in the chapter on 'Native History' in Doug Owram, ed., *Canadian History: A Reader's Guide*, Vol. 2, *Confederation to the Present* (Toronto: UTP, 1994), 179–201, as well as in Robert J. Surtees, *Canadian Indian Policy: A Critical Bibliography* (Bloomington: Indiana University Press for the Newberry Library, 1982).

# The State, the Church, and Indian Residential Schools in Canada

It was a big day for Grace Lavallé. She was selected to meet and be photographed with Louis St Laurent, Canada's prime minister, when he visited her residential school at Lebret, Saskatchewan.[1] Such ceremonial visits were common at the Oblate residential school in the Qu'Appelle Valley, which was easily accessible by rail and road from Regina. On numerous occasions when officials visited residential schools, an elaborate display of amity and cooperation between church and government occurred, for such visits were as much about public relations and promotion of the interests of the Department of Indian Affairs as they were about highlighting the accomplishments of students such as Grace.[2] These carefully orchestrated visits also reinforced the impression that Native residential schools were a harmonious and productive combination of throne and altar for the benefit of both Aboriginal peoples and Canadian society.

While the residential schools that existed in Canada from the 1880s to the 1970s are fairly described in most historical literature as a partnership between the state and the church, within the relationship of throne and altar there were both tensions and differences of emphasis that produced some interesting side effects. Such cross-currents in church-state relations were a feature that Canadian mission schools and their American counterparts shared, although in the United States cooperation of government and churches had been much more short-lived than it was north of the border. And even in Canada the apparent partnership of missionary and bureaucrat that formed the implicit background to the photograph of a grinning Grace Lavallé and a benignly smiling prime minister masked important differences in objectives, and sometimes also in outcomes.

Although these residential schools existed as a state creation from 1883 to Ottawa's decision to terminate them in 1969, there was also a 'prehistory' to the story of residential schooling that stretched back to seventeenth-century New France, with important developments in late eighteenth-century New Brunswick and mid-nineteenth-century Ontario.[3] In this earlier period, leadership was almost invariably provided by Christian missionaries, whether Jesuits and Ursulines in New France or New England Company and Methodists in British North America. In the prehistorical period of residential schooling, Christianity often looked in vain for encouragement and support from the state. Consequently, when the Dominion of Canada turned in the 1870s to the development of a schooling policy for the 'Indians' for whom it had constitutional responsibility, there were missionary precedents and ongoing missionary-run boarding schools in Ontario, the Prairies, and British Columbia.[4]

The immediate inspiration of the Aboriginal educational policy that emerged in the 1880s were the seven treaties that Canada signed between 1871 and 1877 with the First Nations of northwestern Ontario and the Prairies. Since each of these pacts contained a clause obligating the Dominion to provide schooling for the Aboriginal groups, Ottawa was induced to begin a leisurely search for a means of implementing its commitment. Following investigation of American schooling experiments, in particular the famous institution conducted by Captain Richard Pratt in Carlisle, Pennsylvania, the Department of Indian Affairs in 1883 created the first three of what it styled industrial schools in what are now Alberta and Saskatchewan. These initiatives joined and coexisted with a number of small boarding schools that operated under Roman Catholic, Anglican, New England Company, Methodist, and Presbyterian auspices, and in the 1890s the burgeoning system spread to British Columbia. Between 1883 and 1923 the Department of Indian Affairs sponsored both industrial and boarding schools, but in the latter year they were amalgamated into a single category, residential schools, in recognition of the reality that meaningful distinctions between the ambitious industrial and the modest boarding schools had withered to insignificance. At its height in the 1920s the Canadian residential school system totalled eighty institutions, but persistent shortcomings and growing Indian opposition led as early as the 1940s to government efforts to wind the system down, and ultimately in 1969 to a decision to eliminate the remainder of the schools.

Although American practice had definitely had an influence on the

creation of industrial schools in 1883, there was an important difference between residential educational facilities north and south of the
international border. In Canada, all the residential schools were operated on the government's behalf by Christian church bodies, leading to
their usually being described, as noted, as a partnership between
throne and altar. In part this arrangement was motivated by racist ideology and in part by parsimony. As Prime Minister Sir John A. Macdonald explained, 'secular education is a good thing among white men
but among Indians the first object is to make them better men, and, if
possible, good Christian men by applying proper moral restraints ...'[5]
Besides, as the man commissioned by the government to recommend a
school policy after treaty-making had argued, it would be cruel to
deprive Indians of 'their simple Indian mythology' without putting
Christianity in its place. To him it was obvious that 'missionary teachers were essential. The advantage of calling in the aid of religion is,
that there is a chance of getting an enthusiastic person, with, therefore,
a motive power beyond anything pecuniary remuneration could supply.'[6] Cheaper, too, of course.

   In the United States, in contrast, although the churches had a role in
the operation of Indian boarding schools in the latter decades of the
nineteenth century, they were largely eliminated from the field by the
twentieth. From the 1870s until 1900, the Bureau of Indian Affairs supported what were termed 'contract schools,' church-run Indian schools
that existed along with its own day and boarding institutions, by
granting land and funds for construction of the school, and by paying
the missionary body an annual per capita grant for operating expenses.
However, the contract schools became unpopular among American
Protestants, especially as Roman Catholic missionaries availed themselves of the program enthusiastically, and Congress decided to end
contracting in 1897.[7] Although American missionaries continued to
participate in schooling for Native Americans well into the twentieth
century, they never enjoyed the government approval or reliance that
marked the Canadian experience. State dominance and greater distance between government and church were features of the American
approach that were alien to Canada.

   In other respects, though, there were important similarities between
the American and Canadian systems of residential schooling for
Native children. In terms of their day-to-day operation, none was more
important than the 'half-day system' that Captain Pratt had pioneered
at Carlisle and that Canadian schools followed until the 1950s. In fact,

the Upper Canadian pre-Confederation experience with residential schooling had also included this system. As the term suggests, the half-day system meant that most residential school students spent half the day in the classroom receiving academic instruction and the other half working in kitchens, barns, fields, or workshops at tasks whose theoretical purpose was vocational instruction, but whose real *raison d'être* was the subsidization of the operation of the schools. One of the early champions of residential schools, Methodist public school pioneer Egerton Ryerson, had even allowed himself to hope before Confederation that 'with judicious management, these establishments will be able in the course of a few years very nearly to support themselves' thanks to student labour.[8] The half-day system, which was eliminated in the more prosperous mid- and late-1950s in Canada, was the source of many ills: overwork, insufficient classroom instruction, and physical mistreatment at the hands of impatient supervisors.

The other negative feature that Canadian and American schools shared was their denigration of Aboriginal culture and their persistent attempts to assimilate the Native child. Products of the nineteenth century, an era notorious for Euro-American intolerance towards non-White peoples and for virulent theories of Caucasian racial superiority, residential schools were thoroughly imbued with a desire to replace Aboriginal identity, belief, and practice with attitudes and behaviour associated with non-Native communities. In Canada, this was merely the pedagogical manifestation of the thoroughly racist assumptions and objectives that framed all of the state's policy towards the indigenous peoples.[9] The heart of Canadian Indian policy, codified in the Indian Act in 1876 and maintained through innumerable amendments for over a century, was a program chillingly and accurately described by an American Bureau of Indian Affairs official: 'the extinction of the Indians *as Indians* is the ultimate end' of Canadian Indian policy.[10]

Canadian policy, ironically, began by defining some Aboriginal people as separate and distinct. In Canadian law, 'Indian' was a legal category administered by the Department of Indian Affairs, admission to which was determined by the government of Canada. The irony arises from the fact that the definition was made solely for the purpose of identifying who was to be encouraged, tutored, and, if necessary, coerced to exchange the status of 'Indian' for the title of citizen. At the heart of Canadian policy was a procedure known as enfranchisement, by which educated and acculturated 'Indians' would apply and qualify for citizenship, necessitating their loss of 'Indian' status and the removal of a share of reserve land in a freehold grant to the new citizen. And, of course, it was to tutor and encourage young Native people to aspire to and qualify for enfranchisement that Indian schooling in general, and residential schools in particular, existed. Although U.S. policy lacked the concept and practice of enfranchisement, principally because American judicial treatment of Native Americans had been different, residential schools in both countries discountenanced Native ways and promoted Euro-American belief and practice.[11] Schools in both countries, unfortunately, were institutions that denigrated things Aboriginal and exalted everything deemed to be Christian and European.

Although in Canada church and state both appeared to subscribe to a thoroughly assimilative program in the residential schools, a project that was only a portion of the larger campaign for the extinction of the Indians *as Indians*, below the surface there was less than unanimity in the aims and practices of the two non-Native partners in the residential schooling story. To summarize crudely, Canadian state policy sought the assimilation of First Nations society through its young in residential schools primarily to limit, reduce, and ultimately eliminate the federal government's financial obligations to Native society. On the other hand, missionary bodies, who were not unanimous about the desirability and necessity of coercive assimilation through the schools, viewed residential schooling as a component of a broader approach that sought, first, to convert Indians religiously and, second, to assist Native communities to make the difficult adjustment to coexisting with and thriving alongside a newly dominant Euro-Canadian majority. If Ottawa was motivated by the balance sheet, seeing assimilation as an aid to reducing expenditure, the churches were focused upon the afterlife, while simultaneously working to help their Aboriginal charges survive in this world.

For the government of Canada, in dealing with Aboriginal peoples in general, and with status Indians in residential schools in particular, the bottom line was the bottom line. This governmental fixation on financial considerations was true of schooling policy in two distinct, but related, senses. First, so far as government was concerned, the dominant objective in all its policies was to bring or drive Aboriginal peoples to economic self-sufficiency so as to reduce and end Ottawa's financial obligations. So long as status Indians in particular were financially vulnerable, the federal government, which had constitutional responsibility for this group, was potentially liable for the wherewithal to maintain them. During the immediate post-treaty years in the Prairie region, the time and place that gave rise to an industrial schools policy in 1883, this was more than a potentiality, because the total collapse of the bison-based economy by 1879 had devastated the Plains nations. The Department of Indian Affairs (DIA), which was established in 1880, constantly worked to reduce expenditure on the 'wards' for whom it had responsibility, in part because non-Native society did not value Aboriginal peoples very highly and in part because their advancing weakness militarily and politically meant they were no longer regarded as a threat. Residential schools, and DIA schools in general, were expected swiftly to bring Aboriginal communities to a sufficiently acculturated level that Indians would apply for enfranchisement under the Indian Act. Schooling would lead to enfranchisement, which would reduce the number of 'Indians' and the extent of reserve land, eventually rubbing out Ottawa's constitutionally based financial liability for 'Indians and lands reserved for the Indians.'[12]

The second way in which a bottom-line mentality shaped the approach of Indian Affairs to residential schools was that the same thinking caused the Department constantly to look for ways to hold down governmental spending on the operation of the institutions. That thinking was the major underpinning of the half-day system by which residential schools operated from the 1880s to the 1950s, much to the detriment of the health and learning of the students, for the system both reduced the students' time in class and shifted some of the burden of maintaining the schools onto their backs. Similarly, the federal government frequently looked for ways to hold down its contribution to the schools' operation. As early as 1892, for example, it cajoled and strong-armed reluctant missionaries to shift the financing of both industrial and boarding schools from a line-budget basis to a per capita system. The change meant that henceforth school administrators would have to manage on the revenue they derived from approved enrolment, rather than being able to call on the government to make good their expenditures on an authorized set of services and goods. Ottawa's rationale for shifting from the latter to the former basis of financing residential schooling was brutally clear: 'When the whole cost of the Institutions is borne by the Government it follows that the same economy is not used as would be employed under other conditions; demands are made for articles of outfit, and for supplies which, if the outlay was covered by a grant, would be found unnecessary; and employees are engaged who would be dispensed with if the payment of their wages formed a direct charge against the per capita grant.'[13]

The consequences of this shift in funding were enormous: more work for students, poorer facilities and supplies, and the admission of unhealthy recruits for the revenue they would bring, no matter the danger they posed to other students in the schools.

The same governmental attitudes that brought the per capita system into effect in 1892–3 led to periodic reductions in funding at moments of financial stringency. Behind the reductions in the per capita grant during the Great War, Great Depression, and Second World War was the simple fact that Indian Affairs and Indians were not very important politically in Ottawa. When cuts had to be made, the weakest and most vulnerable in Canadian society – Indian children – were forced to bear the worst of them. Although these cuts were restored – often after ferocious, united lobbying by the normally competitive churches – while they were in operation, they caused enormous problems for missionary bodies as well as residential school students. It is fair to say that financial matters were the single greatest and most frequent irritant between missionaries and government throughout the existence of the schools. Government regularly attempted to offload more of the cost of the schools on students and missionaries. The latter absorbed some of the cost through increased contributions by their non-Native adherents, but there were very definite limits to how deep congregations, especially in the non-Catholic churches, were willing to dig to support Native missions and residential schools. As the twentieth century wore on, enthusiasm for these missions and schools ebbed, particularly in the United Church, to a lesser extent in the Anglican communion, and least of all among Roman Catholics. When the government began moving from segregated, largely residential, schooling to an emphasis on 'integrated' schooling – significantly, for financial as well as ideological reasons – after 1945, it was only the Catholics who resisted the move strongly.[14]

Government utilized and appreciated the missionaries' work in the residential schools, but largely for instrumental reasons that were not congruent with the aims that motivated the evangelists. Christian missionaries were desirable as teachers and childcare workers from the government's point of view because ethical instruction was as important as secular learning for Native children and because missionaries could be induced to work more cheaply than non-evangelists. Both these ideas, as noted earlier, had been articulated by founders of the industrial schools in the nineteenth century. Prime Minister Macdonald had said that Indians required instruction by missionaries because 'moral restraints' were what they needed to become 'good Christian men.'[15] Edgar Dewdney, an Indian Affairs official and later cabinet minister, in 1884 argued that the Indian child 'must receive one spiritual training unhampered by any other influence' because otherwise instruction would lower, rather than elevate, the youth.[16] The assumption behind these beliefs, an assumption shared by missionaries and politicians, was that moral weakness, rather than intellectual deficiency, was the principal obstacle to success in Native schooling. 'The Indian problem,' the Department's annual report contended, 'exists owing to the fact that the Indian is untrained to take his place in the world. Once teach him to do this, and the solution is had.'[17] A Presbyterian inquiry early in the twentieth century pinpointed what type of teaching was required: 'His failure in life is not because he is intellectually dull but because of moral weakness.'[18] Another Prairie evangelist agreed that 'moral strength is the element in their natures that is so lacking.'[19]

Besides striving to inculcate this moral strength, missionaries worked cheaply. There were several reasons for this welcome phenomenon. Among the Roman Catholics, clerical celibacy and large numbers of female religious who had taken vows of poverty and chastity ensured that school workers did not have families who had to be housed and fed, and that the workers themselves would accept minimal remuneration. Among Christian missionaries in general, the evangelical motivation that had brought them into 'the work,' as it was usually termed, ensured that they would not expect the same rates of pay that workers in similar lines elsewhere were getting. As the report that Macdonald's government had commissioned in the late 1870s expressed the point: 'The advantage of calling in the aid of religion is, that there is a chance of getting an enthusiastic person, with, therefore, a motive power beyond anything pecuniary remuneration could supply. The work requires not only the energy but the patience of an enthusiast.'[20] From Ottawa's perspective, religion was important in the residential schools for both pedagogical and financial reasons.

From the missionary's viewpoint, such thinking was short-sighted: evangelists saw the primary purpose of the schools as Christian conversion. Indeed, on the missionaries' part, the primacy of evangelization was a consistent and long-standing feature of their multi-denominational labours in Canada. From the days of New France, through the broadening campaign that developed in the nineteenth century, until the 1960s at least, persuading Aboriginal peoples to abandon their animistic worldview and practices in favour of Christianity, whether Catholic or Protestant, had always been the primary motivating aspiration of the thousands who volunteered for 'the work,' whether in schools, missions, or hospitals. The inner proselytizing pulse that made Christianity such a revolutionary force in the world was captured in the biblical Great Commission: 'Go ye into all the world, and preach the gospel to every creature.'[21] Whether the clerical revolutionaries were Jesuits, Church Missionary Society laymen, Sisters of Saint Ann, or Methodist saddlebag preachers, all were animated at some level by this injunction. And it was pursuit of that goal – conversion of Aboriginal society through the Christian schooling of their young – that was the first objective of those who served in residential schools in Canada.

Where Christian missionaries varied was in the details of their methods. Did religious conversion require cultural assimilation? This had been a matter of debate since seventeenth-century New France, although in nineteenth-century Canada evangelists moved towards a consensus in their answer. In New France the first male missionary order, the Récollets, had believed francization was an essential precondition to conversion, but their successors, the more experienced Society of Jesus, eventually came round to the viewpoint 'that the best mode of Christianizing them was to avoid Frenchifying them.'[22] Early nineteenth-century missionaries, both Roman Catholic and Protestant, were much more ambivalent about the notion that conversion required a cultural transformation.

This ambivalence came through most clearly in the language practices and policies that the missionaries of this era followed in their work with Native communities. In the first half of the nineteenth century, at least, all the major denominations utilized Native languages in their missions, including the schools. The Church Missionary Society (CMS), evangelical standard-bearer for the Church of England, followed a 'native church policy' that aimed at the indigenization of Christianity by adapting the new religion to the culture of the foreign field, rather than the reverse. In keeping with this approach, male missionaries were expected by the CMS to learn the Native language that prevailed in the mission field. The CMS missionary who learned Swahili or Ojibwa as part of his early duties was under instructions to promote Native advancement to ordination and control of the mission.[23] The Methodists, too, most notably in Upper Canada before 1850 but also in their labours in the prairie West, had missionaries who learned and used the Native languages in their work. Names like James Evans and McDougall, both George and John, were and are synonymous with facility in Aboriginal languages and customs. As John McDougall once put it in the columns of the *Christian Guardian*, he had 'held service in the schoolhouse, and had the privilege of preaching the glorious Gospel to an earnest people in the "language wherein they were born," which, after all, is the only way to reach the hearts and thoughts of any congregation.'[24] The Jesuits who returned to British North America in the early 1840s, and the Oblates who came a bit later to share the labours in the Catholic mission field, similarly regarded mastery of the language of the Aboriginal group to whom they ministered as their first assignment. Like the Methodists, Church Missionary Society workers, and Jesuits, the Oblates became famous for the facility in Aboriginal languages of some of their missionaries.[25]

Although this missionary proclivity for Native languages did not represent a culturally relativist stance towards Aboriginal communities, it was noticeably different from the post-Confederation governmental attitude. Instructions to indigenize the missionary congregation did not obliterate the assumptions of cultural and racial superiority with which many Englishmen and Canadians came to the evangelical work, and willingness to adopt and employ Aboriginal languages did not imply acceptance of Native peoples' religious beliefs and social customs. Moreover, as will be noted later, missionary openness to Aboriginal languages declined during the late nineteenth and early twentieth centuries. All the same, the existence, however temporarily and however attenuated, of a willingness to make use of Native languages the better to convert was evidence that missionaries placed much greater emphasis on religious motives – evangelization for its own sake – than did the state.

The second most important missionary motive, assisting Native people with economic adjustment, was one on which there was congruence, not just between state and church, but also between those Native groups that desired schooling and the non-Native partners in residential schooling. Among Aboriginal leaders, from Peter Jones and Shinguakonce in Upper Canada to the pro-treaty Plains chiefs like Ahtakakoop and Mistawasis in 1876 to leaders who appeared before the Special Joint Committee on the Indian Act in the 1940s and told the parliamentarians, 'Our greatest need to-day is proper education,' there was a consistent theme.[26] Those First Nations leaders who favoured Euro-Canadian schooling did so primarily for its practical vocational potential. Missionaries strongly supported this objective, and saw schooling as the most effective means of achieving it expeditiously. Where the evangelists differed from the bureaucrats and politicians in Ottawa was that the missionaries wanted to promote economic adjustment because it was beneficial for Aboriginal communities, while the Ottawans favoured it as much because it would benefit government by reducing financial obligations to Indians. The differing motives that the three parties in residential schooling had for supporting vocational training help to explain the varying levels of attachment to the goal. The federal government always subordinated the training goal to its fixation on economy, most notoriously in the 1930s and 1940s when its policy was to promote manual training in the schools but its Indian Affairs administration never provided funds adequate to enable schools to carry the policy out effectively. Churches were more supportive of practical training than government, but by the inter-war period of the twentieth century they were no longer willing or able to provide the funds to make up the shortfall in government financing.

For First Nations communities, the vocational training aspect of Euro-Canadian schooling was probably its most attractive feature. While their leaders often were ambivalent about the religious or moral component of instruction, they usually recognized that literacy and training in agriculture and trades held the potential to advance their people economically. Such thinking had underlain the views of nineteenth-century Native missionaries such as Peter Jones and Plains treaty negotiators in the 1870s.[27] What all of these leaders, missionary and non-Christian alike, shared was an assumption that vocational and rudimentary academic learning could be acquired in the newcomers' schools without loss of Aboriginal culture and identity. This assumption, of course, proved tragically ill-founded.

In sum, the three parties to residential schooling – Indians, missionaries, and government – had multiple motives for supporting, at times equivocally, residential schools. Sometimes their motives overlapped to a greater or lesser degree; at other times there were divergences between them. State and church agreed on the importance of Christian instruction, though for subtly different reasons. All were in favour of using the schools to provide practical instruction that would equip graduates with work skills that would enable them to thrive in the changing world around them; however, Native communities were regularly frustrated by the failure of their non-Native partners to provide adequate funding to enable the schools to accomplish this goal. The frictions, tensions, and open criticisms that became audible over this aspect of the pedagogical program in the post-1945 period constitute but one of many indicators that the supposed partnership of throne and altar in residential schooling was an uneasy one. Another, similar area that taught the same point was the provision of secondary schooling in the twentieth century. As the need for education beyond the elementary level became ever more obvious by the period of the Second World War, the federal government frustrated its partners by dragging its feet in funding more advanced instruction.[28] The reason was straightforward: the governmental parsimony that had marred residential schooling since at least 1892. The logjam was broken only when the Jesuits and Daughters of the Heart of Mary went ahead on their own and provided limited secondary facilities at their schools at Spanish, Ontario, in 1946.[29]

Another topic that revealed the cross-currents in the apparently smooth relations between church and government in residential schooling was the matter of languages, more particularly Aboriginal languages in the schools. This is a topic that is, invariably and rightly, mentioned in any account of residential schooling. What is much less often remarked is the fact that until well into the twentieth century most missionary bodies did not agree with the government's desire for a complete ban on the use of Native languages. This issue actually arose in the prehistory of the story of residential schools, because the government of the Province of Canada in the 1850s had insisted that the Jesuits stop permitting the use of Ojibwa at its mission and schools on Manitoulin Island.[30] During the period of federally supported residential schooling after 1883, government officials applied heavy pressure on school administrators to force uniform use of English (or French in parts of Quebec after the Second World War). As a note to the 'Programme of Studies' in the 1894 annual report of the Department of Indian Affairs put it, 'Every effort must be made to induce pupils to speak English, and to teach them to understand it; unless they do the whole work of the teacher is likely to be wasted.'[31] Researchers into the history of residential schools are treated to the spectacle of missionaries born and educated in France having to correspond from the field in British Columbia or the Prairies in English with bureaucrats in distant Ottawa. Little wonder that one French Oblate was reported to have complained to an Oblate conference that 'French was spoken in Heaven and that we should therefore learn that language.'[32]

Over time, missionary and bureaucratic attitudes on language became more similar, as Native missions became ideologically closer to

Canadian society in general. So far as the Anglicans were concerned, a major stimulus to this process was the switch of administration of the missions, including schools, from the England-based Church Missionary Society to the Missionary Society of the Church in Canada in the early decades of the twentieth century. So far as Methodists and Presbyterians were concerned, after the pioneering generation of evangelists who went west from Ontario in the middle decades of the nineteenth century, their missionary workers had little interest in languages other than English, including Native languages. Part of the nationalizing process that has been observed at work in the Protestant churches was acquisition of the growing intolerance, including impatience with linguistic diversity, that typified Ontario in particular from the late decades of the nineteenth century onward. And even the Oblates found themselves gravitating away from the use of Native languages, as the priests increasingly paid more attention, particularly in western Canada, to their missions to immigrants from Europe and eastern Canada than to the nearby Native missions and schools in the region. (The Oblates attempted after 1936 to restore an emphasis on Native languages in their Prairie missions.)[33]

Whatever the outlook of later evangelists, most early missionaries were ambivalent about Ottawa's insistence on imposing English on the residential school populations. Isaac Stringer, Anglican bishop of the Yukon, commented in his charge to his Synod in 1915, 'The Indian language is good and serviceable as a medium, but the Government has decided that Indian pupils must be taught English and perhaps that is the best policy in the end.'[34] The Oblate vicar apostolic in the territory of Grouard urged 'My dear Little Friends' who produced a newsletter at Blue Quills School to make more room in your 'Moccasin Telegram' for your 'beautiful Cree language. It is your mother-tongue, so let no other one take its place on your lips and in your heart. Be proud of it. When you speak to Almighty God in your prayers and in your hymns, as well as when you speak and write to your dear parents, use the language that God has given your forefathers, as the most suitable expression of their thoughts and feelings.'[35]

And it was not just in the North that the Roman Catholics, in particular, thumbed their nose at Ottawa's will. The Oblate provincial instructed the clerics at the Lestock School in 1909 that 'il faudrait que les enfants apprennent les prières dans leur langue maternelle; les enfants sauteux en Sauteux, and les enfants Métis français en français.'[36] At Spanish in 1935, the Jesuit principal acceded to his provincial's instruction to resume teaching the children their prayers in Ojibwa, even though he was pretty sure that the policy 'would never meet the approval of the powers-that-be.'[37] And, while twentieth-century Protestant missionaries were less accommodating of Aboriginal languages than the Catholics, some of them clearly made little or no effort to extirpate the indigenous tongue. For example, one of the complaints that the Presbyterian principal reportedly levelled at the farm instructor at the Cecilia Jeffrey School in northwestern Ontario was 'that he could not recollect of one occasion that I had sent a pupil into his office for punishment for talking the Indian language.'[38]

In fact, it was in the praying and working areas of the schools, rather than the classroom, that Native languages were most likely to be heard, especially when the supervisors were themselves Native people. A Mohawk woman from Kahnawake recalled that the girls at the Daughters of the Heart of Mary School at Spanish particularly liked a Native woman classroom teacher and a Native woman laundry supervisor who treated them well.[39] At Wabasca in northern Alberta in 1961, the matron, who was also the wife of the principal, was 'often heard conversing with the children in a steady flow of Cree.'[40] Some school administrators, such as a remarkable principal, Earl Anfield, at the Anglican school at Alert Bay in the 1930s, understood the local Aboriginal language, though he could not speak it, and dealt with the local community partially in their tongue during his tenure.[41] Although the Christian missionaries who operated the residential schools shared many of the ethnocentric attitudes towards Aboriginal peoples that bureaucrats, politicians, and Canadians at large held, their approach to linguistic assimilation was significantly different. In large part because their advocacy of assimilation was diluted by their preference for effective methods of proselytizing and by their close, daily contact with Native students in and around the schools, missionaries often were less oppressive about the use of Aboriginal languages than was the federal government.

Not only did the complex area of language in the residential schools reveal subtle differences of emphasis and approach between the state and its church partners, but the same area yielded ironic consequences. For example, Aboriginal groups who were being subjected to heavy pressure by the Indian agent to abandon traditional practices, such as the Sun Dance, could use the statements of the exceptional courageous missionary, such as John McDougall, who spoke out publicly against such attempts at suppression on grounds of freedom of religion.

Describing the Thirst Dance as 'a religious festival,' McDougall added that 'I altogether fail to see why in these days of our much boasted religious liberty anyone should interfere with a few Indians in the exercise of their faith.'[42] And on another occasion, McDougall charged in a letter to the *Christian Guardian* that attacks on ceremonial dancing were a violation of commitments in the treaties that missionaries such as himself had helped persuade Plains nations to sign in the 1870s.[43]

Denominational competition between the various churches, most acutely in cases pitting a Roman Catholic mission against a non-Catholic one, encouraged some missionaries to be more accommodating of Aboriginal interests and sensibilities than they might otherwise have been. The concessions inspired by denominational rivalry ranged from the crass to the pedagogically defensible. Offering inducements – from assistance with transportation costs to a girl's dress to outright bribery of the parents – was common throughout western Canada.[44] Not all the beneficiaries, however, were parents. At the Kamloops School, a former principal admitted in 1935, 'I paid the old Father LeJeune five dollars for every child who came from his missions. He was worth all that and more.'[45] According to Eleanor Brass, a graduate of the File Hills School in southern Saskatchewan, at least one Indian father exploited the competition between the Presbyterian and Roman Catholic schools in the region. 'Dad said that the principals of these schools used to bribe the parents to send their children to their schools,' she recalled. 'He thought his grandfather got paid for him to go to both schools but somehow he landed in the nearest one to the reserve, the File Hills Presbyterian boarding school.'[46] Rivalry could also push missionaries to be more accommodating on the use of Native languages. On the Poorman reserve in Saskatchewan, an Oblate missionary warned his provincial it was vital to have a Cree-speaking missionary 'for recruiting purposes' so as to gain an advantage over the Anglican Gordon's School: 'the great & important need here is one who can speak Cree, to come where we have to compete with the other school.'[47]

This competition for souls could also force missionaries to make better provision, pedagogical and otherwise, for residential schoolchildren. For example, the Oblate principal on the west side of Vancouver Island was so concerned about keeping students from the Presbyterian institution at Ahousat that he urged his provincial, '... we must make the school attractive not by pandering to the children & parents but by giving them a reason to want to send their children. That is why I want a good carpentry & machine shop, a good carpenter & a good mechanic so the boys can learn how to build houses, do carpentry work, learn to repair engines, etc.'[48] First Nations leaders learned to exploit the rivalry, for example, to secure a school closer to their reserve than otherwise might have been the case. A chief in the Battle River region of western Saskatchewan gave the Methodist Church until the autumn to promise a school. 'If there was no prospect of a school, then they would have to put their children in the Roman Catholic School.'[49] A second example came from northwestern Ontario, where the Presbyterians were so desperate to satisfy the desire of the local Ojibwa band rather than see the field occupied by the Roman Catholics that they signed an agreement with Chief Red Sky committing them not to proselytize the children, block the absence of children to participate in their traditional rites, or use the police to bring back runaways.[50] This Ontario case was exceptional, but it demonstrated boldly how First Nations that fortuitously found themselves in a cockpit of church rivalry and competition for students could exploit the situation in ways that stretched from bribes to toleration of Aboriginal spiritual practices.[51]

Another ironic aspect of the language issue was the fact that English frequently served as the lingua franca (pardon the pun!) at residential schools that drew their student body from the territories of First Nations who spoke more than one Aboriginal language. Redfern Louttit, who was to go on to be a distinguished Anglican cleric, journeyed far from his home in the James Bay region to Chapleau School, where he encountered Ojibwa-speaking students who did not understand his Cree.[52] In such situations, use of English was a linguistic common denominator for ethnically diverse school populations. In ethnic 'border' regions such as the stretch from Chapleau to Spanish in Ontario, or Beauval in Saskatchewan, the European language was frequently practical and efficient. British Columbia was an especially acute example of this because of the dozens of distinctive First Nations languages that were to be found there. In coastal regions the development of 'trade Chinook,' or Chinook jargon, had been one early response to this situation. In the residential schools of the province, especially in the interior, the common tongue would be English. As a French Oblate, John Duplanil, explained, 'In B.C. the children came from different Reserves. They spoke different languages and English was the only means of communication between children of different tribes. Those who came from the same tribe were not allowed to speak their dialect. Obvious reasons – no (one) group can be tolerated.'[53] As incidents of this sort clearly indicate, the issue of language in the residential schools and the missions with which they were associated was by no means a simple one, whether in its state-church or other aspects.

The troubled story of residential schooling for Aboriginal children in Canada reveals subtleties and complexities in the roles of state and Christian church that are often overlooked or downplayed. Part of the reason that scholarly commentators place church-state differences in shadow is that observers fear running the risk of appearing to trivialize or dismiss the painfully real damage that these missions and schools often did. Let there be no mistake about it: whatever the subtleties of policies and practices on language in the schools, a very large majority of former residential school students recall their coerced acquisition of English as a scarring experience. No sensitive student of the history of residential schools is likely to forget that reality.

At the same time, a desire to be sensitive to such traumatic phenomena should not drive analysts into being insensitive or unjust towards the non-Native participants in the tale. The historical reality of residential schooling is not that it was a seamless and untroubled partnership between throne and altar against the interests and well-being of Aboriginal populations. There were important, if subtle, differences in objectives between government and church. For the state, the reduction and elimination of financial liability for status Indian populations, especially those in treaty, was the overriding preoccupation. However, for missionaries of all denominations, the schools represented, not an opportunity to improve non-Native Canada's bottom line, but a chance, with governmental support, to save Aboriginal souls for Christ and assist Native society to make a successful adjustment to a world now dominated by non-Aboriginal people and their ways.

In the complex area of the history of relations between the state and the church, the residential schools that were inflicted on First Nations and some Inuit between the 1880s and the 1970s offer important insights. The history of residential schooling indicates clearly that apparent cooperation between throne and altar masked underlying tensions and differences. Although they could agree on the tool to be used, the missionaries and bureaucrats did not necessarily agree on objectives or other means. Both sought assimilation through schooling, but Ottawa's purpose was principally financial while the churches' goals were both religious and humanitarian. They hoped that foisting Euro-Canadian ways on Native society through the coercive schooling of their young would facilitate conversion both to Christianity and to the newcomers' ways of maintaining themselves economically. The underlying differences emerged over financial commitments and language policies. The history of church-state cooperation in Native residential is more complex and subtle than is generally realized.

## Notes

'The State, the Church, and Indian Residential Schools in Canada,' pp. 109–29 in Marguerite Van Die, ed., *Religion and Public Life in Canada: Historical and Comparative Perspectives* (Toronto: University of Toronto Press, 2001). Reprinted by permission.

1 The encounter was captured in a photograph now found in an album loaned by school officials to Professor John Dewar, University of Saskatchewan, who permitted me to have a copy made. Given the period of St Laurent's prime ministry, the photograph is probably from the early 1950s.
2 On the residential schools and the bureaucrats' careful public relations campaign, see J.R. Miller, *Shingwauk's Vision: A History of Native Residential Schools* (Toronto: University of Toronto Press, 1996), 145–6.
3 Ibid., chapters 2–3.
4 See, for example, the report of Indian Superintendent David Laird to the minister of the interior, 2 Jan. 1878, in National Archives of Canada (NA), Records of the Department of Indian Affairs (RG 10), Black Series, vol. 3679, file 12, 046.
5 Canada, House of Commons, *Debates*, 9 May 1883, 1107.
6 NA, MG 26 A, Sir John A. Macdonald Papers, vol. 91, 35428, N.F. Davin, 'Report on Industrial Schools for Indians and Half-Breeds,' confidential, 14 March 1879, 12-15
7 Margaret Connell Szasz and Carmelita Ryan, 'American Indian Education,' in *History of Indian-White Relations*, ed. Wilcomb E. Washburn, Vol. 4 of the Smithsonian Institution's *Handbook of North American Indians* (Washington: Smithsonian Institution, 1988), 291.
8 *Statistics Respecting Indian Schools with Dr. Ryerson's Report of 1845 Attached* (Ottawa: Government Printing Bureau, 1898), 73.
9 For a summary of these polices and their interrelatedness, see J.R. Miller, *Canada and the Aboriginal Peoples, 1867–1927* (Ottawa: Canadian Historical Association, 1997).

10 A.G. Harper, 'Canada's Indian Administration: Basic Concepts and Objectives,' *America Indigena* 5, no. 2 (April 1945): 127.

11 Roger L. Nichols, *Indians in the United States and Canada: A Comparative History* (Lincoln and London: University of Nebraska Press, 1998), 225–6; Frederick E. Hoxie, *A Final Promise: The Campaign to Assimilate the Indians, 1880–1920* (Lincoln and London: University of Nebraska Press, 1984), esp. chapter 6.

12 *Constitution Act (1867)*, sec. 91(24).

13 RG 10, Black Series, vol. 3879, file 91, 833, memo of D.C. Scott to acting deputy minister, 28 June 1892.

14 Miller, *Shingwauk's Vision*, 390–2.

15 Canada, House of Commons, *Debates*, 9 May 1883, 1107.

16 RG 10, vol. 3674, file 11422-2, E. Dewdney to superintendent general of Indian affairs, 14 Feb. 1884.

17 Annual report of the Department of Indian Affairs for 1895, *Sessional Papers (No. 14) 1896*, xxii.

18 Records of the Presbyterian Church (PC), Foreign Mission Committee (FMC), Western Section (WS), Indian Work in Manitoba and the North West (IWMNW), box 4, file 68, Report of Synod's Commission on Indian Affairs, Dec. 1904, United Church of Canada Archives, Toronto (UCA).

19 PC, Board of Foreign Missions (BFM), Correspondence with Women's Foreign Missionary Society (WFMS), box 1, file 25, R.P. MacKay to M. Craig, quoting view of W.E. Hendry, 23 Dec, 1910.

20 Davin, 'Report on Industrial Schools,' 12–15.

21 Mark 16:15.

22 P.F.X. de Charlevoix, *History and General Description of New France*, trans. J.G. Shea, 6 vols (1743; Chicago: Loyola University Press, 1870), 4: 198. More generally, see Miller, *Shingwauk's Vision*, 54–5.

23 On the CMS Native church policy, see Jean Usher [Friesen], *William Duncan of Metlakatla: A Victorian Missionary in British Columbia*, Publications in History, no. 5 (Ottawa: National Museum of Man, 1974), 18-21.

24 *Christian Guardian*, 27 Jan. 1891, p. 51.

25 For example, A.G. Morice, O.M.I. See David Mulhall, *Will to Power: The Missionary Career of Father Morice* (Vancouver: University of British Columbia Press, 1986), esp. 20–1.

26 Canada, Parliament, Special Joint Committee of the Senate and the House of Commons on the Indian Act, *Minutes of Proceedings and Evidence 1947*, 952. The speaker was Joseph Dreaver of the Union of Saskatchewan Indians.

27 For a brief explication of the point, see Miller, *Shingwauk's Vision*, 408–9.

28 For example, on the west side of Vancouver Island: Archives of St Paul's Province of Oblates, Vancouver (Oblates-Vancouver), series 1, box 9, file 4, J.L. Bradley, supervisor of Indian missions in the Diocese of Victoria, report on West Coast missions, 31 March–28 April 1944, 10–11.

29 Miller, *Shingwauk's Vision*, 390–2.

30 Regis College Archives, Toronto, Rev. E. O'Flaherty Papers, file 'Hanipaux-Ferrard Report 1858,' copy of report of Special Joint Indian Commissioners, 1858, Manitoulin Island, 230; ibid., Rev. J. Paquin, SJ, 'Modern Jesuit Indian Missions in Ontario,' 181 and 195. It was not completely clear if the government instruction to use only English was inspired by opposition to the use of an Indian language or by the use of French along with some English in the Manitoulin Island schools.

31 Report of the Department of Indian Affairs for 1894, Canada, *Sessional Papers (No. 14) 1895*, 248–9. The entire curriculum is in ibid., 246–9.

32 Oblates-Vancouver, series 1, box 9, file 3, George Forbes, O.M.I., to father provincial, 4 Aug. 1940. Father Forbes continued: '(his "proof" was that the Blessed Virgin spoke to St. Bernadette in French, – which she didn't).'

33 *Acte général de visite des missions indiennes du Nord-ouest canadien* (Rome: Maison Générale, 1936), 49, 52, 56, 93. *Acte de la visite générale de la Province du Manitoba* (N.p.: n.p., 1941), 72, 77; *Acte général de la visite de la Province d'Alberta-Saskatchewan* (Montreal: n.p., 1942), 18–23; Donat Levasseur, *Les Oblats de Marie Immaculée dans l'Ouest et le Nord du Canada, 1845–1967* (Edmonton: University of Alberta Press / Western Canadian Publishers, 1995), 196–7.

34 Archives of Yukon, Anglican Diocese of Yukon Records, box 19, file 3, *Report of the [Third] Synod of the Diocese of Yukon ... 1915* (n.p., n.d.)

35 Archives Deschâtelets (AD), HR 6618 . C73 R 1, (Blue Quills) *Moccasin Telegram*, Dec. 1938 and Jan. 1939; ibid., 2–3, letter of U. Langlois, O.M.I., vicar apostolic of Grouard, 10 Dec. 1938.

36 AD, L 531 N127C 1, Codex historicus for Lestock, 27 March 1909. (Children should learn prayers in their mother tongue, the Saulteaux children in Saulteux, and the francophone Métis in French.)

37 Regis College Archives, Ontario Indian Missions Papers, file 'Correspondence Spanish 1926–1936,' F.F. Walsh, SJ, to provincial, 4 Feb. 1935; ibid., Charles Belanger to Walsh, 19 Feb. 1936.

38 PC, FMC, WS, IWMNW, box 6, file 131, P.W. Gibson Ponton to R.P. MacKay, 1 Feb. 1911. The dismissed employee denied the accusation. For the school language issue, in general, see J.R. Miller, 'Owen Glendower, Hotspur, and Canadian Indian Policy,' *Ethnohistory* 37, no. 4 (Fall 1990): 398–9.

39 Tape-recorded answers to questionnaire by Margaret Mayo, 16 Jan. 1990.

The Native laundry-room worker, who was from Manitoulin Island, told the students that she took the job at the school to be close to her daughter, a pupil.

40 General Synod Archives, GS 75-103, series 2-15, box 34, Indian schools administration newsletter, Nov. 1962.

41 Interview with Mrs M. Anfield, widow of Earl Anfield, Vancouver, 12 Sept. 1990. See also Vema J. Kirkness, ed., *Khot-La-Cha: The Autobiography of Chief Simon Baker* (Vancouver/Toronto: Douglas & McIntyre, 1994), 41, 100–1.

42 *Winnipeg Free Press News Bulletin*, 27 Nov. 1907, in RG 10, Black Series, vol. 3825, file 60, 511-2.

43 *Christian Guardian*, 8 July 1914, pp. 19–20.

44 Anglican Diocese of Yukon Records, box 11, file 15, H.G. Cook to W.R. Adams, 5 Oct. 1951; ibid., H.G. Cook to C.T. Stanger, 9 Oct. 1951 (copy); UCA, PC, FMC, WS, Indian Work in British Columbia, box 2, file 32, J.W. Russell to R.P. MacKay, 4 Sept. 1901; ibid., box 1, file 21, H. McKay to R.P. MacKay, 9 Jan. 1901.

45 Oblates-Vancouver, series 1, box 10, file 1, J. Duplanil, O.M.I., to Joseph Scannell, O.M.I., 12 July 1935.

46 Eleanor Brass, *I Walk in Two Worlds* (Calgary: Glenbow-Alberta Institute, 1987), 6.

47 AD, L 535.M27L355, Wm Moss, O.M.I., to father provincial, 13 June 1932. Concerning Methodist complaints at the Catholics' effective use of Aboriginal languages in recruiting, see UCA, Alexander Sutherland Papers, box 7, file 135, A.R. Aldridge to A. Sutherland, 18 March 1908; ibid., file 143, A. Sutherland to Joseph H. Lowes, 28 July 1908 (copy).

48 Oblates-Vancouver, series 1, box 9, file 3, George Forbes, O.M.I., to provincial, 16 Aug. 1938. Father Forbes added: 'These & other things will help us fight the Presbyterian school at Ahousat.'

49 UCA, Sutherland Papers, box 7, file 139, E.R. Steinhauer to A. Sutherland, 13 April 1909; ibid., file 135, A. Sutherland to A. Barner, 20 April 1909.

50 Ibid., PC, BFM, Manitoba and the North West, box 2, file 33, J.C. Gandier to R.P. MacKay, 14 Jan. 1902, and 'agreement' of the same date.

51 On this topic generally, see J.R. Miller, 'Denominational Rivalry in Indian Residential Education,' *Western Oblate Studies* 2 (1991): 147–54.

52 Taped response to research questionnaire by Canon Redfern Louttit, November 1989.

53 Oblates-Vancouver, series 1, box 10, file 1, J. Duplanil, O.M.I., to Joseph Scannell, O.M.I., 12 July 1935.

# THE CROWN

# Petitioning the Great White Mother:
# First Nations' Organizations and Lobbying in London

On the Prairies, First Nations' public ceremonies, such as those associated with commemoration of treaty-making, always include an element that seems jarring, even anachronistic. Veterans and elders pray and raise flags to start the day's observances, but among the flags that are ritually run up the improvised poles the Union Jack seems strangely out of place to observers from outside the First Nations' community. However, the raising of Britain's venerable pennant is neither anachronistic nor out of place for First Nations, given their long-standing and still vibrant sense of kinship with the Crown, including what scholars would refer to as the Crown in right of the United Kingdom. This tie was established and grew strong in the eighteenth century, the product of both Aboriginal approaches to external dealings and First Nations' well developed strategic sense. It played a role through the nineteenth and twentieth centuries both in treaty-making and lobbying for imperial support for First Nations' causes. Most recently and most noticeably, it was a prominent element in the hectic campaigning for and against the patriation of the Canadian constitution, which led to the adoption of a new constitutional package in April 1982. In other words, it persisted beyond the 'end of Empire,' the period when both Britain's imperial reach and grasp came to an end. Only very recently have there been signs that Aboriginal groups' penchant for lobbying in London might give way to another form of international activity. Surely any tradition such as this lobbying – petitioning the Great White Mother – is worthy of investigation.

Aboriginal leaders' use of terms such as the 'Great Father' or the 'Great White Mother' is easily explained. Within First Nations communities, interactions almost invariably took place between kin. In societies whose fundamental organization was usually by clan and family, ties of kinship were not only important, they were vital to the conduct of relations of various kinds. It was essential to be in a familial relationship of some kind in order to conduct business with other people in these communities. Examples of the importance and use of kin ties are many and varied. The elaborate alliance system that developed in the northeast woodlands in the seventeenth and eighteenth centuries, the Covenant Chain of the League of the Iroquois and their allies, was a bewildering network whose links were characterized by family relationships. Some paired links in the Chain related as parent to child, while the relationships between others were fraternal (or sororal), and still others were typified by a purported relationship of uncle and nephew or niece.[1]

Each and every one of those different familial links was a metaphorical description of the nature and quality of the relationship: those between brothers were links between equals; but those between father and child, or between uncle and nephew, connoted an inequality in power and status between the two. Much of this relationship was, in the language of the anthropologists, 'fictive,' meaning that it was imputed to describe and facilitate the relationship.

Other examples of the use of kinship in relationships with Aboriginal peoples can be found in the North American fur trade and in treaty-making in the West. As is well known, European male traders often took Native partners, and Native families were often pleased to see their daughters enter a relationship with the newcomers who had the coveted trade goods. Among the reasons for the formation of these fur-trade family units was the reality that in Aboriginal society kinship links facilitated trade. The European trader who married a Cree woman would automatically have a network of trading partners, while the bride's family would enjoy preferred access to that trader and to the company for whom he worked.[2] Finally, in the making of the numbered treaties of the latter decades of the nineteenth century, the use by both government and Aboriginal negotiators of familial imagery is striking. Treaty commissioners such as Alexander Morris talked repeatedly of how the 'Great Queen Mother' desired good for her Indian children and wished to provide for them from her 'bounty and benevolence,' and a suspicious Cree leader like Mistahimusqua (Big Bear) assured the government representative that 'I am not an undutiful child' even as he was rebuffing the commissioner's efforts to get him to sign treaty in 1876.[3]

If use of the language of kinship and family was universal in Aboriginal relations, understanding of the familial terms was often not. Indeed, one of the striking features of commercial and diplomatic relations between the representatives of the Crown and First Nations in Canadian history is the way in which the Europeans over time lost their understanding of how the terminology worked. In the early phases, when the Europeans were represented in their dealings with First Nations by the likes of Sir William Johnson, himself married into the Mohawk nation of the Six Nations Iroquois, the newcomers could use and parse the terms of kinship with all the skill and subtlety of the First Nations leaders from whom they had learned to do so. However, a century later, by the time both government treaty commissioners and First Nations were passing terms like 'Queen Mother' and 'Indian children' across the negotiating table, it is clear that the Euro-Canadians no longer understood completely what the First Nations meant by familial terms. When government representatives referred to the Queen's 'Indian children' in the 1870s treaty talks, the reference was invariably followed by some comment that assumed the subordination of First Nation to the government. This stood in dramatic contrast to First Nations' usage, for their references to themselves as 'children' never occurred in a context that implied Indians' subordination and obedience to the 'Queen Mother' and her government in Ottawa. When First Nations leaders used this terminology, they did so within a First Nations cultural context, a set of social assumptions that treated children as distinct individuals who enjoyed a great deal of autonomy and who could count automatically on the love and protection of their parents.[4] Over time the meaning of the language of kinship and family changed, but what remained constant was the predominance of such language.

If describing the British monarch as the Great White Mother can be understood against the backdrop of Aboriginal insistence on having relations take place within a framework of kinship, real or fictive, why did some leaders consider it necessary to take their petitions to the Great Father or Queen Mother in London themselves? Here the explanation is found in the Native leaders' perception of how critical the Crown's response was to their well-being, and in their desire – a desire that grew ever stronger over time – to avoid intermediaries who they feared would muffle or distort their message. The first major example of petitioning the Crown, Mohawk chief Joseph Brant's pilgrimage to London in 1775, illustrates both the importance of crisis and the desire to transmit the message clearly.

The strategic context for the expedition was the American revolution, and the tactical context was the recent death of Joseph Brant's brother-in-law, Sir William Johnson. The onset of the rebellion cast into doubt both the future of the League of the Iroquois and the security of their lands south of Lake Ontario, directly in the path of the expansionist American colonists, with whom they had had uneasy relations for some time. For security they had relied on imperial instruments such as the Royal Proclamation of 1763, which forbade all settlement beyond a western boundary and restricted entry for trading purposes to the interior to those merchants who obtained a licence from the governor in advance of their foray into Indian Country. Even with the protection of the Royal Proclamation, First Nations in the period after 1763 saw settler pressure on their lands constantly increase. In this situation they relied on William Johnson, superintendent of the Northern Department of the Indian Department that Britain had created in 1755, to try to restrain the land-hungry Americans. Johnson was motivated both by personal inclinations and by his official duty to do what he could to protect the territorial interests of these First Nations. He was a trader and large landowner in the Mohawk River valley, a man who depended on good relations with Indian peoples in order to promote his own interests. He was also married – married in the Iroquois fashion, at any rate – to Molly or Mary Brant, the remarkably talented and courageous Mohawk clan mother who was sister to the then young Joseph Brant. In addition to these ties of self-interest and family, it was Johnson's responsibility as the effective head of the Indian Department in the region to try to conciliate Indian communities and retain their alliance with Britain if possible, or, failing that, their neutrality in any quarrel in which Britain might become involved. Johnson had a remarkable career between his appointment in 1755 and his death in 1774, largely succeeding in maintaining the alliance system in which the League of the Iroquois were such a vital link.

Johnson's death immediately cast into doubt the foundations on which many Mohawk, such as the Brants, had built their strategy. In the Revolutionary War, the Mohawk and the other nations in the Iroquois confederacy were pressed to support Great Britain militarily. However, they were understandably concerned about Britain's reliability. If they fought with Great Britain against the colonists, would Britain support their territorial claims and help to defend their lands? It might have been possible to rely on assurances from a trusted figure such as Sir William Johnson if he were still alive. However, he was gone, and the young Joseph Brant took it upon himself to go to London in the winter of 1775 in search of reassurances about British intentions towards its Indian allies.

Joseph Brant and another Mohawk man travelled to London in the company of Guy Johnson, a nephew of the late Sir William who was in search of his uncle's office as Indian superintendent. In an interview with the colonial secretary, Lord George Germain, Brant outlined the objective of his mission: 'I have come over on purpose to be informed of the real motive which ocasioned the unhappy dispute subsisting twixt Brittain and her American Colonies, as numbers of Rebbles were amongst the Indians circulating various reports which if they had believed would in all probability have ocasioned unhappy consequences. Therefore, [I] begg of your Lordship to inform me of your Intentions respecting the Quelling those disputes, as I mean to return and use my utmost endeavours in favor of Government.' Lest the colonial secretary too easily miss the point and leap to the conclusion that the Mohawk, at least, would support the Crown in the war, Brant continued with grievances and concerns to which he needed reassurances. The previous year the Mohawk had assisted in the defence of Canada but had not received any credit for their contribution. He also impressed on Germain that 'notwithstanding our Attachement to Government we had suffered greatly in our Lands, which had been taken wrongfully away from us, and would be very glad to know, if His Majesty meant to redress the Mohawks respecting said lands.'[5]

Germain was satisfyingly forthcoming. He informed Brant that he was aware of the Mohawk's recent military contributions and grateful for them. And 'he said respecting the Lands which was wrongfully taken, he knew every circumstance that I related to be true, but on account of these disputes, they could not attend to them but that I might rest assured as soon as the troubles were over, every grievance and complaint should be redressed and he hoped the Six Nations would to fulfill their engagement with Government as they ever had done, and in consequence of which, they might rest assured of every support England could render them.' Joseph, not surprisingly, took this assurance as a guarantee that, if the Iroquois supported Britain against the American rebels, the United Kingdom would defend the Indians' lands against American invasions and ambitions. Accordingly, Joseph 'thanked him in the name of the Six Nations and acquainted him that he might depend they would fulfill their engagement with Government.'

This pilgrimage to London proved far more satisfactory to Brant and the Mohawk than its aftermath. In addition to obtaining what he took to be Britain's commitment, he had pledged Six Nations support. Moreover, he had been received at Court by George III – an event that seemed to affect him positively and permanently – and been lionized in London society.[6] Back in North America, Brant found that he could not deliver fully on his promise to Germain. Thanks in no small part to the exhortations of Molly and Joseph Brant, the Mohawk swung loyally and tenaciously to support the British alliance, and the Seneca, Cayuga, and Onondaga somewhat less enthusiastically did as well.[7] However, the Oneida and Tuscarora, who had close ties to Congregationalists in the Thirteen Colonies because of the ministrations of missionaries among them, were sympathetic to the rebels. The result of the division of opinion was the extinguishment of the League Council fire, signifying the end – temporary as it later proved – of the Iroquois Confederacy.

At war's end, it hardly mattered whether an Iroquois nation had fought with Britain or sympathized with the rebels, because all members of the League found their territorial interests surrendered or ignored. Joseph Brant charged that, 'the King had "sold the Indians to Congress."'[8] Another disillusioned Iroquois leader was even more scathing: 'The King surely would not pretend to give the Americans that which was not his to give; and [he] would not believe that the Americans would accept that which the King had not power to give. They were allies of the King, not subjects; and would not submit to such treatment ... If England had done so it was an act of cruelty and injustice and capable only of *Christians.*'[9] Britain obtained lands north of Lakes Ontario and Erie from the Mississauga and created reserves near Belleville and Brantford for their Iroquois allies. However, the sense of betrayal remained strong among leaders such as Joseph Brant.

Because of these developments, Joseph Brant undertook a second trip to petition the Crown in 1785. This journey merely deepened Mohawk disillusionment. For one thing, in contrast to the 1775 pilgrimage, which British officials had facilitated because they were eager to obtain solid Iroquois support in the Revolutionary War, Joseph found this time that Indian Department officials tried to dissuade and ultimately prevent him from sailing from Quebec. It was only with persistence and dissembling that he got to England at all.[10] More serious was the fact that although Joseph was received at Court and made much of, he was unable to obtain even a promise of British redress of losses, including territorial losses, that the Mohawk had suffered during the Revolutionary War or to secure guarantees of imperial support in the event of conflict between the Indians and the United States. He was well received by the King and Queen, consorted uproariously with the Prince of Wales (who took him to some places 'very queer for a prince to go to'), and was invited out by many people.[11] And, while he and his sister Molly had their personal claims compensated and Joseph would eventually be placed on half-pay pension, the larger strategic question of what Britain would do in the event of hostilities between the Republic and the First Nations was not satisfactorily resolved. The written words of Colonial Secretary Lord Sydney were facile but vacuous. Referring to commitments to compensation for individuals, Sydney claimed they signalled goodwill for the future, but he refused to be more specific or concrete about what assistance the future might hold:

> This liberal conduct on the part of His Majesty, he trusts, will not leave a doubt upon the minds of his Indian allies that he shall at all times be ready to attend to their future welfare; and that he shall be anxious, upon every occasion wherein their happiness may be concerned, to give them such farther testimonies of his royal favour and countenance, as can, consistently with a due regard to the national faith, and the honor and dignity of the crown, be afforded to them.
>
> His Majesty recommends to his Indian allies to continue united in their councils, and that their measures may be conducted with temper and moderation; from which added to a peaceable demeanor on their part, they must experience many essential benefits, and be most likely to secure to themselves the possession of those rights and privileges which their ancestors have heretofore enjoyed.[12]

A disappointed and disillusioned Joseph Brant returned to North America shortly after receiving the weak response from the colonial secretary.

The next phase of pilgrimages to London was different in character from Brant's, reflecting the enormous changes that occurred in Native-newcomer relations in British North America between the late decades of the eighteenth century and the middle years of the nineteenth century. Joseph Brant's journeys to the imperial capital had been motivated by strategic concerns. The next phase of journeying to London, which began in the 1850s and continued into the twentieth century, was also motivated on the First Nations' side by concerns about their lands. But, in the later period, they had no diplomatic and military quid pro quo with which to try to negotiate with imperial officers. The diplomatic-military frontier between First Nations and Europeans in Canada had ceased to exist with the end of the War of 1812. It was replaced by an agricultural frontier in which First Nations were regarded as an obstacle to settlement and development, rather than a potentially valuable asset in strategic calculations. In this changed relationship, neither the imperial Crown nor colonial legislatures had much interest in safeguarding Aboriginal lands. Worse still, the advent of colonial self-government meant that First Nations were largely abandoned by Britain to the tender mercies of settler societies. The consequences of this transition – a shift from a military to a settlement relationship – was a concerted campaign by the local farmers and developers to dispossess First Nations of their lands and change them culturally through extensive campaigns of attempted assimilation that would last from the 1830s to at least the 1970s.[13]

This altered relationship, a poisoned colonial atmosphere, was the context for forays such as that of the redoubtable Nahnebahwequa in 1859–60. Nahnebahwequa, also known as Catherine Bunch Sonego or Catherine Sutton after her marriage to the English immigrant William Sutton, was a well-connected Mississauga woman who grew up on the Credit Mission near Toronto.[14] The niece of Mississauga Methodist clergyman and chief Peter Jones (Kahkewaquonaby, Sacred Feathers), she was closely associated with Canadian Methodism throughout her life. She met her husband through the English wife of her uncle, and she and William Sutton lived for a number of years at Credit Mission, where Catherine also acted as a Methodist instructor. In the 1840s she and her family lived near Owen Sound, where they were granted two hundred acres by the Chippewas of Newash, and in the early 1850s they were at Garden River near Sault Ste Marie, a centre of intensive Christian evangelization. After a sojourn in Michigan from 1854 to 1857, they returned to Owen Sound, where they discovered that their land had been taken by the Indian Department in the surrender of the Bruce Peninsula and put up for sale. Furthermore, the Department denied Nahnebahwequa an opportunity to purchase when she sought to get their land back. When Nahnebahwequa and two Indian men, one of them a chief, pursued the matter with the Indian Department in Toronto, a bureaucrat told her that 'Indians where [sic] not allowed to Purchase Land.'[15] No satisfaction was to be obtained from officialdom in the settler society of Ontario.

A petition to the provincial legislature by the three would-be Indian purchasers proved unavailing, and, to add insult to injury, Nahnebahwequa found that the arguments the Indian Department gave for not permitting her to acquire her lands kept shifting. They culminated in a contention that she was no longer an Indian because she had married a 'white man.' Incensed by the treatment she had received, she determined to take her search for redress to London and the Queen. As her petition put it:

> I am an Indian woman born of Pagan Parents but brought up under religious instructions. My Father and Mother where full Blood Indians and my forefathers fought and bled for the British Crown, and the Representatives of Briton have repeatedly told our Fathers that they where the Friends of the Red Man and would continue to be, as long as the grass grew and waters continued to flow. [B]ut for the last Quarter of a Centuary their [h]as been a strange way of showing it.[16]

Perhaps the Queen, a wife and mother herself, would prove more sympathetic than the hard-hearted men in the Indian Department in Toronto.

Authorized by chiefs to represent their land claims, too, and assisted financially by sympathetic Quakers in New York, Nahnebahwequa made her way to England in 1860. With support from prominent figures in the Aborigines Protection Society, she secured an audience with Victoria in late June 1860. Nahnebahwequa was overcome by the occasion and Victoria's graciousness: 'She received me with so much kindness as to astonish me, when I saw her come smiling and so good to a poor Indian.'[17] For her part, the Queen was favourably impressed. 'She speaks English quite well, and is come on behalf of her Tribe to petition against some grievances as regards their land,' Her Majesty noted.[18] Although no immediate action was taken, promises apparently were made, and the Queen did instruct her secretary of state, the Duke of Newcastle, to hear the petition of the other claimants when he accompanied the Prince of Wales to British North America later in 1860. Said Victoria, 'I am happy to promise you my aid and protection.'[19]

Back in British North America, the petitioners made an impressive case to Newcastle, but, again, no action ensued. Methodists who were sympathetic to the Indian cause, several of the claimants being prominent Methodist converts, strongly suspected that the good that the Indians' interview and petition accomplished with the colonial secretary was offset by the pernicious influence of an Indian Department official who had previously resisted the claims and who, as secretary to the governor, accompanied Newcastle everywhere during the prince's tour of the colony.[20] Only Nahnebahwequa received her lands, apparently as the result of a commitment by Victoria herself; the other dispossessed claimants got no redress. Nahnebahwequa spent the last few years till her death in 1865 campaigning against the settler mindset, publicly characterizing 'their ideas of justice' as 'might makes right' and describing as 'wholesale robbery and treachery' the government's efforts to acquire Manitoulin Island from First Nations who had been promised it in perpetuity in 1836.[21]

The other high-profile effort by First Nations to petition the Crown directly for redress from settler rapacity originated in British Columbia in the first decade of the twentieth century. Indeed, early twentieth-century British Columbia in disturbing ways resembled the mid-nineteenth-century Canada West (Ontario) that had produced Nahnebahwequa's expedition. The indigenous population of the Pacific province had been overtaken numerically in the 1880s by non-Native settlement, and First Nations' control of their lands and activities from then on was steadily more circumscribed by the presence of non-Natives and the imposition of laws created by the provincial legislature they dominated.[22] Land matters in British Columbia were complicated by the fact that very little of the province was covered by treaties between the Crown and First Nations. Aside from fourteen small pockets on Vancouver Island for which treaties had been negotiated by Governor James Douglas in the 1850s and the northeast corner of the province that was embraced by the 1899 Treaty 8, British Columbia was unsurrendered First Nations' land. However, the legal status of the lands – or what a twenty-first century authority would regard as their unsurrendered status – did not prevent British Columbians from usurping and appropriating lands, waterways, and natural resources of all kinds. In the British Columbia case, the situation was made even more tangled by an imbroglio that had developed between Ottawa and Victoria after British Columbia entered Confederation in 1871. To put the matter oversimply, the province systematically opposed and frustrated federal efforts to regularize the anomalous situation of Indian lands from the late 1870s onward. The federal government, which was a notorious victimizer of First Nations itself in most other parts of the country, found itself outdone in uncharitable and punitive treatment of Indians in the Pacific province by the settler government that administered matters there.

Eventually, the response of some First Nations in British Columbia was to seek redress elsewhere for most of three decades by petitions and representations to both the provincial and national capitals, but these efforts always proved unavailing, principally because of the stubborn attitude of the province. Through this period, various First Nations in British Columbia had grown accustomed to invoking the Crown in their struggles with intransigent representatives of settler society. So, for example, in 1875 the chiefs of the Coast Salish bands in the Fraser Valley informed the Indian commissioner that they did not want the public funds they had heard had been provided to celebrate the Queen's birthday. They were disgruntled at how they were being treated, and this ploy was intended symbolically to make their point.[23] More positively, in 1879 the Nlha7kápmx (Thompson) invoked the Queen as their ally in their dealings with authorities in settler society that were intended to secure state recognition of a form of indigenous self-rule.[24] British Columbia First Nations grew accustomed to thinking of the monarchy as a potential ally in the early, difficult years after the coastal colony joined Confederation.

By the middle years of the first decade of the twentieth century, some First Nations leaders who had had enough of mistreatment by the federal and provincial governments moved to invoke their potential ally in London. In particular, Coast Salish groups on Vancouver Island and the mainland began to organize to project their claims beyond Victoria and Ottawa to London.[25] Taking advantage of a fortuitous visit to Victoria by Prince Arthur, Duke of Connaught, nephew of King Edward VII, the leadership of the Cowichan, a Salish group on southern Vancouver Island, presented an address of welcome that emphasized their ties to the Crown, their affection for the late Queen Victoria, and their allegiance to the new occupant of the throne:

> We the undersigned chiefs of the Cowichan Indian tribe, representing about seven hundred people, desire to express our sincere gratitude to Your Royal Highness for this unexpected pleasure of seeing a member of the royal family. By our first governor, Sir James Douglas, we were told of Her Most Gracious Majesty, the late Queen Victoria, whom we learned to love as a mother, and whose memory we revere with unspeakable devotion. Whilst we still mourn the death of our beloved Queen, we nevertheless rejoice that in her noble son, King Edward VII, she has found a worthy successor – long may he reign ...[26]

Other preparations for a foray to London included a series of potlatches, the sharing ceremonial of North West Coast peoples, that were used to build solidarity among First Nations and support for the trip to England. Three chiefs – Joseph Capilano (Kayapálanexw), a Squamish chief, Basil David, a Shuswap, and Chillihitza (Chief Charlie), an Okanagan – were selected for the delegation, and a line of argument agreed upon. To the immense frustration of the local press, the Salish leadership refused until just before their departure to divulge the contents of the message they intended to deliver, a strategy apparently adopted to build press interest and prevent government from thwarting their mission by countering their arguments in advance. After a large parade in Vancouver, the chiefs and their interpreter boarded a transcontinental train for the long journey to Montreal and connections with an ocean liner that carried them to the United Kingdom.[27]

After some setbacks, the three chiefs succeeded in laying their views before the 'Great White Chief.'[28] Their arrival in London had coincided with the King's absence on a hunting excursion, but His Majesty agreed to see them first thing upon his return to the capital, not long before the chiefs were scheduled to depart on their return voyage. Their formal message reiterated the theme of allegiance ('We bring greetings to your majesty from thousands of true and loyal hearts'), explained briefly the way in which their land rights had been ignored ('in British Columbia the Indian title has never been extinguished, nor has sufficient land been allotted to our people for their maintenance'), threw their cause on the Crown's mercy ('We are persuaded that your majesty will not suffer us to be trodden upon or taken advantage of'), and asked for an investigation of their grievance. 'We cannot tell your majesty all our difficulties, it would take too long, but we are sure that a good man, or some good men, will be sent to our country who will see, and hear, and bring back a report to your majesty.'[29] As had been the case with Nahnebahwequa, though, there was little concrete action flowing from the appeal, despite how carefully staged it had been.

The aftermath of the Salish chiefs' trip might not have included effective action, but it did pave the way for important political developments among British Columbia First Nations. According to an unverified version of Chief Joseph Capilano's recollections, '... we talk with King and at end he shake my hand hard and ... pat my right shoulder three times so ... and say, "Chief we see this matter righted, but it may take a long time, five years perhaps" ... King he received me like a brother chief and very kind.'[30] The three chiefs' recollections of Edward VII's expressions of sympathy and what they reported as his assurances about their case became a source of political strength and confidence to Salish and other groups in the Pacific province.[31] Moreover, the efforts at political unification among British Columbia First Nations that had preceded the trip continued after the chiefs' return. The 1906 pilgrimage to London is generally regarded as part of the consciousness-raising and coalition-building that were forces behind the emergence in 1916 of the Allied Tribes of British Columbia, the first major pan-Indian political movement in a province marked by the large number and heterogeneity of its First Nations.[32] In this sense, the 1906 trip can legitimately be seen as the harbinger of an increasing emphasis on political topics and tactics among First Nations in Canada, an emphasis that also manifested itself in future ventures to the imperial capital by First Nations delegations.

Although First Nations deputations continued to head to London from British Columbia and other parts of Canada,[33] eventually the focus of the effort shifted to Ontario, more particularly to the Six Nations near Brantford, Ontario.[34] The Six Nations community that produced an international campaign for recognition of their status as a sovereign people was unique among First Nations in Canada. The members of the Iroquois Confederacy had been allies of, first, the Dutch in the seventeenth century and, then, of the British. According to the Iroquois view of the history of their interactions with the newcomers, their relationship with the strangers was both recorded and symbolized by the *gus wenta*, or two-row wampum. Wampum belts were used for a variety of purposes, among them to record and archive important discussions and agreements with other groups. The *gus wenta* contained symbols – two parallel lines that represented canoes – that stood for a relationship of allies and equals who would forever respect the autonomy of the other group. When the War of the American Revolution ended badly for Britain and its Iroquois allies, tensions between them rose dramatically. Those Iroquois who had fought with Britain were angry at their ally's blithe surrender of their territorial rights in the peace settlement. To conciliate the Iroquois and avoid further complications with the young United States, Britain acquired lands from the Mississauga on which they could settle both their Aboriginal allies, such as the Iroquois, and non-Native allies who wished to escape the republic. Significantly, the grant by which Governor Frederick Haldimand conveyed land to the Six Nations referred to their role as 'His Majesty's allies.'[35]

The usefulness of the Six Nations in the eyes of the imperial government ended with the War of 1812, in which they again fought with the British. After the Rush-Bagot Convention ushered in enduring peace with the United States, the Six Nations were no longer valued for their military contribution. The Six Nations land base shrank, in part because the imperial and colonial administrations showed little disposition to protect it from the covetousness of developers and settlers. The community was divided deeply, between religious traditionalists and Christians, and also between those who believed in Iroquois sovereignty and others who preferred to work within the framework of Canadian law, including the Indian Act. In the late decades of the nineteenth century and early decades of the twentieth, there was growing polarization between supporters of hereditary governance and proponents of elective institutions, which the Indian Affairs Department favoured. Although there was not exact congruence between religious traditionalists and supporters of hereditary government or Iroquois sovereignty, there was a high degree of correlation.

Relations between Six Nations and the federal government were seriously strained at the end of the Great War when Parliament amended the Indian Act to permit involuntary enfranchisement at the behest of the Department of Indian Affairs. Enfranchisement was the mechanism by which a male status Indian gave up his status and became a Canadian citizen. Efforts to persuade First Nations to enfranchise voluntarily had been going on since1857, but without much visible success, and by 1920 the government was prepared to adopt sterner measures. The 1920 amendment that authorized involuntary enfranchisement at the will of the Indian affairs minister joined with disputes over governance to provoke a showdown with the Six Nations that quickly expanded into a full-blown confrontation over the issue of Iroquois sovereignty.[36]

The leading spirit in the movement that became the Iroquois sovereignty campaign was Deskaheh, or Levi General, a follower of the traditional longhouse religion and ally of hereditary governance at Six Nations. Disgruntled at the rejection by Indian Affairs of the case for recognition of Iroquois sovereignty, and irritated by the passage of the involuntary enfranchisement provision in 1920, Deskaheh and his followers took their case to London and George V in the summer of 1921. As they had during the Ottawa phase of their campaign for recognition, the advocates of sovereignty showed themselves adept at generating and exploiting newspaper publicity to further their cause, even though the British government was not prepared to support them.

Deskaheh, for example, gained a sympathetic hearing from journalists in the imperial capital, much to the annoyance of senior officials of the Department of Indian Affairs. The publicity and a change of Canadian government in late 1921 from the Unionists to Mackenzie King's Liberals resulted in the repeal of the 1920 involuntary enfranchisement amendment of the Indian Act. This paved the way for another attempt, again futile, to gain recognition of Iroquois sovereignty from Ottawa in 1922.

Deskaheh, his advisers, and his supporters among the hereditary government element next determined on a more ambitious gambit. While they had been negotiating with the Canadian government during 1922–3, they had also been seeking international support. When the Dutch government agreed to support them internationally, Deskaheh broke off talks with Ottawa. He would take the search for recognition of the Six Nations as a sovereign people over the heads of Ottawa and London; with the support of their first European ally, Holland, they would seek recognition in the recently created international body, the League of Nations. When the Dutch representative to the League forwarded the Iroquois petition, without committing his government to verifying or supporting its claims, both Canada and the United Kingdom took defensive action. The Canadian government prepared a reply asserting that the Iroquois were British subjects, and that, therefore, whatever complaints they had were a domestic Canadian matter. For its part, the British Foreign Office made it clear through Holland's ambassador in London that Britain disapproved of the Dutch action and that Holland, as a former imperial power itself, might find that the action it had taken would come back to haunt it at Geneva. These steps seemed successful; by the summer of 1923, it was obvious that the Iroquois petition was going nowhere with the League.

As part of the campaign, Deskaheh in the summer of 1923 made the usual pilgrimage to London, en route to Geneva. As was becoming usual with First Nations from Canada, Deskaheh took some pains to arouse press interest in the matter, issuing a pamphlet and provoking significant journalistic comment in the United Kingdom. At the League, Deskaheh initially confronted a procedural stone wall: no member state had asked that the Iroquois petition be put on the agenda, and therefore it would not be discussed. However, by the spring of 1924 the Iroquois sovereigntist had persuaded a striking group of League representatives to support his case. It was reported that the delegates from Persia, Estonia, Ireland, and Panama were all sympathetic to the initiative. And it was lost on no one that all four of these states were former or actual colonies themselves. At this point the British Foreign Office weighed in heavily, telling the quartet of 'minor powers' that their proposed 'interference' in British and Canadian affairs was 'impertinent.'[37] This had the desired effect, and the four feisty states abandoned their support of Deskaheh and the Iroquois.

Defeated in Geneva, Deskaheh and his supporters once more turned to London. In the autumn of 1924, Deskaheh appealed to George V for justice for the Iroquois, only, as usual, to see his request referred to Ottawa and the unsympathetic ears of the Department of Indian Affairs. The death of Deskaheh in June 1925 removed the energetic Iroquois leader from the struggle, but it did not end the crusade. In the summer of 1930, another group of Iroquois made their way to London in pursuit of claims both for recognition of their sovereignty and redress from what they claimed was the mismanagement by Indian Affairs of their funds. Once again, they employed the tactics that had been developed over several similar forays: they enlisted the support of prominent Britons and staged colourful incidents that captured press attention for them and their cause. The Iroquois, in full regalia, were entertained for tea on Westminster Terrace by sympathetic members of Parliament, and 'the historic pipe of peace was produced and handed around.'[38] Labour MP Fenner Brockway pursued their cause with British officialdom and found their demands, as usual, spurned. Another sympathizer who asked for a hearing was told 'that as the matters referred to in your letter lie within the exclusive competence of His Majesty's Government in Canada, the Secretary of State cannot see his way to receive the deputation or to take any action in regard to these matters.'[39]

Although the Iroquois campaign during the 1920s had a quixotic and futile quality, its significance nonetheless was considerable. The effort was the culmination of a tradition of petitioning the Crown in London that went back at least a century and a half, to the days when Joseph Brant had sought a British commitment to defend Six Nations territorial interests in return for military support from the Iroquois during the Revolutionary War. During the nineteenth century, the pilgrimages continued, but now they often focused on land-related questions. The cause that took petitioners to London now might be grievances of individuals, such as Nahnebahwequa or the Salish chiefs who attended the Court in 1906, and the kinds of strategic considerations that motivated Brant no longer were in evidence. One other change that occurred in the practice of petitioning the Crown was increasing First Nations' reliance on publicity to advance their cause. That had been evident in the preparations in British Columbia in 1906, when the departing chiefs arranged for a parade in Vancouver that attracted considerable attention. Seeking out publicity was a tactic even more in evidence in the struggles in the 1920s to advance the cause of Iroquois sovereignty.[40] Now the argument was not, as it had been in Brant's day, that strategic necessity required British support of the Iroquois. Rather, the contention was that the Iroquois and the British had always been allies, that Iroquois sovereignty had never been surrendered or extinguished, and that Britain ought, as a simple measure of justice, to help the Iroquois secure recognition of their sovereign status. And, of course, by the 1920s First Nations' use of publicity to attract attention to their cause and embarrass the government back in Canada had become very pronounced. By the time of the Statute of Westminster, many Aboriginal political organizations in Canada had become quite sophisticated in their tactics of petitioning the Crown.

It was the reliance on publicity and media manipulation that was most obvious in the last chapter of this saga of First Nations' pilgrimages to London: the lobbying efforts carried out in the campaign over constitutional renewal during 1979–82. In 1976 a Parti Québécois government had been elected in Quebec dedicated to achieving sovereignty for the province, and Canadian prime minister Pierre Elliott Trudeau was determined to frustrate that goal, preferably by renewing the Canadian constitution with a made-in-Canada amending formula and an entrenched bill of rights that would guarantee both basic civil and democratic rights and minority linguistic rights. The struggle over constitutional renewal went on from 1977 till early 1982. Throughout this period, Aboriginal leaders, especially the leaders of the status Indian organizations, whose national representative was known as the National Indian Brotherhood (NIB), sought to become involved in the process in order to advance their own agenda. As early as 1978, the NIB insisted that Aboriginal organizations must play a prominent role in the constitutional talks and that any new constitution must guarantee Aboriginal and treaty rights. If these things did not occur, the NIB warned, they would go to the United Kingdom to ask Queen Elizabeth II to stop the constitutional patriation process.[41] One of the reasons for this stance, according to the president of the Indian Association of Alberta, was a concern 'that treaty rights may not be safeguarded by a new constitution and that the ending of Canada's colonial status could also mean the ending of the Indian people's special relationship with the Crown.'[42] When the NIB leadership became convinced that they were not going to achieve meaningful participation in the constitutional talks, they despatched a large delegation to London in the spring of 1979. The Government of Joe Clark found itself faced with the question of what advice to give the British government on how the delegation should be received. Even though Queen Elizabeth had been the recipient of a carefully negotiated political speech in Alberta when touring Canada in 1973, and a large delegation had gone to England in 1976 and had an audience on the centenary of the signing of Treaty 6, the Clark Government advised Britain that the Queen not meet the delegation. But the two hundred people in the delegation met with various other politicians, especially from the opposition, and once again captured enormous publicity for their cause.[43] Although the Clark Government promised that Aboriginal leaders could attend constitutional talks as participants rather than observers, the Trudeau Government, which returned to power early in 1980, reneged. Worse still, the eagerness of the re-elected Trudeau to complete constitutional renewal meant that Aboriginal issues were going to be deferred to a later round of constitutional talks, after the concerns of Quebec were addressed.

Aboriginal leaders resisted the constitutional juggernaut both by protest in Canada and initiatives in England. In the autumn of 1980, the NIB determined on a widespread lobbying campaign in England and succeeded as early as November of that year in getting a hearing by the Foreign Affairs Committee of the British House of Commons. Unfortunately for the Canadian Aboriginal cause, the committee's report, issued in January 1981, declared that Crown treaty obligations had been transferred to Canada, although no one seemed entirely certain when and how that had occurred. The organizations continued to lobby in London, but their efforts were hampered by a breakdown in the common front they had hammered together for their submission to the Foreign Affairs Committee. Part of the problem was that the Aboriginal movement in Canada was divided among the Inuit Council on National Issues, representing, of course, the Inuit; the Native Council of Canada, representing the Métis and non-status Indians; and the National Indian Brotherhood, representing status Indians. The NIB, the largest and best organized of the three, was having its own internal problems, with differences over strategy being only one of the sources of division. In spite of these difficulties, it appeared that progress was made in Canada early in 1980 when the government and NIB seemed briefly to agree on a formula of words for the new constitution, which said: 'The aboriginal and treaty rights of the aboriginal peoples of Canada are hereby recognized and affirmed.' However, this entente fell apart, too, and the various Aboriginal groups repaired once more to London in the spring and summer of 1981. In the autumn, as is notorious, the climactic First Ministers Conference on the constitution betrayed the Aboriginal organizations by, initially, dropping the proposed entrenchment of 'aboriginal and treaty rights,' and, when there was an outcry over this duplicity, agreeing to restore the clause with the critical limiting adjective 'existing' before 'aboriginal and treaty rights.'[44] That and the failure to include Quebec in the final deal in November 1981 left the supposed triumph of constitutional renewal a shambles.

In addition to public agitation aimed at the politicians, the Aboriginal organizations also entered the courts to try to frustrate the Canadian government. Unfortunately, they did not manage to maintain a common approach in their litigation. The Indian Association of Alberta chose to challenge the decision of the Foreign Affairs Committee, arguing that the Crown in right of Britain retained obligations to Aboriginal organizations. The British Columbia and Saskatchewan First Nations organizations chose to argue merely that Aboriginal agreement was a necessary condition for patriation of the constitution. Alberta lost in the court of first instance, but in December the Court of Queen's Bench, or, more specifically, its chief justice, Lord Denning, granted them leave to appeal. However, Denning eventually ruled that it was, as the British government maintained, the Crown in right of Canada that now bore responsibility to Aboriginal groups.[45] Frustrated and disappointed in court, the Aboriginal groups now swung their attention to Westminster, where the Canada Bill, which embodied the cobbled-together deal on constitutional renewal, was to be debated. The organizations scored a moral victory, inasmuch as their parliamentary champions delayed passage for a time and the debates in both Commons and Lords focused overwhelmingly on Aboriginal issues. However, the Canada Bill passed, and the Queen in April 1982 signed the new constitutional provisions in Ottawa. Aboriginal organizations, as well as the premier of Quebec, boycotted the signing, and the Native groups declared 17

April a day of mourning. The patriation story was another disappointing chapter in the lengthy saga of pilgrimages by Aboriginal people to England.

Although the reasons that Aboriginal organizations, especially First Nations, had for taking their cause to London and the monarch were clear and understandable, the practice never produced much satisfaction for them. In their cultural and diplomatic world, the tie to European powers such as the United Kingdom was fashioned as personal and familial, and they regarded their link to the King or Queen as an important symbol of their relationship to the monarch's people. However, on the British side, where relations with First Nations' leaders and individuals were always fashioned within a framework of constitutional parliamentary government, the links existed for *raison d'état*, and there was nothing familial or personal about them. Accordingly, the British government, in spite of the honeyed words spoken on some occasions by the King or Queen, treated the relationship as instrumental and the interests of the Aboriginal petitioners as a relatively low priority. Over time, Native leaders from Canada began to adjust to that harsh reality, reaching out to opposition politicians, to media outlets that could publicize their cause and perhaps shift politicians' attitudes, and, finally, to international organizations such as the League of Nations that might, if they could not deliver redress, at least embarrass the British and Canadian governments into taking corrective action. The constitutional campaign from 1977 to 1982 certainly revealed the limitations of the strategy of petitioning the Queen. For Britain, if not formally and fully for Canada until 1982, empire had ended decades earlier. Entanglements with Aboriginal groups in Canada, aside from colourful opportunities during royal visits to the Dominion, were an inconvenience and encumbrance.

Certainly, First Nations' leaders have learned the lesson. If the Crown is no longer the answer, perhaps an international forum is, or so both First Nations' intellectuals and political leaders seem to think. Recently, efforts by some First Nations' leaders have focused on talks in Geneva, where a Working Group on the Draft Declaration of Indigenous Populations, a subgroup of the United Nations Human Rights Committee, has been wrestling with the question of Aboriginal peoples' place in the world. And when Matthew Coon Come became grand chief of the Assembly of First Nations in 2000, he promised his followers that he would, if necessary, take their grievances to the United Nations to embarrass Ottawa into doing right by First Nations. The pilgrimages continue, but now, as with so much else in Canadian life, they are to New York or sometimes Geneva, rather than to London.[46]

## Notes

This essay was prepared with the assistance of a Standard Research Grant from the Social Sciences and Humanities Research Council of Canada. Its preparation for presentation at a conference on 'Canada and the End of Empire' at the Institute of Canadian Studies, University of London, was immensely facilitated by the work of research assistant Christa Nicholat. A version of this essay will appear in Phillip Buckner, ed., *Canada and the End of Empire* (Vancouver: UBC Press, 2004).

1  The most comprehensive coverage of this complex matter is found in the Covenant Chain trilogy of Francis Jennings: *The Invasion of America: Indians, Colonialism, and the Cant of Conquest* (Williamsburg, VA: University of North Carolina Press, 1975); *The Ambiguous Iroquois Empire: The Covenant Chain Confederation of Indian Tribes with English Colonies from Its Beginnings to the Lancaster Treaty of 1744* (New York: W.W. Norton, 1984); and *Empire of Fortune: Crowns, Colonies, and Tribes in the Seven Years' War* (New York: W.W. Norton, 1988).

2  Sylvia Van Kirk, *'Many Tender Ties': Women in Fur-Trade Society in Western Canada, 1670–1870* (Winnipeg: Watson & Dwyer, [1980]), esp. chapters 2–3.

3  Alexander Morris, *The Treaties of Canada with the Indians* (1880; reprinted, Saskatoon: Fifth House, 1991), 193.

4  John L. Tobias, 'The Origins of the Treaty Rights Movement in Saskatchewan,' in *1885 and After: Native Society in Transition*, ed. F. Laurie Barron and James B. Waldram (Regina: Canadian Plains Research Center, 1986), 248.

5  National Archives of Canada (NA), MG 11, CO 42 (CO 42), vol. 87, 221, Joseph Brant's notes of speech. I have suppressed some of the exuberant uppercasing in this document.

6  See the account in Isabel Thompson Kelsay, *Joseph Brant, 1743–1807, Man of Two Worlds* (Syracuse: Syracuse University Press, 1984), 161–71; and, as an example of the lionization, James Boswell's gushing account of 'Joseph Thayendaneken, the Mohawk Chief,' *London Magazine*, July 1776.

7  Barbara Graymont, 'The Six Nations Indians in the Revolutionary War,' in *Sweet Promises: A Reader on Indian-White Relations in Canada*, ed. J.R. Miller (Toronto: University of Toronto Press, 1991), 94–6.

8   Quoted in Robert S. Allen, *His Majesty's Indian Allies: British Indian Policy in the Defence of Canada, 1774-1815* (Toronto: Dundurn. 1992), 56.

9   Quoted in D.C. Scott, 'Indian Affairs, 1763–1841,' in *Canada and Its Provinces*, ed. A Shortt and A.G. Doughty (Toronto: Glasgow Brook & Co., 1914), 4: 708.

10  See CO 42, vol. 17, 188–93 and 208–9.

11  William L. Stone, *Life of Joseph Brant* (1838; reprinted, St Clair Shores, MI: Scholarly Press, 1970), 2: 249–60.

12  Lord Sydney to Joseph Brant, 6 April 1786, quotedin ibid., 256.

13  This process is traced in J.R. Miller, *Skyscrapers Hide the Heavens: A History of Indian-White Relations in Canada*, 3rd ed. (Toronto: University of Toronto Press, 2000), parts 2 and 3.

14  The biographical details come principally from Donald B. Smith, 'Nahnebahwequay,' *Dictionary of Canadian Biography [DBC]* (Toronto: University of Toronto Press, 1976), 9: 590–1. I have also benefited from reading drafts of the following two articles: Ian Radforth, 'Performance, Politics, and Representation: Aboriginals and the 1860 Royal Tour of Canada,' *Canadian Historical Review* 84, no. 1 (March 2003): 1–32; and Celia Haig-Brown, 'Seeking Honest Justice in a Land of Strangers: Nahnebahwequa's Struggle for Land,' *Journal of Canadian Studies* 36, no. 4 (Winter 2002): 143–70.

15  NA, RG 10, Records of the Department of Indian Affairs (RG 10), vol. 2877, file 177, 181, petition of Catherine Sutton. Internal evidence indicates that this petition was prepared in 1859 or 1860 (she says she's been married twenty years; *DCB*, 9: 590, says she married in 1839), likely for presentation in England ('but let the British Government order a thorough investigation of all Indian afairs [sic]'). For the petition to the colonial legislature, see *Christian Guardian*, 29 Aug. 1860. I am grateful to Dr Wade Henry, who provided me with a copy of the *Christian Guardian* item.

16  RG 10, vol. 2877, file 177, 181, petition of Catherine Sutton.

17  *Toronto Leader*, 10 Aug. 1860. I am indebted to Dr Wade Henry, who provided me with this item.

18  Quoted in *DCB*, 9: 591.

19  *Toronto Leader*, 10 Aug. 1860.

20  See the *Christian Guardian*'s editorial of 5 Sept. 1860, in Conrad Van Dusen, *The Indian Chief: An Account of the Labours, Losses, Sufferings, and Oppression of Ke-zig-ko-e-ne-ne (David Sawyer), a Chief of the Ojibbeway Indians in Canada West* (London: W. Nichols, 1867), 144. See, too, the *Guardian*'s editorial of 30 Jan. 1861 charging that Indian Department officials deliberately manufactured a misleading image of the Indians by having them parade before the Prince and Newcastle 'everywhere as savages. They were instructed to present themselves half-naked, with painted faces, feathers in their hair, the

most grotesque forms of savage dress, and with every appearance of savage ferocity. The effect of all this would be to make the Duke feel that lands could be no use to them, and that they were incapable of valuing or improving that which might be conferred upon them' (ibid., 147–8).

21  Quoted in *DCB*, 9: 591.

22  The literature on this depressing process is extensive, but a good beginning can be made by referring to Robin A. Fisher, *Contact and Conflict: Indian-European Relations in British Columbia*, 2nd ed. (Vancouver: UBC Press, 1992) esp. chapters 7–8; and Paul Tennant, *Aboriginal Peoples and Politics: The Indian Land Question in British Columbia, 1849–1989* (Vancouver: UBC Press, 1990), esp. chapters 1–7.

23  RG 10, vol. 3612, file 3763, Chief Alexis to Indian Commissioner, 15 May 1875. For detail on this incident, see '"I will accept the Queen's hand": First Nations Leaders and the Image of the Crown in the Prairie Treaties,' in this volume.

24  Douglas Harris, 'The Nlhá7kapmx Meeting at Lytton, 1879, and the Rule of Law,' *BC Studies*, no. 108 (Winter 1995–6): 25. My thanks to my colleague Keith Carlson for this reference.

25  There was an unsuccessful effort to see the King in 1904, when two chiefs from the interior, accompanied by an Oblate priest, failed the get an audience with Edward VII. See R.M. Galois, 'The Indian Rights Association, Native Protest Activity and the "Land Question" in British Columbia, 1903–1916,' *Native Studies Review* 8, no. 2 (1992): 6–7.

26  *Victoria Daily Colonist*, quoted in Daniel P. Marshall, *Those Who Fell from the Sky: A History of the Cowichan Peoples* (Duncan, BC: Cowichan Tribes, 1999), 147. I am indebted to my colleague Keith Thor Carlson for bringing this source to my attention.

27  Tennant, *Aboriginal Peoples and Politics*, 85; Marshall, *Those Who Fell*, 147–8.

28  *London Daily Telegraph*, 25 Aug. 1906, reprinted in *Victoria Daily Colonist*, 31 Aug. 1906.

29  'Indians' Petition to King Edward,' *Victoria Daily Colonist*, 6 July 1906.

30  'A Mirror of Joe Capilano,' in Carolyn Thomas Foreman, *Indians Abroad, 1493–1938* (Norman: University of Oklahoma Press, 1943), 211. Unfortunately, this work has no references that would permit verification of the author's sources. According to other authorities, the members of the delegation were told 'to present their claims to the Canadian Government and if they then received no satisfaction, their complaints would be dealt with further' (*Native Rights in Canada*, ed. Peter Cumming and Neil Mickenberg [Toronto: Indian-Eskimo Association of Canada in association with General Publishing Co. Ltd, 1970], 188).

31  Marshall, *Those Who Fell*, 157–8.

32  Galois, 'The Indian Rights Association,' 7–8.

33  See, for example, the correspondence concerning a trip by three Dakota from Oak River in Manitoba in the summer of 1907, in NA, RG 10, vol. 4035, file 311, 256. The purpose of the trip is not clear from official records.

34  Both the Governor General's Office and the Department of Indian Affairs reacted with alarm in August 1906 when a group from the Six Nations were reported to be on their way to England 'with the hope of seeing the King' (NA, RG 10, vol. 3099, file 301, 224, J. Hanbury Williams to deputy superintendent general of Indian affairs, 8 Aug. 1906). All concerned relaxed when it turned out that the group were merely part of a hired entertainment troupe. The reason for their leader's return to London two years later is unclear.

35  Quoted in E. Brian Titley, *A Narrow Vision: Duncan Campbell Scott and the Administration of Indian Affairs in Canada* (Vancouver: University of British Columbia Press, 1986), 112.

36  The issue is well covered in Titley, *A Narrow Vision*, chapter 7; Richard Veatch, *Canada and the League of Nations* (Toronto: University of Toronto Press, 1975), chapter 7; and Joëlle Rostkowski, 'The Redman's Appeal for Justice: Deskaheh and the League of Nations,' in *Indians and Europe: An Interdisciplinary Collection of Essays*, ed. Christian F. Feest (Lincoln and London: University of Nebraska Press, 1989), 435–53. I have also benefited from Donald B. Smith, 'Onondeyoh: The Grand River and Toronto Backgrounds of Fred Loft (1861–1934), an Important Early Twentieth-Century First Nations Political Leader' (paper presented at the Conference on Twentieth-Century Canadian Nationalisms, Massey College, Toronto, 18 March 2001).

37  Titley, *A Narrow Vision*, 123.

38  *Peterborough Examiner*, n.d. (the item was datelined 'London, June 24'), in NA, RG 25, vol. 1573, file 673 (1930).

39  RG 25, vol. 1573, file 673 (1930), H. Tait to J.R. Ockleshaw-Johnson, 8 July 1930. According to Titley (*A Narrow Vision*, 129-31), Ockleshaw-Johnson was a British adventurer who interested himself in the Iroquois cause until they grew suspicious of his aims and severed their connection with him.

40  For example, see Rostkowski, 'The Redman's Appeal,' 444–5.

41  The Aboriginal role in the patriation process is well covered in Douglas E. Sanders, 'The Indian Lobby,' in *And No One Cheered: Federalism, Democracy and the Constitution* Act, ed. Keith Banting and Richard Simeon (Toronto: Methuen, 1983), 301–32. I have also benefited from an unpublished paper by Michael D. Behiels, 'Aboriginal Nationalism in the Ascendancy: The Assembly of First Nations' First Campaign for the Inherent Right to Self-

Government, 1968–1987' (paper presented at the Conference on Twentieth-Century Canadian Nationalisms, Massey College, Toronto, 18 March 2001). See also Tony Hall, 'What Are We, Chopped Liver? Aboriginal Affairs in the Constitutional Politics of Canada in the 1980s,' in *The Meech Lake Primer: Conflicting Views of the 1987 Constitutional Accord*, ed. Michael D. Behiels (Ottawa: University of Ottawa Press, 1989), 423–56; and Michael Woodward and Bruce George, 'The Canadian Indian Lobby of Westminster, 1979–1982,' *Journal of Canadian Studies* 18, no. 3 (Autumn 1983): 119–43. Also instructive are Peter Jull, 'Aboriginal Peoples and Political Change in the North Atlantic Area,' *Journal of Canadian Studies*, 16, no. 2 (Summer 1981): 53–68; and Simon McInnes, 'The Inuit and the Constitutional Process,' *Journal of Canadian Studies* 16, no. 2 (Summer 1981): 68–80.

42 Joe Dion, quoted in Sanders, 'The Indian Lobby,' 304.
43 Ibid., 305–6.
44 Douglas E. Sanders, 'Prior Claims: Aboriginal People in the Constitution of Canada,' in *Canada and the New Constitution: The Unfinished Agenda, Vol. 1*, ed. Stanley Beck and Ivan Bernier (Montreal: Institute for Research on Public Policy, 1983), 227–8.
45 *R. v. Secretary of State for Foreign and Commonwealth Affairs, ex. P. Indian Association of Alberta* [1982] 1 QB 892 (C.A.).
46 Marie Battiste and James Sa'ke'j Youngblood Henderson, *Protecting Indigenous Knowledge and Heritage: A Global Challenge* (Saskatoon: Purich, 2000), esp. 1–6 and 251–61.

# 'I will accept the Queen's hand':
# First Nations Leaders and the Image of the
# Crown in the Prairie Treaties

According to the official records, the monarch was central to both the process and results of Prairie treaty-making in the 1870s. Alexander Morris, the Ontario lawyer who served as chief negotiator for the Crown in Treaties 3, 4, 5, and 6, highlighted the role of the monarchy in his 1880 account, *The Treaties of Canada with the Indians*. In the section of his exhortatory concluding chapter that dealt with the 'Future of the Indians,' Morris asked, 'What is to be the future of the Indian population of the North-West?' and predicted that with effective Indian administration, 'I look forward to seeing the Indians, faithful allies of the Crown, while they can gradually be made an increasing and self-supporting population.'[1] Moreover, as the reprints of the government version of the various treaties in Morris's book made clear, the Crown was, ostensibly at least, one of the signatories to the agreements. Typical was Treaty 2, the government text for which began, 'Articles of a Treaty made and concluded this twenty-first day of August, in the year of our Lord one thousand eight hundred and seventy-one between Her Most Gracious Majesty the Queen of Great Britain and Ireland, by Her Commissioner, Wemyss M. Simpson, Esquire, of one part, and the Chippewa tribe of Indians, inhabitants of the country within the limits hereinafter defined and described by their Chiefs, chosen and named as hereinafter mentioned, of the other part.' The first paragraph of this text of Treaty 2 mentioned 'Her Majesty's said Commissioner' once more and 'Her Most Gracious Majesty' herself four times, culminating in the statement that the treaty was furnished so that the Saulteaux who had agreed to it 'may know and be assured of what allowance they are to count upon and receive from Her Majesty's bounty and benevolence.'[2] And so it was with all the treaties in Alexander Morris's volume.

Why, apparently, was the Crown so central in treaty-making in the 1870s? Morris, for example, appeared to give only the contributions of missionaries more weight in assuring the 'Future of the Indians.' And Morris seemed to have agreement from some of the First Nations negotiators who entered into treaty in thinking the Queen was significant in the process. Wemyss Simpson, primary Crown negotiator of Treaties 1 and 2, reported after concluding his work that 'the Indians ... have a firm belief in the honor and integrity of Her Majesty's representatives, and are fully impressed with the idea that the amelioration of their present condition is one of the objects of Her Majesty in making these treaties.'[3] Ahtahkakoop, a venerable Cree chief from the Fort Carlton area along the North Saskatchewan, ended a lengthy harangue to fellow First Nations negotiators in favour of making treaty with the words: 'I will accept the Queen's hand for my people. I have spoken.'[4] Why was the Crown so important to treaty-making that two of the Queen's most experienced treaty commissioners and one of the most influential Cree chiefs made allusion to her in their remarks? Why was the Queen so prominent? What role did the symbol of the Crown play? How did Canadian negotiators portray the Crown, and how did First Nations perceive the monarch? In the answers to these questions there are some important insights into the treaty-making history of post-Confederation Canada.

The Crown was important to North American First Nations long before the era of western treaty-making in the 1870s. In the intricate diplomacy that typified Native-newcomer relations in the eastern woodlands, personal relationships were critical to the interchanges between indigenous and European negotiators. So, for example, the Iroquois of what is now upper New York State encapsulated their relations with Britain and France in references to Corlaer and Onontio, their names for the governors of New York and New France respectively. For the League of the Iroquois, this manner of describing external relationships was simply a continuation of what they did with other First Nations in the northeastern woodlands. In the Covenant Chain, the extensive diplomatic network that the Iroquois fashioned with other Indian nations in the system, relations were personalized and familial. So other First Nations were brothers or cousins or even fathers, depending upon their status relative to the Iroquois. This personalization of relationships, including diplomatic associations, was typical of societies in which links of kinship were critical prerequisites to carrying on business. Just as First Nations invented or imputed kinship relationships – fictive kinship to use the anthropologists' term – to trade furs with their brothers in the commerce in peltries, so, too, they thought of and described their diplomatic relationships in familial terms. The link was individualized to the foreign monarch's local governor or to the Crown itself in First Nations' diplomatic language.

After Britain assumed the mantle of suzerainty from France in 1763, these intimate familial ties to the Crown remained important to some First Nations in the northeastern woodlands. Whenever they feared or encountered problems in their relations with the newcomers, they turned to the Crown in London, especially if the monarch's local representative was unavailable, ineffective, or unsympathetic to their cause. An example of this tendency emerged in the early months of the American Revolutionary War, when the Iroquois faced a crisis. The possibility of victory by the rebel Americans threatened them, for the American colonists were viewed as rapacious expansionists who would overrun Iroquois lands and dispossess them if they succeeded. In the recent past, the Six Nations had relied on Sir William Johnson, northern superintendent in the Indian Department that Britain had created in 1755 and husband of a Mohawk clan mother, to protect their territorial interests. However, Johnson had died in 1774, and the future looked threatening. In response, Joseph Brant, a young Mohawk leader and brother-in-law of the late Sir William Johnson, journeyed to London in the winter of 1775–6 to petition Britain for guarantees of Iroquois territory in return for Iroquois military support. Besides securing the assurance he sought, Brant was received at Court by George III, an event that seemed to attach him permanently to Britain's cause, and was lionized by London society. When the Revolutionary War ended badly for the Iroquois and Britain negotiated away their lands – Brant charged that the King had 'sold the Indians to Congress'[5] – Joseph Brant returned to London in 1785. Although again well received at Court and squired about town by the Prince of Wales, Brant this time failed to secure the guarantees of Iroquois territory that he sought.

Although First Nations' practice of personally petitioning the monarch was especially important in the heightened diplomatic and military atmosphere of the late eighteenth century, it did not end with the passing of this military era. In the subsequent phase of colonization and settlement, the era in which British immigrants made farms on lands negotiated from First Nations by treaty in Ontario, the throne was still perceived as a living entity that could be helpful in dealing with the incursions of Euro-Canadian settlement. So, for example, the expedition in 1860 of an Ontario Ojibwa woman Nahnebahwequa (Catherine Sutton) to ask Queen Victoria for assistance in recovering lands that she and her husband, an English immigrant, had been granted but then lost when the Indian Department took over the Bruce Peninsula. As Nahnebahwequa put it, she was 'an Indian woman born of Pagan Parents but brought up under religious instructions' whose 'forefathers fought and bled for the British Crown.' She had learned from her family that representatives of Britain repeatedly told her ancestors that they were 'Friends of the Red Man,' but of late the British had demonstrated 'a strange way of showing it.'[6] Received sympathetically by Victoria, Nahnebahwequa eventually did obtain title to her lands. Others whose interests she had also tried to represent in London did not, however, and Nahnebahwequa spent the rest of her life publicizing and campaigning against what she described as the government's 'wholesale robbery and treachery' over First Nations' lands in Ontario.[7]

On the other hand, the occasional visit of royalty to North American shores could prompt outpourings of fervent loyalty. When the Prince of Wales toured British North America in 1860, for example, First Nations had an opportunity to reiterate their ties to the Crown. Oronhyatekha presented the following address on behalf of the Six Nations to the Prince:

Brother, – We, the Chiefs, Sachems and Wariors of the Six Nations in Canada are glad of the opportunity to welcome to our native land, the Son of our Gracious Sovereign Queen Victoria, and to manifest our continued loyalty and devotion to the person and Crown of your Royal Mother. We return thanks to the Great Spirit that he has put it in to your Royal highness's mind to come to this country, and that He has preserved your Royal Highness safe, that we may meet together this day. He has ordained Princes and Rulers to govern His people; and it is His will that our beloved Queen, Your Royal Mother, is so preeminent in power and virtue.

Brother, – Although we have been separated from our Sovereign by the 'Great Water,' yet have we ever kept the chain of friendship bright, and it gives us joy to meet with the Heir Apparent to the Throne, that we may renew and strengthen that chain, which has existed between the Crown of England and the Six Nations for more than two hundred years. Our confidence in our Sovereign is as lasting as the stars in Heaven. We rejoice at the presence among us to fill the place of your Royal Mother, and her illustrious predecessor, whom we also love.

Brother, – We thank the Great Spirit, that we have had an opportunity of addressing your Royal Highness, and we pray that he who watches over all men may return your Royal Highness in health and safety to your Royal Mother, our Beloved Queen Victoria.[8]

First Nations had reason to continue to believe they needed the Crown as a counterweight to unsympathetic settler society in the decade leading up to western treaty-making in the 1870s. For one thing, in 1860, the year of the Prince of Wales's visit, the United Kingdom transferred jurisdiction over Indian matters to the colonial governments of British North America. This was part of a divestiture and devolution of responsibility that had been going on for several years. Also, in the late 1850s in the Province of Canada, the Indian Department stopped making annual presents to First Nations, a practice that symbolized for Indians the relationship between themselves and the Crown. Then, in 1860, Britain abandoned them to the tender mercies of local governments peopled by men whose interests, especially concerning land, were usually in conflict with those of First Nations. They protested their abandonment by Britain without avail. On the other hand, a few years later a Dakota group on the Prairies was able to invoke their tie to the Crown for much more positive reasons. In 1862, Dakota running from the American cavalry after the Minnesota wars claimed the right to reside north of the 'medicine line,' the international border, when they encountered Europeans. Their entitlement, as they explained, was based on the fact that they had fought with the British in the War of 1812. And they made their case founded on their alliance with the Crown to officials at Red River when they fled there after being defeated by the United States Army.[9]

The tie between First Nations and the Crown could be used negatively for political purposes, too, as was demonstrated by a Fraser River chief in 1875. In 1864 officials in the coastal colony had begun supplying funds to bands with which to celebrate the Queen's birthday.[10] However, on 15 May 1875 Alexis, chief of the Cheam band of Coast Salish, wrote in his own name and 'in the name of the other Chiefs of the River Fraser' to the Indian commissioner in Victoria about a matter that concerned Her Majesty:

We have heard that you have obtained from the Dominion some money in our name in order that we should celebrate properly the Queen's birthday.

We come to inform you that we do not wish to celebrate the Queen's day. She has not been a good Mother and Queen to us. She has not watched over us that we should have enough land for the support of our families. She knows that the British Columbia Government has deprived us of our land leaving but few acres and in some cases not even one acre per head ... If she is so great as we have been told she must be powerful enough to compel the British Columbia Government to extend our present Reserves. In that way Indian family [sic] will have eighty acres of land.

We come to tell you to send back the money the Dominion allowed for the celebration of the Queen's day. We do not wish it to be spent for us as long as our land question is not settled according to our wishes ...[11]

Spurning celebration of the Queen's birthday by these chiefs was a typical gesture of First Nations who believed their relationship to the newcomers had been sullied, dishonoured, or rendered unrewarding. Just as fur-trading leaders who believed they had not been well received and treated in trade would sever their commercial relationship with a Hudson's Bay Company trader by retrieving the pipes that they smoked in ritual ceremony upon arrival at the trading post, so Alexis and his fellow chiefs protested what they viewed as hostile treatment by the colonial government and inadequate protection by the monarch by refusing participation in a British ritual celebration, the twenty-fourth of May. The incident showed how the tie to the Crown could be used negatively as well as positively for political purposes. It also demonstrated the continuing importance of the Crown to First Nations. Clearly, then, the link between First Nations and the Crown was a well-established part of Native-newcomer history in Canada, and First Nations had demonstrated its importance to them repeatedly for a century prior to the post-Confederation treaty-making era.

The Crown was useful for diplomatic and political purposes for non-Natives, too, especially in the negotiation of the seven numbered treaties in the Canadian West in the 1870s. Between 1871 and 1877 Canada, in the name of the Crown, negotiated seven agreements known as numbered treaties for a region stretching from the Lake of the Woods in northwestern Ontario to the foothills of the Rocky Mountains and from the international border in the south to a point about midway up what are now the three Prairie provinces. These pacts were concluded with the Saulteaux (Western Ojibwa), Cree, Assiniboine, and Blackfoot. In making these agreements, Canada was both fulfilling an obligation and avoiding difficulties while acquiring access to a vast patrimony. The Deed of Surrender, the document embodying the transfer of the Hudson's Bay Company lands, or Rupert's Land, to the Dominion in 1870 contained a clause that obligated Canada to deal with any claims or protests by Native groups in the region. Simultaneously, in the period from 1869 to 1875 a succession of First Nations from the Lake of the Woods to Blackfoot country sent warnings to government officials indicating that the resident First Nations regarded the lands they occupied as their own and demanding that the government deal with them prior to authorizing any entry onto the lands by settlers. Also important was the fact that some First Nations' leaders, such as a group at Fort Edmonton headed by an elderly and highly respected chief known as Sweet Grass, sent a message that began with the complaint 'We heard our lands were sold and we did not like it' and concluded: 'Come and see us.'[12] Obviously, then, Canada turned to treaty-making because it was obliged to do so and because it feared that, if it did not, trouble even greater than the difficulty it had had with the Métis at Red River during 1869–70 would ensue. The fact that the Americans in the 1870s were embroiled in a series of Indian wars in their West reinforced the message that negotiation was the preferred method to integrate the newly acquired Rupert's Land and make it available for peaceful and quick settlement by non-Native farmers.

By 1870 Canada had a well-established tradition and methodology for making treaty with First Nations concerning access to Aboriginal land. It is important to remember that the politicians who dominated the federal government in the early post-Confederation decades were from Ontario and Quebec. These men, particularly the Ontarians, had matured politically in an era when treaty-making was almost the only method used to secure access to Indian lands. On the whole, British officialdom had followed the precepts of the Royal Proclamation of 1763 in making treaties in Upper Canada between the 1780s and 1860s. These requirements included a representative of the Crown meeting with Indian people in a public meeting to discuss and agree upon transfer of land from the First Nation to the newcomers. Because of this Upper Canadian treaty-making tradition, even though the Royal Proclamation was not meant to apply in Rupert's Land, its principles effectively did because of the influence of political leaders from Ontario. And it is worth noting that within the Royal Proclamation protocol for treaty-making the Crown had a prominent role: treaties for land could only be made with First Nations by a representative of the monarch. In addition to establishing a tradition based in large part on the Royal Proclamation, Upper Canadian practice also established a template for future treaties. By the time of the Robinson Treaties of 1850. Upper Canadian land agreements had come to include several features later found in western treaties. These were: treaties covered large areas of Aboriginal land; they included the provision of reserves for First Nations signatories; and they carried with them a Crown guarantee of the First Nations' continuing right to hunt, fish, and gather.

Accordingly, when Canada turned to negotiating treaties with western First Nations in 1870, tradition ensured that the Crown would play a prominent role in the process. But it was not just pre-Confederation custom that was at work. Canadian treaty negotiators recognized that associating their efforts with the Crown and the military power of the state could smooth the way to some extent with western First Nations. Alexander Morris said as much to the prime minister in the early months of 1873, not long before he began to negotiate treaties himself. According to Morris, as 'little as Canada may like it she has to stable her elephant,' and with that in mind he argued against reducing the size of 'both a military and police force' in the West. Furthermore, the 'police should also be under military discipline & if possible be red coated, as 50 men in red coats are better than 100 in other colours.'[13] Morris also associated his activities with the Queen, as in his 1873 speech from the throne in the Manitoba legislature because, as he told the prime minister, 'in this country it is important that the authority of the Queen should be brought before the people.'[14] It was no coincidence that a lieutenant-governor for Manitoba and the Northwestern Territory served as a Crown commissioner at negotiation of each of the seven treaties, or that after the North West Mounted Police established themselves in the West in 1874 they were prominent at treaty talks.

One of Morris's favourite tactics in treaty negotiations was to associate himself and his enterprise with the Queen in both positive and negative ways. First, associating the government negotiator with the monarch assured First Nations leaders that he did not represent anyone or anything but the Crown. At the negotiation of Treaty 3, the North West Angle Treaty, in northwestern Ontario in 1873, Morris told Indian leaders, 'I wish you to understand we do not come here as traders, but as representing the Crown, and to do what we believe is just and right.'[15] One reason for assuring Native negotiators that the Queen's commissioners did 'not come as traders' was to dissociate Canada from the Hudson's Bay Company, whose recent deal to transfer Rupert's Land to Canada for £300,000 and one-twentieth of the land was known and deeply resented by many First Nations. Another was to discourage prolonged haggling. Ironically, it was the former Hudson's Bay Company man, James McKay, who at Fort Carlton in 1876 said to persistent Native bargainers, 'My friends, I wish to make you a clear explanation of some things that it appears you do not understand. It has been said to you by your Governor that we did not come here to barter or trade with you for the land.'[16] On the contrary, they were there to tell First Nations leaders what they might expect from Her Majesty's 'bounty and benevolence.'

However, there was a positive aspect to Morris's invocation of the Queen as well. First was his insistence on the direct connection between his mission and the monarch. When the Saulteaux proved reluctant to come to the table at Fort Qu'Appelle in 1874 because of their anger at the Hudson's Bay Company transfer, Morris stressed, 'What I have to talk about concerns you, your children and their children, who are yet unborn, and you must think well over it, as the Queen has thought well over it. What I want, is for you to take the Queen's hand, through mine, and shake hands with her for ever ...'[17] The message was understood and accepted by First Nations. For example, Long Claws, at talks at Fort Pelly in 1874, greeted Morris with the words: 'My father – I shake hands with you, I shake hands with the Queen.'[18]

The assurance of direct representation and monarchical goodwill was a constant refrain. As Morris told Cree leaders at Fort Carlton in August 1876, during the negotiation of Treaty 6, 'I had been sent by the Queen, in compliance with their own wishes and the written promise I had given them last year, that a messenger would be sent to them.'[19] Morris also insisted on the Queen's good intentions towards western First Nations, and on the supposed goodwill of the Queen's Canadian government. After pointing out the efforts that had already been made to negotiate Treaties 3, 4, and 5, he continued:

> ... and now that the Indians of the east understand the Queen and her Councillors, I come to you. And why is all this done? I will tell you; it is because you are the subjects of the Queen as I am. She cares as much for one of you as she does for one of her white subjects. The other day a party of Iroquois Indians were taken to England across the ocean; the Queen heard of it and sent to them, saying 'I want to see my red children,' took their hands and gave each of them her picture, and sent them away happy with her goodness.

Before I came here I was one of the Queen's Councillors at Ottawa. We have many Indians there as here, but for many years there has been friendship between the British, and the Indians. We respect the Indians as brothers and as men. Let me give you a proof of it. Years ago there was war between the British and the Americans; there was a great battle; there were two brave Chief warriors on the British side, one wore the red coat, the other dressed as you do, but they fought side by side as brothers; the one was Brock and the other was Tecumseth whose memory will never die; the blood of both watered the ground; the bones of Tecumseth were hid by his friends; the remains of Brock by his, and now a great pile of stone stands up toward heaven in his memory. And now the white man is searching for the remains of Tecumseth, and when found they will build another monument in honour of the Indian.[20]

Clearly, the treaty commissioner's message associated Canada's treaty-making enterprise with the Queen rather than a trading company, and sought simultaneously to link the Canadian government with Her Majesty's warmth and good intentions towards First Nations.

The Canadian commissioners also insisted that the Queen's good intentions manifested themselves in what was offered to First Nations to enter into treaty. As noted earlier, Canada's representatives associated the Crown with the 'bounty and benevolence' that they proffered in treaty negotiations and in the government's version of the treaty agreement. In a similar fashion, the same notion of the Queen's benevolence was used as a bargaining ploy, particularly when First Nations negotiators were hard to convince. So, for example, when Alexander Morris met a solid wall of Saulteaux opposition at Fort Qu'Appelle in 1874, an opposition largely founded on Saulteaux resentment over the land deal between the Hudson's Bay Company and Canada, the treaty commissioner invoked the Queen:

Must we go back and tell the Queen that we held out our hands for her, and her red children put them back again? If that be the message that your conduct to-day is going to make us carry back, I am sorry for you, and fear it will be a long day before you again see the Queen's Councillors here to try to do you good. The Queen and her Councillors may think that you do not want to be friends, that you do not want your little ones to be taught, that you do not want when the food is getting scarce to have a hand in yours stronger than yours to help you. Surely you will think again before you turn your backs on the offers; you will not let so little a question as this about the Company, without whom you tell me you could not live, stop the good we mean to do.[21]

As described by the treaty commissioners, the Queen's hand contained assistance in the form of schooling for the young and food aid for all.

After 1874, the year the North West Mounted Police arrived on the Plains, the Queen's 'bounty and benevolence' included the aid of her red-coated 'soldiers,' too. During the Treaty 6 talks, Morris emphasized the protective role of the police:

> A Chief has his braves; you see here the braves of our Queen, and why are they here? To see that no white man does wrong to the Indian. To see that none give liquor to the Indian. To see that the Indians do no harm to each other. Three years ago some Americans killed some Indians; when the Queen's Councillors heard of it they said, we will send men there to protect the Indians, the Queen's subjects shall not be shot down by the Americans; now you understand why the police force is in this country, and you should rejoice.[22]

No western leader would have missed the allusion to the Cypress Hills Massacre, in which American wolf hunters murdered a party of Assiniboine in a dispute over stolen horses that was inflamed by alcohol.

Similarly, Canada's representatives assured First Nations negotiators that taking the Queen's hand meant only good things, nothing bad. In his opening statement at Fort Pitt in September 1876, Morris made the unqualified nature of Crown support and assistance unmistakable:

> This is the seventh time in the last five years that her Indian children have been called together for this purpose; this is the fourth time that I have met my Indian brothers, and standing here on this bright day with the sun above us, I cast my eyes to the East down to the great lakes and I see a broad road stretching on to Ellice, I see it branching there, the one to Qu'Appelle and Cypress Hills, the other by Pelly to Carlton; it is a wide and plain trail. Anyone can see it, and on that road, taking for the Queen, the hand of the Governor and Commissioners I see all the Indians. I see the Queen's Councillors taking the Indian by the hand saying we are brothers, we will lift you up, we will teach you, if you will learn, the cunning of the white man. All along that road I see Indians gathering, I see gardens growing and houses building; I see them receiving money from the Queen's Commissioners to purchase clothing for their children; at the

same time I see them retaining their old mode of living with the Queen's gift in addition.[23]

It was a risk-free deal, thanks to the 'bounty and benevolence' of the Queen and her government. 'What I have offered does not take away your living, you will have it then as you have now, and what I offer now is put on top of it. This I can tell you, the Queen's Government will always take a deep interest in your living.'[24] Whenever Morris had to refuse a negotiating demand, he cast responsibility for his negative response on the Canadian government,[25] but when there was a positive message to be delivered he was the Queen's messenger.

If the reasons and methods of the Crown negotiators were fairly clear, could the same be said regarding the First Nations? How did they perceive the role of the monarchy in the negotiations to which they were party between 1871 and 1877? What did they understand by the Crown, and what sort of relationship did they think they had established with Queen Victoria when they entered treaty?

First, as was noted at the outset, by the 1870s First Nations in the northern half of North America were not strangers to the Crown. Some of them in the eastern woodlands had on occasion taken their grievances directly to the throne in London, in an obvious effort either to circumvent or defeat colonial administrators with whom they had difficulties. Furthermore, as the behaviour of the Dakota who crossed the medicine line in 1862 revealed, they understood that there were benefits to be derived from a relationship with the Crown, whose White children were poised to invade the prairies as settlers. In western Canada, the Crown as representative of the new society took some getting used to on the part of First Nations because they had long associated the Hudson's Bay Company with newcomer presence. Indeed, they had succeeded in having the Company adopt Aboriginal diplomatic and mercantile protocols in the fur trade, making formal welcomes, pipe ceremonies, and gift exchange a regular part of the fur trade.[26] Now they would have to adjust their thinking about this external presence. However, in distinguishing the Queen from the Company, they had their vast knowledge of what transpired in other parts of North America, a knowledge transmitted by the famous 'moccasin telegraph' that worked efficiently throughout Indian Country.

It is also important to understand that First Nations approached treaty negotiations with the Queen's commissioners with assumptions and expectations shaped by their own cultural values and prescriptions. Part of that cultural background was the personalization of relations that was noted earlier. Another was a reliance on highly metaphorical language to convey concepts and abstractions in concrete, often personal, terms. One component of First Nations' metaphorical language that was critical to the western treaty negotiations was their reliance on the language of family and of childhood. Personalized relationships required the employment of metaphors of close association, and no ties were more intimate than the relations within the family. Hence, the First Nations who negotiated treaties in the 1870s would not have been offended by references to Queen Victoria as their 'mother' and to themselves as 'Red children' of the Queen. On the contrary, in First Nations societies, children in particular enjoyed a privileged place. Unlike Euro-Canadian society, in which children were dependent and controlled, in First Nations communities children, while dependent on adults, were fairly autonomous and privileged. Indian children were seldom restrained by harsh words or corporal discipline, and the golden years until they reached early adulthood were a time when they had a right to expect support and assistance from parents and older kin. Accordingly, whatever twenty-first-century non-Natives might assume, First Nations negotiators would not have been offended by references to themselves as the Queen's 'children.'[27] If Victoria proposed to behave towards them as they did to their own children, taking treaty was an attractive proposition.

What First Nations knew or assumed about the Crown enhanced the likelihood of their agreeing to enter treaty. In the first place, to them the monarch symbolized power, often personalizing the strength of her white-skinned subjects who were soon to invade the West. So, for example, a chief at the North West Angle in 1873 complained that a treaty medal that the government had given to Treaty 1 negotiators in 1871 was unworthy of the Queen. The treaty commissioner, the chief objected, 'said it was silver, but *I* do not think it is. I should be ashamed to carry it on my breast over my heart. I think it would disgrace the Queen, my mother, to wear her image on so base a metal as this ... Let the medals you give us be of silver – medals that shall be worthy of the High position our Mother the Queen occupies.'[28] Or, as Thomas Sewap of the Peter Ballantyne Cree band replied when he was asked in 1976 what the origin of their treaty was, 'That originated from the Queen herself, from the Queen's representatives.' And, in case there was any misunderstanding of what the Queen represented, he added, 'Ki-choga-mas-kew – GREAT WHITE WOMAN.'[29] Elder Nancy McCallum, interviewed at the same time as Thomas Sewap, underlined the Queen's importance and power when she testified, 'It was the Queen who governed the whole land. You cannot change what the Queen had said, even though she's dead.'[30]

In addition to being strong, the Queen was generous and supportive, qualities that stemmed in part at least from the fact that she was a woman. Mistawasis and Ahtahkakoop, two elderly Cree chiefs who vigorously supported taking treaty at the Treaty 6 talks at Fort Carlton in August 1876, between them made a persuasive case for joining with the Queen because her strength would provide assistance in troubled times. First, in a private caucus of First Nations' negotiators, Mistawasis reminded his fellow leaders that they faced a crisis because of the rapidly declining buffalo herds on which the Plains peoples had always relied:

> I speak directly to Poundmaker and The Badger and those others who object to signing this treaty. Have you anything better to offer our people? I ask, again, can you suggest anything that will bring these things back for tomorrow and all the tomorrows that face our people?
>
> I for one think that the Great White Queen Mother has offered us a way of life when the buffalo are no more. Gone they will be before many snows come to cover our heads or graves if such should be.[31]

Mistawasis left it to Ahtahkakoop, his partner in what was obviously a carefully planned strategy to win the chiefs' agreement to making treaty, to spell out what that 'way of life' the Queen offered them was.

When it was Ahtahkakoop's turn to speak to the caucus, he carried on Mistawasis's argument. They faced a crisis caused by vanishing buffalo and arriving settlers, a crisis to which the Queen and a treaty were the answer. Ahtahkakoop began with a question:

> Can we stop the power of the white man from spreading over the land like the grasshoppers that cloud the sky and then fall to consume every blade of grass and every leaf on the trees in their path? I think not. Before this happens let us ponder carefully our choice of roads ...
>
> We have always lived and received our needs in clothing, shelter, and food from the countless multitudes of buffalo that have been with us since the earliest memory of our people. No one with open eyes and open minds can doubt that the buffalo will soon be a thing of the past. Will our

people live as before when this comes to pass? No! They will die and become just a memory unless we find another way.

And that, Athtahkakoop hammered home, was where the Queen came into the calculation:

> For my part, I think that the Queen Mother has offered us a new way and I have faith in the things my brother Mista-wa-sis has told you. The mother earth has always given us plenty with the grass that fed the buffalo. Surely we Indians can learn the ways of living that made the white man strong and be able to vanquish all the great tribes of the southern nations. The white man never had the buffalo, but I am told they have cattle in the thousands that are covering the prairie for miles and will replace the buffalo in the Long Knives' country and may even spread over our lands. The white men number their lodges by the thousands, not like us who can only count our teepees by tens. I will accept the Queen's hand for my people. I have spoken.[32]

Through a treaty with the Queen, Ahtahkakoop and Mistawasis argued, they could get the help they needed to respond to the imminent crisis brought on by the collapse of the buffalo resource.

When the image of the Queen was projected as a helpful mother, the gender of the monarchy became a critically important issue to Plains negotiators. As Charles Backman, an Alberta Cree elder later recalled, 'That is why they were agreeable to treaty because the promises were so good. The government official was always making references to a woman who had sent them. The Indians sympathized with the woman, the Queen, through her representatives.'[33] As Cree scholar Sharon Venne, relying on the oral history of elders, explains, the monarchy's helpfulness was directly associated with the Queen's gender: the 'Queen's breasts were big enough and could last that long to feed and care for all the Indian peoples. You could never exhaust the supply of them to feed you all. This was the answer the Elder got from the Commissioner.'[34] The chief treaty commissioner at Treaty 4 in 1874 was closely questioned about the Queen's helpfulness:

> Kan-oo-ses [sic] – Is it true you are bringing the Queen's kindness? Is it true you are going to give my child what he may use? Is it true that you are going to give the different bands the Queen's kindness? Is it true that you bring the Queen's hand? Is it true you are bringing the Queen's power?

Lieut.-Gov. Morris – Yes, to those who are here and those who are absent, such as she has given us.

Kamooses – Is it true that my child will not be troubled for what you are bringing him?

Lieut.-Gov. Morris – The Queen's power will be around him.[35]

Clearly Kamooses was attempting at Fort Qu'Appelle to get confirmation that the Great White Queen Mother's protective and helpful embrace was part of the treaty that was proposed.

Finally, to Plains First Nations negotiators the Crown represented justice, or, perhaps, relative justice. Mistawasis, the Cree chief who argued for taking treaty at Fort Carlton in August 1876, pitched his argument partially in terms of the fact that the Queen and British power represented the promise of fair treatment for First Nations. 'Look to the great Indian Nations in the Long Knives' country [the United States] who have been fighting since the memory of their oldest men. They are being vanquished and swept into the most useless parts of their country. Their days are numbered like those of the buffalo. There is no law or justice for the Indians in Long Knives' country. The Police followed two murderers to Montana and caught them but when they were brought to the Montana court they were turned free because it was not murder to kill an Indian.'[36] Alexander Morris played on the Plains peoples' fear of American enmity towards Indians by contrasting during Treaty 6 talks the hostility of the Americans and the fairness of the Queen's law.[37] Plains leaders who remembered the Cypress Hills Massacre would understand that message.

Certainly the venerable Blackfoot chief Crowfoot, who had drawn close to the North West Mounted Police in southern Alberta after they arrived in 1874, was aware of the difference between law south and north of the medicine line. The Mounted Police, wearing the red serge associated with the British military, had cleaned out the American's whiskey forts, sites of contagion and violence, and sent the American peddlers packing across the border. Crowfoot cited the fairness of the Queen's law, represented by her red-coated soldiers, as a primary reason to sign Treaty 7 in 1877. 'The advice given me and my people has proved to be very good,' said the Blackfoot chief. 'If the Police had not come to the country, where would we be all now? Bad men and whiskey were killing us so fast that very few, indeed, of us would have been left to-day. The Police have protected us as the feathers of the bird protect it from the frosts of winter. I wish them all good, and trust that all

our hearts will increase in goodness from this time forward. I am satisfied. I will sign the treaty.'[38] For Crowfoot, as for Mistawasis and no
doubt many other western First Nations' leaders, treaty meant a relationship with the Queen and her people that promised a more just – or
less unjust – treatment than they might expect from the Americans to
the south.

The image of the Queen as it emerges from the treaty discussions in
western Canada in the 1870s is an amalgam of positive qualities. First,
although the monarch's representative hailed from the same country
as the Hudson's Bay Company, he was Her delegate, not the Company's. He and his fellow commissioners were 'not here as traders,'
implying that they were not associated with the land transfer to which
some Plains nations objected and that they had different intentions
from the merchants with whom the Indians had dealt for two centuries. The fact that the treaty commissioners almost invariably conducted the parleys according to Aboriginal protocol – with welcoming
speeches, rituals including the pipe that guaranteed the Creator's over-
sight of their proceedings, and gifts – indicated that they were prepared to accommodate themselves to Native ways, as the Baymen did,
but they still were different.

Second, the speeches and behaviour of the First Nations' negotiators
indicated that they recognized the strength that the Queen and her
treaty commissioners represented. As Mistawasis told his fellow leaders in the August 1876 caucus outside Fort Carlton, the strength of the
Queen was manifested in the effectiveness of her redcoat 'soldiers' in
southern Alberta soon after their arrival in the West. They had come
west because the 'Great Queen Mother, hearing of the sorrows of her
children, sent out the Red Coats.' They had scattered the whiskey peddlers. Mistawasis pressed on to his point about the Queen's power by
pointing out how a few mounties scattered the desperadoes:

> I ask you why those few men could put to flight those bad men who for
> years have defied the whole of the southern Indian nations?
>
> Surely these Red Coats are men of flesh and blood as ourselves and a
> bullet is just as effective on them as on any Blackfoot, but ask yourselves
> why the traders fled in fear from so few men. The southern tribes out-
> numbered this small Police Force one hundred to one, but they were help-
> less in spite of their numbers.
>
> Let me tell you why these things were so. It was the power that stands
> behind those few Red Coats that those men feared and wasted no time in

getting out when they could; the power that is represented in all the Queen's people, and we the children are counted as important as even the Governor who is her personal speaker.

The Police are the Queen Mother's agents and have the same laws for whites as they have for the Indians. I have seen these things done and now the Blackfoot welcome these servants of the Queen Mother and invite her Governor for a treaty with them next year.

Mistawasis expected the Queen to continue to deploy her strength for the benefit of the Indians after treaty: 'I, for one, look to the Queen's law and her Red coat servants to protect our people against the evils of white man's firewater and to stop the senseless wars among our people, against the Blackfoot, the Peigans, the Bloods ... The prairies have not been darkened by the blood of our white brothers in our time. Let this always be so. I for one will take the hand that is offered. For my band I have spoken.'[39]

Finally, treaty meant an association with a Queen who was generous and just. In part because she was a woman, the Queen metaphorically represented generosity and support to her Indian 'children' in the rhetoric of Plains people at treaty time and since. Her treaty commissioners constantly played on both those qualities in their presentations in treaty talks, and their assurances of beneficence and fairness resonated with First Nations who were concerned about their ability to manage a difficult transition to a new way of life after the buffalo were gone. It is not surprising that a great deal of the rhetoric about the Queen's generosity and protection emerged in the Treaty 6 talks, especially at Fort Carlton, because by 1876 Plains nations could see unmistakable evidence that the bison resource was in precipitous decline. It is also no coincidence that the famine clause and the medicine chest clause, treaty provisions that guaranteed Crown support in time of severe hardship and provision of limited medical assistance, were incorporated into Treaty 6. Although these clauses have proven disappointing to the Plains Cree who negotiated them because the Canadian government proved niggardly in its interpretation and implementation of them, at the time of negotiation they would have reassured anxious Plains leaders of the Queen's 'bounty and benevolence.'

Underlying all the rhetoric about accepting the Queen's hand and having the Queen's protection about them in treaty was an assumption on the part of the First Nations that the treaty they were negotiating would establish a family relationship with the Queen and her people.[40]

To them these were not one-shot contracts involving transfer of title to land. Rather they were covenants – the Creator, whose presence was invoked both by pipe ceremonies and repeated rhetorical references by both parties to the deity, the Crown, and the First Nations were the parties – that would last forever. Both Crown commissioners and Indian negotiators frequently said that the treaties were to last as long as the sun shone and the waters flowed, and the annuities, annual payments that were part of treaty compensation, were the tangible symbols of the renewal of the relationship that the numbered treaties fashioned between First Nations and the Crown. It was important for Indian negotiators to perceive the Queen as strong, generous, and just in order for them to have confidence in a future relationship with her and her Canadian people that was to last to eternity. A monarch with a positive image, such as Queen Victoria clearly enjoyed in the treaty talks of the 1870s, was a major asset for Canadian negotiators in persuading western First Nations to enter into treaty.

Although the First Nations were to be bitterly disappointed with the implementation of the treaties they agreed to between 1871 and 1877, they never abandoned their positive image of the Crown, at least at a rhetorical level. The early post-treaty years were difficult ones for the western nations, as a frugal national government took advantage of the collapse of the buffalo economy both to drag its feet in providing the support the treaties promised and in using First Nations' hardship to impose the government's will on Indians. In the aftermath of the Northwest Rebellion of 1885, the Department of Indian Affairs used the crisis to crack down on Plains nations, especially those led by chiefs who had been resisting the imposition of government policies. Besides using the post-Rebellion trials of innocent chiefs such as Mistahimusqua (Big Bear), Poundmaker, Wapahaska (White Cap), and One Arrow politically to deprive Plains communities of effective leadership, they clamped a series of policies on them that lacked any legislative base, such as the pass system, or violated treaty promises of continuing freedom of mobility and harvesting, or interfered with internal governance. Generally speaking, the three decades following the treaty negotiations were among the most difficult western Indians faced.

Despite the Canadian government's treachery in these years, western Indian leaders continued to express loyalty to and support of the Crown, although they frequently wondered aloud about the Queen's wayward children in Ottawa who were making their lives so difficult. As early as 1878 two prominent Treaty 4 chiefs, Kakishiway (Loud Voice) and O'Soup, both of whom had been signatories to the treaty four years earlier, bent the ear of a Canadian member of Parliament who accompanied the government party that came to Fort Qu'Appelle to pay their annuities. Kakishiway told the member of Parliament that four years earlier the treaty commissioner 'told us to keep our ears open. I saw then what our Great Mother gave us, and promised us. Our Great Mother told us to try hard and sustain her. We have done so. Now we ask for our Great Mother to be charitable.' His colleague, O'Soup, was more pointed: he asked for 'all he had said [to be] put on paper and given to our Great Mother, and if what they wanted was not granted the paymaster need not come back next year.'[41] The clear implication of these words was that, if the treaty promises were not properly observed, the annual payments should stop, signalling that the treaty was rescinded.

A particularly revealing moment that indicated the continuing importance of the Crown occurred in 1881, when Governor General Lorne made a tour of the western territories and met with many First Nations delegations. Lord Lorne was no ordinary British noble; he was the son-in-law of Victoria herself, having married the Queen's daughter, the Princess Louise. While the delegations he met welcomed him, they made some important points. For example, Kakishiway emphasized the kin relationship that Treaty 4 had established with the Queen by greeting Lorne at Qu'Appelle with the words, 'I am glad to see you my Brother in Law.' The chief was Victoria's son, brother to the Princess Louise, and therefore brother-in-law to Lorne. Day Bird said he was 'sorry I did not see your lady.' Pahsung similarly remarked, 'If the Princess was here I would like to see her too and shake hands and The Queen – the Mistress of Everything.' Very similar sentiments were expressed at Battleford, where Lorne got another earful from disgruntled chiefs.[42]

In spite of their post-treaty disillusionment, western First Nations continued to express and demonstrate their loyalty to the Queen and even to her wayward government in Ottawa. Poignant examples of this loyalty occurred in Treaty 4 in 1884 and in Treaty 6 much later. Kakishiway, the elderly chief who had signed Treaty 4 in 1874 and greeted Lord Lorne as a kinsman in 1881, lay dying in 1884. Furthermore, his followers faced a crisis, because they were having grave difficulties with the Department of Indian Affairs. Although a reserve had been surveyed for them, and another for Chief Chacachase, not far away in the late 1870s, the tracts were never set aside by order-in-council, as was required by law, as reserves. Consequently, both bands remained land-less and in uncertainty. In spite of the dubious treatment they had received from Ottawa, among Kakishiway's last words were advice to his followers 'to be loyal to their Queen, to take the advice of those over them, and not to leave their reserves.'[43] Their reward? The Department of Indian Affairs took advantage of Chacachase's absence about the same time to combine his band with that of Kakishiway and cram them onto one reserve. Nonetheless, these bands, like all the Plains nations, remained loyal to the Crown during the Northwest Rebellion, which erupted soon afterwards.[44] Similarly, when the great-grandson of Chief Mistawasis, one of the senior advocates of making Treaty 6 in 1876, enlisted in the Canadian forces during the Second World War, according to historian James Dempsey he explained his action as a consequence of the Plains Cree's 1876 alliance with the Crown.[45]

In spite of often difficult post-treaty chapters in the history of Native-newcomer relations, First Nations in Canada have retained their sense of close attachment to the person and office of the Crown. Their politi-cal representatives have always insisted that they made treaties with the British Crown, and have never accepted the legitimacy of the trans-fer of responsibility for treaties and First Nations to Canada when the country achieved autonomy within the Commonwealth. A 1978 hunt-ing rights court case involving a Treaty 9 band in northern Ontario reaf-firmed 'that the Indians thought they were dealing with the king's personal representatives and were relying on the word of His Majesty rather than officials of Government.'[46] Canadian First Nations, both individually and in larger political organizations, have repeatedly attempted to invoke their relationship with the Crown, ostensibly in search of antidotes to federal government policies, but in reality in an attempt to embarrass Canada into taking corrective action by bringing the glare of international publicity to bear on conditions in Canada. The Six Nations did this in the 1920s when they sought British and League of Nations recognition of their claim to sovereignty. First Nations' orga-nizations employed the same tactics at Westminster in the late 1970s and early 1980s in their campaign to prevent the patriation of the Cana-dian constitution until their demands had been met. In the autumn of 2002, some First Nations considered staging protests during Queen Elizabeth's visit to Canada, part of her golden jubilee celebrations, to publicize their opposition to recent government legislative initiatives on financial accountability and governance.[47] The Crown has increasingly taken on the image of a convenient political device that Canadian First Nations could try to exploit in pursuit of their political or constitutional agenda.

To leave this analysis on such a cynical note would be as inaccurate as it would be unfortunate. Western First Nations to this day retain a strong sense of direct connection to and affection for the Crown. It manifests itself regularly in Prairie celebrations when the Union Jack is always flown along with the maple leaf flag in commemoration of First Nations' alliance with the Crown in war service and in treaty. Most recently, in the spring of 2001, Prince Charles met with a rapturous welcome when he toured Saskatchewan. Both non-Native and First Nations groups flocked to his public occasions. And the provincial government, anxiously clinging to power as out-migration swelled and provincial revenues shrank amidst a prolonged drought and slump in commodity prices, saw fit to associate itself with the glory of the Crown and the Prince's visit by distributing broadly a picture-laden commemorative booklet of the tour.[48]

## Notes

This essay is a revised version of a paper given to the Majesty in Canada Conference held at the Centre for Canadian Studies, University of Edinburgh, on 3 May 2002. Research for this essay was funded by a Standard Research Grant of the Social Sciences and Humanities Research Council of Canada. My colleague Keith Carlson commented helpfully on an earlier draft. I would also like to thank research assistant Christa Nicholat, who located many sources for me; and Allyson Stevenson, who kindly allowed me to use citations from her graduate seminar research paper.

1 Alexander Morris, *The Treaties of Canada with the Indians* (1880; reprint, Saskatoon: Fifth House, 1991), 295.
2 Ibid., 316-17.
3 Wemyss M. Simpson to secretary of state for the provinces, 3 Nov. 1871, ibid., 42.
4 Peter Erasmus, *Buffalo Days and Nights*, ed. Irene M. Spry (Calgary: Glenbow, 1989), 250.
5 Quoted in Robert S. Allen, *His Majesty's Indian Allies: British Indian Policy in the Defence of Canada, 1774–1815* (Toronto: Dundurn, 1992), 56.

6  National Archives of Canada (NA), RG 10, Records of the Department of Indian Affairs (RG 10), vol. 2877, file 177, 181, petition of Catherine Sutton. Internal evidence suggests that this petition was prepared in 1859 or 1860 (she says she's been married for twenty years; Donald B. Smith, in 'Nahnebahwequay,' *Dictionary of Canadian Biography* [Toronto: University of Toronto Press, 1976], 9: 590–1, indicates that she married in 1839), probably for presentation in England ('but let the British Government order a thorough investigation of all Indian afairs [*sic*]'). See also 'Petitioning the Great White Mother,' in this volume.

7  Smith, 'Nahnebahwequay,' 591.

8  Presentation reproduced in the exhibition 'Victorian Ideals, Victorian Values: Oronhyatekha, M.D.,' Royal Ontario Museum, 29 May 2002. The exhibition was created by the Woodland Cultural Centre, Brantford, in collaboration with the Royal Ontario Museum.

9  P.D. Elias, *The Dakota of the Canadian Northwest: Lessons for Survival* (Winnipeg: University of Manitoba Press, 1988), 17.

10  Keith Thor Carlson, 'The Power of Place and the Problem of Time: A Study in Aboriginal History Identity' (Ph.D. diss., University of British Columbia. 2003), chapter 6.

11  RG 10, vol. 3612, file 3763, Chief Alexis to Indian Commissioner, 15 May 1875.

12  Morris, *Treaties*, 170-1.

13  NA, MG 26A, Sir John A. Macdonald Papers, vol. 252, 113998–4003, A. Morris to J.A. Macdonald, 16 Jan. 1873

14  Ibid., 114092–5, A. Morris to J.A. Macdonald, 5 March 1873.

15  Morris, *Treaties*, 67.

16  Ibid., 211.

17  Ibid., 90.

18  Ibid., 124. I am indebted to Allyson Stevenson for this citation.

19  Ibid., 183.

20  Ibid., 200–1.

21  Ibid., 113.

22  Ibid., 206–7.

23  Ibid., 231.

24  Ibid., 211.

25  Ibid., 60, 62.

26  Arthur J. Ray, Jim Miller, and Frank Tough, *Bounty and Benevolence: A History of Saskatchewan Treaties* (Montreal and Kingston: McGill-Queen's University Press, 2000), 5–10.

27  John L. Tobias, 'The Treaty Rights Movement in Saskatchewan,' in *1885 and*

*After: Native Society in Transition*, ed. F.L. Barron and J.B. Waldram (Regina: Canadian Plains Research Center, 1986), 248.

28  Morris, *Treaties*, 74

29  Saskatchewan Archives Board, Collection R-834, file 38 c, records of an inquiry at Pelican Narrows, 4 Feb. 1977, conducted by Dr Lloyd I. Barber, Indian claims commissioner, Appendix 3, transcript of interview of Thomas Sewap at Pelican Narrows, 5 Feb. 1976, 171. Sewap's testimony from an earlier interview (5 Feb. 1976) was introduced and added as an appendix at the 1977 inquiry held to collect oral history information about the adhesion of Peter Ballantyne band to Treaty 6.

30  Ibid., testimony of Nancy McCallum, Pelican Narrows, 25 Feb. 1976.

31  Erasmus, *Buffalo Days and Nights*, 247.

32  Ibid., 249–50.

33  Sharon Venne, 'Understanding Treaty 6: An Indigenous Perspective,' in *Aboriginal and Treaty Rights in Canada: Essays on Law, Equality, and Respect for Difference*, ed. Michael Asch (Vancouver: UBC Press, 1997), 192.

34  Elder Lazarus Roan, quoted in Venne, 199.

35  Morris, *Treaties*, 117–18.

36  Erasmus, *Buffalo Days and Nights*, 249.

37  Morris, *Treaties*, 206–7.

38  Ibid., 272.

39  Erasmus, *Buffalo Days and Nights*, 248–9.

40  Jean Friesen, 'Magnificent Gifts: The Treaties of Canada with the Indians of the Northwest,' *Transactions of the Royal Society of Canada*, series 5, 1 (1986): 47.

41  Ray, Miller, and Tough, *Bounty and Benevolence*, 187–8.

42  RG 10, vol. 3768, file 33, 642, notes of Lord Lorne's interviews with chiefs, 1881.

43  A. McDonald, Indian agent, to superintendent general of Indian affairs, 16 Sept. 1884, in 'Annual Report of the Department of Indian Affairs for the Year Ended 31 December 1884,' Canada, *Sessional Papers (No. 8) 1885*, 67.

44  Blair Stonechild and Bill Waiser, *Loyal till Death: Indians and the North-West Rebellion* (Saskatoon: Fifth House, 1997).

45  James Dempsey, 'Alberta's Indians and the Second World War,' in *For King and Country: Alberta in the Second World War*, ed. Ken Tingley (Edmonton: Reidmore Books, 1995), 41. In spite of the title of article and book, Private Dreaver was from the Mistawasis Reserve in central Saskatchewan. I am indebted to Christa Nicholat, who brought this item to my attention.

46  Ontario in *Regina v. Battiste*, (1978) 19 O.T. (2nd) 145 (D.C. Temiskaming); quoted in Douglas Sanders, 'Prior Claims: Aboriginal People in the Consti-

tution of Canada,' in *Canada and the New Constitution: The Unfinished Agenda, Vol. I*, ed. Stanley Beck and Ivan Bernier (Montreal: Institute for Research on Public Policy, 1983), 246.

47  *Star-Phoenix* [Saskatoon], 21 Sept. 2002.
48  Province of Saskatchewan, *Saskatchewan Royal Reflections: The Prince of Wales in Saskatchewan, April 2001* (Regina: Government of Saskatchewan, 2002).

# ACADEME

# Devil's Island, Marijuana U., and the League of the Six Nations: Models for Governing the University

Styles of university governance are like Caesar's Gaul: they are divided into three. One approach to running universities emphasizes the stick: it is authoritarian, punitive, and coercive. A second favours inducing the university's personnel to look upward for rewards: it encourages staff to pander to their superiors in hope of advancement and other forms of favour. Finally, there is a style of governance that stresses consultation, consensual decision-making, and non-punitive sanctions designed to inhibit or prevent negative actions. For simplicity these three styles can be labelled: Devil's Island, Marijuana U., and the League of the Six Nations.

Everyone recognizes the university modelled on Devil's Island, the infamous French overseas prison. Devil's Island U. is run as though it were an isolated prison for the most dangerous and incorrigible offenders. We all know the hallmarks of this penal hell, and everyone thinks they belong to the 'bad old days' of despotic administration. Surely Devil's Island is something out of the early twentieth century, when President Walter Murray of the University of Saskatchewan could have several tenured faculty removed for not being sufficiently loyal to his notion of what was best for the institituion. Or perhaps it is a relic of the early days of the Second World War, when a number of governors at the University of Toronto wanted Frank Underhill fired for gloating on the public airwaves about the inevitable decline of British power. Or maybe – the bad old days are getting closer now – that Devil's Island style was found in the officials at United College who in the 1950s thought it was all right to open a professor's mail and later to force him out of the institution. For those who think that Devil's Island techniques are found only in historic times, reference could be made to a battle in 1990 at Australia's Macquarie University in which the president appointed two individuals to professorial fellowships outside normal procedures and the university's staff association publicly chastised her for doing so.[1]

On the modern Devil's Island such administrative arbitrariness is essential to what is thought to be the efficient running of the place. Contemporary academic penal isles are characterized by an absence of recognized procedures, whether within or outside a collective agreement or procedures manual, and by a large amount of unilateral bureaucratic behaviour. Accountability flows only in one direction. There are elaborate systems for making those lower down in the hierarchy accountable to those above them, but there is no way of making administrators answerable to the general population. Prisoners' committees have no voice in deciding how things are done. The other side of that coin is a set of severe sanctions – denial of tenure, refusal to promote, inability to win merit increases – that in reality is used as an instrument to keep the denizens in line. Of course, administrative arbitrariness is facilitated by a stiff code of punishments, and in turn it depends upon it to survive. The euphemism for rule by bureaucrat's whim is 'administrative flexibility.' In the hands of all but angels, it inevitably turns into repression, suppression, and even oppression. It can happen here; angels are not noticeably more numerous in Canadian universities than anywhere else.

At first glance, viewed from a distance, the institution of higher learning that is governed on the cannabis principle seems far different. In that grove of academe there seems to be a lot of camaraderie and good cheer. But that bonhomie is merely a facade; the reality is in essence little different from the system on Devil's Island. For in Reefer U. the governing rule – indeed that is where the name comes from – is 'The harder you suck, the higher you get.'[2] In other words, in Marijuana U. success is achieved not by attending to the canons of one's discipline or by serving others in the pursuit of their academic goals. Rather, advancement is secured by pleasing those in authority, and the most effective way to do that is to adopt their views, policies, objectives, prejudices, and enmities. Yes-men and yes-women have the best chance of making their way up the academic and administrative ladder. As on Devil's Island, in the happy atmosphere of Marijuana U. the system persists because of a culture that tolerates administrative arbitrariness and a one-way flow of accountability. In this institutional cannabis culture, everyone seems happy, but somehow the institution never seems to go anywhere.

That is not all that is wrong with the Marijuana U. model, of course. The most fundamental objection to it is that it is an utter perversion of the values for which the university is supposed to stand. Rather than pursuing and describing truth as one sees it, the faculty member of Marijuana U. tailors the result of research and the contents of teaching to the views and wishes of those in authority. Before very long, both students and the general public – the faculty are usually the last to recognize it – spot the institutional hypocrisy. Marijuana U. loses its moral credibility and its support. At a more utilitarian level, an academic culture in which pleasing those above is more important than doing what is professionally right ensures stagnation. Heads of major units do not defend their territory lest they displease the authorities who have other plans for the distribution of always-scarce resources. Faculty cease to respect those who are their titular leaders, give up their involvement in the administrative discourse of the campus, and seek refuge in their research and their classes. Over time, Marijuana U. becomes nothing but the hollow shell of a true academy. The outer walls still stand, but there is no vitality or energy within.

But what does the model of the League of the Iroquois have to recommend it in our times? Is this some radical call to academic arms in imitation of the Warriors' Society? Hardly, though it is worth noting in passing that 'warriors' society' is a bit of a misnomer, or at least an imprecise translation, for what might more accurately be rendered as the 'protectors of the earth.' No, the reason for suggesting that the League of the Six Nations might have something to teach us academics now is that that fascinating instrument united diverse groups into an effective unit that provided internal harmony and security against external threats. How it did so is worth considering.

The League of the Six Nations, or the Iroquois Confederacy, was a federal political structure that existed among an eastern agricultural and commercial Indian people prior to the coming of Europeans in the fifteenth and sixteenth centuries. The Iroquois resided south of what we call Lake Ontario and the upper St Lawrence River, and they depended mainly on horticulture, especially growing corn, and on trade with other Indian groups, especially hunter-gatherer groups. Though inhabiting many large, palisaded villages, they were generally recognized as being composed of five principal groupings, until early in the eighteenth century when their number was augmented by refugee Tuscarora who migrated northward from disastrous wars that threatened to destroy them. The Six Nations played critically important roles in the Europeans' imperial wars of the eighteenth century, and included in that group of struggles were the American Revolution and the War of 1812. As a consequence of picking the losing side, they were forced to relocate north of the lower Great Lakes, particularly in large reserves near Brantford and Belleville, but also in smaller mission settlements at such places as St Regis (Akwesasne), Caughnawaga (Kahnawake), and, of course, Oka (Kanesatake). Today, as in the 1690s and the 1790s, they are a force to be reckoned with in Canadian life. Against formidable odds, they have survived, even thrived. What was and is their secret?

The Iroquois League persisted because it was made up of a set of institutions and practices that preserved harmony within the group while ensuring the collectivity's ability to act unitedly against a danger from without. At this point, feminist scholars might interject that the most important of those factors were matrilocalism and matrilineal-ism. And in a sense those feminist scholars would be right. One of the most important features of Iroquois life, one that they shared with many other indigenous peoples, was a shunning of coercion and force among themselves. Village life was regulated by non-coercive sanctions, such as gossip and ridicule, rather than force and punishment. Iroquois learned not to behave in anti-social ways mainly because anti-social behaviour was ridiculed and shamed. Honour and pride were prime virtues; the threatened loss of them was an effective deterrent.

The Iroquois bulwark against their external enemies was not the walls of their distinctive villages – though those were impressive and important in warfare – but rather their federal political structure. The grand council of the Five Nations in the days prior to the coming of the Tuscarora consisted of fifty chiefs representing the Mohawk, Cayuga, Seneca, Oneida, and Onondaga roughly in proportion to the size of their nation. Matters of proposed common policy – principally issues of diplomacy and war – were discussed at lengthy, regular meetings of the council, and no decision was binding that was not unanimous. Finally, as is often noted by environmentalists, Iroquoian political bodies charged specific individuals with the responsibility of considering only the effect of any proposed course of action, not just on the present generation or even upon the children and grandchildren of the contemporary decision-makers, but upon the seventh generation that would follow them. Iroquois policy-making, because of Iroquois political institutions, was consultative, consensual, and far-sighted.

Still there was one more vital element in the governing system of the Iroquois League. As important as non-coercive social and political relations were, as vital as consensual and provident policy-making were, they were not the entire story. The final, essential ingredient in successful governance among the Iroquois was the nature of leadership. As is often noted, leaders were chosen by the clan mothers from particular lineages in which leadership potential was hereditary. (The clan mothers also had a great deal to say about crucial decisions on waging war or making peace, another Iroquoian practice modern-day Canadians might consider adopting.) But what is most significant about Iroquois leadership is the qualities considered most desirable in a leader. What the clan mothers looked for as they surveyed the young adult males from the dominant lines when it came time to select a new chief was someone with a strong sense of service, mature and sound judgment, and proficiency in arms or diplomacy (or both). The reason for this was that leadership in the Six Nations was, and is, an obligation and a burden rather than an opportunity and an advantage.

Leadership among the Iroquoians, as among most First Peoples in the northern part of this continent, was a network of duties and obligations. The leader had to live for, not on, his people. The chief's responsibility was to see that the weak were protected, the disabled were fed and cared for, and the well-being of the group was pursued. His personal convenience and comfort could not be put ahead of the welfare of those whom he nominally led, but in actuality served. So far as giving direction to his people's will was concerned, the chief led by example and by moral authority. There simply were no instruments of coercion or favouritism that he could employ to drive or induce people to follow a path of his, rather than their, choosing. Unlike the commandant on Devil's Island, the Iroquois chief could not make the populace obey by the use of force and fear. In contrast to the head toker in Marijuana U., the sachem could not con the village into a happy herd mentality by a system of favouritism and targeted rewards. Behaviour of the kind employed on the penal isle or in the stoned academic grove would have resulted in loss of authority, weakening of social and political harmony, and perhaps vulnerability to the external foe.

The League of the Six Nations, then, adapted successfully to successive challenges attendant on the coming of a Euro-Canadian majority because of the strength of its social and political institutions. Internally it benefited from an intricate network of structures, values, and sanctions that induced socially harmonious behaviour while promoting effective and self-sacrificing leadership. Its strength against the outside world historically lay in its access to surplus food and its federal political system. Over the last two centuries, of course, it has only been the latter that has given it an advantage. But over all the Iroquois have persisted and even thrived because their apparatus for social and political governance has kept them strong and vital.

And why is the Iroquois League the best of the three styles of governance for Canadian post-secondary institutions? In part the answer lies, of course, in the obvious inappropriateness of the other two models. Even such a timid group as university faculty will not put up for very long with the commandant of Devil's Island. They will either escape or rebel. And the cannabis style has been revealed to be productive of nothing but administrative time-serving and institutional stagnation. Clearly the manifold ills of both Devil's Island and Marijuana U. make them unsuitable for governing the Canadian university nowadays. But not all of the argument for the Iroquois model is negative; there is also a positive case to be made.

The model of the League of the Six Nations is the most appropriate because it is best suited to grapple with the major categories of problems that Canadian universities face now and are likely to encounter in the near future. To summarize, the coming challenges fall under two headings: adjusting to the cost-income squeeze confronting all universities; and accommodating new social and academic imperatives. Everyone who has read a university annual report or an alumni magazine during the last decade will be painfully familiar with the strains generated in our academies by the twin forces of rising demands for services and declining public-sector financial support for universities. During the 1990–1 academic year, for example, full-time university enrolment continued its decade-long march upward, rising by yet another 3 per cent.[3] And, needless to say, the per-student funding of the universities has continued to sag. More serious still is the certainty that post-secondary education's claim on the public treasury will continue to weaken in the face of mounting demands for further expenditures on debt servicing and on health care by an aging population. In short, the first major problem of this era is that the students vote confidence in university education with their feet, while their parents refuse to match that endorsement with their taxes. The inevitable consequence of the resulting stress will be an unavoidable need to restructure and reduce the programs of Canadian universities. And that, of course, will pose the risk of engendering strife between faculties, and between faculty and administration.

The other major category of difficulties stems from universities' need to respond to increasingly insistent demands from society and our disciplines to reorient the way we recruit and treat faculty, as well as redefine our mandate for research and teaching. The former is a problem of equity that our institutions confront as they try to reconcile understandable demands for greater justice for women and racial minorities at a time when growth, the most convenient way to respond to such imperatives, will probably be unavailable. Canadian universities will face personnel and morale problems as they try to find places for greater numbers of female and minority academics during a period of little or no expansion. The other aspect of the problem of the new imperatives is the desperate need to devote greater attention, both in our research facilities and our classrooms, to topics that have shot quickly to the top of the public agenda and, as usual more slowly, are making their way up the academic roster as well. Chief among these program needs are environmental issues and aspects of international relations. It is not that Canada's universities have neglected questions of pollution and conservation, of diplomacy and business challenges from abroad. Rather, the novelty of the situation now is that the tax-paying public is demanding that its universities devote much more attention and resources to these matters. Universities ignore that insistent public at their peril.

But again, as in the matter of accommodating the strains that inevitably flow from the cost-revenue pinch or the need to address equity issues, the need to reallocate resources in light of a revised public and academic agenda holds the potential to disrupt the academy by setting its constituent parts at war with one another. For boards of governors, it will be truer than it ever has been before that 'Gouverner, c'est choisir.'[4] But to govern is not just to choose; it is also to disappoint. When choices are made about reallocating increasingly scarce resources, some people's interests are hurt as others' are advanced. And therein lies the danger of disrupting morale and reducing commitment among those who actually run the universities, the staff and faculty. This menace of employee alienation rises from the impending challenges at precisely the moment when universities expect to encounter recruitment problems stemming from demographic factors. Thanks to the age distribution of the Canadian population and the unenlightened policies of provincial governments, this country faces a shortfall in junior academics just as large numbers of mature researchers and teachers are about to retire. All of this adds up to a university crisis of personnel relations the like of which has never been seen in this country.

What all of this means, of course, is that the key to governing the university successfully in the near future will lie in leadership. Boards of governors and senior administrations who know the importance of their employees and who utilize effective ways of holding and strengthening their commitment to the institution and its mandate will be indispensable. Recent research by the American firm Selection Research, Inc. shows that the most important reason for alienation and resignation is the extraordinarily ordinary: "'My boss didn't care about me.'"[5] Is there anyone who has served in a Canadian university through the stresses and strains of recent decades who does not recognize that the very same sentiment often lay at the heart of the weakening of faculty commitment, the waning of academic involvement, and, ultimately, the reduction in effectiveness and vitality of the university? Well, for the foreseeable future it will be even more important to make faculty and other employees *know* that they are valued and involved, in part because of structural recruitment problems and in part because of the factors outlined earlier. The same article that quoted the Selection Research discovery about the emotional root of employee disenchantment reported the conclusion of the chief executive of a major Canadian corporation: "'People say there's a labor crisis ... I say there's a management crisis. The numbers-oriented manager won't get any support today.'"[6] Because to govern is to choose and to choose is to disappoint, it is the people-oriented administrator and governor who will succeed. It's not enough to know the words of the collective agreement; you have to know the music of effective leadership, too.

And people-oriented leadership was the genius of the social and political structures of the League of the Iroquois. The leader was chosen by the clan mothers because he, out of all the potential chiefs, had demonstrated a knack for the distinctive style of leadership that had evolved in the palisaded villages and around the fire of the grand council of the League. The Iroquois leader led by example and moral authority; the chief of an Iroquoian village discharged his duty by serving the needs and advancing the interests of those who were nominally his followers; and the very essence of leadership was the realization of the group will, or mission, that had emerged by a consultative and consensual process. A leader among the Six Nations could not fall back on what we think of as the usual instruments of power. There were no deliberative bodies that operated by brute majoritarian methods, no coercive code, and little by way of enforcement mechanisms. The Iroquois leader succeeded by being in tune with and at the service of the whole community. And, given the Aboriginal peoples' sense of all existence as a continuum, that meant the leader was in tune with his people's ancestors and expected descendants as well.

The most important thing about leadership in the League of the Iroquois was that it worked. To a degree that modern Western societies would find astonishing, it provided social harmony, not ruthless conformity, but a blending of individual wills and aspirations that avoided destructive conflict. In spite of the dictates of a political culture that required that diplomatic policy be set by an elaborate and time-consuming process that required eventual unanimity, the Iroquois were able to cope with a bewildering array of commercial, religious, and military assaults emanating from the European presence until disease and Euro-American numbers simply overwhelmed them in the late eighteenth and early nineteenth centuries.[7] And even so, as Canadians saw at Oka in 1990, while much diminished in numbers they survive as communities that, though riven by internal disagreements on strategy and political process, maintain a united front to the rest of the world. Truly it is one of most astonishing examples of successful social structures and governance that history reveals.

The most appropriate model for governing the Canadian university is, indeed, the League of the Iroquois. The reason is not just that the other options, Devil's Island and Marijuana U., are illegitimate and unviable. More important is the fact that a style of governance that relies on consultation, consensus, and leadership-by-service is most likely to produce the internal harmony, employee commitment, and institutional loyalty that are the prerequisites for coping with the demands and challenges facing the university. Six Nations leadership resembled nothing as much as the late president of Yale, Bart Giamatti's, description of academic leadership as 'an essentially moral act, not – as in most management – an essentially protective act. It is the assertion of a vision, not simply the exercise of a style: the moral courage to assert a vision of the institution in the future and the intellectual energy to persuade the community or the culture of the wisdom and validity of the vision. It is to make the vision practicable and compelling.'[8]

And that is *what* governing the Canadian university is going to be about!

### Notes

1 *The Australian*, 25 July and 1 August 1990.
2 With apologies to the Sydney, Australia, policeman who described his own

force as similar to a marijuana farm: '"The harder you suck, the higher you get,"' he noted (*Sydney Morning Herald*, 28 May 1986).

3 *Star-Phoenix* [Saskatoon], 5 September 1990.

4 Duc de Lévis, *Politique*, 'Maxime de Politique,' xix; quoted in *Oxford Dictionary of Quotations*, 3rd ed. (New York: Oxford University Press, 1979), 314 (To govern is to choose).

5 Rona Maynard, 'The Next Labor Crisis,' *Globe and Mail Report on Business Magazine*, June 1990, p. 43.

6 Bill Dover, president, General Mills Restaurants of Canada; quoted in ibid., 46.

7 This complicated story can be traced in a remarkable trilogy of historical works known as 'The Covenant Chain' by American ethnohistorian Francis Jennings: *The Invasion of America: Indians, Colonialism, and the Cant of Conquest* (Chapel Hill: University of North Carolina Press, 1975); *The Ambiguous Iroquois Empire: The Covenant Chain Confederation of Indian Tribes with English Colonies from Its Beginnings to the Lancaster Treaty of 1744* (New York: W.W. Norton, 1984); and *Empire of Fortune: Crowns, Colonies, and Tribes in the Seven Years' War in America* (New York: W.W. Norton, 1988).

8 A. Bartlett Giamatti, *A Free and Ordered Space: The Real World of the University* (New York: W.W. Norton, 1988), 36.

# Aboriginal Peoples and the Academy

It is the first week of September 1970. A young and very anxious Susette Bear has arrived on the University of Saskatchewan campus to register for her classes in the first year of an Arts and Science program. Susette is not from Saskatoon, and she does not recognize a single face in the crowds of young people around her. She does notice, however, that almost all those faces are pale, at least by the standards that prevail in her home community. Susette is a young Cree woman from a small village in northern Saskatchewan. She has had relatively little contact with non-Natives prior to this expedition to the big city of Saskatoon. Her early education took place in the village where she was born, in a multi-grade school, although she had to move to La Ronge to complete the last two years of secondary schooling. She was an academically gifted student, and, with the encouragement of her family, including the aunt and uncle with whom she lived in La Ronge, she did well in her senior high school work.

La Ronge had been a bit of culture shock for her, teaching her, among other things, that she was an Aboriginal person and was different from the mostly non-Native people who ran the school, the businesses, and the town. She had never thought much about her identity while she lived with her immediate family in the North, but now she was alert to cultural difference and curious to learn more about it. Obviously, the University of Saskatchewan, where she planned to spend at least three years, would be a good place to find out about her own people, and also about the *Moonias*, and perhaps something about how the two groups dealt with one another.

Susette was shocked to discover that her assumption about some of the things she would be able to study at the University of Saskatchewan in the early 1970s was almost totally wrong. The staff in the Arts and Science Office, where she conducted the first portion of her in-person registration, could not suggest a single academic opportunity to study about Aboriginal peoples, their experience with the newcomers, or any other aspect of their existence. At first she had assumed that the Arts and Science staff were not adequately informed about course offerings and she would do better when she talked to some learned person from the faculty. (She would discover during her university career that things were the other way around: Arts and Science staff were far better acquainted with the program than faculty.) She had hesitatingly mentioned, when pressed to declare a major, that she was interested in history, and therefore found herself across a small table from an affable, though vague, middle-aged man who confessed to having a doctorate in history and something called tenure. It turned out he had been with the university for some years. In spite of all those credentials, attainments, and experience, he was of no use to Susette either.

In the first place, it turned out that there was almost nothing in the history offerings from which she could select an introductory course that dealt with indigenous peoples. Having perused the calendar herself while waiting in a hallway line-up that morning to see the history adviser, she was aware of and drew to the faculty adviser's attention the existence of HIST 103, 'Europe and North America.' Probably there was something there concerning Native peoples; turned out there wasn't.[1] Nor, apparently, were there courses concerning Native peoples in the Departments of Economics and Political Science or Sociology.[2] Similarly the language departments – though Susette could easily understand their lack of offerings, given that they all were concerned with European or Asian tongues. Upon further reflection, the kindly historian across the table recalled that there were a few relevant courses in the Department of Anthropology and Archaeology, but not at the first-year level. Susette would have to satisfy a prerequisite requirement consisting of ANTH 101 (General Anthropology) and one of several 200-level anthropology courses before she would qualify to attend ANTH 331 (Indians of North America) or ANTH 332A (Indians of Canada) in her final year.[3]

Susette asked in some frustration how this academic dearth could exist in the College of Arts and Science. Defensively, the history adviser responded that Arts and Science was typical of the university as a whole: there was little or nothing available in other colleges, although the College of Education did offer a B.Ed. Program for Teachers in Indian and Northern Communities as part of its three-year B.Ed. (Elementary) offerings. However, it turned out that candidates had to take almost two years of Arts and Science subjects before being able to enrol in courses like EdInd 357 (The School Program in Indian and Northern Communities) and EdInd 457 (Curriculum Development in Indian and Northern Schools).[4] In any event, Susette was not certain she wanted to narrow her options to teaching or to commit herself to a return to the North. As Susette walked away after registering in a group of courses of dubious relevance to her real interest, she wondered how she was going to get through the next three years of study.

But she did. And she graduated in 1973 with a B.A. with Distinction and high hopes. By that time she was wise enough in the ways of the academy not to feel bitter as she noticed that the University of Saskatchewan was moving to create exactly the kinds of programs in which she was interested just when she was leaving its precincts. Thanks in no small part to energetic individuals in education and in law, the University of Saskatchewan was just then becoming the academic home of the Indian Teacher Education Program and the Native Law Centre. In fact, the dean of law had arranged the establishment in 1973 of the Programme of Legal Studies for Native People, which provided an eight-week summer program for students of Aboriginal ancestry who had an acceptance from an accredited Canadian law school.[5] It just so happened that Susette Bear was able to avail herself of that preparatory program in 1973 before heading off to the Faculty of Law at the University of British Columbia.

It is September 1997, and Susette's son, William, has arrived in Saskatoon from his home on Vancouver Island to begin his first year of study in the College of Arts and Science. His mother had been astonished when he told her that his perusal of programs, course offerings, and faculty on the University of Saskatchewan's website had yielded an abundance of possibilities. Not only was there an Indian Teacher Education Program now, but also a Saskatchewan Urban Native Teacher Education Program and a Northern Teacher Education Program alongside longer established concentrations in Indian and northern education.[6] Law not only boasted the eight-week summer program and a Native Law Centre, but it also had two 400-level half-year seminars on Indian and Aboriginal law (436.3) and advanced studies in Aboriginal law (437.3).[7] There were special-access programs in several colleges, most notably the College of Nursing, and the College of Arts and Science had experienced an explosion of courses and programs concerning the experience and knowledge of Aboriginal peoples. The Departments of Anthropology and Archaeology, History, and Sociology all had a number of courses that focused exclusively on Native peoples or provided a fair bit of coverage of them. And since 1982 the College of Arts and Science had contained a Department of Native Studies that offered a wide range of courses on First Nations and Métis to an audience of both Aboriginal and non-Native students. Finally, as William discovered when he arrived in September 1997, the University of Saskatchewan now also had an Indigenous Students' Centre, and Arts and Science, a coordinator of academic programs for Aboriginal students. When informed of this, William's mother had said that she hoped these new facilities and academic offerings meant that he would have a more enjoyable and relevant experience than she had had in her time.

What had happened to change the face of the University of Saskatchewan so much between Susette's difficult time in the early 1970s and her son's admission near the end of the century? In particular, where had all the academic courses and programs come from that were available to William? When Susette had discussed the academy's shortcomings from the perspective of an Aboriginal woman with a few sympathetic faculty during her undergraduate days, some of them had told her that the primary reason why the university appeared to be such an alien and alienating place was that the various disciplines or academic subjects had not yet begun to produce much scholarship about Inuit, First Nations, and Métis peoples. If that was so, why and how had the academy changed in the quarter-century that intervened between the start of mother's and son's post-secondary careers? Perhaps even more relevant for us, what might be the future or futures of Aboriginal peoples and the academy in the next twenty-five years?

To begin to appreciate Susette Bear's plight in September 1970, it is helpful to recall how long it had taken the academy to 'discover' Aboriginal peoples, as well as to remember the curious ways in which at first academics examined their discovery. Writing on the First Nations began outside the colleges and universities in the nineteenth century, and remained for a long time the province of Christian missionaries, amateurs, and anthropologists working for federal government agencies. The study of Aboriginal peoples entered English-Canadian universities only very slowly in the twentieth century, the first anthropologist being appointed at the University of Toronto in the 1920s.[8] He, Dr T.F.

McIlwraith, in turn trained an important New Brunswick historian, A.G. Bailey, in the research techniques that are known today as ethnohistory, and Bailey produced the first example of ethnohistorical scholarship in 1934.[9] Historians, as we will see in more detail in a moment, pretended not to notice the publication or its methodology.

The work done in public agencies such as museums and the Geological Survey of Canada in these early days of scholarly examination of Aboriginal peoples made a curious and only partially useful contribution. The early inquiries of a Franz Boas or a Diamond Jenness or a Marius Barbeau fell into a descriptive category usually termed ethnography that was a crucial element in what is sometimes characterized as 'salvage anthropology.' The motivation behind this style of inquiry, which was intended mainly to record as much as possible about indigenous peoples' languages, social structures, and spiritual beliefs, was an assumption that such data had to be gathered before the societies disappeared. This preoccupation had two aspects. Some, such as Daniel Wilson and Diamond Jenness, quite literally believed that Natives were a 'vanishing race.' Others, such as the highly influential German-born scholar Franz Boas, were motivated by a concern that Natives' attributes be recorded before the (assumed) 'purity' of Aboriginal societies was diluted by intermarriage and prolonged contact and interaction with non-Natives.[10]

There were at least two things wrong with this preoccupation. First, it led anthropology to portray Aboriginal peoples as static and unchanging, whereas they had just undergone three centuries of cataclysmic change and were still dealing with its effects. Second, the ethnographic approach steered scholars away from any examination of non-Native governments' policies towards and impact upon Aboriginal communities. The only major exception to this generalization, a perverse and malignant one unfortunately, was the occasional anthropologist such as Diamond Jenness, whose research conclusions were ideologically consistent with and supportive of the Canadian state and its policy objectives.[11] With scholarly friends such as these anthropologists, who in the Aboriginal community needed academic enemies?

Things were no better among the academic lawyers and sociologists, and fairness demands that some extenuating circumstances be noted in the cases of both these social science disciplines. Sociology emerged as a distinct academic discipline in Canadian universities only about the middle of the twentieth century, and for its early decades its research focused on community and institutional studies. Even when sociology's research interest turned towards questions of ethnicity and race, for a long time it fastened on eastern European and Asian nationalities whose admission to Canada had often ushered in lengthy and difficult periods of adjustment. So far as academic lawyers and the law were concerned, the disincentive to pay attention to the Aboriginal peoples was found primarily in Canadian law. The courts had done little to recognize the distinctive interests of Aboriginal peoples, and from 1927 to 1951 Canada's Indian Act made anyone who 'without the consent of the' minister of Indian affairs 'receives, obtains, solicits or requests from any Indian any payment or contribution or promise of any payment or contribution for the purpose of raising a fund or providing money for the prosecution of any claim' guilty of an offence and liable to a fine or incarceration for a period up to two months.[12] In other words, status Indians could not legally hire lawyers, resulting in a dearth of legal work on Aboriginal issues for practising lawyers and a consequent absence of scholarly interest among specialists in the law schools. Under these circumstances, it is little wonder that, as the Supreme Court of Canada noted in its decision on the *Sparrow* case in 1990, 'for many years the rights of the Indians to their Aboriginal lands – certainly as legal rights – were virtually ignored ... For fifty years after the publication of Clement's *The Law of the Canadian Constitution* (3rd ed. 1916), there was a virtual absence of discussion of any kind of Indian rights to land even in academic literature.'[13] It was not until the 1970 publication of Cumming and Mickenberg's *Native Rights in Canada* that this lamentable shortcoming in legal scholarship began to be addressed.

If this overview of academic neglect has been hard on the anthropologists, sociologists, and lawyers, it is only a warm-up to considering the situation among the academic historians. The tone had been set for the followers of Clio by William Kingsford, often referred to as the dean of nineteenth-century historians of Canada. (Professional historians always like to stress that Kingsford was an engineer and amateur historical investigator.) In the second tome of his ten-volume *History of Canada*, which covered the history of the country down to the 1840s, Kingsford pronounced: 'I do not consider it incumbent upon me to enter into an account of the Indian races of North America ... I have ... in these pages confined myself to the record of events, without entering into ethnological details, considering that they would only lead to an undesirable interruption of the narrative.'[14]

What Kingsford meant, and what dominated the little historical scholarship there was that touched on Native peoples, was that First Nations assumed a place in Canadian history only when and where they interacted with European newcomers, such as in the fur trade in New France or the colonial phases of European imperial wars in the eighteenth century. And for the New France phase of Canadian history, scholars' understanding of Native peoples' roles remained dominated until well into the twentieth century by the baleful view of Boston historian Francis Parkman. An example of this can be found in the early career of Donald Creighton, a historian who would influence historical study in Canada profoundly in the 1950s and 1960s. When Creighton was looking around in the late 1920s for a new field of research because he had realized that he could not afford the trips to Paris that his real academic love, revolutionary France, entailed, he went to his friend and colleague Harold Adams Innis, the specialist on Canadian economic history. Innis's advice to his younger colleague was to avoid his first inclination – an examination of New France. Why? asked Creighton. Because 'Parkman's done it,' declared Innis. The older scholar's advice was instead to examine the papers of an obscure colonial governor that had recently been acquired by the Public Archives of Canada. Creighton did so, joined the historical mainstream that was concerned during the inter-war period with constitutional and economic history, and helped to move the profession towards biography and political history.

The result of these sorts of influences was that academic historians from the 1920s to the 1970s considered political and economic history, often from a nationalist perspective and certainly without any involvement of Aboriginal peoples. These emphases in research dovetailed with Quebec historians' preoccupation with the history of the cultural survival of the Québécois, an interest that had led them to adopt a Parkmanesque view of Aboriginal peoples as a threat to New France, even if it caused them to reject the Bostonian's virulent anti-Catholicism. They have never resolved satisfactorily the historical reality that it was First Nations, or at least some of them, that ensured the survival of New France until the British navy brought about its defeat in the 1750s. The exceptions to the generalization that academic historians ignored Aboriginal peoples could be counted on a very few fingers. A.G. Bailey, as already noted, was a ground-breaker who looked back to find he had no followers among his colleagues in other universities. Harold Adams Innis, who managed to study the fur trade without understanding the contribution of Aboriginal peoples very well, was another. And military historian George Stanley, whose 1936 *The Birth of Western Canada: A History of the Riel Rebellions* dominated academic understanding of Plains First Nations for half a century, was a third. Unfortunately, Stanley's benign view of Canadian government policy, particularly in the era of treaty-making, paid little attention to the perceptions, motives, and actions of the First Nations themselves.

As it happened, it was during Susette Bear's first year at the University of Saskatchewan that a young historian at the University of Waterloo exposed his discipline's negligent treatment of Aboriginal peoples. In 1971 Jim Walker gave a paper entitled 'The Indian in Canadian Historical Writing' which summarized Clio's dubious contribution to the study of Aboriginal peoples in devastating language:

> The picture of the Indian as a human being that is presented by writers of Canadian history is confusing, contradictory and incomplete. Clearly he is not often considered to be deserving of serious attention, or his society of scholarly analysis ... The other general histories consulted mention the Indian only in passing, and invariably on occasions of white-Indian contact ... From all of them [general histories of Canada] it is evident that the Indian is considered totally peripheral to the study of Canada.[15]

Inasmuch as history was only the most egregious example of a condition that was general throughout academe, Professor Walker's indictment could be applied to all the disciplines. His judgment also helps us to understand why Susette Bear found a dearth of courses in September 1970, not to mention why the affable but vague faculty adviser from the Department of History got a bit defensive and huffy when she questioned him about the absences.

Between the times that Susette and her son, William, registered, a lot of change within the disciplines had obviously occurred. In fact, it was the decade of the 1970s that ushered in a new, large-scale scholarly interest in Aboriginal peoples. In part, the attention that anthropologists, historians, lawyers, and sometimes also political scientists and sociologists began to pay to Aboriginal peoples reflected a greater consciousness of Native affairs that stemmed from contemporary social, political, and legal influences. The emergence of the civil rights movement, not to mention the American Indian Movement, strengthened a growing awareness of Third World and indigenous peoples' conflicts with the more prosperous nations of 'The West.' This trend in the 1960s

and beyond simply built on and amplified the spreading consciousness of such frictions that had originated in the decolonization movements in Asia, Africa, and Central and South America after 1945. In
Canada specifically, government inquiries such as the Hawthorn
Report of the mid-1960s involved many more social scientists, especially anthropologists, in a consideration of socio-economic conditions
in which Aboriginal peoples found themselves in modern, affluent
Canada. The election of the first Trudeau government in 1968, with its
promise to create a 'Just Society,' excited youthful hopes, while that
ministry's White Paper of 1969 provoked united Indian protest and
sparked reflection about social scientists' complicity in federal government policies that were now being revealed as duplicitous in their origins and dangerous to First Nations in their effects. If such incidents as
the White Paper fiasco especially affected anthropologists and sociologists, academic lawyers found inspiration in the 1973 landmark decision on Aboriginal title in *Calder*. The subsequent creation of an Office
of Native Claims also attracted the attention of a steadily widening circle of historians.

As influential as these contemporary forces, particularly among academic historians, were methodological fashions and interests that came
to North America from Britain and western Europe in the 1960s and
later. Thanks in no small part to pioneering work by French and English
social historians, academic history found itself being reoriented from a
concern with the high-born and influential in society to detailed study
of the marginal, the dispossessed, and the alien. In short, Canadian historians from the 1970s onward were moving steadily away from political, constitutional, diplomatic, and military history towards various
branches of social history. So one now found more systematic study of
women, the working poor, immigrants, minority ethnic and racial
groups, and increasingly the indigenous populations of Canada. And
to some degree this change in intellectual fashion mirrored a demographic change in the universities, as large numbers of women, working-class, and minority students flooded into the academy in the 1960s.

As historians moved into these forms of social history in the late
1960s and beyond, they found their research agendas and sometimes
their methodologies starting to mesh with those of scholars with whom
they had seldom associated in the days when history was fixated on
monarchs and generals. In particular, historians pursuing new social
history topics began to look to cultural anthropologists for clues that
would allow them to practise the new technique known as ethnohis-

tory, to sociologists for a better understanding of social processes, to historical geographers for an improved appreciation of the impact of the terrain and environment on collectivities in remote regions, and even to legal scholars for the beginnings of an understanding of how some of the ordinary people the historians were now studying found themselves enmeshed in the coils of the law and with what results. For those of the historians whose special research interest was Native peoples and their relations with European newcomers, this blurring and blending of disciplinary boundaries was a startling experience.

Progress in reporting on research results on Aboriginal peoples was slow at first, but during the last fifteen years it has been accelerating, particularly among historians. As late as 1982, a bibliographical essay on Canadian Indian policy by historian Robert J. Surtees had to admit that in spite of the importance of the topic 'it is a field of study that has attracted remarkably little attention from historians and other scholars.'[16] In fact, a change was going on just as Surtees wrote. The year before publication of his bibliography, the anthropologist Sally Weaver stunned social scientists interested in relations between government and First Nations with her *Making Canadian Indian Policy: The Hidden Agenda, 1968–1970* (University of Toronto Press, 1981), which demonstrated convincingly how Ottawa had deceived leaders from the National Indian Brotherhood during months of spurious 'consultations' that culminated in the disastrous 1969 White Paper. The year after publication of Surtees's bibliography, John Tobias of Red Deer College published his 'Canada's Subjugation of the Plains Cree' in the *Canadian Historical Review*, with intellectual consequences similar to those of Weaver's work. Tobias had become involved in researching the historical experience of the Plains nations in the late nineteenth century during a stint as a researcher on land claims for the Federation of Saskatchewan Indians (now Indian Nations) in the early and mid-1970s. His 1983 article documented federal dishonesty in implementing the numbered treaties and in using the courts to crush innocent Plains leaders such as Poundmaker and Big Bear after the Northwest Rebellion. The relevance and import of the work that Weaver and Tobias had produced were amplified in the 1986 publication of a 'public biography' of Indian Affairs bureaucrat D.C. Scott by educational historian Brian Titley, who is now at the University of Lethbridge. The work of Titley, Tobias, and others in the 1980s made what is sometimes called 'the Prairie school' of history covering Indian-government relations a major influence in historical and other circles.

In the 1990s, this enhanced intellectual interest in Aboriginal peoples has been powerfully increased by public events. The role of Elijah Harper in defeating the Meech Lake Accord on behalf of Aboriginal peoples in June 1990 was soon followed by the trauma at Oka/Kanesatake that summer. And through the rest of the decade of the 1990s and beyond, a combination of political-constitutional processes such as the Charlottetown Accord (1992), confrontations (Ipperwash and Gustafsen Lake, 1995), land-claim settlements (Nisga'a, 1997), and crucial legal decisions (*Delgamu'ukw*, December 1997) have maintained both public and academic interest at a high level. In other words, the apparently expanded offerings available to Susette's son, William, in September 1997 can be explained by reference to changing academic interests and the emergence of Aboriginal peoples and their issues on the public agenda, as well as the fact that there is a direct connection between the latter and the former.

Perhaps more important than how Aboriginal peoples got from the unhappy experience that Susette Bear had in the early 1970s to what we hope will be a more satisfying experience for her son in the last few years of the century is the question of how matters are likely to evolve in the next quarter-century. When William's children are considering options in post-secondary education in the 2020s, what is likely to be the situation with Aboriginal peoples and the academy? What is the future likely to hold in this important area?

Perhaps the first thing to notice is that there are several paths available to Aboriginal peoples and the academy on the eve of the twenty-first century. One of the most obvious directions in which our institutions should move is a continuation of efforts to recruit qualified Aboriginal academics. The arguments for this are obvious and well known. For the student, both Native and non-Native, Aboriginal scholars provide an important role model, and for Native students, in particular, such a positive influence can make the academy a less intimidating and forbidding place. From the point of view of the research community generally, the presence within the academy of more qualified Aboriginal scholars promises enrichment of our understanding of both Aboriginal peoples and their relationship to non-Aboriginal peoples. Within the field of history, for example, one can cite both curiosity-driven and applied-research examples of the contributions to knowledge that Aboriginal researchers are making. In the first category, a book by a colleague at the Regina campus of the Saskatchewan Indian Federated College, Georges Sioui, has deepened our understanding of European-Wendat (Huron) relations in the seventeenth century and sketched a new form of relationship for the future. *For an Amerindian Autohistory* was completed as a master's degree, and subsequently published by McGill-Queen's University Press in 1992. His doctoral dissertation has appeared in French, and is expected soon in English as well. In the area of applied or policy-related research, I should mention the work that Harold Cardinal has been doing on the oral history of the Saskatchewan treaties for the Office of the Treaty Commissioner in this province. The insights and understanding that elders with a direct connection to the treaty-making process can make available through the work of Harold Cardinal will undoubtedly improve the Euro-Canadian understanding of those agreements.

There is every reason to hope and expect that Aboriginal scholars will swell the ranks of faculty and enrich both research and teaching in the coming decades. Aboriginal faculty can bring to both their teaching and their research a familiarity with indigenous culture and Native communities that enable them to add a bicultural perspective to what they write and teach. Their close links with Aboriginal leaders and communities give them access to elders and current chiefs and councillors, both of them important sources for understanding the past, present, and future of Aboriginal peoples and their interactions with non-Natives. As I have learned from my teaching experience over the last decades, the presence of significant numbers of Native students in history classes adds a dimension to classroom discussion that benefits all students. Similarly, the diffusion of Aboriginal faculty and scholarship throughout the university and its curriculum will strengthen and deepen understanding. The presence of a stronger Native voice in teaching, research, and administration will make universities, especially in western Canada, more inclusive, more interesting, and more effective in carrying out their educational mandate.

Beyond such sensible steps as continuing efforts to recruit and to retain qualified Aboriginal academics, there are other important issues to address. Perhaps the one that is both most difficult and most important is how we collectively will define what 'Aboriginal Peoples and the Academy' will mean in the future. Should we plan on seeing Aboriginal peoples in the academy, *Aboriginal peoples with the academy*, or **Aboriginal peoples against the academy**? In other words, should both Aboriginal students and the study of Aboriginal peoples be submerged in an unaltered university, integrated into the operations of the university on mutually acceptable terms, or function only in separate, parallel institutions beyond the university? My own choice would be the second – Aboriginal peoples with the academy – for reasons and in ways I would like to outline briefly.

First, the notion of simply submerging Aboriginal peoples within a traditional university would be as unwise and unhelpful as it is unthinkable. As the earlier sketch of the evolution of research and writing during the last thirty years should demonstrate, our research and teaching have already moved beyond the state that Susette Bear encountered and Jim Walker analysed in 1970. The consequence of that change has been the enrichment of the understanding that all students now have available of law, cultures, politics, and history. To take only Canadian history as an example, the understanding that we have now of fur-trade society and economic relations, of the purpose and impact of federal government policy on First Nations, or of the dramatic ways in which Aboriginal peoples have used their traditions to maintain their identity in a hostile environment means that every student who studies the history of this country at an advanced level has more complex and, in some ways, more disturbing material to absorb.

Turning to the second – my preferred – option, there are at least two obstacles to promoting the further involvement of Aboriginal peoples with the academy. They are resistance on the part of the university and impatience on the part of Aboriginal peoples. As any Aboriginal person interested in post-secondary education will tell you, universities are slow to change. Some Native people have given up on the institution, thinking it cannot change quickly enough to accommodate their needs. However, I would argue both that universities should be slow to change, and that they have made and are making important adjustments.

The university is one of two institutions that are critically important to the transmission and preservation of what we usually refer to as Western society. An offshoot of the Christian church, it emerged in the High Middle Ages and early Renaissance. It slowly incorporated the insights and agenda of the scientific revolution and the Enlightenment by the end of the eighteenth century, and by the late nineteenth century it was a powerful institution in the societies of western Europe and North America. However imperfectly, it has maintained some of the best of Western traditions, while over time grafting onto them new insights, new pedagogical and economic purposes, and new social objectives. It has incorporated training in the professions, promoted technology transfer from the results of curiosity-driven research to the market place, and continued to harbour the social and political critics who are essential to the health of the liberal democratic system that we all, I hope, cherish.

Against this positive view of the evolution and contribution of the academy, two arguments are sometimes advanced by those who have become impatient with its slow movement towards embracing Aboriginal and other non-traditional forms of knowledge. First, it is sometimes said that the university is the product of the 'Enlightenment Project' and shares with that historical phenomenon responsibility for capitalism, imperialism, and oppression in many forms. However, the university is not the product of the Enlightenment; it pre-existed the Age of Reason; and it incorporated some of that Age's most important insights and values, as earlier it had the intellectual and artistic fruits of the Renaissance. In our century, it has continued to criticize and modify the obnoxious features that anti-colonial critics detest. Where do those critics think the critique of the so-called 'Enlightenment Project' – modernism, imperialism, oppression – originated? Where is it being refined and modified?

Second, some critics charge that the university cannot change quickly enough to accommodate the needs and aspirations of Aboriginal peoples. The validity of that criticism remains to be seen. Susette Bear's grandchildren will know what we cannot at this stage. But before writing off the possibility of significant change, consider just one tiny area of inquiry that has evolved in the last thirty-odd years. Thirty-five years ago, C.B. Macpherson, a political philosopher at the University of Toronto, revolutionized our understanding of early market societies and polities in a volume he entitled *The Political Theory of Possessive Individualism: Hobbes to Locke* (Oxford University Press, 1962). That book was based on wide reading of English political writers, but it also relied on a new methodology that probed beyond the words of Harrington or Hobbes or Locke to the unarticulated assumptions that must have underlain them. It seems clear that Macpherson's seminal work in some ways anticipated the way anthropologists and historians in the following decades would interrogate culturally tongue-tied sources in search of the Native voice. And if there is a similarity between Macpherson's methodology and the ethnohistorical method, is there not also a striking similarity between those and one of postmodernism's favourite tools, discourse analysis? And notice, too, that postcolonial analysts and critics are among the most frequent and effective users of that instrument from the postmodern tool kit.

Of course there is resistance and obstructionism still in some quarters. However, the hardest battles have been won; there is no longer objection in principle to devoting more attention and effort to Aboriginal topics. It was heartening, for example, to note the response of this institution to a request from the Office of the Treaty Commissioner in 1997 to facilitate my release from some of my teaching duties to join Frank Tough and Arthur J. Ray in a research project on the Saskatchewan treaties. That is the project that I described earlier as involving the Aboriginal legal specialist Harold Cardinal in the oral history sector. When the Federation of Saskatchewan Indian Nations suggested my partial release, most elements of the university administration readily responded. The president, the head of history, and the director of libraries all cooperated to make my full participation possible. Of course, there was opposition from a senior member of the Dean of Arts and Science Office that jeopardized my ability to be involved. However, what is striking is how quickly and enthusiastically this institution responded to a request to help with an innovative research project. As I said, there is still some obstructionism, but overall this university, like most universities I should think, was accommodating.

Universities can change. Universities always have; they are doing so now. And universities will continue to do so if they are not undermined or destroyed. And that is why I am more optimistic than some that the university, one of the oldest products of a Western civilization that is being displaced, can adapt to a changing order that understandably is attempting to reflect and transmit the values of other societies. This is not meant to suggest that independent, Aboriginal-controlled institutions such as the Saskatchewan Indian Federated College, renamed the First Nations University of Canada in 2003, or Gabriel Dumont Institute should or will disappear and their functions be absorbed by a more inclusive university system. There are and will remain for the foreseeable future needs and functions that such post-secondary institutions can perform better than traditional universities. There is no reason why they should not exist alongside universities, just as the Saskatchewan Indian Institute of Technology operates in an environment it shares with the Saskatchewan Institute of Applied Science and Technology. As the chief justice of the Supreme Court of Canada has said in the *Delgamuukw* decision, 'Let us face it, we are all here to stay.'[17] Why not teach, learn, and research together, too?

And so, when William's children and Susette's grandchildren are considering their options for post-secondary education or training some twenty-five or thirty years from now, perhaps they will look at the University of Saskatchewan as one of a number of possible locations for further study. They will if this institution and other universities continue to make space in their curricula and classrooms for Aboriginal peoples, Aboriginal traditional knowledge, and research both by and concerning Aboriginal peoples. With effort, goodwill, and not a little luck, the next generation of students will find that the form that the relationship of Aboriginal peoples and the academy takes in their time will be one in which Aboriginal scholarship occurs in and with the university, with resulting benefits to both Aboriginal and non-Aboriginal students.

## Notes

1 University of Saskatchewan, *Calendar 1970–71*, E-105: 'A survey of the historical development of North America from the expansion of Renaissance Europe to the Second World War.' None of the Canadian history survey courses (206, 207, 208) mentioned Aboriginal peoples in their course descriptions, either (ibid., E-106).
2 Ibid., E-75. A promising-looking ECON 366 explained in a description that it was 'a study of the significance of economic factors in the growth of western civilization on the North American continent with principal emphasis on Canadian economic problems.' Sociology (ibid., E-147-9) had SOC 201B (Social Issues), 203 (Race and Ethnic Relations), and 227 A or B (Canadian Society), but the course descriptions for all of these offerings contained no mention of Aboriginal social groups.
3 Ibid., E-35.
4 There was also a requirement of a course in linguistics or a second language (Cree 'if available') in the program, as well as three electives. Finally, a prescribed course was EdFdt 407 (Anthropology and Education) or 408 (Sociology and Education), though the descriptions for these courses did not contain any explicit reference to Native peoples (ibid., J-28).
5 University of Saskatchewan, *Calendar 1973–74*, M-6.
6 University of Saskatchewan, *Calendar 1997–98*, 147 and 139. There was also a Northwest Territories Teacher Education Program and an Aboriginal Teacher Associate Certificate (ibid., 139).
7 Ibid., 232–3, 236.
8 B.G. Trigger, *Natives and Newcomers: Canada's 'Heroic Age' Reconsidered* (Montreal and Kingston: McGill-Queen's University Press, 1985), 39;

Douglas Cole, 'The Origins of Canadian Anthropology, 1850–1910,' *Journal of Canadian Studies* 8, no. 1 (Feb. 1973): 33–45, esp. 35.

9  It was published in shortened form by the New Brunswick Museum in 1937 under the title *The Conflict of European and Eastern Algonkian Cultures, 1504–1700: A Study in Canadian Civilization.*

10  Cole, 'Origins,' 34, 40, 43–4; Trigger, *Natives and Newcomers*, 18–20; Diamond Jenness, *The Indians of Canada*, 7th ed. (Toronto: University of Toronto Press, 1977; first published by National Museum of Man, 1932), 264: 'It is not possible now to determine what will be the final influence of the aborigines on the generations of Canadian people still to come. Doubtless all the tribes will disappear. Some will endure only a few years longer, others, like the Eskimo, may last several centuries.'

11  P. Kulchyski, 'Anthropology in the Service of the State: Diamond Jenness and Canadian Indian Policy,' *Journal of Canadian Studies* 28, no. 2 (Summer 1993): 21–50, esp. 27–30 and 38.

12  *17 George V, chap. 32*, 149A.

13  *R. v. Sparrow [1990] I S.C.R. 1075* at 1103.

14  William Kingsford, *History of Canada*, vol. 2 (Toronto: Rowsell & Hutchinson, 1888), 166.

15  James W. St G. Walker, 'The Indian in Canadian Historical Writing,' in Canadian Historical Association, *Historical Papers, 1971*, 21, 38–9.

16  Robert J. Surtees, *Canadian Indian Policy* (Bloomington: Indiana University Press, 1982), 1. Similarly, J.R. Miller, 'Native History,' in *Canadian History: A Reader's Guide*, Vol. 2, *Confederation to the Present*, ed. Doug Owram (Toronto: University of Toronto Press, 1994), 182–3.

17  Supreme Court of Canada, *Delgamuukw v. British Columbia*, reasons of Chief Justice Antonio Lamer, paragraph 186.

# Bibliography

## Primary Sources

Rather than trying to list all the primary sources that have been consulted for the essays in this volume, it makes more sense to comment on the categories of sources that have been the most useful. Research for the history of residential schools relied on archival collections, oral history, and printed primary sources. Archives of most of the Christian denominations that operated schools were consulted, as well as the Records of the Department of Indian Affairs (RG 10), both Central Registry Files Black Series and School Files, in the National Archives of Canada. The manuscript collections of particularly influential figures such as Sir John A. Macdonald, Edgar Dewdney, and Hayter Reed were also important. As useful for the history of the schools were the questionnaires and interviews with former staff and students of the residential schools that I collected, oral sources that told more about day-to-day life in the institutions than could be extracted from government and/or church archives. Finally, published primary sources such as the annual reports of the Department of Indian Affairs and *Hansard* were useful for the official view. So, too, were a limited number of memoirs of former students and church officials.

For the history of policy and treaty-making, the chief primary sources were RG 10, interviews, and published primary sources. The last group included accounts of policy-makers and other government officials, in particular. Naturally, published primary sources in the form of government reports and position papers were also essential for understanding this area. Finally, for the history of Native-newcomer relations more generally, published primary sources were, along with the archival and oral history sources mentioned above, the most important. Contemporary published documents from the seventeenth century through to the twentieth century figure regularly in the notes that support the sections of these essays that deal with general Native-new-comer history. Since their number is large, the reader is asked to consult the notes for further guidance.

## Secondary Sources

Abel, Kerry. *Drum Songs: Glimpses of Dene History.* Montreal and Kingston: McGill-Queen's University Press (MQUP), 1993.

Allen, Robert S. His *Majesty's Indian Allies: British Indian Policy in the Defence of Canada, 1774–1815.* Toronto: Dundurn, 1992.

Anderson, Karen. *Chain Her by One Foot: The Subjugation of Women in Seventeenth-Century New France.* New York and London: Routledge, 1991.

Asch, Michael, ed. *Aboriginal and Treaty Rights in Canada: Essays on Law, Equity, and Respect for Difference.* Vancouver: UBC Press (UBCP), 1997.

Axtell, James. *The Invasion Within: The Contest of Cultures in Colonial North America.* New York: Oxford University Press (OUP), 1985.

– *Natives and Newcomers: The Cultural Origins of North America.* New York and Oxford: OUP, 2001.

Bailey, Alfred G. *The Conflict of European and Eastern Algonkian Cultures, 1504–1700: A Study in Canadian Civilization* 2nd ed. Toronto: University of Toronto Press (UTP), 1969 (1937).

Barman, Jean. *The West beyond the West: A History of British Columbia.* Toronto: UTP, 1991.

Barron, F. Laurie, and James B. Waldram, eds. *1885 and After: Native Society in Transition.* Regina: Canadian Plains Research Center, 1986.

Boswell, M.J. '"Civilizing" the Indian: Government Administration of Indians, 1876–1896.' Ph.D. diss., University of Ottawa, 1977.

Brown, G., and R. Maguire. *Indian Treaties in Historical Perspective.* Ottawa: Indian and Northern Affairs, 1979.

Brown, Jennifer S.H. *Strangers in Blood: Fur Trade Company Families in Indian Country.* Vancouver: UBCP, 1980.

Buckley, Helen. *From Wooden Ploughs to Welfare: Why Indian Policy Failed in the Prairie Provinces.* Montreal and Kingston: MQUP, 1992.

Cairns, Alan C. *Citizens Plus: Aboriginal Peoples and the Canadian State.* Vancouver: UBCP, 2000.

Cardinal, Harold. *The Unjust Society: The Tragedy of Canada's Indians.* Edmonton: Hurtig, 1969.

Carter, Sarah A. *Lost Harvests: Prairie Indian Reserve Farmers and Government Policy.* Montreal and Kingston: MQUP, 1990.

Chute, Janet, E. *The Legacy of Shingwaukonse: A Century of Native Leadership*. Toronto: UTP, 1998.

Coates, Ken S. *Best Left As Indians: Native-White Relations in the Yukon Territory, 1840–1973*. Montreal and Kingston: MQUP, 1991.

– *The Marshall Decision and Native Rights*. Montreal and Kingston: MQUP, 2000.

– ed. *Aboriginal Land Claims in Canada: A Regional Perspective*. Toronto: Copp Clark Pitman, 1992.

Cole, Douglas. *Captured Heritage: The Scramble for Northwest Coast Artifacts*. Vancouver: Douglas & McIntyre, 1985.

Cole, Douglas, and Ira Chaikin. *An Iron Hand upon the People: The Law against the Potlatch on the Northwest Coast*. Vancouver: Douglas & McIntyre, 1990.

Crowe, Keith J. *A History of the Original Peoples of Northern Canada*. Montreal: Arctic Institute of North America, 1974.

Cruikshank, Julie, with Angela Sidney, Kitty Smith, and Annie Ned. *Life Lived like a Story: Life Stories of Three Yukon Native Elders*. Vancouver: UBCP, 1990.

Cumming, Peter A., and Neil H. Mickenberg. *Native Rights in Canada*. 2nd ed. Toronto: Indian-Eskimo Association of Canada, 1972 (1970).

Daniel, R. *A History of Native Claims Processes in Canada, 1867–1979*. Ottawa: Indian Affairs, 1980.

Delâge, Denys. *Bitter Feast: Amerindians and Europeans in Northeastern North America, 1600–74*. Trans. Jane Grierley. Vancouver: UBCP, 1985.

Dempsey, Hugh A. *Big Bear: The End of Freedom*. Vancouver: Douglas & McIntyre, 1984.

– *Crowfoot: Chief of the Blackfeet*. Edmonton: Hurtig, 1972.

– *The Gentle Persuader: James Gladstone, Indian Senator*. Saskatoon: Western Producer Prairie Books, 1986.

– *Red Crow: Warrior Chief*. Saskatoon: Western Producer Prairie Books, 1980.

Dempsey, James. *Warriors of the King: Prairie Indians in World War I*. Regina: Canadian Plains Research Center, 1999.

Devens, Carol. *Countering Colonization: Native American Women and Great Lakes Missions, 1630–1900*. Berkeley and Los Angeles: University of California Press, 1992.

Dickason, Olive P. *Canada's First Nations: A History of Founding Peoples from Earliest Times*. 3rd ed. Toronto: OUP, 2002 (1992).

Duffy, R. Quinn. *The Road to Nunavut: The Progress of the Eastern Arctic Inuit since the Second World War*. Montreal and Kingston: MQUP 1988.

Dyck, Noel. *What Is the 'Indian Problem'? Tutelage and Resistance in Canadian Indian Administration*. St John's: Institute of Social and Economic Research, Memorial University, 1991.

Edmunds, R. David. 'Tecumseh's Native Allies: Warriors Who Fought for the

Crown.' In *War on the Great Lakes*. Ed. W.F. Welsh and D.C. Skaggs. Kent, OH: Kent State University Press, 1991.

Elias, P.D. *The Dakota of the Canadian Northwest: Lessons for Survival*. Winnipeg: University of Manitoba Press, 1988.

Fingard, Judith. 'The New England Company and the New Brunswick Indians, 1786–1826: A Comment on the Colonial Perversion of British Benevolence.' *Acadiensis* 1, no. 2 (1972): 29–42.

Fisher, Robin A. *Contact and Conflict: Indian-European Relations in British Columbia, 1774–1890*. 2nd. ed. Vancouver: UBCP, 1992 (1977).

Flanagan, T. *First Nations? Second Thoughts*. Montreal and Kingston: MQUP, 2000.

– *Louis 'David' Riel: 'Prophet of the New World.'* Toronto: UTP, 1979

– *Metis Lands in Manitoba*. Calgary: University of Calgary Press, 1991.

– *Riel and the Rebellion: 1885 Reconsidered*. Saskatoon: Western Producer Prairie Books, 1983.

Foster, Hamar. 'Honouring the Queen's Flag: A Legal and Historical Perspective on the Nisga'a Treaty.' *BC Studies* no. 120 (Winter 1998–9): 11–35.

Francis, Daniel, and Toby Morantz. *Partners in Furs: A History of the Fur Trade in Eastern James Bay, 1600–1870*. Montreal and Kingston: MQUP, 1983.

Friesen, Gerald. *The Canadian Prairies: A History*. Toronto: UTP, 1984.

Friesen, Jean. 'Magnificent Gifts: The Treaties of Canada with the Indians of the Northwest, 1869–1876,' *Transactions of the Royal Society of Canada*, series 5, 1 (1986): 41–51.

Fumoleau, René. *As Long As This Land Shall Last: A History of Treaty 8 and Treaty 11, 1870–1939*. Toronto: McClelland and Stewart, [1975].

Getty, Ian A.L., and A.S. Lussier, eds. *As Long As the Sun Shines and Water Flows: A Reader in Canadian Native Studies*. Vancouver: Nakoda Institute and UBCP, 1979.

Giraud, Marcel. *The Métis in the Canadian West*. 2 vols. Trans. George Woodcock. Lincoln: University of Nebraska Press, 1986.

Goddard, John. *Last Stand of the Lubicon Cree*. Vancouver: Douglas & McIntyre, 1991.

Grant, John Webster. *Moon of Wintertime: Missionaries and the Indians of Canada in Encounter since 1534*. Toronto: UTP, 1984.

Haig-Brown, Celia. *Resistance and Renewal: Surviving the Indian Residential School*. Vancouver: Tillacum Library, 1988.

Hawthorn, H.B., ed. *A Survey of the Contemporary Indians of Canada: Economic, Political, Educational Needs and Policies*. 2 vols. Ottawa: Indian Affairs, 1966–7.

Innis, Harold A. *The Fur Trade in Canada: An Introduction to Canadian Economic History*. New ed. Toronto: UTP, 1999 (1930).

Jaenen, Cornelius J. *Friend and Foe: Aspects of French-Amerindian Cultural Contact in the Sixteenth and Seventeenth Centuries.* New York: Columbia University Press, 1976.

Jenness, Diamond. *The Indians of Canada.* 7th ed. Toronto: UTP, 1977 (1932).

Jennings, Francis. *The Invasion of America: Indians, Colonialism, and the Cant of Conquest.* Chapel Hill: University of North Carolina Press, 1975.

Kulchyski, Peter. '"A Considerable Unrest": F.O. Loft and the League of Indians.' *Native Studies Review* 4, nos. 1–2 (1988): 95–117.

Leslie, John, and R. Maguire, eds. *The Historical Development of the Indian Act.* 2nd ed. Ottawa: Indian Affairs and Northern Development, 1983 (1975).

Loo, Tina. 'Dan Cranmer's Potlatch: Law as Coercion, Symbol, and Rhetoric in British Columbia, 1884–1951.' *Canadian Historical Review* 73, no. 2 (1992): 125–65.

Lux, Maureen K. *Medicine That Walks: Disease, Medicine, and Canadian Plains Native People, 1880–1940.* Toronto: UTP, 2001.

Macklem, Patrick. *Indigenous Difference and the Constitution of Canada.* Toronto: UTP, 2001.

Manuel, George, and M. Posluns. *The Fourth World: An Indian Reality.* Toronto: Collier-Macmillan, 1974.

Martel, Gilles. *Le Messianisme de Louis Riel.* Waterloo, ON: Wilfrid Laurier University Press, 1984.

Martin-McGuire, Peggy. *First Nation Land Surrenders on the Prairies, 1896–1911.* Ottawa: Indian Claims Commission, 1998.

Miller, J.R. *Big Bear (Mistahimusqua).* Toronto: ECW Press, 1996.

– *Canada and the Aboriginal Peoples, 1867–1927.* Ottawa: Canadian Historical Association, 1997.

– *Lethal Legacy: Current Native Controversies in Canada.* Toronto: McClelland and Stewart, 2004.

– *Shingwauk's Vision: A History of Native Residential Schools.* Toronto: UTP, 1996.

– *Skyscrapers Hide the Heavens: A History of Indian-White Relations in Canada.* 3rd ed. Toronto: UTP, 2000 (1989).

– ed. *Sweet Promises: A Reader in Indian-White Relations in Canada.* Toronto: UTP, 1991.

Milloy, John S. *A National Crime: The Canadian Government and the Residential School System, 1879 to 1986.* Winnipeg: University of Manitoba Press, 1999.

– *The Plains Cree: Trade, Diplomacy and War, 1790–1870.* Winnipeg: University of Manitoba Press, 1988.

Morris, Alexander. *The Treaties of Canada with the Indians.* Toronto: Belfords, Clarke 1880; Saskatoon: Fifth House, 1991.

Mulhall, David. *Will to Power: The Missionary Career of Father Morice*. Vancouver: UBCP, 1986.

Nichols, Roger L. *Indians in the United States and Canada: A Comparative History*. Lincoln and London: University of Nebraska Press, 1998.

Pannekoek, Frits. *A Snug Little Flock: The Social Origins of the Riel Resistance*. Winnipeg: Watson & Dwyer, 1991.

Paul, Daniel. *We Were Not the Savages: A Micmac Perspective on the Collision of European and Aboriginal Civilization*. Halifax: Nimbus, 1993.

Payment, Diane Paulette. *'The Free People – Otipemisiwak': Batoche, Saskatchewan, 1870–1930*. Ottawa: Parks Canada, 1990.

Peterson, Jacqueline, and Jennifer S.H. Brown, eds. *The New Peoples: Being and Becoming Métis in North America*. [Winnipeg]: University of Manitoba Press, 1985.

Pettipas, Katherine. *Severing the Ties That Bind: Government Repression of Indigenous Religious Ceremonies on the Prairies*. Winnipeg: University of Manitoba Press, 1994.

Plaice, Evelyn. *The Native Game: Settler Perceptions of Indian-Settler Relations in Central Labrador*. St John's: Institute for Social and Economic Research, Memorial University, 1991.

Ray, Arthur J. *The Canadian Fur Trade in the Industrial Age*. Toronto: UTP, 1990.

– *I Have Lived Here since the World Began: An Illustrated History of Canada's Native Peoples*. Toronto: Key Porter, 1996.

– *Indians in the Fur Trade: Their Role As Hunters, Trappers, and Middlemen in the Lands Southwest of Hudson Bay, 1660–1870*. Toronto: UTP, 1974.

Ray, Arthur J., Jim Miller, and Frank Tough. *Bounty and Benevolence: A History of Saskatchewan Treaties*. Montreal and Kingston: MQUP, 2000.

Richardson, Boyce. *Strangers Devour the Land: A Chronicle of the Assault upon the Last Coherent Hunting Culture in North America, the Cree Indians of Quebec, and Their Vast Primeval Homelands*. New York: Knopf, 1975.

Ross, Rupert. *Dancing with a Ghost: Exploring Indian Reality*. Markham, ON: Octopus, 1992.

Royal Commission on Aboriginal Peoples (RCAP). *Partners in Confederation: Aboriginal Peoples, Self-Government, and the Constitution*. Ottawa: Ministry of Supply and Services, 1993.

– *Final Report*. 4 vols. Ottawa: RCAP, 1996.

Ryan, Joan. *Wall of Words: The Betrayal of the Urban Indian*. Toronto: Peter Martin Associates, 1978.

St Germain, Jill. *Indian Treaty-Making Policy in the United States and Canada, 1867–1877*. London: University of Nebraska Press, 2001.

Salisbury, R.F. *A Homeland for the Cree: Regional Development in James Bay, 1971–1981*. Montreal and Kingston: MQUP, 1986.

Samek, Hana. *The Blackfoot Confederacy, 1880–1920: A Comparative Study of Canadian and U.S. Indian Policy*. Albuquerque: University of New Mexico Press, 1987.

Sealey, D.B., and A.S. Lussier. *The Métis: Canada's Forgotten People*. Winnipeg: Pemmican Publications, 1975.

Sioui, Georges. E. *For an Amerindian Autohistory: An Essay on the Foundations of a Social Ethic*. Montreal and Kingston: MQUP, 1992.

Smith, Donald B. *Sacred Feathers: The Reverend Peter Jones (Kahkewaquonaby) and the Mississauga Indians*. Toronto: UTP, 1987.

Sosin, J.M. 'The Use of Indians in the War of the American Revolution: A Re-Assessment of Responsibility.' *Canadian Historical Review* 46, no. 2 (1965): 101–21.

Sprague, D.N. *Canada and the Métis, 1869–1885*. Waterloo, ON: Wilfrid Laurier University Press, 1988.

Stanley, George F.G. *The Birth of Western Canada: A History of the Riel Rebellions*. 2nd ed. Toronto: UTP, 1960.

– 'The Indians in the War of 1812.' *Canadian Historical Review* 31, no. 2 (1950): 145–65.

Stonechild, Blair, and Bill Waiser. *Loyal till Death: Indians and the North-West Rebellion*. Calgary: Fifth House, 1997.

Sugden, John. *Tecumseh: A Life*. New York: Henry Holt, 1998.

Surtees, Robert J. *Canadian Indian Policy: A Critical Bibliography*. Bloomington: Indiana University Press, 1982.

Tennant, Paul. *Aboriginal Peoples and Politics: The Indian Land Question in British Columbia, 1849–1989*. Vancouver: UBCP, 1990.

Thistle, Paul C. *Indian-European Trade Relations in the Lower Saskatchewan River Region to 1840*. Winnipeg: University of Manitoba Press, 1986.

Titley, E. Brian. *A Narrow Vision: Duncan Campbell Scott and the Administration of Indian Affairs in Canada*. Vancouver: UBCP, 1986.

Tough, Frank. *As Their Natural Resources Fail: Native Peoples and the History of Northern Manitoba, 1870–1930*. Vancouver: UBCP, 1996.

Treaty 7 Tribal Elders with Walter Hildebrandt, Dorothy First Rider, and Sarah Carter. *The True Spirit and Original Intent of Treaty 7*. Montreal and Kingston: MQUP, 1997.

Trigger, Bruce G. *Natives and Newcomers: Canada's 'Heroic Age' Reconsidered*. Montreal and Kingston: MQUP, 1985.

Upton, Leslie F.S. *Micmacs and Colonists: Indian-White Relations in the Maritimes, 1713–1867*. Vancouver: UBCP, 1979.

Usher, [Friesen], Jean. *Duncan of Metlakatla: A Victorian Missionary in British Columbia*. Ottawa: National Museum of Man, 1974.

Van Kirk, Sylvia. *'Many Tender Ties': Women in Fur-Trade Society, 1670–1870*. Winnipeg: Watson & Dwyer, [1980].

Walker, James. 'The Indian in Canadian Historical Writing.' In Canadian Historical Association. *Historical Papers, 1971*.

Washburn, W.E., ed. *Handbook of North American Indians. Vol. 4. History of Indian-White Relations*. Washington: Smithsonian Institution, 1988.

Weaver, Sally M. *Making Canadian Indian Policy: The Hidden Agenda, 1968–1970*. Toronto: UTP, 1981.

White, Richard. *The Middle Ground: Indians, Empires, and Republics in the Great Lakes Region, 1650–1815*. Cambridge: Cambridge University Press, 1991.

Whitehead, Ruth Holmes. *The Old Man Told Us: Excerpts from Micmac History, 1520–1950*. Halifax: Nimbus, 1991.

Wise, Sydney F. 'The American Revolution and Indian History.' In *Character and Circumstance: Essays in Honour of Donald Grant Creighton*. Ed. J.S. Moir. Toronto: Macmillan, 1979.

Woodcock, George. *Gabriel Dumont: The Métis Chief and His Lost World*. New ed. Peterborough, ON: Broadview Press, 2003 (1975).

York, Geoffrey, and Loreen Pindera. *People of the Pines: The Warriors and the Legacy of Oka*. Toronto: Little, Brown, 1991.